*The Columbia University
College of Physicians
and Surgeons*

COMPLETE
GUIDE TO
PREGNANCY

The Columbia University College of Physicians and Surgeons

MEDICAL EDITORS

Donald F. Tapley, M.D.
*Senior Deputy Vice-President for Health Sciences
and Alumni Professor of Medicine, Columbia University*

W. Duane Todd, M.D.
*Professor of Clinical Obstetrics & Gynecology,
Columbia University*

EDITORIAL DIRECTOR

Genell J. Subak-Sharpe, M.S.

ASSOCIATE EDITOR

Diane M. Goetz

COMPLETE GUIDE TO PREGNANCY

Crown Publishers, Inc.

NEW YORK

Table 3.1 originally appeared in *Obstetrics and Gynecology*, vol. 58, no. 3, 1981, pp. 282-285. Reprinted by permission of Ernest B. Hook, M.D., and The American College of Obstetricians and Gynecologists.

Table 9.8 originally appeared in "Food, Pregnancy, and Health," Washington, D.C., 1982. Reprinted by permission of the American College of Obstetricians and Gynecologists.

Published by Crown Publishers, Inc., 225 Park Avenue South, New York, New York 10003 and represented in Canada by the Canadian MANDA Group.

CROWN in a trademark of Crown Publishers, Inc.

Manufactured in the United States of America

Library of Congress Cataloging-in-Publication Data

Complete guide to pregnancy.

   1. Pregnancy. 2. Pregnant women—Health and hygiene. 3. Obstetrics—Popular works. I. Tapley, Donald F. II. Todd, W. Duane. III. Columbia University. College of Physicians and Surgeons complete guide to pregnancy. RG525.C686   1988   618.2   88-7079 ISBN 0-517-57030-0

Contents

Acknowledgments

THE CREATION OF ANY BOOK inevitably requires the skill, knowledge, and devotion of scores of people, and this one is no exception. Over the last two years, more than a dozen busy and dedicated medical specialists at the Columbia University College of Physicians and Surgeons have freely shared their expertise and knowledge. Without them, this book would never have been possible. They have given up weekends, vacation time, and spare moments snatched from already overloaded schedules. To each and every one, we are indeed grateful.

We also have had the unstinting cooperation of a team of highly skilled medical writers and editors. They include Doreen DeFlorio, Rebecca Hughes, Susan Ince, Franca LeBow, Caroline Tapley, Antonia van der Meer, and Josleen Wilson.

A team of extraordinarily talented medical artists and illustrators also have worked on this book. The original drawings have been provided by Lauren Kestwick and Hilda Muinos. Other illustrations have been provided by Robert Demarest and John W. Karapelou from the Columbia Audio Visual Service, Glenna Deutsch, and Beth Ann Willert.

Behind the scenes, we have had the invaluable help of Laura Rosenfeld, Emily Fraenkel, David, Sarah, and Hope Subak-Sharpe to type, check facts, and lend all-round support.

Again, Diane Goetz as the Associate Editor has overseen the myriad details in putting together a book of this complexity. Simply keeping track of who is doing what and where it all is has been a monumental task.

The staff at Crown has pooled its talents to take the manuscript and turn it into a highly readable, handsome volume. Particular credit goes to our editors, Betty A. Prashker, David Groff, and Laurie A. Stark. Also our appreciation to Ed Otto, Joan Denman, Jim Davis, and Peggy Goddard.

Finally, a special tribute is due our patient spouses and children—their support throughout this project has helped make this book happen.

The Editors

DONALD F. TAPLEY, M.D., Alumni Professor of Medicine and Senior Deputy Vice-President for the Health Sciences, has spent most of his medical career at the College of Physicians and Surgeons. After completing a fellowship at Oxford University, he joined the P&S faculty as an assistant professor of medicine in 1956, rising to dean in 1974. During his 10-year tenure as dean, Dr. Tapley presided over the tremendous growth of the institution and is widely acknowledged as one of the most notable medical school deans in the nation. His medical specialty is endocrinology, and over the years he has published a number of papers in this field, with special emphasis on the role of the thyroid hormones.

W. DUANE TODD, M.D., began his medical career as a student at the Columbia University College of Physicians and Surgeons and has since remained an active member of the Columbia medical community. After completing his internship at Columbia Presbyterian Medical Center, Dr. Todd spent his residency at the Sloane Hospital for Women. Certified by the American Board of Obstetrics and Gynecology in 1961, Dr. Todd presently serves as attending obstetrician and gynecologist at The Presbyterian Hospital, Columbia Presbyterian Medical Center. He is also a Professor of Clinical Obstetrics and Gynecology at the College of Physicians and Surgeons. In addition to coauthoring numerous articles, Dr. Todd is a past president of the New York Obstetrical Society.

GENELL J. SUBAK-SHARPE, M.S., is a medical writer and editor who began her journalism career on the metropolitan staff of the *New York Times*. Since then, she has served as vice-president of Biomedical Information Company and as editor of a number of magazines for both physicians and consumers and is the author, coauthor, or editor of more than 20 books in health and medicine. She is now president of her own medical communications company and editorial director of the *Health and Nutrition* newsletter.

DIANE M. GOETZ is a medical writer and editor who specializes in preventive health topics for the general public. She was on the staff of the American Heart Association, New York City Affiliate, for 10 years, ultimately serving as vice president for communications. She holds a B.A. in journalism from the University of Wisconsin and an M.B.A. from New York University. She is editor of *Weight Watchers Women's Health* and *Fitness News*, a monthly newsletter.

List of Editors and Contributors

MEDICAL EDITORS

DONALD F. TAPLEY, M.D.

Senior Deputy Vice-President for Health Sciences and Alumni Professor of Medicine

W. DUANE TODD, M.D.

Professor of Clinical Obstetrics and Gynecology

EDITORIAL DIRECTOR

GENELL J. SUBAK-SHARPE, M.S.

ASSOCIATE EDITOR

DIANE M. GOETZ

CONTRIBUTORS

LAXMI BAXI, M.D.
Associate Professor of Clinical Obstetrics and Gynecology

FREDRIC M. BOMBACK, M.D.
Clinical Professor of Pediatrics

EDWARD BOWE, M.D.
Professor of Clinical Obstetrics and Gynecology

HAROLD FOX, M.D.
Associate Professor of Clinical Obstetrics and Gynecology and Clinical Pediatrics

GEORGIANA JAGIELLO, M.D.
Virgil G. Damon Professor of Obstetrics and Gynecology

RAPHAEL JEWELEWICZ, M.D.
Associate Professor of Clinical Obstetrics and Gynecology

MARY ANN JONAITIS, R.N., M.ED.
Specialist, Maternal Nutrition Department of Ambulatory Obstetrics

AMALIA KELLY, M.D.
Assistant Professor of Obstetrics and Gynecology

RICHARD U. LEVINE, M.D.
Associate Professor of Clinical Obstetrics and Gynecology

JACK MAIDMAN, M.D.
Associate Professor of Clinical Obstetrics and Gynecology

ELYNNE MARGULIS, M.D.
Assistant Professor of Clinical Obstetrics and Gynecology

MORTIMER G. ROSEN, M.D.
W. C. Rappeleye Professor of Obstetrics and Gynecology
Professor and Chairman
Department Obstetrics and Gynecology

PAMELA TROPPER, M.D.
Assistant Professor of Obstetrics and Gynecology

Preface:
How to Use This Book

Pregnancy is one of the most exciting, and perhaps most doubt-ridden, periods for any couple. The arrival of a baby suddenly transforms a couple into a family, and overnight, the parents assume the total responsibility for nurturing and guiding a new being. Of course, you are not alone in this monumental venture; typically there are grandparents, aunts, uncles, friends, colleagues, and many others all too willing to give advice and perhaps even lend a helping hand.

Your doctor and other health care professionals are ready to provide medical treatment and answer questions. Still, no matter how extensive the prospective parents' support system, there are bound to be hundreds of questions. What do these funny twinges mean? Is it safe to take my usual medication? What should I be eating? Can I continue my daily jogging? Obviously, your doctor is the best person to answer these questions. But there will be many times when you will want to know more. This is why you should keep this book close at hand throughout the entire process—from planing your pregnancy until after delivery.

In compiling *The Columbia University College of Physicians and Surgeons Complete Guide to Pregnancy*, the editors have enlisted more than a dozen of the most experienced and knowledgeable specialists at the Columbia Presbyterian Medical Center and Sloane Hospital for Women as contributors. From their extensive experience both in treating patients and research, they have special insight into the concerns of prospective parents as well as the problems that may arise.

The information in this book should not be used to alter your own physician's recommendations—your doctor knows and understands your own medical needs. Instead, this book is intended to help you understand what is going on as your pregnancy progresses. If your doctor has told you something you do not fully understand, look it up in this book to get a more detailed explanation. You also can use this book as a basis for discussions with your doctor about the aspects of your pregnancy that may be troubling to you.

We think you will find the information in this book reassuring. Simply knowing that what you are experiencing is normal and shared by millions of other prospective parents can be very comforting.

Finally, this book is designed to be used as a companion to *The Columbia University College of Physicians and Surgeons Complete Guide to Early Child Care*. That guide picks up where this one ends and provides invaluable advice and information on caring for your new baby through early infancy until school age.

1 Planning Your Pregnancy

Pamela Tropper, M.D.

INTRODUCTION

WITHOUT A DOUBT, having a baby is one of life's most rewarding events. Parenthood is also one of the most serious undertakings for both mother and father. Suddenly a couple becomes a family, with all of the joys and responsibilities that entails. Although millions of babies are brought into the world each year with little or no planning, this is hardly ideal for either the parents or the child. How well the pregnancy goes depends a lot on the mother's health and well being, beginning well before she decides to have a child. Even more important, a couple's advance planning can have a tremendous impact on the baby's future.

As much as possible, a couple should be sure that both partners are ready for parenthood before planning a pregnancy. In planning a pregnancy, there is a tendency to focus on the most pleasurable aspects of parenthood; couples also should consider that raising a child takes time, effort, money, and, above all, commitment. Although several factors—careers, finances, and physical health—can be weighed somewhat objectively before pregnancy, having a baby is still largely an emotional decision, and emotions are more difficult than material factors to catalog. For example, couples struggling with marital problems often think that having a child will revive their marriage and bring them closer together. In the beginning, when all attention is focused on the new baby, the marital problems may seem to fade, but instead of actually resolving the problems, the child is more

likely to become entwined in its parents' difficulties. Babies born into troubled marriages often become the focal point of tension and quarrels. The time for couples to work out problems in their intimate relationship is before pregnancy. Counselors urge that a couple carefully evaluate their relationship and why they want a child before embarking on a pregnancy. Table 1.1 lists the types of questions that couples should ask themselves.

Effect on Marriage

Having a baby forever alters the nature of marriage. Whether you have a baby at age 20 or 40, after 1 year of marriage or 10, the marriage shifts from a relationship that caters to 2 adults to a relationship that nurtures a child. When a couple become parents, a family is born, and the family evolves a personality all its own. Invariably, new parents marvel at the many ways in which a new baby brings new purpose and meaning to their lives. Over and over we hear such exclamations as, "It's a miracle!" or "How did we manage without this wonderful little person?"

Still, parenthood is not just fun. Parents are expected to make sacrifices in terms of time, money, and attention. With the arrival of a baby, a couple must expect to give up some of the time they have had exclusively for each other. Now the family comes first, and all other obligations are second. A couple must balance their own intimate relationship within a new family structure. The transition from

Table 1.1
QUESTIONS TO ASK BEFORE STARTING A PREGNANCY

Before starting a pregnancy, couples might ask themselves the following questions about parenthood and discuss their responses together:

● Why might you want a child?

● What do you think pregnancy will be like?

● How do you imagine yourself with a child?

● What do you expect from your partner?

● How would you like to see the responsibility shared?

● Are these reasonable expectations?

● Are your expectations fairly well matched?

● How do you feel having a baby will affect your relationship?

● If you already have children, what will a new child mean to them?

● If you are single, what support system is available in your community?

● How would you support and care for a child?

● Where would you live? With whom, if anyone, would you live?

● As the child grows up, what do you expect will be important to you in terms of your career and other interests?

months before and during pregnancy. Before pregnancy, couples can contemplate making changes in lifestyle, talk about their hopes and fears, plan the kind of family life they want. Later, such activities as studying nutrition, reading books about pregnancy and childbirth, taking childbirth classes together, and planning the baby's room and wardrobe all help couples anticipate change and make impending parenthood more real. Although there is a tendency to become so wrapped up in the wonders of a new baby, it is important that new parents strive to nurture not only the baby, but also each other. In doing so, the parents will be providing the kind of environment in which the entire family can thrive and grow.

A Choice for Both Partners

Although the decision to have a baby seems to rest primarily with women, obviously it is a choice that a couple should share. Readiness to bear children does not always come to both partners at the same time, however. Differences in desire can make the decision more difficult.

If one partner is worried about finances or jobs, the other must take these concerns or fears seriously and be willing to talk about them. Certainly the decision about when to have a baby can be a difficult one for couples trying to juggle work, marriage, and parenthood. In many ways, however, the problem solving is easier today than it was even 10 years ago. Both men and women today have a clearer notion of shared responsibilities than in the past, and old attitudes about parental roles are changing, making the adjust-

couple to parents can be difficult, but it will be much easier if both partners have begun to build a sense of family in the ment to parenthood somewhat easier.

Still, it would be foolish to downplay the ambivalence about parenthood experienced by many, if not most, couples. Because today there is more latitude than ever about if and when to marry and have a family, the decision to have a baby can seem more complicated than in the past.

In fact, such freedom offers important options. When a couple decides to have a baby today, it is likely to be because both partners feel the right time has arrived and consequently they share the conviction that the child will be wanted and cherished.

SPECIAL CONSIDERATIONS

Age Factors

There is no one ideal age for parenthood that applies to all couples. The mother's age, however, is an important consideration for many couples today. The standard age range for marriage and childbearing traditionally has been in the early to mid-20s. In the past 2 decades, however, there has been a trend toward postponed parenthood that allows women time to complete their educations and become established in careers before becoming mothers. There are many other benefits to postponing pregnancy until age 30 or older. A couple who wait to have a baby have more time to stabilize the marriage. Older parents also tend to have more patience and more experience in life. They are likely to have a stronger sense of their own identities, so that their own growing pains are not tied up with those of their children.

On the other hand, older parents are often absorbed in full-time careers or committed to expensive or glamorous styles of living, so it becomes all the more difficult to make the sacrifices that a baby

demands. Younger couples just starting out may find it easier to accommodate child rearing into their lives, and their financial expectations may not be as great as those of older, more established couples. Younger parents also tend to have more energy and more time to devote to children.

In short, the best time to have a baby is when a couple feels it is right for them. The trend toward older parenthood is neither right nor wrong. It is simply another option. Couples can weigh the various components of the decision-making process—education, income, work, other family responsibilities—and judge them against their own emotional readiness. The decision they make may not be right for someone else, but it will be right for them.

There is, however, one important age factor that should be considered in making the decision. Physiologically, the optimal years for childbearing are those between 18 and 35. Women who postpone pregnancy until their mid- to late 30s may find their fertility is somewhat reduced. Although most will still conceive, it may take longer because some women do not ovulate as regularly or as often at that age.

Older mothers also have an increased risk of complications during pregnancy and of having a child with a congenital anomaly, such as Down syndrome. (See chapter 13, The High-Risk Pregnancy.) These risks, however, are small and often can be managed with appropriate medical care. On the other hand, a very young mother also risks a problem pregnancy and has a far greater than average risk of bearing a low-birth-weight infant.

A MEDICAL CHECKUP

THERE ARE MANY reasons for a woman, before she becomes pregnant, to have a medical checkup that includes genetic screening, an assessment of nutritional needs, and advance preparation if she falls into a high-risk category. The most important part of such a checkup is to rule out infection or other gross anomalies that may have a detrimental effect on pregnancy and the fetus.

It is a good idea to have this pre-conception medical evaluation performed by an obstetrician. If the checkup is done by a family physician or internist, the woman should tell the doctor that she is planning to become pregnant and request a pre-conception checkup, which is similar to an initial prenatal examination. It includes a family history of both partners, a general physical examination, a vaginal and pelvic examination, and laboratory tests on blood and urine.

Medical History

Family Tree. A family history acts as a preliminary genetic screen and suggests whether either partner is at risk to transmit any genetic diseases to offspring and whether there is any background of twins or multiple births. The woman should obtain this information in advance from her partner or ask him to attend the checkup. If either partner can trace an unusual incidence of a disease or birth defect in the family, for example, hemophilia or cystic fibrosis, the couple may want to consult a genetic counselor before pregnancy to assess the chances of passing along the disorder.

Occupational Hazards. One might also consider at this time hazards and toxins to which either partner may be exposed in the workplace. Such hazards should be avoided before conception.

Reproductive Status. The physician will want a description of the female partner's menstrual pattern. Menstrual difficulties may suggest a number of fertility problems, such as endometriosis, erratic ovulation, unbalanced hormonal cycles, and premature menopause. If any of these problems exist, the physician may suggest that it be treated before the woman tries to become pregnant. (See chapter 5, Infertility Problems.)

A woman will also be asked if she has ever had pelvic inflammatory disease, an infection that can damage the reproductive organs. The contraceptive method a couple uses may also be important in determining reproductive status and timing. Prior use of an intrauterine device (IUD) may make conception more difficult or increase the chance of tubal or ectopic pregnancy.

The couple's previous sexual experiences also may be important. A number of sexually transmitted diseases, including genital herpes and chlamydia, may affect the management of a particular pregnancy and possibly the mode of delivery. Increasingly, obstetricians are suggesting that a woman undergo an HIV antibody test if there is any possibility that she may have been exposed to the AIDS virus in the past. This is still a highly controversial issue, but since a significant proportion of the babies born to women carrying the AIDS virus will develop the disease, many experts feel that testing before pregnancy is well advised for any women in a high-risk category.

General Illness. Any serious illness or chronic disease should be carefully described. A woman who has kidney disease, high blood pressure, diabetes, or a convulsive disorder will require special pre-conception care and careful follow-up throughout her pregnancy. For example, a diabetic woman, even if her disease is in good control, may require special modifications in her regimen prior to conception.

Medications. Medications taken soon before conception or during pregnancy can cross the placental barrier and may harm the fetus. The physician should review all medications, including over-the-counter drugs, that the woman may be taking. If she is on prescription medications such as oral hypoglycemics, insulin, anticonvulsants, or antihypertensives, the regimen may have to be altered before pregnancy to minimize any risk to the baby. This includes vitamins and minerals, since some high-dose products, especially vitamin A, can cause harm to the developing fetus.

Previous Pregnancies. The physician will want to know about any previous pregnancies and will ask particularly about complications. Tubal pregnancy, miscarriage, induced abortion, premature birth, and preeclampsia are just a few of the conditions that may have a bearing on future pregnancies.

Genetic Screening. Race or ethnic background may suggest a predisposition for certain genetic problems. If either partner is black or Hispanic, his or her blood should be tested for sickle cell trait. If both partners carry the sickle cell trait, there is an increased risk of the baby having sickle cell disease, a severe form of anemia. (See chapter 3, Genetic Considerations.)

If either partner is of southern Mediterranean ancestry, his or her blood may be tested for thalassemia, another hereditary blood disease that can cause severe anemia in the baby. Or, if either partner is of Eastern European Jewish descent, a screening test for a metabolic disorder called Tay Sachs disease should be considered. It is important that Tay Sachs screening be carried out *before* pregnancy, as the test results may be difficult to interpret when performed on pregnant women. As noted earlier, a family history of genetic disorders may require special testing and counseling.

Height and Weight

On this visit the physician will also measure the woman's height and check for any posture problems or physical abnormalities that might affect her pelvis. Preconception weight is particularly important. A significant weight problem in either direction can cause problems and a woman will want to gain or lose weight *before* she becomes pregnant.

Pelvic Examination

The internal exam will detect structural abnormalities of the pelvis, vagina, or cervix that might affect the pregnancy. During the exam the physician will also take cervical swabs for a Pap smear and to test for the presence of infections.

Infections

The physician may take a vaginal culture to check for infections such as trichomonas or yeast and for more serious sexually transmitted diseases (which may not exhibit symptoms) such as gonorrhea or chlamydia. A history of genital herpes is important. A woman should make sure her doctor knows that she has had this viral infection, and the doctor should check carefully for any signs of an active herpes lesion.

Urine Tests

A urine specimen can be analyzed for protein (which may indicate kidney disease), glucose (for diabetes), and pus and blood (for urinary tract infection).

Blood Tests

A blood sample is analyzed to identify blood group and to test for syphilis (a required test in most states), anemia, and the rhesus (Rh) factor. If a woman is Rh negative and her partner is Rh positive, she should be aware of the potential incompatibility problem, particularly if it is a second or third pregnancy or if she has received blood transfusions in the past. Incompatibility problems are unusual since the introduction of treatment with rhesus gamma globulin.

Infectious Diseases

There are a number of infectious diseases that can pose problems for a fetus. One of the most common is toxoplasmosis, a parasitic infection that may cause spontaneous abortion, stillbirth, and fetal abnormalities. It is often transmitted to humans via a cat's litter box or, more commonly, from eating raw or very rare beef. Some physicians may check for toxo-plasmosis immunity, but many find the current test to be unreliable and needlessly alarming or confusing. Instead, they recommend precautionary measures such as avoiding raw or undercooked meats, wearing gloves when gardening, and, if there is a cat in the household, having someone else empty the litter box.

Although a relatively trivial illness in children and adults, rubella (or German measles) can have grave consequences for an unborn baby. If a pregnant woman contracts it during the first month of pregnancy, there is a 50 percent risk of significant damage to the fetus. Later in pregnancy, the risk to the baby progressively decreases, with only 1 to 2 percent of babies being affected in the fifth month of pregnancy.

Even when a woman believes she has had rubella or was vaccinated against it, her doctor should confirm that she is still immune. Rubella is a mild, highly infectious illness that lasts for only a few days. It often resembles other viruses—slight rash and fever—and may have been in-correctly diagnosed or the vaccination may not have established immunity. If a woman is not immune to rubella, she should be immunized *at least 3 months before* attempting pregnancy. Vaccinations against rubella cannot be carried out after conception because the live vaccine might harm the unborn child. However, as long as an unvaccinated woman does not contract rubella during pregnancy, the baby will be all right.

Vaccines

It is safe to give certain vaccines in pregnancy if absolutely necessary. If a woman is planning a trip abroad, she should try to make certain her immunizations are up to date before she tries to conceive. As all adults should have tetanus and diphtheria boosters every 10 years, this is a good time for a woman to update her immunity. Some women may not have been immunized against polio in childhood; if this is the case, she should also ask her doctor about polio vaccine at this time.

A DENTAL CHECKUP

THE DENTAL PROBLEMS some women encounter during pregnancy are usually related to gum ailments rather than calcium deficiencies. A woman should have an evaluation of her mouth and complete any major dental work before she becomes pregnant. Although it is safe to have dental work during pregnancy, some precautions, such as shielding the abdomen for dental X rays and more careful selection of medications, should be observed. Most, however, would rather avoid the stress of extensive or prolonged dental treatment at this time.

DIET, EXERCISE, AND LIFESTYLE

BEFORE CONCEPTION couples will want to assess their lifestyle to pinpoint changes that might benefit the pregnancy. Ideally, any necessary changes—such as losing or gaining weight, beginning an exercise program, quitting smoking, or cutting down on drinking—should be made well in advance of pregnancy.

Good nutrition and physical fitness help to ensure a comfortable and healthy pregnancy. If a woman is not at her ideal weight, she should make every effort to become so before conception. If she feels that she is out of condition, she should exercise and tone her muscles.

Pre-Conception Nutritional Status

Weight. A woman who starts pregnancy markedly underweight is more likely to deliver prematurely or to have a baby of low birth weight, even if she gains weight normally during pregnancy. A little extra weight does not appear to cause difficulties, but a woman who is obese before conception is more likely to develop complications, such as gestational diabetes, and to encounter difficulties in delivery that could jeopardize both the baby and herself.

No matter how overweight a woman is when she becomes pregnant she should not cut down drastically on eating during pregnancy. Dieting during pregnancy may deprive the baby of nutrients necessary for normal development. Also, losing weight causes body fat to be broken down

into substances called ketone bodies, which may interfere with the development of the fetus. In addition, potentially toxic substances, such as PCBs, are stored in body fat; thus, in the best interest of the fetus, it is a good idea to avoid breaking down stored fat.

If a woman determines that she needs to lose weight before pregnancy, she should avoid crash diets or any extreme or limited regimen that is contrary to a nutritious, balanced diet. A diet high in complex carbohydrates, low in fat, and with a moderate amount of protein is the best approach. Calorie intake levels need to be balanced against the activity level to allow a gradual weight loss, preferably 1 to 2 pounds a week until ideal weight is achieved.

Remember, too, that nutritional requirements increase dramatically during pregnancy. A person entering pregnancy significantly overweight may still need to increase food intake to ensure proper nutrition for the fetus. (See chapter 9, Nutrition During Pregnancy, for a more detailed discussion.)

Vitamins and Minerals. Of course, weight is only one aspect of the nutritional preparation for pregnancy. Certain key vitamins and minerals,—specifically folic acid, calcium, and iron—are critical for pregnancy and may be lacking in the typical American diet. Thus, some obstetricians today recommend preconception supplements. A word of caution, however: Vitamin and mineral supplements should be taken only on the advice of a physician since megadoses can cause more harm than good.

Folic Acid. Folic acid, a B-complex vitamin, works along with vitamin B_{12} to promote the formation of healthy red blood cells in the mother. Good natural sources of folic acid are liver, dark-green vegetables, legumes (especially lima beans), and whole grains. Vitamin B_{12} is found naturally in meat, fish, shellfish, organ meats, egg yolks, and milk and milk products.

The recommended dietary allowance (RDA) for folacin is 400 micrograms (mcg) for adult women. This increases to 800 mcg during pregnancy, 500 mcg if the mother is breastfeeding. Folacin supplements are often included in prenatal vitamins. There is some evidence to suggest that folic acid supplements before conception may decrease the incidence of neural tube defects.

Calcium. Calcium may be supplemented during pregnancy, although a diet that provides adequate dairy products and other natural sources is sufficient for most people. Calcium from the mother's body is crucial for development of the baby's bones and tooth buds. If adequate calcium intake is not maintained, the mother will be relatively calcium deficient and this may influence her future risk for osteoporosis. Women planning a pregnancy can build stores of calcium naturally by increasing their consumption of milk, yogurt, and other dairy products. (Skim milk provides as much—or even a little more—calcium as whole

milk, but without the fat and extra calories.) Calcium is also found in dark-green leafy vegetables, sardines, dried peas and beans, and canned salmon.

Iron. Few women start pregnancy with enough iron stored in their bodies. Iron is necessary to make hemoglobin, which carries oxygen in the blood. It is especially critical during pregnancy when a woman's blood volume approximately doubles and thus her body must produce extra hemoglobin to ensure an adequate amount for both herself and the fetus. Although during pregnancy the body is able to absorb more iron from food sources than it normally can, it still cannot absorb an adequate amount. Consequently, prenatal iron supplements are commonly recommended.

Natural foods that contain substantial amounts of iron are liver and other organ meats, lean meats, dark-green leafy vegetables (especially parsley and kale), beets and beet greens, dried fruits (apricots, prunes, or figs), egg yolks, shellfish, molasses, and whole grains. Many breads and cereals are fortfied with iron.

Physical Fitness

Exercise promotes good health, but during pregnancy, keeping fit is particularly important. Good muscle tone not only makes a pregnant woman feel better, but it helps prepare her body for labor. A healthy fitness program before and during pregnancy also promotes good bowel function, aids in sleep, and ultimately helps a mother regain her figure more easily after pregnancy.

A regular exercise program improves circulation, tightens flabby muscles, and improves posture. Regular exercise might also help to reduce emotional stress and alleviate anxiety and depression. It is safer and easier for a woman to continue exercising during pregnancy when her body is already in shape. Women who wait to start a vigorous exercise program until after they become pregnant are adding additional stress to the body. Because exercise tolerance is decreased during pregnancy, it is best to get in shape before pregnancy and then modify exercise routines as pregnancy advances. (See chapter 10, The Pregnant Lifestyle.)

At least 10 to 15 minutes should be set aside each day for some form of exercise. If daily sessions are impractical, 15 to 30 minutes 3 times a week is adequate. Shorter, regular workouts are better than an hour once or twice a week.

Many different kinds of exercise can increase general fitness, but a woman planning a pregnancy should choose a program that can be continued in some form throughout pregnancy. The American College of Obstetricians and Gynecologists has recently suggested that the safest and most beneficial exercises for pregnant and newly delivered mothers are brisk walking, swimming, and stationary cycling. Tennis and jogging in moderation are also safe, as long as a woman becomes active in these sports before pregnancy.

All extreme forms of exercise should be avoided. A doctor should be consulted before making any major change in an exercise routine, especially if the woman has been sedentary up to this point or if she has any chronic medical condition such as asthma, hypertension, or arthritis.

Smoking, Alcohol, and Caffeine

The time to stop smoking and to avoid or reduce alcohol consumption is *before* pregnancy is achieved. This is good advice for both partners, although it is the mother's smoking and alcohol consumption that has the most direct impact on the fetus. There are indications, however, that secondhand smoke is a health hazard to both the mother and her baby. The timing is crucial because the embryo is at its most vulnerable in the early weeks of intrauterine life, before a woman even knows she is pregnant.

Women who smoke have an increased risk of miscarriage, stillbirth, and premature or low-birth-weight babies. Crib death is also more common among babies whose mothers smoke. Some studies have suggested that children of mothers who smoked during pregnancy score lower on neurological and intellectual tests than those of nonsmokers and are more likely to be hyperactive.

Heavy drinking has been associated with miscarriage, low-birth-weight babies, and birth defects, including mental retardation. The safe level of alcohol consumption during pregnancy has not been established, nor is it known exactly how the extent of fetal damage relates to the quantity of alcohol consumed. Most scientists believe that an occasional drink is not harmful to the pregnancy, but heavy drinking, especially in the early weeks of pregancy, is clearly dangerous.

Much more dangerous than an occasional drink is binge drinking. All medical researchers agree that consuming large quantities of alcohol in a concentrated period of time is extremely hazardous to the fetus at every stage of development, especially during the early embryonic stage, when the vital organs are being formed.

The evidence regarding caffeine consumption is not as grave as for alcohol or tobacco, but most doctors recommend that intake be limited to 1 or 2 cups of coffee or their equivalent a day. If a woman drinks more than 4 or 5 cups or glasses of coffee, tea, or soda that contains caffeine a day, the months before conception are also a good time for her to begin cutting back gradually. Switching to naturally decaffeinated coffee or tea, herbal tea, postum, or caffeine-free colas is one way of cutting back. Alternating cups of caffeine-containing and caffeine-free beverages, or mixing ground regular coffee with decaffeinated coffee first and gradually increasing the amount of decaffeinated are other ways of reducing caffeine intake.

Changing well-ingrained lifestyle habits can be stressful, so it is best to begin well in advance of pregnancy. While it may be difficult to stop smoking and drinking, cut down on caffeine, optimize nutrition, and begin an exercise program all at once, keep in mind that no one can control life's events—especially those involving reproduction—down to the last minute. It may take a woman a year or longer after discontinuing contraception to conceive; on the other hand, it may only take a month, so procrastination over adopting better health habits is not a good idea.

Drugs

As noted earlier, a woman should check with her doctor about the safety of any drugs, both prescription and over-the-counter, that she may be taking. Drugs taken for a specific medical condition should not be stopped or the regimen altered without consulting a physician, but the medication or regimen may be changed to one that is best for both the mother and baby.

Some drugs are known to be potentially harmful to the fetus and some, such as thalidomide or megadoses of vitamin A, can produce serious birth defects. But most drugs on the market have never been tested for safe use during pregnancy. Therefore, a woman who is planning a pregnancy or who is already pregnant should be aware of these hazards and take steps to guard against them in every way she can. She should not take any medications, even nonprescription ones such as antacids or cough medicines, without checking first with her obstetrician. Drugs prescribed by a dentist or another doctor should also be approved first by the doctor attending her pregnancy.

Illicit or Addictive Drugs. Addictive drugs such as heroin, cocaine, and methadone also cross the placental barrier and reach the fetus. Women who use these drugs often have low-birth-weight babies, and the infant of an addicted mother may be born addicted and suffer seizures during the period of withdrawal after birth. Cocaine use also has been linked to miscarriages and prematurity. Marijuana seems to decrease fertility in men, which may make it more difficult for the couple to conceive.

MISCELLANEOUS FACTORS

Toxins and Pollutants

If either partner works with toxic materials, or if the couple live or work in a polluted atmosphere, they may need advice from an obstetrician about possible hazards to the proposed pregnancy. Occupational hazards are difficult to evaluate, and in many instances the risks are not clear. Known hazards include radiation, anesthetic gases, chemical solvents, and heavy metals; less well understood are the effects of numerous other toxins, as well as high-stress jobs.

Heat

Heat seems to have a deleterious effect on a man's sperm production. Recent evidence shows that heat can also damage a developing fetus in the early days of pregnancy. Pregnant women and women trying to conceive should avoid saunas, hot tubs, and steam baths. Regular baths are not dangerous, however.

Interim Contraceptives

A couple planning a pregnancy may need to use an alternative form of contraception before actually attempting pregnancy. For example, if the female partner has been using oral contraceptives or if she has an IUD in place, it is a good idea to switch to a barrier method of contraception (condom, diaphragm, or sponge) for 2 or 3 months, until she is ready to conceive. This gives her body a chance to resume its normal hormonal levels (if she has used the pill) or allows the uterus to repair any effects from an IUD.

Using a diaphragm, sponge, or condoms just before conception has not been shown to affect pregnancy. There is some question about a possible link between spermicidal creams or foams and birth defects. To date, however, there is no good evidence to support this concern.

Ambivalence

Even when they have wholeheartedly made a decision to have a child, it is not unusual for ambivalence to flare up when a couple stops using contraceptives. Nor does stopping contraceptives mean instant pregnancy. It can take several months or longer to achieve pregnancy. Many couples begin counting days and timing ovulation if they do not conceive in the first month. In fact, it can take a year, and sometimes longer, to achieve pregnancy. The best advice is to relax and enjoy this period of trying.

SPACING CHILDREN

ALTHOUGH THE BODY can restore itself in about 3 months, it is generally recommended that a woman wait at least a year after the birth of one baby before trying to conceive again. Her body needs ample time to replenish its nutritional reserves, and her reproductive organs need time to prepare for another baby. If she is nursing, she should wait longer. The combination of nursing and pregnancy are physically stressful and it is very difficult, if not impossible, to get all the nutrients needed to sustain both at once. Although it is possible to become pregnant while nursing, the conception rate is lower. In any event, breastfeeding should not be considered an adequate alternative to birth control.

New research studies suggest that children born within 1 or 2 years of each other seem to fare well psychologically. Accepted theory has it that firstborns and only children do better in life—scholastically, professionally, and financially—

than do subsequent children. Those born in the middle seem to fare the worst, having a poorer sense of self-esteem than do their older and younger siblings. Recent studies, however, indicate that the length of time between births might override many effects of the child's position in the birth order. New research suggests that optimum spacing between children is either about 1 year or so apart or else 5 or more years apart. Very close—or very wide—spacing seems to reduce intense feelings of competition betwen siblings.

Some parents, too, feel they would like to have all their babies at one time in order to get through the difficult phases of diapering, bottle-feeding/nursing, and toilet training in 1 massive undertaking. For many, however, the idea of caring for 2 or more infants and toddlers at one time is overwhelming. The spacing of children, like many other facets of pregnancy and childbirth, is largely a matter of family choice.

UNPLANNED PREGNANCIES

EVEN WITH THE widespread availability of contraceptive methods, many women unexpectedly become pregnant and are unprepared to continue the pregnancy. The earlier the pregnancy is confirmed the more time will be available to resolve the conflicts and issues. When a pregnancy is advanced, the mother or the cou-

ple may be forced into making a decision that is not in her, or their, best interests.

Although relatives, family friends, and even physicians may try to influence the choice, the prospective parents themselves should make their own decision about whether to continue the pregnancy. Some difficult considerations they may have to deal with include finances, marriage, adoption, health considerations, single-parenthood, living arrangements, and employment.

Abortion

Abortion is a highly charged issue, and one in which there are no easy answers. Ultimately, whether to have an abortion or not must be a woman's decision, and ideally, it should be made along with her male partner. If a couple chooses abortion, there are several options. The woman's physician may perform the abortion as an outpatient or inpatient procedure, depending on timing. If not, the woman's gynecologist may refer her to another doctor. Referrals to an outpatient center can also come from Planned Parenthood and similar organizations, or from some municipal health centers.

An outpatient women's center that performs first-trimester abortions (up to 12 weeks) will usually offer pre- and postabortion counseling, as well as advice about contraceptives. Outpatient clinics usually provide pelvic exams and pregnancy tests, pre- and postabortion counseling, and any necessary laboratory tests. For example, if a woman is shown to be Rh negative, she will receive a small dose of rhesus gamma globulin at the time of the abortion to prevent complications in future pregnancies. Local anesthesia is usually given. Some clinics will arrange to perform second-trimester abortions, usually in a nearby hospital. The staff usually comprises obstetrician/gynecologists, anesthesiologists, nurse practitioners, and trained counselors.

One drawback is that some of these facilities may not provide good follow-up care. If something goes wrong after the woman leaves, she may have to go to the emergency room of a hospital for treatment. For that reason, it is wise for a woman to select an outpatient center recommended by her private physician if she has one, and to return to her physician for follow-up. Any woman who has an abortion should have adequate follow-up by her physician or at the clinic where the procedure was performed within 1 to 2 weeks following the termination, even if no apparent complications arise.

Women with preexisting medical problems—diabetes, heart disease, or bleeding disorders—should have an abortion performed in a hospital. Abortions at hospitals, even when performed on an outpatient basis, are usually more expensive because the procedure is carried out in an operating room.

Less than 1 percent of all early abortions and 10 percent of second-trimester procedures result in serious complications. Early complications occurring within the first 24 hours of abortion include bleeding, uterine damage, and anesthesia-related problems. If bleeding is caused by incomplete emptying of the uterus, a dilation and curettage (D&C) will have to be performed. In this procedure, the cervix is dilated under anesthesia and a spoon-shaped instrument called a curette is used to scrape out the uterine cavity.

Occasionally (1 in 1,000 abortions) the uterus is perforated during the abortion and will require at least an overnight stay in the hospital. If the cervix is damaged by forceful dilation, it may be repaired by a single suture. Rarely, bleeding or perforation requires more extensive surgery. These complications reveal themselves within 24 hours of the abortion.

Delayed complications are often more serious. Pelvic pain, heavy bleeding, fever, chills, or foul-smelling discharge—which may begin several days to 2 weeks after the abortion—may indicate infection and require immediate medical attention. Minor infections tend to respond well to a course of oral antibiotics. However, the infection may be severe enough to spread throughout the pelvic cavity and invade the fallopian tubes; in that case, a woman will require hospitalization and intravenous antibiotic treatment.

Methods of Abortion

Suction Abortions. These are performed in women who are up to 12 weeks pregnant (first trimester). These early abortions are, in general, safe procedures that carry very little risk. First-trimester abortions may be performed appropriately in a clinic, an ambulatory care facility, or a hospital. There are 2 types of suction abortions:

Menstrual Extraction or Miniabortion. These can be performed as early as 1 week after conception but no later than 2 weeks after a missed period. Menstrual extraction, unlike other suction abortion methods, puts very little pressure on the cervix and requires only minimal dilation, if any. The cannulae used to evacuate the uterine contents are very small in diameter. A woman requesting menstrual extraction may not be certain she is pregnant; a urine test is likely to be negative at this early stage, but a blood pregnancy test can verify pregnancy.

The main drawback to menstrual extraction is that it has a failure rate of 2.5 to 3 percent. For this reason, the woman should have a follow-up examination in 1 to 2 weeks to confirm that she is no longer pregnant.

Vacuum Curettage. This is the most common method of first-trimester abortion and is normally performed between 7 and 12 weeks of pregnancy, counting from the first day of the woman's last menstrual period. The procedure, which can be done under either local or general anesthesia, involves dilating the cervix with small metal rods of progressively increasing diameter. Dilation can also be achieved by means of *Laminaria japonicum*, a water-absorbing dried seaweed, which is inserted into the cervix prior to the procedure. The sterile seaweed gradually swells over a period of several hours as it absorbs fluid, and gently dilates the cervix.

After the cervix is dilated, the doctor positions a plastic tube through the cervix, attaches the free end to an electric suction pump, and then suctions out the uterine cavity in 3 to 5 minutes.

Dilatation and Evacuation (D&E). This procedure is used for abortions during the second trimester of pregnancy (between 14 and 23 weeks). D&E requires greater dilation of the cervix than suction methods; *Laminaria japonicum* often is used for a more gentle, less damaging, dilation. The procedure is still usually one of suction curettage, but larger instruments are needed.

D&E is usually done in the hospital under general anesthesia. A woman choosing a second-trimester abortion should find a skilled, experienced surgeon. Not all physicians are trained to perform this procedure, and in the wrong hands it can be a hazardous technique.

Instillation Abortions. These take place between weeks 16 and 24 of pregnancy and involve the injection of saline, prostaglandin, or urea into the amniotic fluid sac. Prostaglandin suppositories may also be used. After the injection, labor begins, and the fetus is delivered, usually within 24 hours, although it can take longer. Instillation abortions are naturally very stressful for the woman; some physicians speed the delivery process by using *Laminaria japonicum* to dilate the cervix or giving intravenous oxytocin—a hormone that promotes labor—to stimulate uterine contractions. Common side effects of instillation abortion are nausea, vomiting, and diarrhea.

Frequently, delivery of the placenta or afterbirth is delayed. When the placenta does not follow the delivery of the fetus within 1 or 2 hours, there is danger of bleeding. In these cases, the doctor may perform a D&C to complete the abortion procedure.

Prostaglandin suppositories are the most widely used of the second trimester abortion substances. Prostaglandins should not be used in women with lung disease, such as asthma, because this hormone may cause spasm of the breathing tubes in the lungs. Saline instillation is contraindicated in women with serious heart or kidney disease because of its tendency to promote fluid retention.

Impact on Future Pregnancies

There is still debate about whether having had an abortion affects a woman's future childbearing capability. For now, the consensus is that an early abortion seems to have no effect on future childbearing, unless the procedure was improperly performed or complicated by infection. Severe infection following an abortion may involve the Fallopian tubes and lead to sterility, but with modern surgical techniques such infections are rare. Theoretically, repeat early abortions might result in an incompetent cervix, which increases the risk of premature deliveries in future pregnancies, or might create scarring within the uterus, making conception difficult. Again, there is no proof of serious incidence of either of these problems after uncomplicated abortions.

Abortions carried out later in pregnancy, however, are more likely to affect future pregnancies. The forceful dilation of the cervix carried out during a D&E may damage the cervix, which may lead to late miscarriage in subsequent pregnancies. The risks, however, are still low.

Emotional Aftermath

Often, when a couple chooses to have an abortion, they do not realize how long they carry emotional feelings about the pregnancy with them. It is usual for both women and men to have thoughts and feelings about the abortion long after the event. Late abortions tend to cause more prolonged grieving. Also, women who feel they were forced into an abortion because of external circumstances often experience intense feelings of stress, anger, and grief afterward. Even those who have made the decision freely often struggle with guilt feelings. Women who subsequently become pregnant and miscarry may feel that they are being punished. The best advice is to recognize that these feelings are normal and to allow a period of mourning. Most clinics, women's centers, and Planned Parenthood centers offer counseling before and after termination of pregnancy as part of the overall cost of the procedure.

SUMMING UP

GOOD PREPARATION FOR PREGNANCY is rewarding physically and emotionally and can make pregnancy and childbirth a pleasure. Preparation includes having a complete check-up, including a physical exam, a family and medical history, laboratory tests, and any necessary immunizations. It also means adopting a healthy lifestyle that includes good nutrition, weight control, exercise, foregoing cigarettes, and modifying alcohol and caffeine consumption.

Having children today means fully understanding the promises of parenthood. By taking an overview of their circumstances ahead of time, a couple can enjoy pregnancy more and at the same time create a more stable and relaxed environment for their entire family.

2 Choosing Your Health Care Team

Edward Bowe, M.D.

INTRODUCTION

AT THE BEGINNING OF THE CENTURY, virtually every American was born at home. Gradually, as medical care became more widely available, women began having their babies in hospitals. By the 1950s, almost every pregnant woman entered a hospital to give birth. Sterile conditions, new drugs and delivery practices, and new technology made childbirth safer for both mother and baby. But gradually the technology developed for high-risk situations began to be used even for healthy, normal pregnancies. Childbirth became an event closely controlled by physicians and hospital staff.

In the 1970s, some women and even some physicians began to argue that most births did not require, nor benefit from, intrusive technology. New parents began to complain that hospital procedures were stressing technology unnecessarily and at the expense of human needs. Their attitude reflected an overall change in attitude among patients toward taking more interest in and more responsibility for their own health care. Along with some innovative physicians, these couples said that pregnancy was a healthy, normal condition and that babies and mothers do best when childbirth takes place in a comfortable, relaxed environment, accompanied by as little medical interference as possible.

Most obstetricians, on the other hand, argued that when things go wrong during delivery they go wrong suddenly and often without warning. Having the latest and best technology available at a moment's notice is the best way to ensure the safety of mother and baby.

As a result, in the early 1980s, largely in response to changing patient wishes, the concept of family-centered childbirth emerged as an integral part of obstetrical care in most hospitals. Many hospitals have tried to become more homelike for mothers and babies, offering birthing rooms, flexible visiting hours, and rooming in for the newborn. (A birthing room, in which delivery as well as labor takes place, often looks like a living room or bedroom.) A family-centered hospital usually encourages a woman's husband or a friend to participate in labor and delivery and may allow family members liberal visiting hours. Some hospitals have midwife programs, where a trained nurse-midwife stays with the woman from the begining of labor all the way through delivery. This personalized approach is complemented by technological advances that make childbirth today safe even for many complicated pregnancies.

Couples planning to have a baby in the United States today have a variety of options not only as to where and how the baby will be delivered, but also as to who will be the primary maternity care provider. They may choose a physician in private practice—a general practitioner, family doctor, or obstetrician. That physician may be in solo practice or part of a group. The mother may choose to receive prenatal care at a hospital obstetrics clinic, where she will be seen by resident obstetricians in training or by nurse-midwives, or both.

Ninety-seven percent of pregnant women receive their care from physicians and deliver their babies in hospitals. About 2 percent receive care from a childbirth center, which is staffed by nurse-midwives, and a few American women choose to have their babies at home. Regardless of the type of care they choose, the couple should look for total maternity care. The person they choose should be thorough and competent, with a desire to know as much as possible about the mother. And the mother should do everything she can to learn about pregnancy and childbirth so she can make an enlightened choice.

CONSIDERATIONS IN CHOOSING MATERNITY CARE

NOT EVERY OBSTETRICIAN or hospital today takes a family-centered approach. It is still up to parents to search for maternity care that meets their own personal preferences. Prospective parents today have a lot to say about the manner in which they would like to have their baby delivered, particularly if the pregnancy is low risk. Different approaches to labor and delivery appeal to different people. Stratification of care available in the United States runs the gamut from medical centers specializing in high-risk pregnancies to community hospitals to free-standing childbirth centers—all the way to having a baby at home with a midwife in attendance.

While there are many options in the type of maternity care a couple might choose, in one significant way maternity care is harder to find than ever. Due to rising costs of malpractice insurance associated with obstetrics, many physicians are abandoning this specialty in favor of less demanding, less potentially risky fields. Nurse-midwives are also faced with similar escalating insurance costs that are forcing many out of practice. This combination of events—a wide variety of types, but limited availability—makes the search for maternity care a major concern, and one that requires time.

The choice of maternity care provider should be made when a woman has the time to consider alternatives and evaluate impressions—not, as is often the case, under conditions of stress and urgency. Ideally, the search should begin before conception so that prenatal care can begin as soon as a woman becomes pregnant.

A couple's choice of care should be based primarily on the woman's age and her risk factors. The young, low-risk woman, especially if it is her first baby, is perfectly well—or perhaps better—cared for by a nurse-midwife who can take extra time educating her about pregnancy and childbirth. Some nurse-midwives work in conjunction with obstetricians. Others work independently, with physician backup, or are employed by childbirth centers. If anything arises during the antepartum course that would impinge upon the outcome of the pregnancy, the midwife transfers the woman to the care of an obstetrician.

An older woman, a woman with a preexisting medical condition, or one who has experienced complications in a previous pregnancy, however, requires care by an obstetrician, and perhaps by a maternal and fetal medicine specialist. (See table 2.1.) She will benefit if she delivers in a technologically advanced hospital.

Regardless of a woman's age or physical condition, however, the most important aspect of her maternity care is consistent prenatal checkups over the course of the pregnancy. Because complications may arise, both the patient and the care provider must have an attitude of flexibility. A breech presentation of the baby, for example, may mean that a woman receiving care at a childbirth center must be referred to a specialist. In these situations, the woman should be willing to accept referral in her own best interests.

A woman's personal preference will also influence the kind of care she chooses. For example, a young and healthy woman may still prefer to have her baby in a sophisticated hospital setting. Or a woman who has some risks may still look for care that emphasizes simplicity and a homelike environment

---

Table 2.1
HIGH-RISK PREGNANCIES

Most obstetricians consider the following conditions to be high risk, requiring prenatal care by a physician and delivery in a well-equipped hospital:

- Age—mother is over 35 or under 18
- Diabetes
- High blood pressure
- Epilepsy
- Heart disease
- Multiple gestation
- Previous difficult pregnancy
- Previous cesarean delivery

(For more information, see chapter 13, The High-Risk Pregnancy.)

---

rather than technology. Even though such personal preferences are important, the most important objective for both patient and doctor is a happy outcome for child and mother.

TYPES OF MATERNITY CARE PROVIDERS

A Physician in Private Practice

General practitioners (GPs), nonspecialists who have delivered many Americans, are now few and far between. General practitioners graduating from medical school today may have only limited knowledge of obstetrics and gynecology because these areas of study are now electives in some medical schools. For licensure, they are only required to take one year of postgraduate study (formerly called "internship," now called "PGY-I"), which may or may not include a period of study in obstetrics and gynecology.

Family practice is a relatively new specialty that is replacing general practice in many parts of the country. The family practitioner has 3 years of training following medical school, including a minimum of 3 months of obstetrics and gynecology. Both the GP and the family practitioner are primary-care physicians, which means that they can give basic, comprehensive care to any person of any age. They are likely to know other family members and to be familiar with a woman's overall background and medical history. Most family physicians have obstetrical experience and some specialize in obstetrics. They have delivery room privileges in most community hospitals. They may not, however, have the experience to handle a high-risk obstetrical case, and in such circumstances they may make referrals for obstetrical and gynecological care.

The obstetrician-gynecologist (OB-GYN) is the most likely choice for women who choose a physician in private practice. An obstetrician has had a minimum of 3 years of specialty training in obstetrics and gynecology after medical school. The OB-GYN may also have additional subspecialty training in areas such as maternal and fetal medicine (high-risk pregnancy) or reproductive endocrinology. When serious medical problems occur in conjunction with pregnancy, obstetrician-gynecologists guide patients to the appropriate health care professional.

Many obstetricians are board certified by the American Board of Obstetrics and Gynecology, or are board eligible. Board certification means that an obstetrician has spent 4 to 5 years in postgraduate training after receiving a medical degree and has passed several difficult examinations. Board eligibility means that a physician has completed postgraduate training but has not yet been in practice for 2 years, the minimum required before taking the certifying examination, or has not yet passed the board examination.

Specialists in Maternal and Fetal Medicine

A maternal and fetal medicine specialist is an obstetrician who has received additional training in high-risk pregnancies. A woman who has a preexisting medical condition before she becomes pregnant—such as heart disease, high blood pressure, diabetes, or cystic fibrosis—might receive her maternity care from such a specialist, who often works in conjunction with her regular doctor.

A young, healthy woman who develops complications over the course of pregnancy may be referred to a maternal medicine specialist or other specialist, if her health care provider feels this is necessary. A woman who is carrying multiple fetuses, for example, automatically falls into a high-risk category. So does a woman who develops diabetes or high blood pressure during pregnancy.

Solo and Group Practices

Solo practice, particularly for obstetricians, is decreasing, except in isolated areas. The obvious advantage to the patient of a solo practice is a more personal relationship with a doctor and less fragmented care. The disadvantage is that the doctor may not be available when the baby is due, in which case another doctor will attend the delivery.

To ease the heavy workload of obstetrics and also to provide consistent maternal care, many physicians today join in partnership or group practices. Even those obstetricians who persist in solo practice have informal arrangements with other doctors to cover each other on weekends, vacations, and during the week for night calls.

A formal group practice is a financial and contractual agreement. A group may have as few as 2 doctors, or as many as 10. By reducing the workload, a group practice may allow the doctor to spend more time with each patient. It is generally more economical to the doctor, a savings that may be passed on in lower fees. The shared economics of the group practice may also allow better equipped offices and may support ancillary services such as laboratories. Finally, the availability of other physicians for consultation is an important advantage.

The group may be a single-specialty group, such as 3 obstetrician-gynecologists, or it may be a multispecialty group including an obstetrician-gynecologist, an internist, and a pediatrician.

In a group practice, the patient has the advantage of having a backup doctor who is known to her. If a couple choose an obstetrician in group practice, it is important for them to know every obstetrician in the practice, even if just one follows the woman through her pregnancy. There is always the possibility that a different member of the group will be on call at the time of delivery.

Each birth is a once-in-a-lifetime experience for a couple, and the attending physician is an integral part of that experience. A woman who feels uncomfortable with one member of the group can request that another doctor attend her labor and delivery, even if the doctor with whom she lacks rapport is on call. If this cannot be promised, the woman should consider looking further.

Nurse-Midwives

A certified nurse-midwife is a registered nurse who has taken at least one year of additional specialized training in a program approved by the American College of Nurse-Midwives and passed the national certification examination.

Nurse-midwives specialize in low-risk pregnancies. Many pregnant women do not want—or need—the latest and best technology. That is where midwives come in. Midwives are qualified to provide complete obstetrical care, including delivery in uncomplicated pregnancies. They do not perform complicated obstetrical care such as forceps, breech, or cesarean deliveries. The nurse-midwife typically remains with the mother throughout labor to provide psychological as well as medical support. Nurse-midwife programs have been instituted at some hospitals in response to patient demand, and nurse-midwives are the major care providers at out-of-hospital childbirth centers.

In a hospital setting, the nurse-midwife usually works closely with an obstetrician, who is usually (but not always) present at the birth. In childbirth centers, the nurse-midwife is in complete charge of prenatal checkups and delivery; an obstetrician is available as backup in case of complications.

Lay Midwives

A few women receive their care at home from lay midwives. The lay midwife, not to be confused with the certified nurse-midwife, traditionally has assisted at childbirth in areas where medical care has been unavailable. Historically the lay midwife received her training on the job and had little formal education.

Because training and experience of lay midwives varies, someone planning to use a lay midwife should carefully check her qualifications and those of her backup doctor. No matter how normal the pregnancy seems, nor how competent the midwife, a woman should not use a lay midwife—or any midwife—who does not have an established medical backup.

WHERE TO HAVE A BABY

A WOMAN'S CHILDBIRTH options may be affected not only by what type of care provider she prefers, but also by *where* she would like to have the baby and what she can afford.

Hospital Clinics

Some couples opt for maternity care in a hospital clinic staffed by resident physicians, obstetrical nurses, and often nurse-midwives. These care providers are supervised by board-certified physicians. It is likely that the woman will be seen by a different doctor on each prenatal visit, and her child may be delivered by someone she has never met.

Pregnant women visit the clinic just as they would a private obstetrician, beginning with prenatal checkups and continuing straight through delivery. Clinics also offer childbirth preparation classes.

Several types of hospitals offer maternity clinics. When a hospital clinic is affiliated with a medical school, technical services—the lab tests and procedures—are more likely to be available and may be superior. The level of obstetrical care offered by such hospital clinics is generally very good. Women are usually closely supervised by resident OB-GYN physicians trained in the latest available techniques. In hospital maternity clinics, various specialists are also available who are called in if complications arise during the course of pregnancy or during delivery.

A high-risk patient choosing a clinic should look for a university medical center. Here she will be seen by obstetricians trained in maternal and fetal medicine. These doctors have completed their obstetrical residency and are closely supervised by attending specialists. In these teaching hospitals there is more attending backup than in community hospitals.

Clinic costs are generally lower than those for private care, but they vary considerably. Generally, a flat fee is charged for the clinic; there is no obstetrical fee. A woman who does not have health insurance or a prepaid health plan might consider using a county or university hospital that uses a sliding scale, rather than a flat fee, for service.

Choosing a Hospital

Often, when a woman chooses an obstetrician or a clinic, she automatically chooses the hospital. Conversely, she may choose a hospital and then find an obstetrician who is affiliated with it. If she is considered a low-risk patient and she values family-centered care, she may find it at either a community hospital (more likely) or at a university medical center. If she is a high-risk patient, however, she should limit her choices to hospitals with the facilities (such as a neonatal care unit), staff, and equipment to handle her care.

One good way to evaluate a hospital is to take a tour of the maternity unit, including labor and delivery rooms, or birthing room, if one is available. Couples should be aware that if they choose a hospital because it offers a birthing room (a homelike setting in which delivery as well as labor takes place), there is no guarantee that the room will not be in use at the time a woman is ready to give birth.

During the tour, nurses should be willing to describe visiting hours, policies about rooming in, early discharges, and other regulations that would affect the delivery or stay.

The hospital selected should be equipped to handle an emergency should one arise. The hospital should also allow the family's chosen pediatrician to come in to examine the baby immediately following birth. Early and accurate diagnosis of any difficulties is important, so that the baby can either be treated or moved for treatment immediately. Prospective parents should find out how far away a neonatal transfer unit is and if the mother will be moved with the child should difficulties arise.

Childbirth Centers

A relatively new phenomenon is a small out-of-hospital facility called a childbirth center. Because these centers are staffed only by nurse-midwives, only healthy, young, low-risk mothers are accepted for care; those with risk factors are referred to a private physician or hospital clinic. Because of such careful screening, childbirth centers have an excellent record. If something out of the ordinary develops during the course of a woman's pregnancy, she is referred to a specialist.

Care at childbirth centers is provided by experienced and well-trained midwives who adhere to established standards of care. Although an obstetrician is not present during the delivery, there is always an obstetrician backup. Costs are generally lower than those of hospital delivery. Total cost of inclusive maternity care—prenatal visits, prepared childbirth classes, a 24-hour stay after delivery, and a postpartum checkup—is around $1500. Most medical insurance programs now cover childbirth centers.

A woman considering a childbirth center for her prenatal care and delivery should check the qualifications of the staff and the reputation and location of the backup hospital. Although most centers provide excellent care, standards do vary, and there are no uniform regulations. The local health department should be able to provide information about a center's safety record.

The main drawback of childbirth centers is that they are only equipped to handle routine deliveries. If the mother must be transferred to a hospital—even one a few blocks away—time is lost and the health of the mother and baby may be endangered.

Although a few emergency cesarean sections have been performed at childbirth centers, if a complication develops, the woman usually will be transported by ambulance to a hospital. Women should request written guidelines detailing the circumstances under which transfer to a hospital will be made and how quickly transfer can be accomplished.

At the present time there are only about 125 such facilities nationwide. A list of birthing centers can be found in the Yellow Pages of the telephone book; on request, the American College of Nurse-Midwives (1522 K Street NW, Washington, D.C. 20005) will provide a list of local nurse-midwife services.

Home Births

Home births enjoyed something of a vogue a few years ago but are now less common, perhaps because of the more personal approach of many hospitals. Home delivery is safe only for "normal" births; the problem is that a birth can be safely said to be normal only after the event. In addition, it is more difficult to ensure an adequately germ-free environment to protect both the mother and baby from infection.

Even a low-risk mother may experience complications during labor or birth. Approximately 10 percent of low-risk women who attempt home births need to be transferred to a hospital facility because of conditions arising during labor or delivery. In that transit time, lives can be lost.

Supporters of home birth believe that technological intervention, such as IVs, internal fetal monitors, and forceps during labor and delivery, is a barrier to the natural process of birth. But the main reason couples choose to remain at home is their desire to have more control of the birth experience.

If a couple chooses a home birth, it is mandatory that they be thoroughly familiar with the process of pregnancy and birth and that the woman receive excellent prenatal care. Choosing the right birth attendant is also vital to a good outcome.

A home birth is usually attended by a certified nurse-midwife or a lay midwife. Because laws and standards governing midwifery vary from state to state, it is up to the couple to evaluate the skills of the birth attendant. A midwife is trained to manage normal births and has the skill to detect abnormalities; she cannot replace an obstetrician if complications arise.

The couple should talk with as many attendants as possible and select the person with the most experience and training, as well as someone with whom they feel comfortable.

With any birth, it is important for a woman to have confidence in those who care for her during labor and delivery. Therefore, if she chooses a midwife for home birth, she should also meet with the backup physician several times during pregnancy.

Only a few doctors today actually deliver at home routinely, due in part to re-strictions placed by insurance companies on malpractice coverage. A few doctors are ardent practitioners of home deliveries, however. A doctor who attends home births need not be an obstetrician, but should be a practitioner for whom home birth is routine.

Regardless of whom the couple chooses as a birth attendant, the woman should see a doctor simultaneously throughout her pregnancy. Any couple planning a home birth should also have a backup plan. They should know what emergency equipment the birth attendant will provide on the scene. They should also make advance arrangements to get to a hospital if an emergency arises. If other children are at home, care should be available if the parents have to go to the hospital unexpectedly.

SOURCES OF NAMES OF HEALTH CARE PROVIDERS

ONE RELIABLE SOURCE of doctors' names is a good hospital—a teaching hospital, a large medical center, or a local community hospital. Any of these can provide the names of obstetricians on their staff who practice in the community. Many hospitals now have referral services that are able to make recommendations based on specific requests from the patient (such as a request for a female obstetrician who has evening office hours). A medical school is another good source: Many faculty members, in addition to their teaching responsibilities, practice privately.

The local medical society can also provide a list of obstetricians in the area (the same list may be available at the local library). In some communities, public-interest groups provide lists of obstetrical care providers—obstetricians, clinics, childbirth centers—along with background information.

Friends and relatives are another source of names. Although they are not always familiar with the recommended doctors' credentials (which can and should be checked elsewhere), they can provide useful information about a doctor's personality and attitude toward maternity care.

Checking a Doctor's Qualifications

The best indicator of a doctor's competence is good medical training. Medical directories, including the *Directory of Medical Specialists* published for the American Board of Medical Specialties and the *American Medical Directory*, available at public libraries, are excellent source books that list both qualifications and affiliations of specialists. They include the medical school a doctor attended, where he or she did postgraduate training, board certifications, and the doctor's present hospital appointments. Affiliation with a well-known hospital, especially one with an approved residency program for obstetrics or one attached to a medical school, is a highly reliable indicator that a doctor is well qualified.

INTERVIEWING PROSPECTIVE DOCTORS

TO A GREAT EXTENT a doctor's competence can be checked by such preliminary research. But competence is only one factor in selecting an obstetrical care provider. Certainly, a doctor or midwife should instill confidence and offer superior care and technical expertise. But he or she should also have time to answer questions and to discuss various kinds of labor and delivery methods. The doctor should want to know how the patient is feeling and be genuinely concerned with her welfare.

The doctor's sex and age also may have some bearing on the choice. Some women feel more comfortable in the care of a female health professional. Ten years ago, only a small percentage of obstetricians in the United States were women. This is changing rapidly, however. Many women physicians are coming into this field, and women make up an increasing percentage of the obstetrical residents currently training in university teaching centers. At the Columbia Presbyterian Medical Center, for example, 75 percent of obstetrical residents now in training are women. Most physician extenders (midwives and nurse-practitioners) are also women.

Some young couples may feel that a younger physician will be more in tune with their views of contemporary lifestyles, particularly as they affect pregnancy and childbirth. Or a high-risk woman may feel that an older doctor will have more experience. In fact, the age of the physician is important primarily as it affects the rapport between patient and doctor. Good rapport is a critical factor in choosing an obstetrician.

It is important for couples to find someone they like—someone with whom they are glad to share this most important experience—and someone who likes them, too. And the only way to discover whether a particular doctor is someone with whom the couple can be comfortable is a face-to-face meeting.

Before making any decision, a couple may want to meet with more than one doctor or go to more than one clinic. Usually a brief interview will be enough. In most cases, they will be charged for these consultations, but in the long run it can save expense and unhappiness. If possible both partners should be present at the initial meeting with a prospective health care provider. Before meeting the doctor the couple should make a list of questions they want to ask.

Practical and Personal Considerations

A pregnant woman will visit her doctor approximately 12 to 15 times over a period of 9 months, which means that practical considerations play an important part in the choice of a doctor. The doctor's office or clinic should be conveniently located, and the hours should be compatible with a woman's schedule. The hospital in which she will deliver should not be too far away.

The atmosphere of the doctor's office is also important. How long must patients wait before seeing the doctor? How quickly are telephone calls returned? What is the attitude displayed by nursing and office staff? All these details reflect the general tone and efficiency of the doctor's practice, and they will also affect a woman's mood and overall well-being as she progresses through the course of pregnancy.

By analyzing qualifications and practical considerations, the couple should be able to arrive at a short list of competent, well-trained physicians. From that point, their decision should be based on their personal response to the doctor.

Establishing Rapport

As they speak with practitioners, the couple should aim to communicate well from the start, asking questions clearly and tactfully, and asking for equally clear and specific answers. It is a good idea to prepare a list of questions beforehand to ask during the initial physician interview. (See table 2.2.) It takes information to ask good questions. Men and women both can prepare themselves for the meeting with physicians by reading current magazine articles and other publications about pregnancy and delivery methods. Even if a couple knows what approach they would like, they should keep an open mind and listen to what the doctor has to say. If they are not sure, they should be informed enough to discuss various possibilities with the doctor in order to reach a mutual decision.

In return, the couple should expect the doctor's full attention. The doctor should willingly answer questions and listen to any anxieties expressed by the patient. He or she should offer information as well as reassurance.

When recommending a prenatal procedure—whether vitamin supplements or specific tests—the doctor should clearly

Before making the final choice, the hospital or childbirth center where the baby will be delivered should be notified about the kind of delivery method the parents have chosen. (Prospective parents should be aware that even when everyone has agreed on the method of delivery, during labor circumstances may arise that demand a change of delivery method.) If the doctor or hospital staff will not agree to the initial request, or if the couple feels uncomfortable with the place or person they have chosen, they should look further.

Changing Obstetricians

Over the course of a pregnancy, various circumstances may arise that indicate that the couple has made a poor choice of obstetricians. Incompetence is one obvious reason for changing physicians. A doctor who fails to answer questions or does not explain clearly what to expect during the course of pregnancy is not doing an adequate job. The patient should feel comfortable talking to the doctor and asking for clarification. She should never be made to feel hesitant about telephoning a doctor. After each prenatal examination the doctor should offer a full discussion of the findings and answer all questions.

In certain circumstances—if the patient has a preexisting medical condition, such as diabetes or heart disease, or if she develops a serious complication during the course of pregnancy—the doctor should willingly refer her to a specialist. A pregnant woman should not, however,

---

Table 2.2
QUESTIONS TO ASK YOUR DOCTOR

A couple will probably want to ask the doctor some of the following questions:

- What is the doctor's usual fee and will it be higher if there are complications, such as a cesarean birth?
- What is the doctor's philosophy about obstetrical care?
- How does the doctor feel about internal fetal monitoring during labor?
- Does he or she cut episiotomies during delivery?
- Do all of his or her patients have an IV?
- How many of the doctor's patients have cesarean deliveries?
- Who covers when the doctor is unavailable?
- Can the couple meet that person?
- The last question a woman should ask herself is "Can I relate to this particular doctor?"

---

explain the risks and benefits involved.

Both partners should feel free to talk about the type of birthing experience they want. At the initial visit, they should ask about any special desires they have, such as Leboyer delivery, rooming in, or breastfeeding. The physician should share at least some of the couple's beliefs and be willing to fulfill their wishes as long as they are medically safe. Both the couple and the physician should be open to talking about alternatives.

be referred to a specialist for minor complaints.

Among the reasons women commonly give for changing obstetricians is incompatibility or lack of rapport. Sometimes a doctor's own lifestyle and point of view are at odds with those of the couple. It is up to the doctor to be flexible in these circumstances. If, for example, the patient makes an informed choice about a prenatal treatment or test, the doctor should accept the choice. If the doctor cannot accept the patient's choice, or does so in a negative manner, it is appropriate for the patient to choose another physician.

Some problems can be resolved if the patient discusses them with the doctor. But when a patient feels uneasy or dissatisfied with the doctor's response, she should change doctors. When a woman is uncomfortable with her obstetrician—for whatever reason—the partnership should be dissolved. While switching can be hard, it can be accomplished at any time during the pregnancy.

When a woman decides to change, she should tell the doctor personally of her decision. Knowing the reason why a woman changes to another doctor can be important to the physician's relationship with future patients, and also makes the woman feel that she has handled the situation in the proper manner. If the relationship has deteriorated too far, however, she may be unable to discuss it. In either case, a woman's medical records belong to her; in order to transfer these records to another physician, all she has to do is make a request in writing.

INSURANCE AND OTHER ECONOMIC FACTORS

MEDICAL COSTS BEGIN with the first prenatal visit to the doctor. Obstetrical bills are usually paid in installments *before* birth. Sometimes the total payment is divided in three parts, with the final payment made after the delivery. An obstetrician's fee, which covers office visits and the actual delivery, plus a postpartum checkup, range from $700 to $2,000 and up. Some obstetricians charge a flat rate, no matter how many visits or how complicated the delivery. Others have one fee for a normal delivery, but charge extra for a cesarean delivery. Hospital costs for both the mother's and the baby's stay are billed separately, as are any special prenatal tests and lab work, such as amniocentesis and ultrasound scans. The fee for the anesthesiologist, if one is needed (for a planned or emergency cesarean), will also be billed separately. The sum total of physician and hospital expenses averages $3,000 to $4,500. If the delivery is by cesarean—and more than 20 percent of deliveries now are—the maternity and nursery stay can be 6 or 7 days, more than doubling the usual 2- or 3-day stay.

All of this means that financial factors play an important part in a couple's choice of care provider. Significant numbers of American women have either no insurance or inadequate insurance to cover maternity fees. (According to a 1984 Currrent Population Survey conducted by the U.S. Census Bureau, 17 percent of women between 15 and 44 years old have no form of health insurance.)

Whatever health plan a woman has when her pregnancy is confirmed is the one she will be covered by; a pregnant woman cannot switch to a different, better policy with higher coverage after she becomes pregnant. So the time to investigate health insurance is before pregnancy.

Some people have excellent coverage and are unaware of it. For example, some women who have Blue Cross & Blue Shield think that only their hospitalization is covered, while in reality they are eligible for complete, private prenatal maternity care under the Blue Shield portion of their policies.

On the other hand, many women assume that because their employer's group health insurance plan provides some maternity benefits, every pregnancy-related bill will be covered. Unfortunately, this is often not the case. Many policies do not include such items as special tests, additional hospital stay, hospital nursery costs, and medications. Some policies will cover nursery costs and extraordinary expenses such as neonatal intensive care if the baby is sick, but will not cover normal well-baby nursery care. Also, some policies require that the patient pay the bills and then await reimbursement, which often can create a serious financial burden. The practice of requiring that a couple wait until after delivery has been successfully challenged in several state courts. Check with your state insurance commissioner to determine local regulations.

Maternity insurance benefits vary significantly from one company to another. Any health insurance plan for employees, however, must pay pregnancy expenses on the same basis that it pays other medical expenses. If both partners work, they should ask about the exact coverage provided by their corporate and private health insurance plans. Most group policies provided through employment cover husband, wife, and all children up to age 19 (or as long as they are students). If both husband and wife are covered by their employers, they cannot collect double benefits. Each must inform the insurance company concerned that he or she is carried on the other's plan so that their benefits can be coordinated. In some cases this coordination can still produce a benefit. If each spouse is covered for 80 percent of a given medical expense, and both file claims when that expense is incurred, the primary claimant will be reimbursed 80 percent and the spouse 20 percent, so that the expense will be 100 percent covered.

It is important for both partners to know exactly what kind of protection is offered by their policy. It is unlikely that any health insurance policy will cover all the costs of pregnancy. Charges for the nursery, or circumcising and conducting routine tests for the infant, may not be included in either policy unless the couple belongs to a health maintenance organization where all costs are covered in a comprehensive fee. The couple should also allow additional money to cover routine monthly visits to the pediatrician through the baby's first year, because most policies do not cover well-baby care.

Some company insurance plans include major medical coverage, protection in case of catastrophic, long-term illnesses or injuries that require extensive treatment and many months in the hospital. In the rare event that something is seriously wrong with the baby after it is born, such a policy can relieve parents of severe financial problems. If a couple is not covered by major medical at work, they should consider buying supplemental coverage on their own.

Other Kinds of Insurance Coverage

Health maintenance organizations (HMOs) are a departure from the traditional system of third-party insurance where medical costs are reimbursed according to services rendered. The HMO plans vary slightly, but basically, for a fixed monthly or annual fee, the HMO provides all necessary health services, including hospitalization. The consumer or her family joins the HMO—often through place of employment, union, consumer group, or insurance company. She receives comprehensive health care including hospitalization and surgery; referral to medical specialists is provided when the need arises. Some HMOs own their own hospitals outright; others contract for a specific number of beds in a local hospital or negotiate a per diem room rate.

For the most part, HMOs have a good reputation; they attempt to reduce hospitalization and lower health care costs, while maintaining good quality of care. One drawback to such prepaid plans is that a patient is limited in her choice of health care provider or hospital or both. And in the case of maternity care this can be an important consideration.

Many HMOs conform to federal standards, others to varying state regulations. Two major plans come under the HMO umbrella. The first is prepaid group practice (PGP), in which the member doctors are salaried. The second is the individual (or independent) practice association (IPA), comprising private physicians in private offices who generally bill the HMO on a fee-for-service basis.

Preferred Provider Organizations (PPOs)

Preferred provider organization (PPO) is a group of independent physicians who individually contract with an employer or insurance company to offer health servives at set prices, usually less than other comparable services. Unlike HMOs, PPOs charge on a fee-for-service basis.

Disability Benefits

If a woman was employed during her pregnancy, she may be entitled to disability payments from the time she stops working to have a baby until she returns to her job following delivery, or for some portion of that time.

A pregnant woman is entitled to the same disability benefits as every other employee at her workplace. For example, if her employer offers other partially disabled employees lighter work, he or she is obliged to do the same for pregnant women. If other employees can be reinstated in their jobs after they have recovered from a disability, a pregnant woman is also entitled to return to her job after childbirth. These rights are guaranteed under the Pregnancy Discrimination Act passed in 1978 as an amendment to Title VII of the 1964 Civil Rights Act. They apply to every business that employs more than 15 people.

Unfortunately, although the law specifically prohibits discrimination because of pregnancy, childbirth, or related conditions, prejudice against pregnant women still exists in the workplace. A pregnant woman might be passed over for promotion or, on a more direct level, she might not receive specific disability benefits granted other employees temporarily disabled by accident or illness.

Every pregnant woman should know the kind of disability protection her employer offers to all employees. Disability benefits vary from company to company —ranging all the way from substantial weekly payments to no benefits at all. If her company does not provide disability benefits, she may qualify for full or partial temporary disability benefits from the state. Not every state, however, provides such coverage, and payments vary significantly.

Disability payments cover the period of time from when a pregnant woman stops working to have her baby until she is judged able to return to work following delivery. If she does not return to work then—or at all—she forfeits benefits. The insurance carrier can require the woman to undergo a physical examination by a doctor of the carrier's choice (at the carrier's expense) if the carrier believes that she is fit to return to work and has not done so.

Anyone who believes she has received unfair treatment or inadequate compensation during pregnancy may seek help from her company's personnel director or from her union representative. Her chance of success may be improved if she joins with other women at work to express their concerns as a group. If the company does not comply, government agencies can be consulted. A state's human rights commissioner, a local chapter of the National Organization of Women (NOW), the American Civil Liberties Union, or the federal Equal Employment Opportunity Commission will help women seek recourse.

While the Pregnancy Disability Act demands that a pregnant woman have the same rights as other workers in her company, in most states she is not legally entitled to any special benefits by virtue of her pregnancy. (A few states have made special provisions for pregnant workers, but their laws are being challenged in the United States Supreme Court.)

The United States lags far behind other countries in this regard. For example, no law guarantees job-protected time off for new mothers. Almost all other countries provide a *paid* leave of absence for new parents. A diverse group of lobbyists, including the Children's Defense

Fund, Association of Junior Leagues, the American Civil Liberties Union, the United Auto Workers, and other feminist, labor, and children's groups, have joined together to promote a bill to establish a national unpaid parental leave policy. As of now, only 40 percent of new mothers have access to any maternity benefits, and those who do rarely receive full wage replacement and more than 6 weeks' leave. The new measure would mandate 18 weeks of job-protected leave for employees who have a newborn, newly adopted, or seriously ill child. It would also allow 6 months' leave for workers with short-term disabilities arising from pregnancy.

SUMMING UP

THE 9 MONTHS OF PREGNANCY are filled with preparation and anticipation, which begins with choosing an obstetrician and a hospital. The trend in maternity care in the United States is toward a family-centered approach that offers a wide variety of options in maternity care. Even with the many kinds of care available, availability may be limited. For this reason, it is important for couples to choose the type of care they want early, so that prenatal care begins soon after conception and continues uninterrupted through the pregnancy. High-risk mothers—those over 35 or under 18 and those with pre-existing medical conditions—require special obstetrical care, which may be available in either a university medical center clinic or private medical practice. Above all, when a woman chooses a doctor (and hospital), although competence is crucial, personal rapport is equally important. She is choosing a person to share the most important 9 months of her life: That person should be someone she genuinely likes and who genuinely likes her.

3 Genetic Considerations

Georgiana Jagiello, M.D.

INTRODUCTION

PLANNING A PREGNANCY is a time of hope for the future, looking forward to welcoming another family member, and taking positive steps to help protect the health of the new baby. It is also a time when couples may look back at their own family histories with anxiety, wondering if past medical problems will recur in the new generation. Their concerns may be very specific, resulting from a known inherited disease in the family or from a previous child with a birth defect. Sometimes the source of concern may be more vague but equally worrisome—an uncle who was "never quite right," one side of the family with a tendency toward early heart attacks, or a relative with a baby born dead.

Over the past 2 decades the study of heredity, or genetics, has rapidly expanded. Myths about the causes of many illnesses and birth defects have been replaced by a greater understanding of underlying inherited factors. For example, certain types of mental retardation, previously unexplained, can now be predicted in advance. Others can be successfully treated if diagnosed early in infancy. This new information is available to concerned couples through *genetic counseling*, a medical specialty that uses family history and laboratory tests to assist couples in protecting their own health and in planning their families. Even in families with no unusual pattern of medical problems and no children with birth defects, considerations of age or ethnic background may be reason enough for a couple to seek genetic counseling when planning a pregnancy.

THE GENETIC BLUEPRINT

As MODERN MEDICINE has become increasingly able to treat infections, the scope of genetic influence on disease has become more apparent. More than 3,000 purely genetic disorders have been described, and researchers are gaining an appreciation of the important influence of inherited factors on common adult diseases, such as heart disease and cancer. About 30 percent of admissions to pediatric hospitals are for treatment of genetic disorders.

From conception, every cell in the body (except sperm and egg cells) contains a complete set of genetic instructions coded in submicroscopic structures called *genes*. Totaling about 100,000, these genes direct the formation and proper function of body parts, as well as determining inherited characteristics like height and eye color. Genes are organized into 23 pairs of tightly coiled *chromosomes*, each referred to by a number. When sperm and egg cells are formed, they include only one copy of each chromosome, so that when fertilization occurs, the resulting embryo will have a full set, half from the mother and half from the father.

Serious birth defects can result if a mistake in egg or sperm formation means the developing embryo has too few or too many chromosomes. Because of the tens of thousands of genes involved, chromosomal errors generally affect many systems of the body. Down syndrome, the most common chromosomal defect seen in newborns, results from an extra copy of the number 21 chromosome. (See figure 3.1.) Children with Down syndrome, also called Down's syndrome or Trisomy 21, share many characteristic features, such as a distinct facial appearance, short stature, mental retardation, and sometimes heart and vision defects.

Down syndrome involves one of the smallest chromosomes. If there is an abnormal number of one of the large pairs,

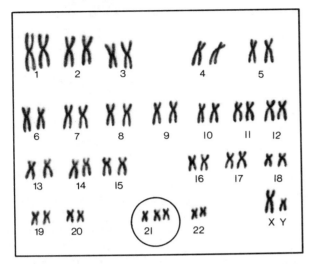

Figure 3.1. **The chromosomal pattern of Down syndrome, or Trisomy 21, so named because of the abnormal 3 chromosomes in pair 21.**

The chance of a chromosome error in a pregnancy is small, but it increases significantly with the age of the mother. (See table 3.1.) Because of the age-related odds, women in their 30s and 40s may wish to seek genetic counseling. In about 1 in 4 cases, the origin of an extra or missing chromosome can be traced to an error during sperm formation. The chance of a chromosome error also increases with the age of the father, although it is a later and less striking phenomenon than in women. Couples may wish to seek genetic counseling if the father is over 55 years of age.

the imbalance in the genetic blueprint is often so great that the embryo cannot develop and a miscarriage occurs. More than half of early miscarriages are thought to be due to chromosome errors in the fetus. When a woman has 2 or more miscarriages, chromosome tests can sometimes explain the reason.

One chromosome pair determines sex. Women have a pair of chromosomes called Xs, while men have 1 X and 1 Y. When egg cells are formed, 1 of the female's X chromosomes is always included. When sperm are formed, either the man's X or Y is passed on. If it is the X, the offspring will be female; if it is the Y, male. Although throughout history women have often been blamed for having a child of the "wrong" sex, it is the sperm that determines the sex of the offspring.

Frequent Chromosomal Abnormalities

● Trisomy 21 (Down syndrome): about 1 in 750 births. Children are small, have a characteristic appearance, and are mentally retarded to some degree (for more information, see *The Columbia University College of Physicians and Surgeons Complete Guide to Early Child Care*).

About one-third have serious medical problems, such as heart defects, frequent infections, and early aging. Many live to 40–60 years of age.

● Trisomy 18 (Edwards syndrome): occurs in 1 in 8,000 newborns. Infants are small, mentally retarded, and fail to gain weight. Most have severe heart defects and do not live past infancy, dying at an average age of 2 months.

● Trisomy 13 (Patau syndrome): occurs in 1 in 15,000 births. Infants have severe abnormalities of the brain, eyes, ears, hands, and internal organs. Many

Table 3.1
THE RISK OF ABNORMALITIES

The risk of Down syndrome and other chromosomal abnormalities increases with the mother's age.

Risk of Significant Chromosomal Abnormality	Risk of Down Syndrome	Maternal Age
1:455	1:1,000	15 or under
1:526	1:1,429	18
1:526	1:1,429–1:2,000	21
1:476	1:1,111–1:1,429	24
1:455	1:1,000–1:1,250	27
1:385	1:833–1:1,111	30
1:323	1:667–1:909	32
1:244	1:417–1:526	34
1:179	1:256–1:400	35
1:149	1:200–1:313	36
1:123	1:156–1:244	37
1:105	1:123–1:192	38
1:81	1:95–1:152	39
1:63	1:73–1:118	40
1:49	1:56–1:93	41
1:39	1:43–1:72	42
1:31	1:33–1:57	43
1:24	1:25–1:44	44
1:18	1:19–1:35	45
1:15	1:15–1:27	46
1:11	1:11–1:21	47
1:9	1:9–1:17	48
1:7	1:6–1:13	49

Reprinted with permission from Ernest B. Hook, M.D., and The American College of Obstetrics and Gynecologists. (*Obstetrics and Gynecology*, Vol. 58, No. 3, 1981, pp. 282–285.)

have cleft lip and palate. Most die in the first month.

• Turner syndrome (only one X chromosome): occurs in 1 in 2,500 female births. Girls with only one X chromosome are short in stature and have undeveloped ovaries, requiring hormone supplements when they reach adolescence. Heart defects and extra skin in the neck may also be present.

● Klinefelter syndrome (XXY, male with an extra X chromosome): occurs in 1 in 1,000 male births. Boys are often tall, have small testes, and tend to be sterile. They may also be psychologically unstable.

● Triple X syndrome (XXX, female with an extra X chromosome): occurs in 1 in 750 births. Girls are relatively tall and normal in appearance, but may have learning and behavioral problems.

● XYY syndrome (males with an extra Y chromosome): occurs in 1 in 1,000 births. Boys are likely to be tall, but display the full normal range of IQs and behaviors. Early studies reporting that XYY men are likely to have criminal records have been shown to be flawed.

SINGLE-GENE INHERITANCE

Dominant Inheritance

Individual genes, as well as entire chromosomes, can cause inherited medical problems that tend to recur in families. Not surprisingly, everybody has a few malfunctioning genes among the tens of thousands, but whether a genetic disorder will appear depends on the mode of inheritance.

Genes work in pairs—a person has 2 copies of each, 1 received from the father and 1 from the mother. If a gene makes its effect known no matter what its partner's genetic message, that is known as *dominant* inheritance. Curly hair, certain kinds of dimples, and having an Rh-positive blood type are all dominant traits. So are such diseases as Huntington disease, neurofibromatosis, and certain types of dwarfism. (See table 3.2.) In general, if either member of a couple has a dominant trait that causes medical problems (see table 3.2 for some common examples), it could show up in a child.

Because both genes in each pair have an equal chance of being passed on, each child (whether boy or girl) has a 50/50 chance of inheriting a dominant condition from an affected parent.

Many dominant disorders are variable in their severity and in the age at which symptoms occur. Healthy people who have a parent with a dominant disorder often seek genetic counseling to understand better how to protect their own health and that of their unborn children.

Sometimes a dominant disorder appears spontaneously, with no family members showing even subtle signs of carrying the disorder-causing gene. In some disorders, these new changes (or mutations) account for about one-third of new cases. There is no way to predict a new mutation in advance, but once it occurs the affected person is capable of passing on the gene to future generations. New mutations are more likely to occur when the father is over 55 years of age.

Table 3.2
EXAMPLES OF DOMINANT DISORDERS

(Note: The numbers given in parentheses are frequencies for the United States as a whole. If a parent has one of these conditions, each child has a 50 percent chance of inheriting the gene and the disorder.)

Achondroplasia (about 1 in 25,000) is a form of dwarfism with short arms and legs and an average-sized head and torso. Skeletal deformities may require surgery.

Polydactyly (about 2 in 10,000), a condition that produces extra fingers or toes, is dominantly inherited.

Familial high cholesterol (hypercholesterolemia) is an inherited tendency to high cholesterol levels, increasing the chance of a heart attack or stroke in middle age. It affects about 1 in 500. Cholesterol-reducing medications and a healthy lifestyle can reduce the risk. A person of any age can be tested.

Marfan syndrome (about 1 in 10,000) is a disorder of the body's connective tissue. Affected individuals are tall and lanky, with a long arm span. The lens of the eye may be dislocated, and nearsightedness is common. Abnormalities of the heart valves and muscle can result in sudden death as a young adult. This condition is sometimes labeled "sudden athlete death syndrome," because of its occurrence in successful basketball and volleyball players who were unaware they had it. Surgery for skeletal, eye, and cardiovascular problems is sometimes needed. Medication can reduce the strain on heart muscle.

Huntington disease (about 1 in 25,000) is a degenerative disease that produces abnormal movements of the face, arms, and legs. There is progressive deterioration of the brain tissue, leading to severe incapacity and death. Scientists have recently learned to detect a *gene marker* that allows them to predict (with 90 percent accuracy) whether the Huntington gene is present. In some families, the presence of this marker can indicate whether a person will eventually develop Huntington disease *before* symptoms appear. It can also be used for prenatal diagnosis.

RECESSIVE INHERITANCE

THE EFFECT OF SOME GENES is only noticeable when both genes of the pair match—these are referred to as *recessive* genes. If a recessive gene is abnormal, it does not matter as long as a properly functioning gene from the other parent is present. A genetic disorder only occurs when *both* parents pass on the same malfunctioning gene. Examples of recessive disorders include cystic fibrosis, sickle cell anemia, and Tay-Sachs disease. (See table 3.3.)

Everyone carries in his or her genetic blueprint a few recessive genes that could cause a serious problem if they were paired. People generally become aware that they carry problem recessives only if

Table 3.3
EXAMPLES OF RECESSIVE DISORDERS

Beta thalassemia (also called Cooley's anemia) is a blood disorder that results in severe anemia, enlarged liver and spleen, recurrent infections, and the need for blood transfusions. About 1 in 25 people of Italian or Greek origin are carriers (carriers are often referred to as having thalassemia trait or thalassemia minor). A simple carrier test is available. If both parents are carriers, prenatal testing is available. Some carriers have symptoms of anemia, especially during pregnancy.

Cystic fibrosis is a condition, frequently fatal before adulthood, in which the body produces too much mucus, which clogs the lungs and digestive tract. The cause is not understood and as yet there is no screening test available, although prenatal diagnosis has recently become possible for some families planning pregnancy after the birth of an affected child. About 1 in 25 whites is a carrier.

Gaucher disease (adult type) is a chronic disorder that affects the spleen, liver, bones, and blood. About 1 in 25 Eastern European (Ashkenazi) Jews in the United States is a carrier. A simple carrier test is available and, if both parents are carriers, prenatal testing is available.

Sickle cell disease is a blood disorder that causes anemia, frequent infections, and occasional painful crises. In the United States, 1 in 10 blacks and 1 in 16 Hispanics of Caribbean origin is a carrier (or may be referred to as having sickle cell trait). A simple carrier test is available. If both parents are carriers, prenatal testing is available.

Tay-Sachs disease is a disorder of body chemistry that renders a child blind, mentally retarded, and paralyzed. It is fatal by about 5 years of age. In the United States, 1 in 25 Jews (specifically Eastern European, or Ashkenazic) is a carrier. A simple carrier test is available. If both parents are carriers, prenatal testing is available.

---

they have a child or close relative with the disorder. There is no comprehensive genetic checkup, but for some recessive conditions, geneticists are able to test whether an unaffected person carries the gene. Screening tests for certain conditions may be recommended, depending on a person's family history and ethnic group, because some recessive genes are more common in some populations than in others.

If both parents are carriers for a recessive disorder, each of their children has a 25 percent chance of having the disorder and a 50 percent chance of being a healthy carrier. If only one parent carries the gene, the couple's children will not be affected. (See figure 3.2.)

Many recessive disorders involve enzymes needed for proper digestion and metabolism. Treatment, via food restriction or supplements, can prevent the damaging effect of these genes if babies are diagnosed and treatment is started soon after birth. For that reason, many states require that every couple be offered newborn screening for several of these disorders.

Figure 3.2. How genetic defects are inherited.

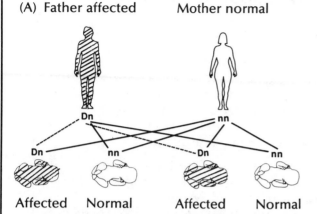

(A) Father affected   Mother normal

Dn   nn

Dn   nn   Dn   nn

Affected   Normal   Affected   Normal

(A) *Dominant Inheritance:* One parent, who has the condition, carries a faulty gene (D) that is dominant, which means it will dominate the normal gene (n). The other parent has 2 normal genes. Each child has a 50 percent chance of inheriting the condition.

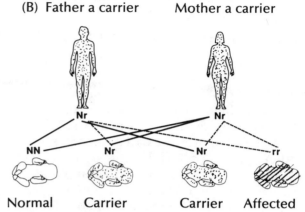

(B) Father a carrier   Mother a carrier

Nr   Nr

NN   Nr   Nr   rr

Normal   Carrier   Carrier   Affected

(B) *Recessive Inheritance:* Both parents are carriers of the condition. Each has a normal dominant gene (N) and each has a faulty recessive gene (r). Each child has a 25 percent chance of inheriting the condition.

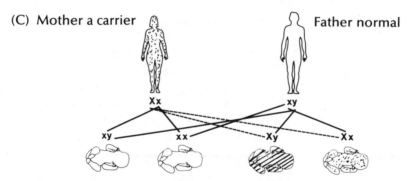

(C) Mother a carrier   Father normal

Xx   xy

xy   xx   Xy   Xx

Son normal   Daughter normal   Son affected   Daughter a carrier

(C) *X-Linked Inheritance:* One of the mother's sex chromosomes carries a faulty gene (X), while her other sex chromosome is normal (x). The father's sex chromosomes (x and y) are both normal. Each male child has a 50 percent chance of inheriting the condition. (Source: March of Dimes Birth Defects Foundation, 1275 Mamaroneck Avenue, White Plains, New York 10605.)

X-LINKED INHERITANCE

A SPECIAL CATEGORY of recessive genes are those located on the X chromosome. There are some 240 known or suspected disorders transmitted by an X-linked gene or genes. They include color blindness, hemophilia (a blood-clotting defect), agammaglobulinemia (lack of immunity to infection), and Duchenne muscular dystrophy (a progressive, crippling muscle weakness usually fatal by age 20).

A woman may inherit a faulty X gene from either her mother or father. Because the faulty X gene will be overshadowed by the healthy X gene, she will not inherit the disease, but she will be a carrier, capable of passing the gene on to her children. (The chances of a woman inheriting 2 faulty X genes, one from each of her parents, is relatively rare. Therefore women are much more likely to be carriers than to exhibit the disease itself.)

If a woman is a carrier, each of her male offspring has a 50 percent chance of being affected by the disease and each female offspring has a 50 percent chance of being a carrier.

Men, who have only one X chromosome, will show the ill effects of any malfunctioning X-linked gene. If a male is affected, none of his male offspring will be affected because they will inherit his Y chromosome. All of his female offspring, however, will inherit his X chromosome and will be carriers.

If a woman has a brother, uncle, or father with an X-linked disorder, she may want to consider genetic counseling. Carrier testing and prenatal diagnosis are available for some X-linked disorders.

One X-linked condition, fragile X syndrome, was discovered in the late 1970s and offers an explanation for many cases of mental retardation in families. This malfunctioning gene makes the end of the X chromosome look "loose" when it is viewed under the microscope after special laboratory treatment. Boys with this fragile X are usually shorter than average, with a relatively large head, ears, and testes. Fragile X syndrome causes no medical problems, but about 80 percent of these boys are mentally retarded, with disability ranging from mild to severe. A few boys (fewer than 5 percent) with fragile X syndrome are labeled autistic.

Girls who carry the fragile X usually do not have serious problems, since their other, normal X covers up for the malfunction, but about one-third of fragile X carriers have serious learning disabilities or mild mental retardation.

If a woman has a brother, uncle, or father with known fragile X syndrome, or mental retardation without known cause, she may request genetic counseling and receive the specialized tests to see if she carries the fragile X gene. If a mentally retarded relative had chromosome tests prior to 1980, it is likely that he or she was not tested for fragile X syndrome.

MULTIFACTORIAL INHERITANCE

MESSAGES FROM MANY individual genes, as well as environmental factors, contribute to proper fetal development and complex human characteristics like growth and intelligence. Some of the most common birth defects, such as heart defects and cleft palate, are multifactorial in their cause.

Neural tube defects are multifactorial disorders caused when the developing spinal column, or neural tube, does not close properly. Spina bifida means the opening is in the back, usually resulting in partial paralysis. Anencephaly is a lethal condition that occurs when the skull and brain do not completely form. One in 1,000 babies in the United States has a neural tube defect—and 95 percent of these defects occur in families in which there has never been an incidence before. Many doctors now offer all pregnant women a blood test for alpha-fetoprotein (AFP), a chemical that is present in higher amounts if the fetus has a neural tube defect. Although the odds are still about 20 to 1 that the fetus is unaffected, after 2 high AFP readings a women is usually referred for genetic counseling and more sophisticated tests.

If a multifactorial genetic problem has occurred in a family, a genetic counselor can determine the odds of it happening in a subsequent pregnancy. Generally, the likelihood is no higher than 1 to 5 percent. Prenatal tests are available for some multifactorial disorders.

FINDING GENETIC COUNSELING

MORE THAN 200 comprehensive genetic service centers are available in the United States, usually located within obstetric or pediatric departments at large medical centers or teaching hospitals. In addition, staff from genetics programs regularly travel to smaller communities to offer "satellite" clinics, consulting with local health professionals and seeing patients and families who do not have easy access to larger centers. (See table 3.4.)

Genetic counseling and planning for pregnancy may be provided by an obstetrician or family practitioner. However, since information and technology in genetics change so rapidly, and the evaluation often requires the careful interpretation of sophisticated laboratory tests, most doctors refer couples to one of the specialized centers.

Counseling at these centers may be provided by a physician or nurse with expertise in genetics or by a specially trained genetic counselor. These latter health care professionals hold a master's or doctoral degree in medical genetics and are experienced in helping families to understand genetic inheritance and to think through personal decisions on pregnancy and child care.

For help in identifying local genetic services, prospective parents can contact:

● The nearest hospital associated with a medical school
● An obstetrician or pediatrician
● A local chapter of the March of Dimes Birth Defects Foundation
● Members of a support organization for a specific condition of concern (such

Table 3.4

GENETIC COUNSELING IS AVAILABLE FOR :

- People who have an inherited disorder or birth defect

- Women pregnant or planning pregnancies in their late 30s or 40s

- Couples who have a child with an inherited disorder or birth defect

- Women who have had an infant death or 2 or more miscarriages without a known obstetrical cause

- Couples concerned that either parent's exposure to radiation, medications, chemicals, infection, or known cancer-causing substances might pose a risk to pregnancy

- Couples who have a child or other family member with mental retardation or delayed development of unknown cause

- Couples who are blood relatives, such as cousins

- Couples who would like testing or more information about gene defects that occur more frequently in their ethnic group

- Pregnant women who have been told, based on blood tests for alpha-fetoprotein, that they may be at increased risk for complications or birth defects

- In short, *anyone* concerned that he or she may be at increased risk of having a child with a birth defect or inherited disorder

as a local chapter of the Muscular Dystrophy Association)

- The American Board of Medical Genetics, which certifies genetics professionals and publishes a geographic listing of board-certified members (15501-B Monona Drive, Derwood, Maryland 20855, 301-762-1992)

- The National Center for Education in Maternal and Child Health (3520 Prospect Street, N.W., Washington, D.C. 20057); this government resource center produces an up-to-date guide to genetic services centers and satellite clinics

WHAT TO EXPECT FROM GENETIC COUNSELING

The Family Pedigree

During the initial counseling session, a pedigree—a family tree of medical information—is created as the couple answers questions about their health and that of their relatives. Prior to the counseling, the couple may wish to confirm or supplement their knowledge by asking relatives about miscarriages, children who died young, chronic medical problems and surgery in family members, and the age and reason for death in deceased relatives. They should also ask about ancestors' countries of origin. Even if one of the couple is adopted or if little is known about one side of the family, genetic counseling can still be helpful.

An accurate diagnosis is critical in order to provide accurate genetic counseling. Inherited and noninherited diseases sometimes look alike, and similar conditions may follow different inheritance patterns. When a specific disorder is the reason for counseling, a complete medical examination may be part of the process. In addition, the counselor may request medical records or autopsy reports on affected relatives. It often helps to bring photographs. In some situations (such as mental retardation without a known cause), new diagnostic techniques may warrant suggesting that an affected family member be reexamined.

Depending on the family history, the couple may be offered certain laboratory tests that aid genetic counseling. Blood tests can often tell whether a person carries a recessive, or hidden, gene for a disorder that has occurred in the family or is more common in his or her ethnic group, such as Tay-Sachs disease or sickle cell disease. Chromosome tests can sometimes explain miscarriages or birth defects in a previous child.

Particularly when the age of the mother is the only concern, genetic counseling can be relatively straightforward. But, if the family history is complicated, the information-gathering stage may involve several weeks of waiting for lab results or medical records. Thus, planning ahead and seeking genetic counseling *before* pregnancy can prevent anxiety and guesswork. If a woman is already pregnant and thinks she could benefit from genetic counseling, she should discuss it with her obstetrician as soon as possible.

RISKS AND OPTIONS

PRIOR TO PREGNANCY, information received during genetic counseling often takes the form of risks and probabilities that a specific birth defect or inherited disease might occur. This information is always placed in the context of the risk inherent in any pregnancy, because no amount of counseling and testing can guarantee that a child will be born without a serious birth defect. About 3 in every 100 babies are born with a serious problem.

Beyond understanding the numbers, genetic counseling helps couples weigh the risks in terms of their personal values and decision making. Identical odds may have very different meanings to different couples, depending on the severity of the defect and on their personal beliefs and experiences. How much a couple chooses to learn, and what they do with that information, remains their decision.

Many couples will have their fears about a particular birth defect alleviated and will enter the new pregnancy reassured. Others will learn that new treatments render a disorder much less serious than they had realized. Still others may decide that the risk of an inherited disease is unacceptably high and they would rather create their family via adoption, artificial insemination, or other reproductive options.

For chromosomal abnormalities and many other genetic diseases, advances in prenatal diagnosis allow couples to move from evaluating risks to knowing for certain whether a fetus will be affected. The tests themselves carry a small risk to the pregnancy, and so the decision usually involves a careful discussion of risks and options with the genetic counselor. If age or family history indicates increased risk of a chromosomal defect, the entire chromosome picture (karyotype) of the fetus can be evaluated. Tests for any of more than 100 specific disorders of body chemistry can be ordered if genetic counseling reveals an increased risk.

Amniocentesis is a technique in which the doctor takes a sample of the amniotic fluid surrounding the fetus. In the laboratory, the chromosomes of fetal cells in the fluid can be examined and tested for specific biochemical abnormalities if indicated. The fluid itself is checked for AFP to detect neural tube defects. Amniocentesis is performed around the sixteenth week of pregnancy, with results available within about 3 weeks.

Chorionic villus sampling (CVS) is a newer diagnostic technique, which can be done in the eighth to eleventh week of pregnancy. A thin catheter is inserted through the vagina and cervix (in some cases through the abdomen), and a small fragment of the early placenta is removed for study. Except for alphafeto protein, the same lab tests can be performed on these fetal cells. Villus sampling is still considered an experimental test. It may carry a greater risk of miscarriage than amniocentesis, but studies of its safety are ongoing.

More than 95 percent of couples undergoing prenatal diagnosis receive reassuring news. If prenatal diagnosis reveals an abnormality, a genetic counselor will share whatever information is available on the outlook for and treatment of a child with the problem. Only rarely can an abnormality be treated in utero. In most cases, a couple is faced with the difficult choice of either terminating the pregnancy or preparing for the birth of an affected child. The genetic counselor can put a couple in contact with members of the clergy who are sensitive to these issues and with parents who have chosen differing options. Whatever their decision, a couple can expect their wishes to be respected.

In some cases, a definitive diagnosis cannot be made prenatally. Further tests may be recommended, or a decision may need to be based on the probability of a defect.

A second-trimester abortion following amniocentesis involves either a medication-induced labor or surgical removal of the fetus. Both physically and emotionally, the experience is painful and difficult. Increasingly, genetic counseling services offer special support groups for couples who have made the decision to terminate a pregnancy after prenatal diagnosis.

TOWARD THE FUTURE

OUR KNOWLEDGE OF GENETICS is changing every week. Since individual genes cannot be seen, scientists have traditionally detected malfunctioning ones by their effect, such as the absence of an important enzyme or the presence of a disease. Now, using a process called *gene mapping*, scientists have pinpointed the location of more than 800 genes on the chromosomes. In some disorders, such as cystic fibrosis and muscular dystrophy, we are learning to detect the defective gene without knowing exactly what it does wrong. This is an important step in improving our understanding and ability to treat these serious conditions.

Treatment for genetic disorders takes many forms—replacing a missing chemical, surgically correcting a malformed limb, transplanting bone marrow or liver, or providing special education and training to improve quality of life. Increasingly, scientists are working toward a more basic cure—gene therapy: transplanting a healthy, functioning gene into a person whose genetic blueprint is defective.

4 How to Tell If You Are Pregnant

Amalia Kelly, M.D.

INTRODUCTION

A HUMAN BEING develops from a single fused cell that divides millions and millions of times. Newborn cells quickly become specialized. Some make blood; others grow hair. Some are sensitive to light, and others detect odors. Some distinguish taste, and still others digest food.

Regardless of their function, all human cells have a common ingredient: Each contains the same 46 chromosomes that carry the genetic code. Of the 46, 2 are "sex" chromosomes. In most cells, the first 44 chromosomes dominate the 2 sex chromosomes. But in a few unique cells, dominance is reversed and the 2 sex chromosomes control the destiny of the cell. These "reproductive" cells are fundamentally different from the rest.

Reproductive cells in men are the millions of sperm-generating cells that line the seminiferous tubules of the testicles. In women, reproductive cells are the ova, or eggs, that fill the ovaries. When 2 of these cells meet, they are able to join together—and this union creates a single hybrid cell with only 46 chromosomes. How this is achieved is a miracle of biological engineering.

Conception occurs when two cells, an ovum and a sperm, unite within one of the two Fallopian tubes in a woman's body. They may also unite outside a tube, resulting in an abdominal pregnancy. The ovum is the largest cell in the female body; the sperm is one of the male body's smallest cells. These two miniscule cells travel through an intricate maze to reach the place in the body where fertilization usually takes place.

FEMALE REPRODUCTIVE ORGANS

THE VITAL ORGANS of the female reproductive system are hidden within the pelvic cavity. (See figure 4.1.) The vagina is the outside passageway to the internal organs. It is connected to the uterus by a small, tight valve called the cervix. The uterus itself, a small flat envelope, is suspended within the pelvic cavity by long bands of ligaments. A Fallopian tube opens off each upper corner of the uterus and the ends of the two tubes swing free. Attached to either side of the uterus by short, muscular stalks are the small,

white ovaries, each no more than 1¼ inches across.

When a baby girl is born, each small ovary contains the full complement of about 1 million primitive follicles. None of these primitive egg cells can be fertilized. Only after puberty, when the brain begins to send out hormones to stimulate the ovaries, do the eggs become mature enough to leave the ovaries in preparation for fertilization—a process known as ovulation.

THE REPRODUCTIVE CYCLE

A GIRL USUALLY BEGINS to menstruate somewhere between the ages of 10 and 13, although there is wide variation. The interval between cycles also varies considerably among women, but is usually 26 to 32 days. Once established, the number of days between periods stays roughly the same month after month.

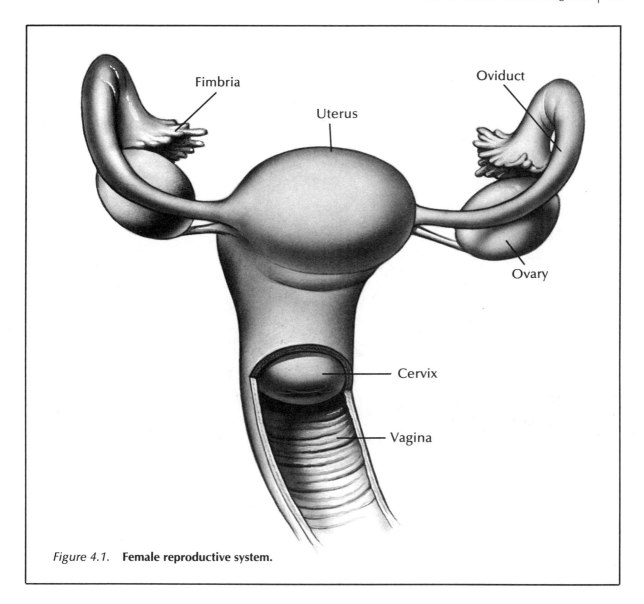

Figure 4.1. **Female reproductive system.**

The Hormonal Axis

The menstrual cycle is divided into hormonal phases, controlled by signals that originate in the hypothalamic section of the brain. (See figure 4.2.) Operating along a hormonal axis, the brain sends signals to the pituitary gland, the pituitary gland signals the ovaries, and the ovaries send hormonal signals back again to the brain. These signals switch midway through the cycle, and it is this switch

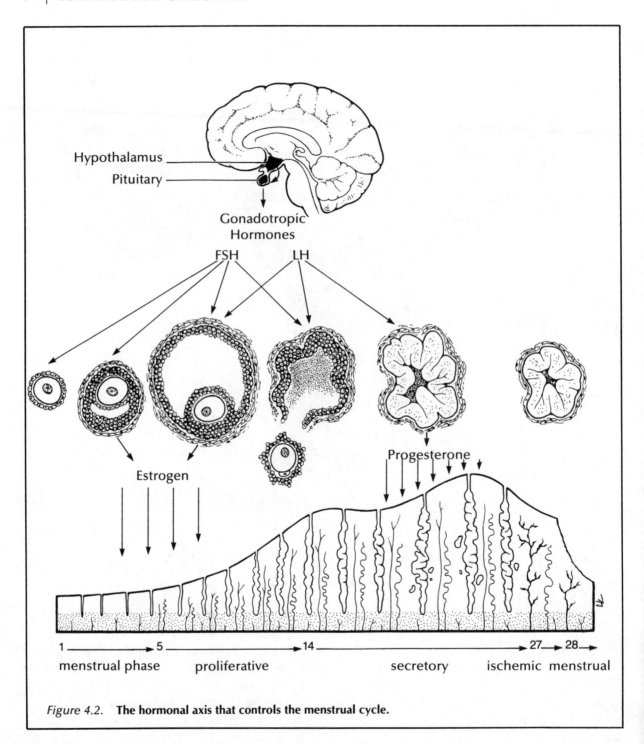

Figure 4.2. **The hormonal axis that controls the menstrual cycle.**

that controls ovulation. During the course of a menstrual cycle a single ovum will mature and ovulate, and the endometrial lining of the uterus will grow and thicken in readiness to receive a fertilized egg. If the egg is not fertilized, the lining sheds at the end of the cycle.

The menstrual cycle begins on the first day of bleeding. On day 1, under the influence of follicle-stimulating hormone (FSH) sent by the pituitary gland, a large number of unripened eggs start to develop in the ovaries. How a group of eggs is selected for development is unknown. As they develop, all of the eggs begin producing estrogen and feeding it into the bloodstream.

Like all cells in the body, each tiny egg carries 46 chromosomes. Before it can be fertilized, an egg must somehow reduce its nuclear contents to 23 chromosomes.

This unique cell division, called meiosis, takes place only in reproductive tissue. Sperm also must go through a similar process. (See figure 4.3.)

Each growing egg divides and spins off 23 chromosomes into a duplicate cell, retaining the other 23 for itself. This duplicate cell, called a polar body, shrivels up. Although it continues to travel alongside the egg, it is useless.

Now, in 1 ovary, 1 follicle of the many chosen for that month begins to grow faster than all the others. As this egg burgeons, the rest fall back. The shell around the egg cell thickens and separates into 4 layers. The 2 inside layers cling tightly to the egg, providing special protection. The 2 outer layers balloon away from it and the sac fills with fluid.

Ovulation

About 14 days into the cycle the lead ovum—called the graafian follicle—reaches its bursting point. The mature follicle bulges on the surface of the ovary, its smooth outer skin stretched tight. The brain detects the high levels of estrogen in the bloodstream and recognizes that the egg is ready to be released. The pituitary switches signals and dispatches a surge of luteinizing hormone (LH). A complex chemical reaction causes the sustaining wall of the follicle to weaken and collapse. The egg rolls out, carrying its 2 closest shell layers with it for nourishment. This is ovulation.

At this point, the menstrual cycle enters its luteal or progesterone phase, when it is dominated by the LH and the hormone progesterone. The outer shell of the egg, called a corpus luteum, remains behind on the ovary. Under the continuing influence of LH, the dying corpus luteum pours out progesterone (Latin for gestation). Progesterone helps the cells of the thickened endometrium build protein and store sugar, as it prepares to receive and nourish a fertilized ovum.

The Egg Enters the Fallopian Tube

For a moment the egg just released from the ovary seems suspended in space. This is a critical point, for now it must drop into the open end of a slender Fallopian tube that will carry it to the uterus. To broaden its portal, the fringed open end of the narrow tube, called the fimbria, splays open like a flower. The "petals" open like long fingers. If the egg drops

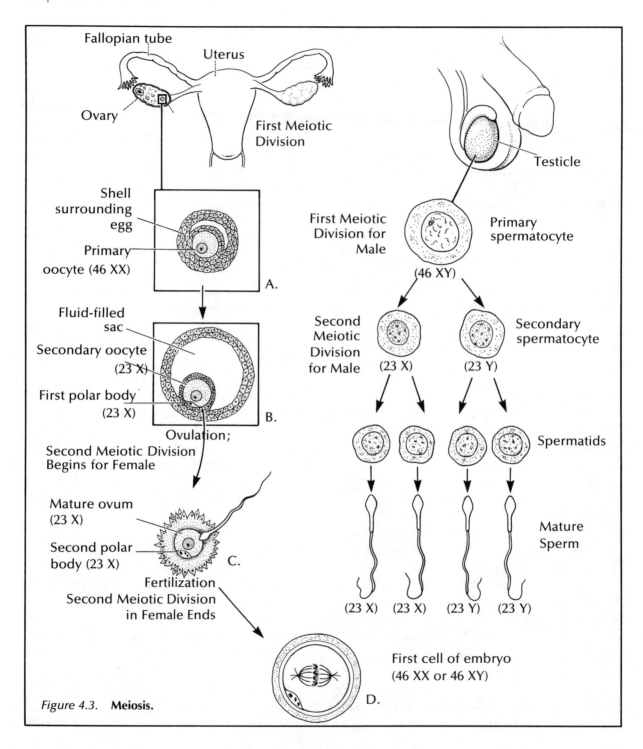

Fallopian tube

Uterus

Ovary

First Meiotic Division

Testicle

Shell surrounding egg

Primary oocyte (46 XX)

A.

First Meiotic Division for Male

Primary spermatocyte

(46 XY)

Fluid-filled sac

Secondary oocyte (23 X)

First polar body (23 X)

B.

Ovulation;

Second Meiotic Division Begins for Female

Second Meiotic Division for Male

Secondary spermatocyte

(23 X)   (23 Y)

Spermatids

Mature ovum (23 X)

Second polar body (23 X)

C.

Fertilization

Second Meiotic Division in Female Ends

Mature Sperm

(23 X)   (23 X)   (23 Y)   (23 Y)

First cell of embryo (46 XX or 46 XY)

D.

Figure 4.3. **Meiosis.**

onto any part of a petal, it will be drawn inside by millions of cilia, tall cells with hairlike tips that brush the egg along toward the uterus. The egg has no momentum of its own and must rely on the sweeping motion of the cilia to carry it toward the high reaches of the tube, the one point in the body where it usually can be fertilized. The egg has about 12 to 24 hours in which it can be fertilized; after that, it will have passed the fertilization point. Whether or not fertilization takes place within those 24 hours depends on the presence of sperm in the tube.

The egg still carries 23 chromosomes, each composed of 2 strands of DNA. Before fertilization can take place, one strand of DNA in each chromosome must be eliminated. But nothing further will happen unless a sperm punctures the egg's shell.

MALE REPRODUCTIVE ORGANS

A MAJOR PURPOSE of a man's reproductive organs is to manufacture, store, and deliver sperm. (See figure 4.4.) Sperm are manufactured in the testicles, two small organs wrapped in membranes and suspended in the protective pouch of the scrotum. This vulnerable position outside the body cavity helps keep these important organs cooler than the rest of the body. Theoretically, this somewhat cooler temperature promotes sperm production and survival.

Within the testicles are thousands of tightly coiled threads called seminiferous tubules. These microscopic tubes are lined with "germ" cells. When a male reaches puberty these cells respond to new hormonal signals from the pituitary gland and begin generating millions of sperm every day.

The hormones that initiate sperm production in men are identical to those that stimulate egg development in women. The primary difference is that the outlying target organs are testicles, rather than ovaries. In men, however, the hormonal action is relatively constant, rather than cyclical, so that sperm are steadily produced.

Like ova, sperm must also reduce their complement of 46 chromosomes to 23 strands of DNA. As hormones flow along the axis, they are picked up by the sperm-generating cells (spermatogonia) that line the tubules of the testicles. As soon as a mother cell gets the hormonal message, it generates a duplicate of itself. As a generator of new sperm cells, the mother cell remains in place, receiving hormonal messages. The new duplicate cell, which also has 46 chromosomes—44 plus an X and a Y sex chromosome—moves forward.

The duplicate cell, called a primary spermatocyte, now becomes unique. The duplicate cell divides again, but this time

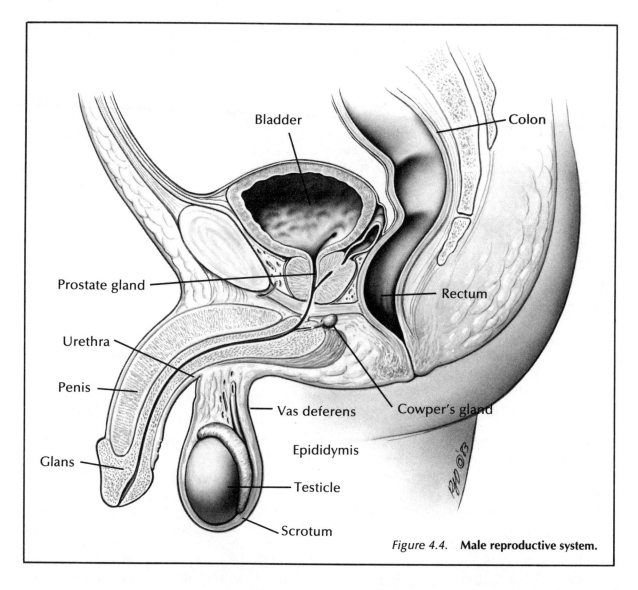

Figure 4.4. **Male reproductive system.**

it halves its number of chromosomes. The two new cells, called secondary spermatocytes, have 23 double-stranded chromosomes each—22 plus either an X or a Y sex chromosome. Before it can fuse with an egg, each cell must first reduce each double strand to a single strand. Thus, the 2 secondary spermatocytes divide once

more, separating the two strands of DNA. The 4 new cells that result, called spermatids, have only 23 single-strand chromosomes each. Two of the cells carry an X sex chromosome and two carry a Y.

The 4 new spermatids, which for the first time begin to look like sperm, will grow into mature cells capable of fertilizing an ovum. In the female, the ovum goes through a similar process of cell division, but it throws away its 3 extra bodies. If it did not, twins, triplets, and quadruplets would proliferate.

The newborn sperm are later transported out of the tubule to mature in the adjacent holding area called the epididymis. The mother cell remains behind, ready to produce 4 new sperm through this unique process.

Each mature sperm cell has an oval head, a midpiece, and a long whiplike tail that propels it through seminal fluid. The head contains a vast data bank of genetic information; stored there are the 23 single-stranded chromosomes, including the X or Y that will determine the sex of a new life when the sperm unites with an ovum. The head is topped by a cap that houses chemicals to help the sperm penetrate an ovum.

With each ejaculation, the testicles release up to 400 million sperm, with the goal that one will meet and fertilize the single egg produced each month by a woman's ovaries.

When a man ejaculates, sperm are ejected from the pocket of the testicles up through a series of ducts. Seminal fluid pouring into the ducts from the prostate gland and adjacent storage areas flushes the sperm through the urethra and out the tip of the penis. Before fertilization can take place, the sperm must be deposited in the vaginal vault, pass through the tiny opening of the cervix, swim through the uterus, and reach the Fallopian tubes.

This pathway is an obstacle course designed to eliminate all but the best. Most of the sperm are destroyed immedi-ately by the acidic fluids that cleanse the vagina. Only a few thousand make it to the cervix, and even fewer reach the Fallopian tubes. Most of the time the sperm are turned back by a hard wall of mucus that normally blocks the cervix and prevents bacteria from invading the abdominal cavity. Only for a few days each month, near the time of ovulation, does this thick cervical mucus change into a fluid stream that sperm can penetrate.

Those sperm that pass through the cervix now have about 48 hours remaining to reach and fertilize the ovum before they die. They can travel this distance in only a few minutes. So another series of obstacles arise to keep as many sperm as possible within the vicinity of the egg for as long as they remain alive. Little crypts inside the walls of the cervix collect some sperm. The gauzy folds of mucus within the Fallopian tubes entrap others.

Although the difficulty of the journey helps ensure that only the most healthy sperm reach the fertilization point, sometimes a poor-quality sperm and egg do fuse; most of these fertilized eggs stop developing and are lost spontaneously without a woman being aware of the pregnancy.

Capacitation

Those sperm that journey as far as the Fallopian tube undergo a final transformation. The head of every mature sperm is veiled by an invisible membrane that holds its chemicals in check until the right moment. As the sperm swims toward the fertilization point, the coating

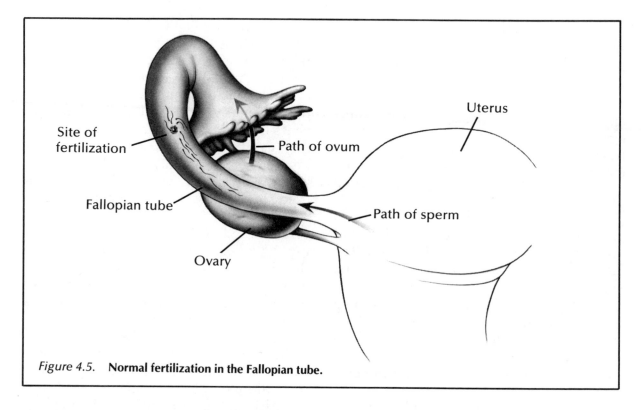

Figure 4.5. **Normal fertilization in the Fallopian tube.**

slowly wears away until the head is bared.

One final obstacle faces sperm that make it this far: the egg itself. As the egg slowly tumbles through the Fallopian tube, all the remaining sperm rush to meet it. Each of these sperm is capable of penetrating the egg, but only 1 can succeed. (See figure 4.5.)

FERTILIZATION

TO REACH THE EGG'S NUCLEUS, a sperm must first dig through several layers of shell. Spraying chemicals from its head, the sperm dissolves a hole in the sticky outer layer, only to find another, tougher membrane underneath (the zona pellucida). The sperm concentrates its chemicals in a fine stream and drills a small hole in this underlayer.

The moment a sperm punctures the egg's shell, several events simultaneously occur. The membrane surrounding the egg is immediately transformed into a rigid barrier that no other sperm can enter. Should the barrier fail and more than one sperm penetrate, the egg will die from a lethal excess of DNA. Twins are never formed by 2 sperm entering 1 egg. Two eggs may be fertilized by two different sperm (fraternal twins), or a fertilized egg may divide into 2 separate embryos (identical twins). But only 1 sperm can enter 1 egg in which a human develops.

At the moment of penetration, the egg splits its double-stranded chromosomes in half, throwing off the excess strands into another polar body. The original, withered polar body imitates the egg, and also splits its chromosomes. The egg now contains 23 single-stranded chromosomes. Its 3 small polar bodies continue to ride alongside.

The sperm locks onto the egg and its DNA slips through the tiny opening in the egg's shell. The membranes of the 2 cells fuse like 2 touching bubbles. The nucleus of the sperm now lies inside the egg, and the 2 cells—1 from the mother and 1 from the father—begin to merge into a hybrid cell. In the next few moments the 23 single strands of sperm DNA begin to pair up with compatible strands of ovum DNA. The new pairs of DNA immediately generate duplicates of themselves to create 46 perfect chromosomes, the full chromosomal array of the first cell of a new person. The sperm and egg are one, and fertilization is complete.

Sexual Imprint

The moment that the 23 chromosomes of the sperm cell pair up with 23 compatible chromosomes of the ovum, all the properties of a new human life are determined, including its sex. Whether the fetus will be a boy or a girl is determined by which sperm enters the ovum. Although rare aberrations arise, the ovum itself almost always carries an X sex chromosome. Sperm cells, however, are about equally divided between Xs and Ys. If the sperm that unites with the egg also carries an X, the baby will be a girl. If it carries a Y, the baby will be a boy.

Implantation

The fertilized egg continues to move through the Fallopian tube. Within 3 days' time it divides into 2, 4, and then 8 cells. At this point the cell cluster sails from the narrow tunnel of the Fallopian tube into the relatively huge cavern of the uterus. On entering the uterus, the cell cluster clings to the inside wall of the uterus and buries itself in the spongy endometrium, where it derives nourishment from the energy-packed cells. The fertilized ovum shoots out an early pregnancy signal, the hormone human chorionic gonadotrophin (HCG), that tells the brain and pituitary gland to continue sending LH to support the endometrium.

For the next 40 to 60 days the pregnancy will be supported by progesterone manufactured by the empty egg sac (corpus luteum) that was left behind on the surface of the ovary following ovulation. After that, the placenta will be developed enough to take over the hormonal work load.

LIKELIHOOD OF ACHIEVING PREGNANCY

THE MOST FERTILE days are during ovulation. Although ovulation occurs approximately midway through the menstrual cycle, it has very few outward signs. The precise time when the egg leaves the ovary and enters the Fallopian tube cannot be known. (See chapter 5, Infertility Problems.)

Even when a couple has intercourse on the right day and sperm are present when the egg drops off the ovary, conception does not necessarily occur.

The Fallopian tube may not catch the egg as it falls. Rarely a dropped catch becomes fertilized outside the Fallopian tube; this is one site of an ectopic pregnancy. Ectopic pregnancies may develop for a while, but ultimately rupture, leading to maternal hemorrhage. (See chapter 14, Complications in Pregnancy.) About 15 percent of the time, even if the ovum enters the tube, it is incapable of being fertilized; and about 25 percent of the time the egg is fertilized and then silently aborts. Scientists estimate that a couple has only a 20 percent likelihood of conceiving in any given month. With these odds, it may take up to a year for an average couple to conceive.

THE HORMONES OF PREGNANCY

ALMOST FROM THE MOMENT an ovum is fertilized, hormonal changes occur to support the pregnancy. The levels of normal hormones may rise or fall, and new hormones also begin to appear. These changes have many effects on the mother's body.

The fertilized ovum itself triggers this hormonal upheaval when it immediately begins to send out an early pregnancy hormone (HCG), which tells the hormonal axis (brain/pituitary/ovaries) to continue the supply of LH/progesterone to the uterus.

With this action, the 2 dominant hormones of pregnancy—progesterone and estrogen—begin to rise. Progesterone increases gradually, reaching its peak between 30 and 32 weeks of pregnancy and remaining at that level until delivery. Progesterone supports the uterus and relaxes smooth muscle fibers, which allows the uterus to grow and expand until it can accommodate a full-sized baby. The estrogen level rises slightly at the beginning of pregnancy and gets higher as pregnancy continues. Estrogen aids the growth of the fetus and placenta, as well as the development of the mother's breasts.

In the early weeks of pregnancy, progesterone is supplied by the corpus luteum on the ovary. After about 6 to 8 weeks, however, there is a shift in dependency as the placenta develops enough to take over and produce its own progesterone. The corpus luteum fades, and the placenta continues to produce progesterone throughout the pregnancy. The placenta also works in tandem with the fetus to secrete estrogen.

Other Pregnancy Hormones

Human placental lactogen (HPL), a peptide produced by the placenta, also rises as the placenta develops. HPL affects metabolism and aids in fat breakdown. It also appears to inhibit the absorption of glucose by the mother's cells, leaving glucose as a source of energy for the fetus. As a result this hormone may have an anti-insulin action and may possibly account for the incidence of gestational diabetes in some pregnant women.

Another hormone, prolactin, is produced by the pituitary gland of a pregnant woman. Prolactin is normally suppressed, but begins to increase early in pregnancy and is very high when the baby is born. Although much remains unknown about this hormone, its primary purpose seems to be preparation of the breasts for milk production. After childbirth, prolactin levels fall slowly, but rise again each time the baby suckles.

The hormone oxytocin is also produced by the mother's pituitary gland. This pregnancy hormone stimulates uterine contractions and also initiates the flow of breast milk. In synthetic form, oxytocin is sometimes given to speed labor during childbirth.

These are some of the hormonal interactions involved in pregnancy. The many physical symptoms pregnant women describe are often attributed to "hormonal changes," but how each hormone triggers specific symptoms is unknown.

EARLY SIGNS OF PREGNANCY

HORMONAL CHANGES cause a variety of reactions in the body, although the first symptoms of pregnancy may not appear until several weeks after conception. A missed period may be the first sign, but it is by no means an accurate barometer. A missed period can be the result of discontinuing birth control pills, strenuous exercise, a major weight loss (20 pounds or more), emotional stress, or illness. Even worry about becoming pregnant or extreme eagerness to have a baby can blunt menstruation. However, ovulation and conception can take place in the absence of menstruation.

Conversely, it is possible to be pregnant and still have menstrual bleeding. A partially suppressed period, caused by insufficient progesterone, may occur once or twice but seldom continues throughout pregnancy. About 22 percent of pregnancies that result in healthy babies involve some bleeding during the first 3 months.

If a woman has been keeping a temperature chart, her temperature, which usually drops at the end of the menstrual cycle, will remain elevated if she has become pregnant. (See chapter 5.) Many experience fatigue and dizziness soon after the first missed period. Breasts may feel heavy and full. Nausea and vomiting (pregnancy or morning sickness) are also common.

Most of these symptoms are attributed to the action of hormones in the bloodstream working to support the new pregnancy. Progesterone, while relaxing the smooth muscle fibers that allow the uterus to expand, also relaxes the walls of blood vessels to accommodate the extra volume of blood during pregnancy. In the early days of pregnancy, the gradual increase of progesterone slows down intestinal motility, so that food does not empty out of the intestine as rapidly, which can lead to constipation. As the fetus grows larger, the pressure it creates against the stomach can cause reflux and heartburn, both common in pregnancy.

During the first 12 weeks of pregnancy, a frequent need to urinate is common and is probably due to hormonal changes affecting kidney function, or the enlarging uterus pressing slightly on the bladder.

Even very early on, a swelling of the lower abdomen may be noticeable. There may be a 5- to 10-pound weight gain long before the fetus and organs involved are anywhere near that big. This swelling and weight gain all probably caused by increased water retention and blood flow to the abdomen. Even without the weight gain, the abdominal swelling may be noticed. An increase in the production of cervical mucus is common, as blood flow is increased to the vaginal area.

Any or all of these symptoms may appear in the first weeks and months of pregnancy. But the earliest and most common symptoms to appear, even before a pregnancy test is done, are fatigue, dizziness, and often nausea.

PREGNANCY TESTS

As soon as pregnancy is suspected, a confirming test should be done. If it is positive, early prenatal care can begin.

When the fertilized egg implants in the uterus 7 to 9 days after ovulation, it begins immediately to secrete HCG into the mother's blood. HCG is cleared by the kidney and comes out in the mother's

urine. This hormone, which can be measured in either the mother's blood or the urine, is the basis for all pregnancy tests.

Urine tests are quick and inexpensive to perform. They are about 98 percent accurate, but false results sometimes occur if the test is done too soon or if the sample is not properly handled. A family doctor or a clinic can perform urine pregnancy tests, or a home testing kit can be used. The waiting time for test results ranges from a few minutes to a few hours.

The least reliable urine test is a simple slide preparation, which can be carried out in a few minutes. This test requires a high HCG level to get a true result, and therefore is not usually accurate until at least 2 weeks after a missed period. A step up is a 2-hour tube urine test, which is more sensitive and can detect a pregnancy about 1 week after a missed period.

All urine pregnancy tests should be done on a sample of the first urine passed in the morning (known as the first void) when the concentration of HCG is at its peak. Before collecting the sample the woman should not have anything to drink, nor should she have urinated during the night. She collects the urine in a clean jar, free of any trace of soap or detergent, then closes the lid tightly, and stores the jar until the sample can be tested. Although urine tests can be done in the doctor's office, most are sent out to a lab; blood tests are always performed by a lab.

Blood pregnancy tests can detect a pregnancy with accuracy as early as 8 days after ovulation—or 5 days before a period is due. These new tests also provide more information about the pregnancy because they measure not only the presence of HCG, but the level of the hormone in the blood.

Even though they are more expensive than urine tests, there is an increasing reliance on blood pregnancy tests because they give the physician a little more information, and because many couples are eager to confirm a pregnancy as soon as possible.

All pregnancy tests detect a pregnancy, but do not show the location of the fertilized ovum. If the pregnancy is misplaced (ectopic) the test will not reveal this dangerous condition. Because blood tests give the physician an actual level of HCG, they can suggest the presence of an ectopic pregnancy. (Ectopic pregnancies tend to have lower levels of HCG for the stage of pregnancy than normally developing pregnancies.)

The doctor may be able to feel the pregnancy, or ask the woman about symptoms (staining, pain) that suggest an ectopic pregnancy; with these signs present the physician may then suggest a sonogram to identify and locate the misplaced pregnancy.

The question of location is one important reservation that physicians have about at-home urine tests. Urine tests only give a yes or no answer to pregnancy. Without an examination by a physician, an ectopic pregnancy may go undetected until the pregnancy ruptures, a life-threatening situation.

Home Tests

The at-home pregnancy tests available now are greatly improved over earlier types. New tests can be done within 1 to 2 days of a missed period (approximately 2 weeks after conception). Instructions are easier to follow and the accuracy rate of positive tests can run as high as 99 percent. (Negative test results tend to be a little less accurate, and so it may be worth repeating a negative test in a few days if menstruation does not start.)

Most home kits cost approximately $10 and give the result in less than 1 hour. Although they vary slightly in method, they all work on the principle of adding chemicals to urine in a test tube, leaving it undisturbed for a specified time, and then reading the result.

FIRST PRENATAL VISIT

THE FIRST PRENATAL checkup should be scheduled as soon as the pregnancy is confirmed. (Many women today have a prenatal checkup before they become pregnant.) The first prenatal visit involves a complete medical workup, beginning with a thorough medical history that includes family background and history of previous pregnancies. The standard prenatal examination includes taking blood pressure, an internal vaginal examination, breast exam, blood tests, and urinalysis. (See chapter 1.)

DATING THE BIRTH

AFTER THE PREGNANCY has been confirmed, the obstetrician works out the date the baby is due to arrive. The average period of gestation is 266 days—or 38 weeks—from the date of fertilization. However, since the exact time of fertilization is impossible to determine, doctors count 280 days, or 40 weeks, from the date of the woman's last menstrual period. Therefore, 4 weeks after she probably conceived (during ovulation) she is considered 6 weeks pregnant.

Obviously, not everyone's cycle conforms to a 28-day pattern and, even if it did, this method is open to slight inaccuracies. In addition, the duration of an individual pregnancy may vary considerably from the average and still be normal. As a result of these variations, as many as 40 percent of all labors start more than 7 days before or after the estimated date of delivery.

5 Infertility Problems

Raphael Jewelewicz, M.D.

INTRODUCTION

IN THE PAST 20 years, the incidence of infertility in the United States has nearly tripled, so that today 1 in 5 American couples—about 15 percent of all adults—is designated as infertile. Understandably, this has led to considerable anxiety among couples who, after a few months of trying, still have not achieved pregnancy. Despite this marked increase in infertility, it should be stressed that most couples eventually achieve pregnancy, although it may take a year or more to do so. In a large population of couples of all ages, about 80 percent will achieve pregnancy within 1 year of actively trying. An additional 5 percent will conceive at some point during another year of trying.

Infertility, therefore, is defined as an inability to achieve pregnancy after 2 years.

Determining that a couple is indeed infertile does not necessarily erase their dreams of parenthood. At last count, there were 16 means of achieving parenthood in addition to the age-old traditional union. Some of these are experimental and others are highly controversial, raising very difficult social issues. In this chapter, the most common causes of infertility and their diagnosis and treatment, with a brief overview of some of the newer methods of achieving parenthood despite established infertility, will be reviewed.

TRENDS IN INFERTILITY

TWO SIGNIFICANT SOCIAL TRENDS are contributing to the increased infertility, especially among American women. One is the marked rise in sexually transmitted diseases such as chlamydia and gonorrhea, which can cause pelvic inflammatory disease (PID) and, consequently, fertility problems. A second factor is the growing number of women who are delaying childbearing until their 30s or even later. A woman's fertility begins to decline in her late 20s and early 30s, making pregnancy more difficult to achieve. In addition, older women are more likely to have had multiple sexual partners, which also increases their risk of PID. Many of these women may also have used intrauterine devices (IUDs); these devices are associated with increased fertility problems. Endometriosis—the abnormal growth of endometrial tissue outside the uterus—increases with age and is another major cause of infertility. Finally, an older woman is more likely to have had some kind of abdominal surgery, which may create scarring around the reproductive organs, thus increasing her risk of infertility.

Of course, infertility is not confined to women. Today about 55 percent of the time infertility can be traced to the female partner, about 35 percent of the time to the male partner, and in 10 percent of cases, no known cause can be discovered for the failure to conceive. Frequently—about 30 percent of the time—both partners will be found to have a fertility problem. (Table 5.1 lists the most common causes of infertility. Figures 5.1 and 5.2 show common causes of female and male infertility, respectively.)

Table 5.1
MOST COMMON CAUSES OF INFERTILITY

Female	Male	Female	Male
General		**Genital Disease**	
Overweight	Overweight	Infection (PID,	Infection
Underweight	Underweight	chlamydia,	(gonorrhea, other
Anemia	Excessive alcohol	gonorrhea,	sexually
Hostile mucus	use	cervicitis, etc.)	transmitted
Turner syndrome	Excessive smoking	Tubal scarring,	diseases)
	Klinefelter	other	Injury to testes
	syndrome	abnormalities	Hydrocele
Developmental		Endometriosis	Orchitis
		Cervical polyps	Prostatitis
Uterine	Undescended	Uterine fibroids	
malformations	testicles		
Undeveloped	Varicocele		
ovaries	Underdeveloped		
Incompetent cervix	testicles		
	Poor sperm count	**Both Sexes**	
	Defective sperm		
	Impotence	Marital maladjustment	
	Ejaculatory	Poor timing of intercourse	
	disorders	Immunological incompatibility	
Hormonal		Genetic disorders	
Pituitary failure	Pituitary failure		
Thyroid disease	Thyroid disease		
Ovarian failure	Adrenal disorders	(Adapted from *Why Can't We Have a Baby* by Albert Decker, M.D., and Suzanne Loebl, Dial Press, 1978.)	
Adrenal disorders			

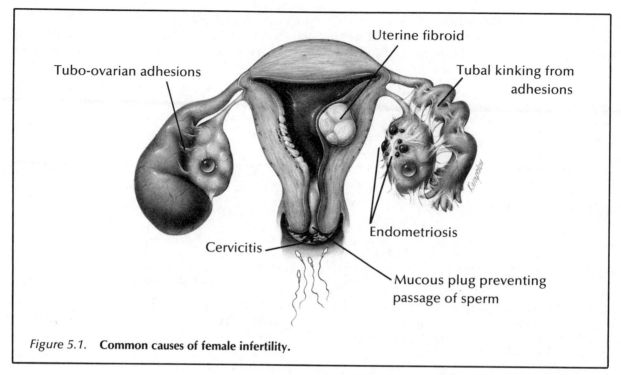

Figure 5.1. **Common causes of female infertility.**

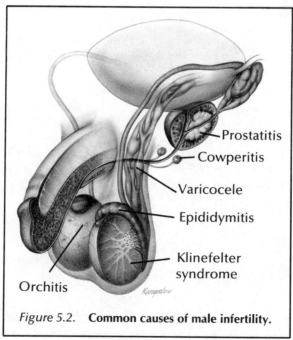

Figure 5.2. **Common causes of male infertility.**

WHEN TO SEEK HELP

THE AWARENESS of the infertility "epidemic" has led many couples, especially those in the older age group, to seek help from fertility specialists after a few months of unsuccessful attempts to conceive. Just because a couple does not achieve pregnancy in a specific length of time, it does not necessarily follow that there is an infertility problem or that they need the services of a specialist. Given the many factors affecting fertility, many specialists suggest waiting for 2 years to seek professional help if the woman is in her 20s. This is shortened to 1 year if she is between 30 and 35, and to 6 months if she is over 35. Professional help may be sought earlier if there are specific causes of concern, for example, if the woman has a history of pelvic infection, missed periods, or unusual menstrual pain that suggests endometriosis, or if the man has suffered scrotal injury or a genital abnormality.

Even when a couple determines that professional help is needed, it is a good idea to start with a gynecologist, internist, or urologist, rather than a fertility specialist. Very often the problem can be resolved by something as simple as timing intercourse to coincide with ovulation or other nonmedical steps. Such problems usually can be resolved by a gynecologist or other primary-care physician without undergoing an extensive fertility examination.

Under the best of circumstances, couples seeking a fertility evaluation are committing themselves to a process of several months, during which their intimate lives, along with their bodies and feelings, may be subject to scrutiny. It is a trying time for most people, and selecting the right health professional(s) is important. The treatment of infertility has been recognized as a medical subspecialty for only about 12 years, and even now there are only about 200 fertility specialists who have been board certified by the Division of Reproductive Endocrinology of the American Board of Obstetrics and Gynecology. Most of these specialists are associated with medical schools or major teaching hospitals. However, a number of other specialists, including gynecologists, urologists, endocrinologists, geneticists, and even psychotherapists and nutritionists, may be involved in the treatment of infertility.

When a couple determines that they need the help of a fertility specialist, they should ask their primary doctor for a referral. Alternatively, they can seek names from the department of obstetrics and gynecology at a medical school or teaching hospital, or from an organization devoted to fertility problems. In selecting a specialist, a couple should look for a doctor who devotes at least 80 percent of his or her practice to infertility, and preferably one who works with other specialists. A health care team offers the best approach to fertility because it provides a range of services in an organized manner. For example, in a fertility team or clinic, one doctor acts as the team leader, working with a group of specialists. Ideally, the team includes both male and female physicians and counselors, and treats both partners. The couple may not need the services of every specialist on the team, but the doctors will be able to consult each other as needed to review the overall picture.

The goal of a fertility workup is to provide precise answers within a given period of time. The physician(s) should have an orderly plan to recommend after the initial visit and should outline for the couple what can be done and how long it will take. At this time, the physician should also indicate the costs involved.

Determining whether pregnancy is possible, and what must be done to make it probable, requires more cooperation on the part of the patients than almost any other medical specialty. However, with modern medical advances many of the causes of infertility can be diagnosed and treated. Thus if the couple is eager to have a baby—or to find out for sure that they cannot—the effort, which is expensive and may not be covered by medical insurance, is well worth it.

A full fertility workup that includes both partners can cost roughly $1,500 to $3,000, involves several office visits, and often a 1-day stay in the hospital. A total evaluation may take 6 to 12 months to complete, although much depends on the approach of the fertility expert as well as the attitude and determination of the couple. For example, if the woman is over 35, it is important to complete the evaluation as quickly as possible. Also, when a specific problem stands out early in the investigation, the evaluation may be completed more quickly. For most cou-

ples, however, it is less stressful to proceed slowly and allow some time to pass between tests. It also should be noted that about 25 percent of couples seeking help from fertility experts achieve pregnancy during the evaluation without any specific treatment.

The Initial Steps

Several tests and examinations are required to provide a complete picture of a couple's reproductive status. Even though the woman usually must submit to many more tests than the man, full cooperation of both partners is crucial, especially since both partners may have a fertility problem. Or both partners may be subfertile: A man may have a somewhat reduced sperm count and a woman may ovulate irregularly. With other partners, achieving a pregnancy may not be a problem, but together they have major difficulties. Therefore, for both emotional and physical reasons, it is important to consider infertility a shared concern, and not a "problem" that rests with one or the other partner.

A fertility evaluation begins with obtaining a careful medical history and then a physical examination of both partners. The medical history is particularly important because it often provides important clues. Particular attention is paid to family history and genetic disorders that might have been passed down. Also a history of certain medical conditions— mumps, measles, whooping cough, diphtheria, rubella, thyroid disease, diabetes, tuberculosis, epilepsy, and the presence of infections—can affect fertility. The doctor will ask about use of certain medications that affect fertility, as well as the use and abuse of alcohol or "recreational" drugs—all of which can affect a man's sperm count.

Both partners will be asked to describe their sexual history. This aspect of the medical history probably should be taken privately, since many people may be reluctant to speak frankly in front of their partners. Abortion, venereal disease, past birth control practices, and previous sexual encounters or pregnancies are all subjects relevant to the fertility evaluation, but may be topics that one partner does not want to reveal to the other. While open and frank communication between partners may be important to the marriage relationship, the real issue here is that each party be totally honest with the physician.

During a fertility interview, both partners should expect extensive questioning about their sexual behavior: how often they have sex, orgasmic patterns, and preferred positions. Occasionally an infertility case is solved immediately when it is learned that the couple is not engaging in vaginal intercourse or is not having intercourse at the optimal time of the woman's monthly cycle. Such factors may seem obvious, but fertility experts agree that a very large percentage of

"cases" are resolved by correcting the obvious.

The timing and sequence of the tests ordered by the fertility specialist are important. Diagnostic tests should be performed in a specific sequence and by expert technicians. Sequence may depend on a patient's age or previous medical history. The sequence also may be altered if the cause of infertility is obvious. Generally, however, nonsurgical tests are performed first.

Certain tests are almost always performed for every couple: a thorough medical history and physical exam of both partners, a semen analysis for the man, a postcoital test, and an endometrial biopsy for the female partner.

However, depending on the circumstances, additional tests may be required. These are discussed in detail in the following sections, and table 5.2 outlines the typical sequence of tests. Because both partners may have more than one problem, some fertility experts like to perform all the tests to make sure nothing is missed. However, if one cause is apparent early in the evaluation, most doctors forego further testing, at least temporarily. They will correct the known problem and wait to see if pregnancy results before further testing.

INFERTILITY IN MEN

THE MALE PARTNER is usually tested first because a semen analysis is the least stressful—and most informative—of the many fertility tests. Some men are reluctant to undergo a semen analysis and other fertility tests, often because they

Table 5.2
TYPICAL SEQUENCE OF FERTILITY TESTS

Women	Men
PHASE 1—FACT FINDING	
History	History
Review of previous fertility tests	Physical examination
Physical examination	Varicocele screening
PHASE 2—DIAGNOSTIC STUDIES	
Temperature chart	Semen analysis
Postcoital test	Stress counseling
Hormone blood studies	Hormone blood studies
Ultrasound	
Endometrial biopsy	
Stress counseling	
PHASE 3—SURGICAL INVESTIGATION	
Hysteroscopy	Testicular biopsy
Laparoscopy	Vasogram (X-ray study)
Hysterosalpinogram (X-ray study)	
PHASE 4—MISCELLANEOUS TESTS AND COUNSELING	
Chromosome analysis	Chromosome analysis
Genetic counseling	Genetic counseling

fear, perhaps subconsciously, that the results will reflect on their masculinity. It should be stressed that sexual prowess has little or no bearing on fertility—the hormonal systems that drive libido and control sperm production function independently of one another. A man can have a minimal libido and be fully fertile and vice versa.

Low Sperm Count

The most common cause of infertility among men is a low sperm count. Although fewer than 2 percent of all infertile men are sterile with no sperm production, a relatively large number will have a lower than normal number of sperm in the semen. There are many causes of an abnormal sperm count and, not uncommonly, a number of ordinarily insignificant factors can cluster together to reduce the sperm count. Hormonal problems, chronic illness, and medications may affect sperm production. As sperm cells grow and mature they become increasingly sensitive to radiation and pollutants such as toxic pesticides and industrial chemicals. Alcoholism or chronic drug abuse have been implicated in some cases of lowered sperm counts. Severe and prolonged stress may also reduce fertility. Although a man's fertility does not decrease with the dramatic finality of a woman's at menopause, advancing age does affect both sperm quality and performance.

Sometimes injury or other conditions may affect function of the testicles and reduce or eliminate sperm in a man's semen. For example, an injury may reduce the blood supply to the area and cause death to the surrounding tissues. (Occasionally such damage results from a hernia operation.)

Infection

The most common known cause of a low sperm count (20 to 30 percent) is a bacterial infection of the prostate or ductal system, which clouds the seminal fluid and affects the quality of the sperm. A semen analysis may find there are adequate numbers of sperm, but that they are sluggish or dead. In such cases, treatment with antibiotics can clear the infection, and sperm usually resume their healthy pattern.

Varicocele

The second most common cause of a low sperm count is a varicose vein of the testicle, called varicocele. In this condition, the tiny valves inside the veins that carry blood away from the testicles fail to function properly. This allows blood to pool around the testicles. This pooled blood produces extra heat around the sperm production centers. Theoretically, this overheating reduces sperm production. However, not every man who has a varicocele is infertile. About 10 percent of all men have a varicocele, and no one knows how many ultimately become infertile. However, 30 percent of men who are infertile have a varicocele.

A varicocele often can be detected during the physical examination, but diagnosis sometimes requires the help of a heat-sensitive photograph called a thermogram. When an infertile man is discovered to have a varicocele the condition can be corrected by a surgical procedure in which the vein is tied off. A new, healthy network of veins then forms. Surgery improves sperm counts for about 70 percent of infertile men with varicocele; about half of these go on to become fathers.

Structural Abnormalities

About 10 percent of male infertility problems are traced to the transport system, the series of passageways through which sperm must pass to get from the testicles into the penis. Ducts may become blocked by scar tissue resulting from previous infection, although venereal disease and other infections are not nearly as dangerous to men as they are to women. Such blockages can often be cleared by surgery.

Some structural abnormalities prevent proper deposit of semen in the vagina. For example, men born with hypospadias—a congential malformation in which the urethra opens on the under side of the penis—may not be able to ejaculate into the vagina. In such cases, pregnancy may be achieved by artificial insemination using the husband's semen.

Voluntary Sterilization

About 500,000 vasectomies are performed in the United States each year, and these men are voluntarily sterile. Vasectomies may be reversed about 50 percent of the time, but this is an expensive procedure requiring the services of a skilled microsurgeon, and even then, the failure rate is high. Thus, any man who undergoes a vasectomy should assume that it is going to be permanent.

FERTILITY TESTS FOR MEN

Semen Analysis

The premier test of male fertility is the semen analysis, which is actually a series of tests carried out on a sample of seminal fluid collected during masturbation. Because a man's reproductive system is relatively constant, the semen analysis can be performed at any time. However, it is best performed after 2 days of abstinence from intercourse because it may take 24 to 48 hours for his supply of sperm to be replenished to normal levels.

The semen analysis reveals the number of sperm in the sample, as well as their shape and swimming ability. The quality of the sperm is often more important than their actual numbers. The sperm must be moving rapidly and easily. The volume and quality of the seminal fluid also are examined.

All men produce some deformed sperm; in general, a man is considered fertile if most of his sperm are healthy and their number exceeds roughly 50 million per milliliter of semen, with more than half the sperm still swimming 4 hours after ejaculation. If the semen analysis does not meet this criteria, additional tests may be needed to determine why.

Infection and Antibody Tests

Before the semen analysis is considered complete, tests are made to identify any bacteria present in the semen, including ureaplasma (mycoplasma) and chlamydia.

One unique and controversial fertility problem involves a so-called antibody reaction. For unexplained reasons, some women seem to produce antibodies in their cervical mucus that kills sperm. Similarly, some men are believed to produce sperm-killing antibodies in their seminal fluid. Male or female antibodies may also cause sperm to clump together (agglutination) and hamper their natural swimming ability. Such clumping, however, may also occur naturally or be caused by infection.

If sperm are dead or clumping, cultures for bacteria are performed on the semen sample. If no infection is found, the laboratory analyst may then proceed with antibody testing. These tests are complicated and expensive, and are usually carried out only when other tests have not revealed a diagnosis.

Postcoital Tests

In a postcoital test, samples of mucus are removed from the woman's cervix within several hours after intercourse to see if healthy, moving sperm are present. If sperm are healthy and moving during semen analysis, but appear dead or sluggish on the postcoital test, it is possible that sperm-killing antibodies are present in the woman's cervical mucus. In this case, antibody testing is carried out on the mucus sample.

TREATMENT FOR MEN

GENERALLY SPEAKING, infertility in men is relatively easy to diagnose, but often difficult to treat. Because there is often a clustering of problems, treatment is much less precise and effective than it is in women. A low sperm count can sometimes be improved with fertility drugs, but these drugs are often overused. However, if blood tests reveal a lack of the pituitary hormones that control the male reproductive system, Pergonal—the same fertility drug that is sometimes used to treat female infertility—may be effective. A blockage in the ductal system can often be surgically corrected. For men who have a varicocele, surgery to tie off the varicose vein is highly successful. In general, the fertility specialist usually works with the overall system to improve con-

ditions in the hope that even a slightly elevated sperm count might be enough for pregnancy.

Occasionally, simple practical advice helps solve the problem. There is speculation that excess scrotal heat lowers sperm production. When no other specific cause can be identified, infertile men are advised against tight underwear that holds the testicles close to the body. They are also advised to avoid saunas and soaking in a hot tub. In the same way, jobs involving long hours of exposure to unusual heat may contribute to a lowered sperm count.

Some of the new experimental treatments show promise in correcting problems dealing with poor seminal fluid. For example, in some instances the fluid may be too thick or may contain substances that hinder the sperm's movement. Pregnancy may then be achieved by collecting a semen sample and using special processes to improve the quality of the seminal fluid, and then using it for artificial insemination.

INFERTILITY IN WOMEN

OCCASIONALLY A WOMAN is infertile because of a problem originating during fetal development or childhood, but most often causes of female infertility arise in adult life. Once identified, many are readily corrected. One of the major problems is arriving at a correct diagnosis.

When a physician is attempting to track down possible causes, a woman will be asked many of the same general questions as her male partner. In addition, she should be prepared to trace her menstrual, sexual, and reproductive history. Questions will include: How old where you when you began menstruating? Are your periods regular? What are they like? Do you experience severe cramps? Have you had a previous pregnancy? Miscarriage? Induced abortion? Questions about pelvic infections, any sexually transmitted disease, previous contraceptive practices, pain during intercourse, and other aspects of her sexual or reproductive life also may be revealing.

FERTILITY TESTS FOR WOMEN

THE FEMALE REPRODUCTIVE system is one of nature's most sophisticated and delicately balanced, and so the first step in tracking down the cause of a woman's infertility involves making sure that her finely tuned biological clock is in sync. There are dozens of factors, many of them seemingly irrelevant, that can upset this biological clock. Quite often, the woman herself can pinpoint problem areas if she knows what to look for. Unfortunately, many women are not very well attuned to their bodies and they simply may not be aware of subtle changes that take place during the different phases of the menstrual cycle. Keeping a careful diary of these phases is an important starting point for both the woman and the physician who is attempting to find the cause of her fertility problem.

The Menstrual Cycle

Record keeping should start at the beginning of the woman's menstrual cycle, which is the first day of menstrual bleeding. The cycle ends on the day before bleeding starts again. Monthly cycles vary considerably among women, but usually fall into a pattern somewhere between every 26 and 32 days. Once established, the number of days between periods stays roughly the same month after month for an individual woman, although there are many exceptions. Most women menstruate regularly, but a large number have irregular cycles. Each phase of the cycle is characterized by distinct hormonal factors. Generally, the average 28-day cycle is as follows. (See figure 5.3.)

Days 1 to 5—The Menstrual Phase. Estrogen and progesterone are at their lowest levels, signaling the hypothalamus and pituitary to secrete luteinizing hormone (LH) and follicle-stimulating hormone (FSH), which in turn stimulate the ovaries to step up estrogen production and to begin developing a new egg or ovum.

Days 6 to 12—The Proliferative/Follicular Phase. Levels of estrogen rise, signaling the pituitary to reduce production of FSH and to step up production of LH.

Days 12 to 13. Estrogen surges, causing a further increase in LH. When LH reaches a certain level, estrogen falls and there is a rise in FSH.

Day 14—Ovulation. The LH surge causes the final maturation of the ovum, and within 36 hours ovulation takes place. The egg breaks away from its follicle and enters the Fallopian tube to begin its journey to the uterus. During this phase, fertilization can occur if the ovum and sperm unite.

Days 15 to 27—The Luteal Phase. The ruptured egg follicle becomes the corpus luteum and begins secreting progesterone, the hormone that prepares the uterus lining for pregnancy. If fertilization does not take place, progesterone peaks at about day 22 and then falls off, causing the endometrium to begin to loosen and break down. On about day 27, estrogen, progesterone, FSH, and LH are at their lowest levels of the cycle.

Day 28. Menstruation starts, beginning a new cycle.

Very few women have a precise 28-day cycle—anything from 20 to 40 days is within the normal range. Many women mistakenly assume that ovulation takes place in the middle of the cycle. This is true only for one that is 28 days long—no matter how long or short the cycle, ovulation occurs about 14 days before menstruation. Thus a woman with a 22-day cycle will ovulate on the eighth day, while one with a 40-day cycle will ovulate on the twenty-sixth day. It is important for a woman to keep track of her cycles so that she knows their average length and can make sure that intercourse coincides with ovulation.

Throughout the cycle, the shifting hormonal levels result in changes in a

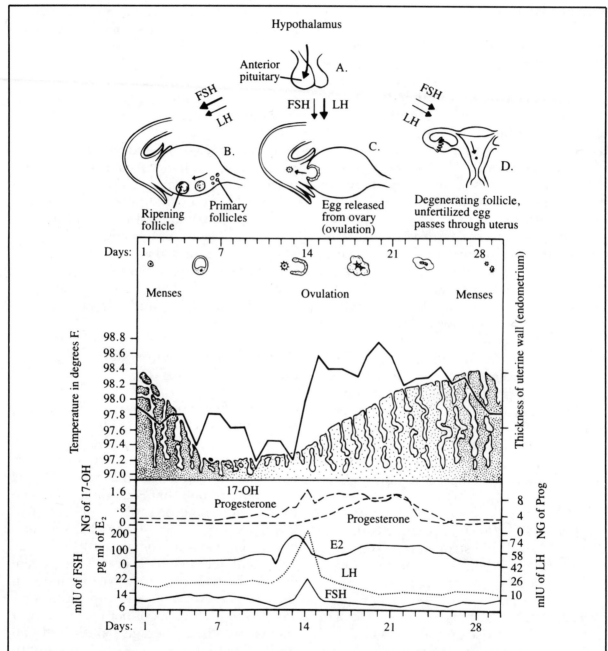

Figure 5.3. **Overview of the menstrual cycle. (Drawing by Beth Ann Willert. Adapted from *Hormones: The Woman's Answer Book,* by Lois Jovanovic, M.D., and Genell Subak-Sharpe, Antheneum, 1987.)**

woman's body, some of which are obvious if a woman knows what to look for, while others may go unnoticed. For example, during the first proliferative phase of the cycle, the rising estrogen stimulates the thin lining of the uterus to grow thicker; by the time of ovulation, the endometrium may be 10 times thicker than it was at the beginning of the cycle. The surge in estrogen also may cause the body to retain salt and water, accounting for the bloating and swelling that some women experience in their premenstrual phase. The high estrogen levels also may cause a flare-up of acne and a worsening of breast cysts. After ovulation, when the corpus luteum begins to produce large amounts of progesterone, the endometrium grows spongier, increasing its blood system as it prepares to receive a fertilized egg. The cervical mucus also undergoes changes during the menstrual cycle. Immediately after menstruation, the mucus is usually scanty, becoming somewhat thicker until just before ovulation, when it becomes thinner and more profuse. Some women experience *mittelschmerz*—a pain that ranges from a mild twinge to severe cramps—at the time of ovulation. The pain results from the bleeding that may occur when the mature egg breaks away from the follicle.

The most common sign for ovulation, however, is the slight change in basal temperature that occurs with shifting hormone levels. Basal temperature is the body's lowest temperature, which can be measured immediately after waking up in the morning and before getting out of bed. When levels of estrogen and progesterone are low during the first phase of the cycle, the basal temperature is also low—typically about 97 to 97.5°F. There is a slight dip in estrogen just before the big surge preceding ovulation, and at this time there will also be a slight drop in basal temperature. The surge in hormones that takes place immediately before and during ovulation results in a rise in basal temperature, perhaps by a full degree or even more. The basal temperature stays higher than usual until menstruation, although there is a gradual decline as progesterone and estrogen drop toward the end of the cycle. If conception occurs, there will be no fall in basal temperature; instead, it will tend to rise even more at the time that menstruation would normally take place because of the surge in hormones needed to establish the pregnancy.

If the ovum has not been fertilized, it is absorbed into the body and disappears, and the corpus luteum ceases to produce progesterone. The abrupt loss of hormone causes the endometrium to break down; the walls of the uterus contract and push out the lining as the menstrual flow.

Even the slightest disruption in the fine-tuned hormonal system described above can result in erratic or absent ovulation. A woman who is not ovulating may not realize there is a problem because she may still menstruate regularly. Thus, one of the first areas of investigation by a fertility specialist will be the hormonal axis, to make sure that ovulation is taking place. This will include the following tests.

OVULATORY TESTS

Basal Temperature Record

Even before seeking the help of a fertility specialist, it is a good idea for a woman to keep a basal temperature chart for 2 or 3 months. (See figure 5.4.) Although the temperature chart is not absolutely conclusive, it is still a good indicator of ovulation. Some women try to use the temperature chart to pinpoint the most optimal time for intercourse. This can be difficult because the rise in basal temperature occurs after ovulation and a woman's most fertile days are just before the rise. To use a temperature chart as a timing device for intercourse, then, a woman must anticipate the rise. If her menstrual cycles are regular, it is relatively easy to predict when the rise is about to occur. Some women show a noticeable dip in temperature just before the upward shift. This dip, if it occurs, coincides with ovulation.

At-Home Ovulation Tests

These new self-tests predict when ovulation will take place much more accurately than a basal temperature chart. The tests are designed to detect the surge in LH that occurs just before ovulation. A

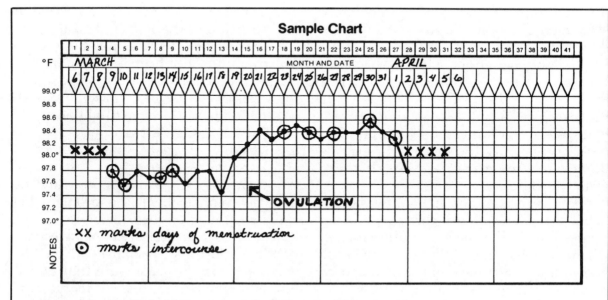

Figure 5.4. **Sample basal temperature chart.** (Courtesy of Serono Laboratories, Inc., 280 Pond Street, Randolph, Massachusetts 02368.)

woman tests her urine for several days before the anticipated time of ovulation. The chemically treated dipstick will change color according to the amount of LH in the urine. By referring to the color code included in the test kits, a woman can determine her most fertile time of the cycle. Conversely, no rise in LH indicates that ovulation is not taking place. These tests tend to be rather expensive, costing $35 or more per cycle. Even so, they are less expensive and more convenient than tests performed in a fertility clinic or specialist's office.

The Postcoital Test

The postcoital is a subtle test of compatibility and potential. Postcoital analysis reveals the condition of the cervical mucus just before ovulation, when mucus should be thin and profuse, thereby enhancing the sperm's ability to swim through it. Careful analysis can also reveal the presence of infection, the activity of sperm, and possibly also the presence of antibodies against the sperm. The postcoital test is performed midcycle. Usually the husband and wife abstain from sex for 2 days before the test. Then, on the night before the test, they have intercourse without using any lubricants or douches. After sex, the woman remains in bed for a half hour or so to allow the sperm to ascend from the vaginal pool into the cervical mucus.

The woman then goes to the doctor's office, usually within 8 to 12 hours of intercourse. The physician suctions out a sample of cervical mucus into a thin tube for microscopic examination, during which the number of sperm and their activity can be observed. The hallmark of a good postcoital test is a thin, watery mucus without white blood cells or other debris. The mucus pH must be alkaline enough to let sperm survive from 24 to 48 hours. The postcoital test cannot prove that a woman actually ovulates, but does show whether enough estrogen has built up in the bloodstream to set the stage for ovulation.

Endometrial Biopsy

The next step in the testing sequence is an endometrial biopsy, which should prove conclusively that ovulation has taken place. The endometrial biopsy is performed late in the menstrual cycle, a few days before a woman's period is expected to begin. The endometrial biopsy is an analysis of a few cells scraped from the uterine lining; it shows whether progesterone has adequately matured the endometrium for conception. Such a progesterone imprint will only be visible if the hormonal cycle has shifted to its second phase. If cells show such an imprint, the specialist can be reasonably sure that ovulation has occurred. If the cells show only the influence of estrogen, the specialist can be certain that ovulation has not occurred.

Besides demonstrating probability of ovulation, the biopsy also shows the quality of the endometrium. A few infertile women (3 percent) have what is called a short luteal phase defect, meaning that progesterone falls too soon, breaking down the endometrium before an embryo can successfully implant.

Ideally, progesterone has primed the endometrium to its maximum, and the biopsy shows that ovulation has occurred and that the uterus is prepared to receive a fertilized ovum. If it has not, the biopsy is repeated in the next cycle to confirm the diagnosis.

Blood Tests

The only way to measure the rise and fall of hormones accurately is by analyzing blood levels. These analytical tests require daily visits to the laboratory and are prohibitively expensive. Laboratory blood tests are not routinely performed, although the new home tests to detect the LH surge may be useful. In certain circumstances—for example, when a woman has no menstrual periods or when her temperature chart and home tests indicate that she is not ovulating—many fertility experts will perform blood tests at the beginning, middle, and end of the menstrual cycle, the critical points.

Ultrasound

In some research settings, ultrasound is occasionally used to determine whether ovulation has occurred. With ultrasound the physician can first track the development of the follicle, and later observe its disappearance, indicating that the follicle has ruptured and that ovulation has occurred. Thus, ultrasound is usually targeted around midcycle.

TESTING FOR STRUCTURAL PROBLEMS

IF THE HORMONAL axis appears to be functioning normally with regular ovulation, the next step in the fertility evaluation is to test for structural or mechanical problems that may be preventing conception from taking place, most commonly nonfunctioning or blocked Fallopian tubes. These tests, which are more complex than those for ovulatory problems, usually involve surgical procedures and include the following.

Hysterosalpingogram

A hysterosalpingogram, an X-ray study using dyes to make internal structures visible, is designed to show whether the Fallopian tubes are open. About three tablespoons of a radio opaque dye are pumped through the vagina, into the uterus and Fallopian tubes. X-rays are then taken; if the tubes are open the dye moves through the length of both tubes and out the open ends. The test is best performed in the early part of the cycle, immediately after menstruation is complete. At this time, the lining of the uterus is at its thinnest and it is unlikely that a woman might be pregnant. Thus, the test has less chance of producing a false-negative result. Usually a false-negative occurs when a thickened endometrium blocks the small openings of the Fallopian tube and creates an impression that the tubes are blocked when, in fact, they are open.

The hysterosalpingogram also shows the size and shape of the uterus and whether it has fibroids, benign growths that can interfere with fertility. The procedure itself is sometimes therapeutic—for a few women pumping dye through the tubes and uterus appears to encourage conception. This test is normally an office procedure, although some specialists do it in an outpatient clinic, usually in conjunction with other more invasive tests.

Hysteroscopy

Hysteroscopy is a telescopic view (via the cervix) into the inside of the uterus to see if any defects, such as polyps, fibroids, or weblike scarring across the entrance to the tubes, are present. Hysteroscopy is also best performed in the early days of the menstrual cycle. To do the test, a thin tube with fiber-optic viewing devices (an endoscope) is inserted into the vagina and through the cervix into the uterus. The endoscope also can be equipped with devices to collect tissue samples for a biopsy.

Laparoscopy

Laparoscopy is a surgical procedure that allows a direct view of the internal reproductive organs via a telescopic instrument (laparoscope) inserted through a small abdominal incision. (See figure 5.5.) The procedure is usually performed during the latter part of the cycle, after ovu-

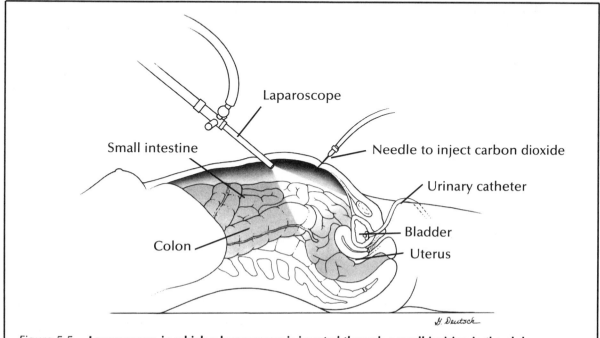

Figure 5.5. **Laparoscopy, in which a laparoscope is inserted through a small incision in the abdomen, permitting the examiner to view the abdominal and pelvic organs.**

lation has taken place. Laparoscopy can detect scar tissue around the reproductive organs and the extent of the damage. The presence of a corpus luteum on the surface of the ovary also confirms whether ovulation has occurred. Endometriosis, if present, can be seen when it is at its most active stage due to the hormonal stimulation at this phase of the menstrual cycle.

Laparoscopy may be performed even when other tests have demonstrated that the tubes are blocked. For example, a surgeon may want to assess the extent of the damage and the overall anatomy of the reproductive organs before performing major abdominal surgery. In such instances, the laparoscopy is carried out early in the menstrual cycle. Based on the findings, the surgeon determines if reconstructive surgery is actually warranted.

Laparoscopy is performed in a hospital, usually under general anesthesia. This is the last test in the fertility evaluation. After laparoscopy, the fertility specialist will have a diagnosis 90 percent of the time.

CAUSES OF FEMALE INFERTILITY

Ovulatory Failure

Identifiable fertility problems in adult women are about equally divided between ovulatory failure or other hormonal problems and blocked tubes or other structural abnormalities. Once a proper diagnosis is made, treatment of female infertility is usually straightforward, with a high degree of success.

Sometimes failure to ovulate is part of the natural course of events. A woman's most fertile years are between the ages of 19 and 28, when ovulation is most regular, usually every 26 to 30 days, or 13 times a year. As a woman ages, ovulation becomes less reliable—instead of ovulating 12 or 13 times a year, she may ovulate in only 9 or 10 cycles, even though she may still menstruate just as often.

There is also a steady decline in the number of eggs or ova. A baby girl is normally born with about 2 million follicles, or egg-forming cells. By the time she reaches puberty, only about 300,000 will be left. During each menstrual cycle, one or two follicles mature and others wither and die. With the approach of menopause, the average woman will still have about 8,000 follicles, but with the passage of time, most lose their capability for fertilization. By the time a woman reaches menopause, even though her pituitary produces more FSH, ovulation does not take place.

In addition to this natural decline in fertility, there are dozens of other factors that can affect ovulation. It is as if the body senses that all systems must be properly functioning in order for a healthy pregnancy to occur. Almost any upset in the body's delicate hormonal interrelationships can affect ovarian function. In addition to primary ovarian failure, thyroid disease, diabetes, and adrenal or pituitary disorders are examples of hormonal causes of infertility.

Illness, stress, excessive underweight or obesity, cigarette smoking, certain drugs, and nutritional deficiencies are among the many factors that can hinder ovulation. Women who engage in extraordinary exercise conditioning—for example, ballet dancers or marathon runners —frequently fail to ovulate, primarily because of their very low percentage of body fat. Similarly, women who are very overweight also may fail to ovulate because their excess fatty tissue causes them to produce too much estrogen.

Some errors in the hormonal axis occur spontaneously; others are perpetrated by illness or drugs, particularly the birth control pill. It is not unusual for a woman to have trouble resuming her normal pattern of ovulation after stopping the pill. Generally this condition cures itself within a few months, but occasionally hormonal treatment is needed to reestablish normal ovarian function. Sometimes the ovarian system fails to resume normal functioning after childbirth or breastfeeding. In these instances, time or, if needed, hormonal therapy usually can resolve the problem.

Fertility Drugs

It is in the treatment of ovulatory problems that the greatest advances have been made, thanks to the development of drugs that help regulate reproductive hormones. For many years the only treatment for ovulatory problems was a surgical technique called ovarian wedge resection. In this procedure a portion of the ovary was removed, and as a result ovulation resumed in a small percentage of women, mostly those with polycystic ovaries (Stein-Leventhal syndrome). This is a condition in which the follicle thickens and continues to produce estrogen instead of releasing the matured egg. If the condition becomes chronic, the ovaries become enlarged with cysts and thickened thecal cells—the structures that secrete estrogen and androgens. The matured eggs are unable to break through the thickened thecal cells, and ovulation does not take place. Removing a portion of ovaries that contain the cysts and thickened thecal cells sometimes permits ovulation to resume. Many times, however, the surgery diminishes fertility by creating scar tissue around the tubes and ovaries. Thus the development of hormonal drugs that can diminish the formation of the cysts and promote resumption of ovulation is more effective than surgery, which is now used mostly for women who do not achieve an adequate response from fertility drugs.

Clomiphene (Clomid) is the drug used most often to treat ovarian failure. Studies have found that about 80 percent of women who have ovaries capable of producing eggs, but who are not ovulating, are helped by clomiphene, although up to 25 percent of these women still will not become pregnant. The drug, which has now been in use for more than 20 years, works directly on the hypothalamus, where it blocks the estrogen receptors and, in effect, prompts the pituitary to secrete FSH. This stimulates the follicle to ripen an egg, a process that results in even more estrogen production. The hypothalamus still does not sense the very high levels of estrogen until the drug is abruptly stopped; this results in a surge of LH, which in turn causes the egg to break free of the follicle, thereby completing ovulation.

Typically, clomiphene is taken for 5 days, beginning on day 5 of the menstrual cycle. If the woman does not conceive within 6 months of treatment, another hormone, HCG (human chorionic gonadotropin, a pregnancy hormone that has a chemical structure similar to that of LH), is given on day 8 or 9 of the cycle to help boost the release of the mature ovum from the ovary.

Sometimes clomiphene will be given before a full fertility workup is carried out, especially if there is a strong suspicion that the problem is failure to ovulate. The drug is considered safe, although some women experience temporary side effects, including blurred vision, hot flashes, bloating, nausea, and enlargement of the ovaries. Most side effects can be avoided by starting therapy with a low dosage and gradually building up.

Clomiphene greatly increases the incidence of multiple births, mostly twins. Two of 50 women using the drug will have twins, compared to a normal twinning incidence of 1 of every 90 pregnancies.

When clomiphene fails, some specialists recommend the more potent fertility drug Pergonal, which is a combination of LH and FSH. Pergonal acts directly on the ovaries, and its use must be very carefully monitored to make sure that the ovaries are not overstimulated, which can cause the release of too many eggs or even, in rare instances, ovarian rupture. The drug should only be administered by a fertility specialist who has experience with its use. In the usual regimen, a woman will take Pergonal for 5 to 10 days at the beginning of the cycle. During this time, she should be checked daily to ensure that the ovaries are not being overstimulated. This is done by blood tests to measure estrogen levels or by ultrasound, which can show how many eggs are ripening. When ultrasound shows that 1 to 3 eggs have matured, a second hormone, HCG, will be given to prompt the ovaries to release the mature eggs from the ovary. Ovulation will not take place without the HCG. Virtually all women with ovaries capable of producing eggs will ovulate with Pergonal and HCG; 3 to 4 cycles may be needed to achieve pregnancy, which occurs in about 65 percent of women taking the drugs. Pergonal therapy tends to be expensive: On the average, costs, which include office visits and tests for monitoring, run about $1,500 to $3,000 for each cycle of treatment. Between 3 and 4 cycles are required per pregnancy.

The most common problem encountered with Pergonal is the overproduction of mature eggs, which can result in excessive multiple births. This is why the ultrasound checks are so important. If more than 2 or 3 eggs are maturing, most specialists recommend that HCG be withheld for that cycle because of the danger of all the eggs becoming fertilized. Although the birth of septuplets, quintuplets, or even greater multiple births creates considerable attention in the media, the sad reality is that these multiple pregnancies are dangerous to both the mother and fetuses and should be avoided if at all possible. If ultrasound shows that too many embryos have implanted, many specialists will advise interrupting the pregnancy at that stage and trying again at a later date. The current rate of multiple births with Pergonal is over 20 percent.

Other Ovulatory Problems

Elevated Prolactin. Prolactin is a hormone that stimulates milk production in new mothers and also blocks ovulation. Many circumstances other than childbirth may stimulate prolactin release, including stress, the use of hallucinogens, excessive alcohol intake, antidepressant drugs and certain other medications, brain tumors, and lack of thyroid hormone. When prolactin is elevated, a woman may cease to menstruate and will not ovulate. She may have some milky discharge from her breasts, but frequently there are no obvious symptoms. A blood test, however, can detect the presence of prolactin.

If the elevated prolactin is due to a pituitary tumor, treatment will involve its surgical removal. Otherwise, a relatively new drug called bromocryptine is used to suppress prolactin production. The drug is given daily in varying doses until prolactin levels fall. Should pregnancy occur, the drug is stopped immediately. A woman may have to take bromocryptine for 3 or 4 months or longer; if the prolactin level does not fall, further studies for an undetected tumor may be indicated.

Other Hormonal Disorders

Infertility due to thyroid or other hormonal disorders usually can be corrected by treating the underlying problem. Problems stemming from hormonal imbalances in the luteal phase of the cycle are relatively easy to detect and resolve. For example, if the infertility is due to low levels of LH, HCG may be given. Sometimes a woman will be found to have too little progesterone to establish the pregnancy. This can be resolved by using vaginal suppositories containing the hormone. Clomiphene may be prescribed to correct low levels of LH and estrogen due to defects of the corpus luteum.

BLOCKED TUBES AND OTHER STRUCTURAL PROBLEMS

THE SECOND MAJOR CATEGORY of fertility problems for women is structural or "mechanical" failures, in which the reproductive organs themselves are damaged. Blocked tubes, pelvic adhesions, and other obstructions account for about 30 percent of infertility problems in women. Less common are developmental problems, such as uterine malformations or an incompetent cervix.

Pelvic Inflammatory Disease

Pelvic inflammatory disease, or PID, is the most common cause of scarred or blocked Fallopian tubes. As noted earlier, there has been a marked increase in PID in recent years, due largely to the rise in chlamydia, gonorrhea, and other sexually transmitted diseases. Rapid treatment can stop massive damage, but even a little scar tissue in the wrong place can interfere with pregnancy. It is estimated that a woman who has had 1 episode of PID has a 15 percent risk of becoming infertile, and the rate increases with each subsequent infection.

Some pelvic infections have such mild symptoms that a woman may not even know she has PID. For example, chlamydia, an increasingly common sexually transmitted disease, often produces only very mild symptoms that may be overlooked until the tubes are severely damaged. Gonorrhea also can be overlooked in its early stages.

During the fertility evaluation, the specialist may ask at what age the woman first had sexual intercourse. A young girl is more susceptible to pelvic infection than an adult woman. A woman who had her first sexual experience in her early teens may have developed a pelvic infection without knowing it, or she may recall being treated for some unexplained infection. The number of sexual partners a woman has had over her lifetime is another critical question. The number of partners is directly related to the risk of sexually transmitted disease and pelvic infection. The more sexual partners a woman has had, the more likely she is to develop PID. For this reason it is now routine for physicians to take a cervical culture of a woman, along with a Pap smear, once or twice a year, especially when a woman has multiple sex partners.

The method of contraception a woman uses may also increase her risk of developing PID. IUDs have been associated with a higher incidence of pelvic infections, especially among women with multiple sex partners. An IUD also appears to alter the uterine lining in such a way as to make it more difficult to establish a pregnancy.

Endometriosis

Another major cause of scar tissue and adhesions within the pelvic cavity is endometriosis, a disease in which bits of endometrial tissue, which is normally found only in the lining of the uterus, begin to grow in various sites throughout the abdomen. How the endometrial tissue appears in these locations is controversial, but somehow the cells implant on sites outside the uterus and continue to grow just as if they were in their normal place. Every month, the implants, stimulated by the same hormones that build the endometrium of the uterus, grow and spread throughout the pelvic cavity. At the end of the monthly cycle the tissue bleeds just like the endometrium, and bleeding creates scar tissue. Remnants of the misplaced tissue burgeon again the following month. The disease can spread through the pelvic cavity until the ovaries and tubes are smothered in scar tissue and adhesions. But infertility can result from even small amounts of misplaced endometrial tissue, explaining why some women without obvious endometriosis are unable to achieve pregnancy while some others with extensive implants are able to have a baby.

About 15 percent of all women have endometriosis, and the incidence of infertility among them is nearly 50 percent. Endometriosis can occur at any age, and for many women it may start just after puberty. Although pregnancy temporarily "turns off" the disease, it often recurs following childbirth.

At this time there is no dependable cure for endometriosis. The goal of treatment is to confine the disease and prevent damage to the vital organs. Treatment may include surgery or drugs, or both. The designed course usually depends on the extent of the disease, as well as the woman's age. Since endometriosis tends to worsen with age, most fertility experts recommend that a woman with the disease attempt pregnancy at as early an age as practical.

Surgical Scarring

Another cause of tubal scarring is previous abdominal surgery, particularly if the operation was complicated by infection. Women who had appendectomies when they were children are often surprised to discover years later that they are infertile as a result.

Ectopic Pregnancy

An ectopic pregnancy, in which the embryo develops in the Fallopian tube or some other site outside the uterus, is still another relatively common cause of infertility. Unless a tubal pregnancy is detected in its very early stages, it can lead to a rupture and consequent destruction of the tube. If the remaining tube is intact, pregnancy is still possible. PID, the use of an IUD, and a previous ectopic pregnancy are among the factors that increase the risk of a tubal pregnancy. Very often, however, there is no obvious cause, and it is impossible to predict who is likely to have an ectopic pregnancy.

Sterilization

In recent years, voluntary sterilization has become the most common form of birth control for married couples. Not uncommonly, a woman will undergo sterilization, which entails cutting or blocking the Fallopian tubes to prevent passage of the ovum to the uterus, and then later want to conceive. Reversal is possible in a small number of cases, but any woman considering sterilization should understand that it is most likely to be permanent and be very sure that she will not want to have children at some future date.

Microsurgery

Many structural problems can be corrected by microsurgery. The female reproductive organs are small and delicate, and difficult to operate on in the conventional manner. Micorsurgery—which combines high-powered lenses with refined surgical techniques—allows surgeons to rebuild a damaged Fallopian tube, remove microscopic bits of endometrial tissue, and correct other defects that may prevent conception. Increasingly, lasers are used in delicate fertility surgery, which decreases scarring. This type of surgery is still in its infancy, however, and success rates vary depending on the extent of the damage and the skill of the surgeon.

CERVICAL AND UTERINE PROBLEMS

A THIRD, less frequently seen group of problems involves the route traveled by sperm as they swim from the vagina through the cervix and uterus and into the tubes. Occasionally problems here originate during fetal development when, for various reasons, the uterus or vagina may not have formed properly. Such birth defects often can be corrected with surgical reconstruction.

Five percent of fertility problems in women involve the cervix, which must produce good-quality mucus to provide a proper environment for sperm. Should even a mild infection set in, the cervix can produce a hostile, killing mucus that destroys sperm on contact. Sometimes a woman does not produce enough mucus; in this case, production usually can be increased by giving estrogens.

The uterus, too, must be in good shape to allow for implantation and proper growth of the fertilized ovum. In the uterus a rare inflammation of the uterine lining, called chronic endometritis, can interfere with implantation. Such infections of the cervix and uterus can be treated with antibiotics; occasionally a dilation and curettage (D&C) of the uterus is needed to remove endometrial tissue.

Uterine fibroids—benign growths— can also cause fertility problems. These growths are quite common and, depending on the size and placement, may not interfere with implantation and fetal development. More often, however, they create problems. Surgical removal often can be accomplished. Very small ones can be removed with a laser; larger ones require a conventional operation.

In recent years, a number of infertility cases have been attributed to the use of DES (diethylstilbestrol) by the patients' mothers during pregnancy. Until the late 1960s and early 1970s, DES was sometimes given to women to prevent a miscarriage; the practice was stopped when it was discovered that many of their daughters had unusual disorders involving their reproductive organs. Some developed a rare type of vaginal cancer; more common, however, are fertility problems among DES daughters. Many have smaller-than-normal uteri; others have cervical or vaginal malformations that make pregnancy difficult to achieve. Even when DES daughters do get pregnant, many tend to have a high miscarriage rate and low-birth-weight babies. It should be noted that most DES daughters do not have problems, but when one fails to conceive, DES should be considered as a possible cause.

PSYCHOLOGICAL FACTORS

NOT LONG AGO thousands of women were told that their inability to conceive was caused by psychological problems. Modern science has shown that most of these women probably had undiagnosed physical problems that caused their infertility. In fact, today 90 percent of all cases of infertility can be accurately diagnosed, compared with only 40 percent 10 years ago. However, we now know that many fertility problems stem from ovulatory failure, which can theoretically be traced to activities in the lower brain (hypothalamus).

We also know that the hypothalamus is sensitive to psychological trauma, which can severely deplete the chemical signals that it sends to the pituitary gland, and ultimately to the ovaries. Certain drugs, particularly the psychiatric class of tranquilizers and mood modifiers, can override the hypothalamus and disturb the hormonal axis. Usually, as soon as the drug is stopped, the axis returns to normal. Illness and stress also can interfere with hormone production and thus temporarily stop ovulation. The influence of the emotions and the brain on reproduction is a prime area of research. As specific reproduction activities of the brain are identified in the future, the elusive role of psychological stress may eventually be accurately defined.

While psychological factors are today not often considered a direct cause of infertility, they are definitely considered a result. Infertility creates emotional stress for both partners, and the stress increases as the couple goes through the workup and subsequent treatment. Stress can create new problems in the marital relationship and also make existing problems worse. For these reasons, a professional psychological evaluation is part of many fertility workups today. The ongoing research involving the effects of stress on infertility may ultimately help scientists learn why some couples, for unknown reasons, cannot conceive.

FERTILITY ENHANCEMENT TECHNOLOGIES

ABOUT 90 percent of the time, the cause of infertility can be diagnosed. But in the remaining 10 percent, the cause will not be identified, even after a perfectly designed workup. Researchers are constantly adding to our understanding of the many facets of reproduction, but many unanswered questions remain.

Even when the cause is known, it is not always possible to correct the problem, although modern fertility drugs and microsurgery often appear to work miracles, making parenthood possible today when even a few years ago it would have been hopeless. Increasingly, couples for whom drugs and surgery do not work are turning to new fertility enhancement technologies, many of which are still experimental and often controversial. Men who have a low or absent sperm count may turn to artificial insemination. For women whose Fallopian tubes are irreparably damaged, in vitro fertilization is a possible alternative. And a woman whose ovaries cannot produce healthy eggs might be able to bear a child by embryo transfer.

Before pursuing these new technologies, couples need first to resolve their feelings about infertility. Not every person is able to cope with the sometimes arduous medical procedures that accompany these technologies. Nor should infertile couples feel they must seek out these treatments simply because they are available. Wanting a baby and not being able to have one can be intensely painful; society may pressure some women to go through time-consuming and expensive medical manipulations that they are unable to bear emotionally.

At their best, fertility enhancement technologies give couples who want children choices. And the long-range potential of reproductive science holds great hope for the future. But for now, such techniques are experimental, meaning that they have a high failure rate. Before deciding to pursue fertility enhancement, couples should try to envision how they will feel if the process does not work and decide how long they will keep trying if the technique fails the first time. These issues should be talked over before agreeing to enter a program, because once involved in treatment it is difficult to examine options clearly. The following are condensed descriptions of currently available fertility enhancement technologies.

Artificial Insemination

Artificial insemination is the oldest, least complicated, and most successful alternative to natural conception. In artificial insemination from the husband or from a donor, a physician uses a small plastic tube to implant sperm directly into a woman's cervical canal.

Artificial insemination using the husband's sperm has limited application and is used primarily when the male partner produces a low volume of semen. Collecting the sperm and implanting them at the cervical neck lets sperm bypass the possibly hostile fluids of the vagina. More sperm survive to enter the uterus and tubes, increasing the chance of fertilization. By special washing and separation methods, the technique can also be used when a man's sperm are hampered by overly dense semen, when he produces only a few good-quality sperm, or when the sperm clump together instead of swimming individually.

Artificial insemination is so simple that the technique can also be performed at home, although the success rate is somewhat reduced. The procedure is carried out just prior to or on the day of the woman's ovulation, which can be detected by home testing. Women who ovulate irregularly may need drug therapy to help develop and release the egg before they receive artificial insemination.

On the proper day, the husband masturbates into a sterile glass jar, usually in a private room at the physician's office. Within about a half hour, the physician inserts a warm speculum into the woman's vagina and uses a syringe to push the semen into the neck of the cervix. Next, a silicone cup is inserted to hold the semen in place for several hours, until the sperm can swim through the cervical canal into the uterus. There is no discomfort, and the woman removes the cup herself after about six hours.

Artificial insemination with donor sperm is the more common type and is used when the male partner has little or no sperm. A history of certain genetic disorders or Rh incompatibility also leads some couples to seek this method of fertilization. Donor insemination may also be a choice when a couple has a long history of unexplained infertility. Currently, 10,000 to 20,000 children are born in the United States each year as a result of donor artificial insemination.

Donor sperm usually come from a sperm bank, which screens potential donors to some extent and collects their semen. The extent of screening varies among sperm banks, and a couple considering this method should always ask what kind of screening is performed. This is particularly important in light of the current AIDS epidemic, since the AIDS virus can be transmitted via semen. Fertility experts recommend that frozen sperm be used for artificial insemination to minimize any risk that the donor may be carrying the AIDS virus but has not yet formed antibodies that are detected by current tests.

Typically, the donor receives a nominal fee, usually about $100. A record is often kept of the donor's physical traits so that the physician can match some traits to those of the husband. Before artificial insemination, the couple is usually asked to sign an agreement to absolve the physician and donor of responsibility for any abnormalities the child may have.

Donor sperm today are also supplied in a frozen state, provided by the 16 major cryobanks in the United States. Typically, a physician orders frozen sperm from an anonymous donor in some other part of the country. Frozen sperm are often more carefully screened for diseases and genetic defects. Further, the wide choice of donors lessens the possibility that two children fathered by the same donor might meet later in life and marry. Donor characteristics also can be more easily matched to the husband's physical characteristics.

The quality of the pregnancy does not appear to be affected by freezing of sperm, and the incidence of birth defects is no higher. However, defrosted sperm have a somewhat shorter lifespan than fresh sperm, and insemination must be precisely matched with ovulation.

Pregnancy rates with artificial insemination correspond to those of natural pregnancy. A woman has about a 20 percent chance of pregnancy in the first month, a 50 to 70 percent chance by the third month, and an 80 percent chance by the end of the sixth month.

However, success rates vary widely among physicians. After 6 months of trying to achieve pregnancy via artificial insemination, the physician should re-evaluate the situation. Poor timing may be at fault, in which case more sophisticated (and expensive) tests might be used to pinpoint ovulation precisely. Or the wife may have an undetected fertility problem that would require further testing and treatment.

Artificial insemination by donor has raised numerous legal issues. Donors are not informed about the use of their sperm, making it unlikely that a biological father will turn up years later and intrude into family relationships. Likewise, donors have never been held legally responsible for any resulting children, and in most cases today, courts consider that the husband who consents to artificial insemination with donor sperm for his wife is the legal father of the child.

Although about half the states have laws covering artificial insemination, none addresses all the legal issues that the practice could entail. In general, the procedure involves these legal promises:

Before contributing semen each donor signs a form waiving all parental rights to any child conceived with his sperm. The husband promises in writing to accept the child as his own son or daughter. The agreement, usually signed by both husband and wife, spells out their understanding of the procedure; the husband accepts the offspring as his child; and the physician is not responsible for birth defects or other genetic abnormalities should they occur in the child. This agreement is not necessarily legally valid; nor does it take into account the multitude of variables that may arise later. And given the changing nature of today's families, it is likely that more complex issues will arise in the future. For example, there are instances in which lesbian couples have used artificial insemination to achieve pregnancy of 1 of the partners. There also are instances in which an unmarried woman wants to have a child without a male partner. Such cases raise complex ethical and legal questions that have not yet been resolved.

Because of these complex issues, both partners should have a fertility evaluation before selecting donor artificial insemination to make sure there is no possibility of conception with the husband's sperm. Even when artificial insemination seems to be the best option, many physicians suggest waiting at least 6 months after male infertility has been established to give the couple time to think things through. Obviously, artificial insemination should be chosen only when both partners agree. When the circumstances are right and the decision carefully considered, artificial insemination is a rewarding alternative to natural pregnancy.

In Vitro Fertilization

Fertilization normally takes place in a woman's Fallopian tubes when a newly released egg meets and fuses with a sperm cell. If the tubes are so damaged that either cell cannot reach the rendezvous point, conception will not occur. The in vitro fertilization (IVF) procedure, sometimes referred to as test-tube fertilization, brings the sperm and egg together outside the woman's body.

To achieve in vitro pregnancy, couples must be prepared to invest much time and money, and the chances of success are low. Today there are approximately 200 IVF clinics around the world, 121 of them in the United States. Many of these clinics, although they are in business, have never had a successful pregnancy—that is, one that resulted in a live birth. Thus, anyone considering this method of fertilization needs to ask many questions before selecting an institution. Overall, although some clinics claim higher rates, a woman has only about a 10 percent chance that the procedure will result in a living baby.

While the main reason couples choose IVF is to achieve pregnancy for women who have badly damaged Fallopian tubes, other fertility problems may also be solved with this method. Some clinics accept couples who have prolonged and unexplained infertility (5 years or longer) or women who have persistent endometriosis. A few programs accept couples if the man has a low sperm count, although in these cases artificial insemination should be tried first, since it is far less expensive and less traumatic than in vitro fertilization. Many clinics now accept women up to 40 years of age and older, though their chances of success are even less than those of a younger woman.

In every case, regardless of other problems, at least 1 ovary must be normal and accessible. If a woman's ovaries are obscured by scar tissue or cysts, she may first have to undergo surgery to free them. If she has difficulty ovulating, fertility drugs may be used to normalize her hormonal system. Even if she does ovulate normally, fertility drugs are often used to increase the number of eggs that can be harvested at 1 time. Above all, both partners must be free of infection of any kind.

In vitro fertilization is a last option, not a first choice for infertile couples. Before a couple is accepted into a program, most clinics require a full workup from a fertility specialist. The medical records are then turned over to the in vitro clinic. Most clinics prefer to work through a referring physician, primarily because it ensures good follow-up care after leaving the clinic.

The basic steps of the in vitro procedure are these: Remove as many matured eggs as possible from a woman, mix them with sperm until they are fertilized, and then reimplant 1 to 3 eggs into the woman's uterus. Success depends on precision timing. Since the failure rate is so high, most specialists prefer to try to implant at least 3 eggs in the hopes that 1 will survive. Many sets of twins have been born through in vitro fertilization, and there have been a few sets of triplets.

In vitro fertilization requires that both partners go to the clinic, although the woman's stay is usually longer. She will be given fertility drugs and then monitored by ultrasound scans and blood tests to measure the rise of estrogen and LH in the blood. These tests help the fertility specialist gauge the growth of the eggs and determine the precise moment at which they are ready to be released from an ovary. The eggs need to be nearly mature, but not so mature that they leave the ovary spontaneously. Often HCG (human chorionic gonadotropin) is given to boost the eggs of the ovary at a precise time. Just before the eggs burst out of their follicles, usually on day 13 of the cycle, the woman is taken to the operating room and the eggs are suctioned off the ovary via laparoscopy. Occasionally, the eggs have failed to mature and the woman must try again in a subsequent cycle. If all goes well, the eggs will be harvested and bathed in a special culture medium and allowed to mature fully while the sperm are prepared. The sperm are collected by masturbation and then, after 5 or 6 hours, mixed with the eggs. This maturing process—which normally takes place in the woman's Fallopian tubes—strips away the outer covering of the sperm and bares the head for egg penetration. Each egg is then combined with a quantity of sperm in a glass dish and placed in an incubator. Fertilization usually takes place within 12 hours. The fused cell begins to divide, a sign that the embryo is developing normally.

Up to this point, the in vitro procedure is successful 75 to 90 percent of the time. The most difficult part of the process begins when the fertilized ovum is transferred to the uterus. When the fertilized ova have grown to 4 to 12 cells, they are drawn up into a catheter, along with a little neutral culture medium; the physician gently pushes the tip of the catheter through the woman's cervix and ejects the fluid column.

Following the transfer, a few days of bed rest are required to give the embryos time to implant. Many doctors order hormone testing over the following week to ensure that enough progesterone is reaching the uterus to support a pregnancy. Overall, a fertilized egg implants only about 20 percent of the time in any cycle. Of those that do implant, 1 of 3 spontaneously abort within the first 12 weeks, and another 10 to 15 percent abort later.

Although many clinics try to implant up to 3 eggs, researchers are still trying to decide exactly how many transfers improve the chances of pregnancy without drastically increasing the chances of multiple births, which can place both mother and fetuses at risk. The medical issue is complicated by the moral implications. Since guidelines concerning the legal status of "extra embryos" have not been established, American clinics transfer all embryos—as many as 4 or 5 at a time. This issue may be resolved by the recent advances in embryo freezing, which means that fertilized eggs would not have to be transferred at one time.

In vitro programs can be very costly. Most insurance policies do not cover the procedure, which can cost $5,000 to $7,000 for each cycle, including hospital fees. To these medical fees must be added hidden costs—time off from work, travel, and hotel accommodations for 2 weeks or longer in each cycle. The critical question is, how many cycles are needed to achieve pregnancy? And at what point should a couple stop trying? If the pregnancy takes and aborts several months later, the couple must decide whether they want to try again. Many clinics limit the number of attempts to 3 cycles; others will perform as many cycles as necessary to achieve pregnancy. Most couples try for 2 or 3 cycles before giving up. Most experts recommend that no more than 3 or 4 attempts be made, although there are instances in which success has been achieved on the sixth or seventh try. In the future, the lengthy and complex in vitro process may be considerably streamlined, leading to a much shorter and less expensive process.

Gamete Intra-Fallopian Tube Transfer

Commonly referred to as GIFT, this technique is the newest concept in fertility enhancement. With GIFT, although ova are surgically removed from the woman's ovary, eggs and sperm are placed directly into the Fallopian tube and fertilization takes place in its natural environment.

GIFT depends on one crucial factor: A woman must have at least 1 open Fallopian tube with healthy cilia and at least 1 healthy ovary, but the tube and ovary do not have to be on the same side.

GIFT can be used when the male partner has a low sperm count or sperm motility problems, or where antibodies have reduced the number of sperm to subfertile levels and artificial insemination has failed; it may also be used when no identifiable cause of infertility has been found.

GIFT is still so new that few procedures have been performed throughout the world. But based on past experience and taking into account that union of egg and sperm in the body's natural fertilization site reduces some of the obstacles to pregnancy, the live birth success rate for GIFT is projected to be about 30 percent.

The first part of the GIFT treatment cycle is similar to in vitro fertilization: the growth and retrieval of a mature egg(s). As with in vitro fertilization, even if a woman's ovaries are functioning normally, infertility specialists help the process along by using fertility drugs to make the ovaries produce several mature ova in a single month. The growth of the eggs is monitored by blood tests and ultrasound.

Just before the eggs erupt from the ovary, usually on day 13, the woman is taken to the operating room and the ripening follicles are aspirated via laparoscopy. The eggs are quickly passed to the laboratory, where they are combined with washed sperm in a strawlike catheter attached to a syringe. While the woman remains on the operating table, the surgeon gently inserts the catheter into the delicate folds of the tubal opening, and pushes the eggs and sperm into the Fallopian tube.

If all goes well, the actual union of sperm and egg should take place within a few hours. A woman can expect to go home about 36 hours after GIFT. Within 2 to 3 days the newly fused cell cluster moves from the narrow tunnel of the Fallopian tube into the relatively large uterus, where it implants into the endometrial lining. This implantation is the critical point of all fertility enhancement techniques and the point where GIFT is expected to show significant improvement over other techniques.

Tests for pregnancy can usually begin 10 days later. Ultrasound should be performed in about 4 weeks to determine that the pregnancy is actually in the uterus and not trapped in the Fallopian tubes. Because many GIFT patients will have had damaged Fallopian tubes, they are expected to have a higher incidence of ectopic pregnancy. If a tubal pregnancy is detected, it will require surgery to remove the misplaced fetus and surrounding membranes (conceptus). There is no way to save an ectopic pregnancy. Thus far, the chances of delivering a baby are about 30 percent. Like in vitro fertilization, GIFT costs between $5,000 and $7,000 per cycle.

OTHER EXPERIMENTAL TECHNOLOGIES

Surrogate Parenting

Surrogate parenting, although physiologically simple, is the most controversial of all fertility enhancement methods. In this case, the husband is fertile, but the wife is not. Another woman volunteers to become pregnant with the husband's sperm via artificial insemination and carry the baby to term. When the baby is born, the surrogate mother allows the couple to adopt the child. Although the husband is the biological father of the child, in some states he is legally classified as a sperm donor, meaning that he has no legal right to or responsibility for the child. To guarantee a husband's rights, then, both husband and wife usually formally adopt the child of a surrogate mother.

Like all fertility enhancement methods, surrogate parenting requires careful consideration of the deepest feelings of all 3 participants. There are many social and religious pressures on both the couple and the surrogate. The surrogate, after going through the additional stress of carrying a child for 9 months, may be faced with sadness and guilt when the time comes to give the child up for adoption.

A survey of 173 surrogates has shown that they are motivated primarily by a desire to help an infertile couple, and also because they enjoy the experience of pregnancy without the responsibility of caring for the child. Money, a motivation they all shared, was seldom the dominant factor. Most surrogates request only a modest amount of money ($5,000 is average), but third-party fees, usually to lawyers, are often much higher.

At present there is no state or federal legislation governing surrogate parenting. The few states that have any laws on the subject mainly prohibit payment for such an act, not necessarily the act itself. The couple and the surrogate sign a contract, a standard part of the surrogate procedure, spelling out the costs, risks, and responsibilities of each person. Even though these contracts are devised with the help of a lawyer, they are not necessarily legally valid. The major risk, from the viewpoint of the couple, is that the surrogate mother will decide to keep the baby after giving birth. Several cases have reached the courts, but there is not enough legal precedent to determine which party is likely to win.

Embryo Transfer

Embryo transfer may be the solution for couples who are infertile because the woman's ovaries cannot produce healthy eggs, but she has a functioning uterus. In this case, another woman volunteers to be inseminated with the husband's sperm. If she conceives, the doctor flushes the embryo from her uterus 5 to 6 days later and implants it into the uterus of the wife. Because embryo transfer requires no surgery to retrieve the ova, it is physically easier on the recipient mother. Fertilization occurs in the natural fertilization site, the Fallopian tubes. The key to the transfer process is the precise matching of menstrual cycles of the 2 women.

There are some serious risks to the donor: The embryo may not be washed out with the fluid, leaving the donor pregnant; or the embryo may be flushed back into the tube, leaving the donor with an ectopic pregnancy.

The embryo transfer technique has been successful in animal breeding for many years. But so few embryo transfers have been attempted in humans, it is difficult to predict the potential success rate.

THE FUTURE

CURRENT TECHNOLOGY suggests numerous parenting combinations for the future: Donor eggs can be fertilized in vitro and the embryos frozen and stored in an "embryo bank." Embryos could be transferred to the uterus of any infertile woman at the appropriate time.

The same principles of embryo transfer could be used in reverse: A woman who has a defective uterus or a medical condition such as severe hypertension that prohibits carrying a child could have her own egg fertilized with her husband's sperm in vitro and then implanted in another woman, who becomes the surrogate.

Although these medical advances are promising, the future of fertility enhancement is closely tied to the viewpoints of religious leaders, physicians, lawyers, and politicians. Women's groups are also becoming more outspoken in questioning the validity of the high costs charged to infertile couples for these advances and the pressure put on women to do everything possible to bear a child. In the future, fertility enhancement may be limited not by medical technology but by decisions made by society at large through court decisions.

6   What Is Safe?

Jack Maidman, M.D.

INTRODUCTION

OF ALL BODY ORGANS, the reproductive systems of both women and men are especially vulnerable to toxins. Reproductive hazards are among the most important issues in health care today; unfortunately, there are still many unanswered questions and even governmental guidelines are often ignored or unenforced.

A reproductive hazard is any environmental agent that endangers the male or female reproductive system, the sperm or ova, or the developing fetus. Among these agents are cigarette smoke, alcohol, drugs ("social," prescription, and over-the-counter), pollutants of air and water, and a growing list of chemicals and other substances encountered in the workplace. Infertility in either sex, spontaneous abortion, a baby born with birth defects, or a stillborn child may all be results of exposure to such hazards at home, in the community, or at work.

Reproductive hazards may threaten directly or indirectly. In men, for example, a chemical may directly kill the spermatogonia, the sperm-generating cells that line the testicles, causing infertility. Or toxins may invade the nuclei of these cells and damage the deoxyribonucleic acid (DNA) located there. The damaged cells may produce genetically damaged sperm. Should such damaged sperm succeed in fertilizing an ovum, birth defects could occur.

The agents that produce structural defects in the fetus fall into 2 broad categories: mutagens and teratogens. Mutagens affect DNA in the egg or sperm, creating permanent mutations and leading to spontaneous abortion. Teratogens are toxins that can cross the placenta and damage a developing fetus, causing birth defects or even death in utero. (The best-documented examples are ionizing radiation, alcohol, excessive vitamin A, thalidomide, and certain viruses, such as rubella.)

Teratogens do most of their damage in the first 3 months of pregnancy, when cells are dividing rapidly and the limbs and internal organs of the fetus are being formed. The earliest days of pregnancy, even before a woman knows that she is pregnant, are among the most crucial. By 12 weeks after conception, the fetus's internal organs, arms, and legs are fully formed, although, of course, much further growth will occur before birth. Once formed, they are no longer subject to the influence of teratogens, and thus the risk that gross structural abnormalities will develop in the remaining months of pregnancy is very small. However, a bombardment of toxins in the second and third trimesters may severely inhibit growth, especially growth of the brain, for which the fifth and succeeding months are all-important. When born, a baby subjected to such a bombardment will have a low birth weight, with all the associated behavioral or developmental problems that may not show up until years later. Or, if the toxin is strong enough, the pregnancy will end in spontaneous abortion or a stillbirth.

SMOKING

SMOKING NEGATIVELY affects the whole spectrum of reproduction: fertility, conception, the development of the fetus in the uterus, labor and delivery, and the child's maturation. It is the most common environmental hazard in pregnancy.

The principal effect of smoking during pregnancy is that the fetus does not grow adequately and is considerably smaller at birth than a baby born to a nonsmoker. In the worst cases, low-birth-weight babies may have difficulty breathing, poor temperature control, low resistance to infection, and a reluctance to feed. (One study has shown that, in the United States, intensive care for babies born too small because their mothers smoked during pregnancy costs $152 million a year in medical expenses.)

Smoking during pregnancy has also been directly related to an increased rate of spontaneous abortion—women who smoke have a 25 percent greater chance of miscarriage than do nonsmokers—premature birth, and stillbirth. There is a higher incidence of sudden infant death syndrome (SIDS or "crib death") among babies born to women who smoke, but smoking has not been directly linked to birth defects.

The effects of smoking during pregnancy appear to be long lasting. One study has shown that low-birth-weight babies born to women who smoke do not seem to catch up later in life. Even at the age of 11, children of mothers who smoked during pregnancy were, on the average, shorter and scored lower on tests of intellectual functioning than those whose mothers did not smoke. The differences were small, but distinctly measurable.

Another study, this one on animals, demonstrated a deleterious effect of smoking on the development of the lungs and liver. What the long-term effect of

poorly developed lungs will be as an infant grows to maturity is unknown.

Cigarette smoking during pregnancy interferes with the supply of blood, and consequently of nutrients, to the fetus. It does so via several pathways. Carbon monoxide reduces the amount of oxygen available to the fetus by tying up the oxygen carrying hemoglobin. Nicotine constricts the placental blood vessels, diminishing the life-supporting blood flow. And cyanide, a third element in cigarette smoke, a toxic agent in itself, deprives the fetus of nutrients and oxygen. This loss of oxygen and vital nutrients is believed responsible for retarding fetal growth. Oxygen deprivation also has more immediate results. When a pregnant woman smokes 2 cigarettes in succession, the fetal heart beats faster and the fetus demonstrates abnormal breathing-like motions—both signs of fetal distress.

Heavy passive smoking—that is, the smoke a pregnant woman breathes in from others—also affects the fetus. And after being born a baby continues to suffer from the smoking of those around it. A nursing baby may receive nicotine in breast milk or by inhaling smoke. Secondhand smoke makes a child vulnerable to a host of ailments, including ear, nose, and throat infections; bronchitis; pneumonia; asthmatic attacks; and decreased lung efficiency.

Because breaking habits takes time, the time to stop smoking is in advance of pregnancy. To protect their child, both parents should stop smoking. Whenever possible, pregnant women should also avoid staying too long in a smoky environment.

ALCOHOL

ALCOHOL is the second most common environmental hazard for the fetus. A woman who drinks heavily during pregnancy—5 to 6 drinks a day—runs a significant risk of giving birth to a baby with fetal alcohol syndrome (FAS), a cluster of irreversible physical and mental defects caused by alcohol damage to the developing fetus. (See table 6.1.)

It is not known exactly how the extent of fetal damage relates to the quantity of alcohol consumed. However, the infants of mothers who drink heavily, especially early in pregnancy, are likely to suffer the most severe abnormalities. From 5 to 10 percent of the babies of heavy drinkers are born with full-blown FAS. Many more babies, including many of those born to moderate consumers of alcohol, may have more subtle defects. These include small size, reduced intelligence, learning disabilities, hyperactivity, eye and speech problems, and sometimes organ abnormalities.

Studies have shown that a woman who consumes about 10 drinks a week, which is classified as moderate drinking, doubles her risk of having a low-birth-weight baby. "Softer" data suggests that growth retardation can occur when a pregnant woman has as few as 2 drinks a week. One study (at Emory University in Atlanta, Georgia) showed that babies born to women who drank this small amount throughout pregnancy appeared more agitated and stressed and less responsive to people and the environment. The behavioral problems persisted until at least 1 year of age, the length of the study. In addition, some studies have shown that mothers who had as few as 2 drinks a week during pregnancy were more likely to experience miscarriage and stillbirth. However, it is difficult to establish a cause and effect relationship with such a low level of consumption. There are other elements in an individual woman's lifestyle—nutrition, stress, occupation, as well as a variety of medical problems—that might contribute to the problem.

In the developing fetus, alcohol is a cellular toxin. It readily crosses the placenta and reaches the fetal blood and body cells in the same concentration as in

Table 6.1

ABNORMALITIES LINKED TO FETAL ALCOHOL SYNDROME

- Growth retardation (both before and after birth)
- Facial abnormalities (e.g., widely spaced eyes, flat bridge of the nose, flat cheeks, narrow upper lip lacking the vertical groove, a blunt small chin)
- Brain damage and mental retardation
- Abnormally small head and brain
- Poor muscle coordination
- Abnormal development of various body organs (e.g., heart defects, underdeveloped genitals in girls, urinary tract, kidney defects)
- Hyperactivity and learning disabilities

the mother's bloodstream. It depresses the fetus's central nervous system and must be metabolized by the fetus's liver. But the fetal liver, not yet fully developed, metabolizes alcohol inefficiently, and alcohol remains in the fetus's bloodstream after it has been eliminated from the mother's. In pregnant women, binge drinking is especially dangerous—alcohol is passed in a massive dose to the fetus, which cannot process the overload. Even a single episode of heavy drinking can cause severe damage.

Should a woman drink at all during pregnancy? It is known that 5 or 6 drinks a day presents a major risk of serious problems to the fetus. (However, heavy drinkers who stop drinking in the first trimester—and continue to abstain throughout pregnancy—markedly improve their infants' chances of being born healthy.) At 3 or 4 drinks a day, the risk appears to be significantly lower, but still present. The current Food and Drug Administration (FDA) position is that: "Presently, there is no known safe level of alcohol consumption below which no risk is present," and it urges that no alcohol be consumed during pregnancy. The advice of many obstetricians is that a woman should give up drinking altogether, before becoming pregnant. Some studies have suggested that women who drink *before* pregnancy tend to have smaller babies. Other studies with animals have shown that alcohol may damage newly fertilized ova and that the embryo is endangered after even a single episode of heavy drinking at the time of conception. These studies have not been confirmed in pregnant women.

No form of alcohol is safer than any other. Wine and beer are no less damaging than hard liquor. Fortunately, many women dislike the taste of alcohol when they are pregnant. But a woman who feels she needs help to stop drinking should talk to her physician, who may recommend a self-help program such as Alcoholics Anonymous.

CAFFEINE

HIGH DOSES OF CAFFEINE have been linked to numerous abnormalities in newborn rats, mice, and rabbits, but to date there is no solid evidence that the caffeine contained in tea, coffee, chocolate, and soft drinks causes birth defects in humans. Nevertheless, the FDA has issued a warning to pregnant women to stop or modify their consumption of caffeine-containing foods and beverages.

One recent study of 3,135 pregnant women has shown that women who consumed moderate to heavy amounts of caffeine daily (151 mg or more) were significantly more likely to have late first- and second-trimester spontaneous abortions. Those who consumed less than 150 mg daily did not show an increased risk of spontaneous abortion, unless they had miscarried in their last pregnancy. The sources of the caffeine included coffee, tea, cocoa, chocolate, cola beverages, and caffeine-containing drugs (Excedrin, Anacin, Dristan, Fiorinal, Dexatrim, and

Table 6.2
CAFFEINE-CONTAINING SUBSTANCES

Substance	Amount of Caffeine
Coffee	29 to 176 mg/cup
Tea	8 to 107 mg/cup
Cocoa	5 to 10 mg/cup
Milk chocolate	6 mg/ounce
Colas	32 to 65 mg/12 ounces
Cold tablets, pain killers, allergy preparations	50 to 200 mg/U
Appetite suppressants	50 to 200 mg/U
Stimulants	100 to 200 mg/U

Dietac). Table 6.2 lists common sources of caffeine.

Coffee was the major source of caffeine for the moderate to heavy caffeine users, but not for the light caffeine users, which suggests that either a threshold effect or some component in coffee other than caffeine may be associated with spontaneous abortion. Benzo(a)pryrene and chlorogenic acids, for example, found in roast coffee, may increase the risks. All types of coffee contain other substances that may have effects that are separate from that of caffeine.

Additional studies are needed before the association of caffeine with spontaneous abortion or other harmful effects can be more definitively evaluated. In the meantime, most physicians would advise that a pregnant woman stop consuming caffeine or limit herself to 1 cup of coffee or other caffeine-containing drinks a day. Since caffeine is tolerated less well in pregnancy and appears to have a stronger effect on pregnant women, a woman who normally drinks 4 or 5 cups of coffee may find that 1 or 2 cups is all she can tolerate, from the standpoint of "jumpiness," when she is pregnant.

"SOCIAL" AND ADDICTIVE DRUGS

THE USE OF social and addictive drugs —marijuana, cocaine, heroin, among others—continues to be one of our most pressing social problems. Their use during pregnancy has a number of well-documented adverse effects on the developing fetus, and some also interfere with fertility. More recently, intravenous drug use has been associated with an alarming rise in the number of babies born with AIDS or carrying the AIDS virus. It is vitally important for a woman who uses any "social" or addictive drug to seek medical advice before trying to conceive and to stop using the drug(s) before attempting pregnancy.

Marijuana

Although marijuana use is associated with decreased fertility in both men and women, it does not appear to have a negative effect on the course of pregnancy itself in humans. However, pregnant monkeys who received THC (9-tetrahydrocannabinol), the active ingredient in marijuana, in a dose equivalent to that obtained by a person smoking 2 marijuana cigarettes a day, experienced a high percentage (40 percent) of fetal death, stillbirth, and early infant death. Further, examination of the living infants of the THC-treated monkeys revealed abnormalities of the nervous system, heart, and urinary tract.

Experience with women who smoke marijuana during pregnancy is limited. There is no solid evidence that marijuana damages the chromosomes of either egg or sperm. But it is known that THC readily crosses the placenta and is also found in maternal milk. A study in Canada found that women who regularly used marijuana were likely to give birth to an infant with tremors, unusual startle reactions, and abnormal visual and auditory responses. These symptoms did not disappear for several weeks. Their severity appeared to be directly related to the amount of marijuana smoked by the mother. Physicians at the University of California at Los Angeles found that marijuana users experienced a higher incidence of prolonged and difficult labor than nonusers. And investigators at Boston University School of Medicine found that marijuana users were more likely to give birth to low-birth-weight infants and babies with abnormalities similar to those found with FAS.

These studies, although limited in scope, suggest that marijuana smoking should be eliminated throughout the course of pregnancy The best recommendation is to stop smoking at least 1 month before attempting conception.

Heroin and Other Addictive Drugs

Narcotics such as heroin cross the placental barrier: Babies born to drug-addicted mothers are themselves addicted. Approximately 70 percent of all babies born of mothers addicted to heroin show some evidence of a withdrawal reaction within a few hours after birth. The distressing and difficult-to-treat symptoms include irritability, tremors, vomiting, respiratory distress, and diarrhea. Even with the best medical care, some of these babies do not survive.

High concentrations of heroin appear in breast milk, and there are reports that the babies of heroin-addicted mothers show withdrawal symptoms every time breast feeding is delayed and when it is discontinued. (Infants whose mothers are on methadone maintenance receive only minimum amounts of the drug.)

Many complications of pregnancy—ectopic pregnancies, low-birth-weight babies, premature rupture of the membranes, toxemia, premature separation of the placenta—are associated with drug addiction. These devastating problems may not be caused directly by the drug, but by elements in the lifestyle that usually accompany addiction: venereal infections and pelvic inflammatory disease, poor nutrition, and little or no prenatal care.

Cocaine

The babies of women who use cocaine, like those of heroin addicts, will be addicted. These babies may require sedation for several weeks after birth. Their withdrawal symptoms, however, seem less severe than those suffered by babies born to heroin-addicted mothers.

Studies of the effects of cocaine on pregnancy are just beginning. This drug may prove to be the most dangerous of all to the unborn. One study has linked cocaine to severe birth defects, but the major identified risk with cocaine use is that the drug may kill the fetus in utero. There is evidence that a single massive dose of cocaine can cause the placenta to separate, bringing sudden death to the fetus.

PRESCRIPTION DRUGS

VIRTUALLY ALL PRESCRIPTION and over-the-counter drugs cross the placenta and reach the fetus. Drugs taken near the time of conception can be especially hazardous, since a baby's vital organs are forming in the first few weeks of life. Unfortunately, most of the drugs on the market today—up to 85 percent in all—have never been tested for safe use during pregnancy. Therefore, a pregnant woman should take no medication—not even an over-the-counter laxative or cold remedy—that has not been prescribed or approved by her doctor. Medications prescribed by a woman's dentist, or by a doctor other than the one attending the pregnancy, should not be taken without approval. (Exceptions are listed in table 6.3.)

Three factors determine whether a drug will harm the fetus: the type of drug, the amount taken, and the stage of pregnancy. The fetus is most susceptible to drug effects during the first trimester of pregnancy. Since most drugs have not been specifically studied to determine safety during pregnancy, not much is known about whether they will cause birth defects. The tragic consequences of thalidomide in the early 1960s serve as a reminder to avoid the use of nonessential drugs during pregnancy. Worldwide, hundreds of women who took this mild sedative during pregnancy gave birth to babies with missing or malformed limbs. More recently, studies have found that the use of Accutane, a drug used to treat severe acne, results in a 25-fold increase in having a baby with a major malformation.

In animal studies, tranquilizers such as Valium, Librium, and Miltown have been shown to cause the development of a cleft lip or cleft palate. The problem with animal studies such as these is that the rapid growth rate of the rats and mice used in the tests makes them more susceptible than humans to drugs (for example, sedatives) that inhibit food intake. It is possible that birth defects in these instances may be due not to the drug itself but to lack of proper nutrition. However, at this point we frequently rely on the results of animal studies, since a real gap exists in human observations. Most drugs are not tested on humans for safety dur-

Table 6.3
NONPRESCRIPTION DRUGS CONSIDERED SAFE DURING PREGNANCY

- *Acetaminophen* (Tylenol, Anacin 3, and others) may be taken as directed for the relief of cold or flu symptoms, headaches, muscle strain, or a fever. If these symptoms persist for more than a day, however, a pregnant woman should call her doctor. A high fever (over 101°F) should be treated by a doctor and should be brought down as quickly as possible. Self-medication with aspirin should be avoided, because aspirin interferes with the blood-clotting mechanism and its use can result in bleeding in both mother and fetus. Moreover, aspirin inhibits prostaglandins, a group of hormonelike substances important in the development and maintenance of fetal circulation.

- *Gelusil or Mylanta* may be taken for the relief of heartburn if other measures are not effective.

- *Preparation H* may be used for relief from hemorrhoids.

The use of these medications should be discussed with the doctor during the regular prenatal visits.

---

ing pregnancy because such testing would subject unborn children to unacceptable risks.

The greatest drawback to animal studies is that a drug that is apparently harmless for animals may cause birth defects in humans and vice versa. Again, thalidomide is the prime example: Tests on several animal species had given no hint of the drug's potential danger to an unborn baby.

Anticonvulsant drugs that contain phenytoin have also been associated with a variety of birth defects, such as cleft lip or cleft palate, as well as facial growth and other physical and mental disturbances. However, most women who suffer from seizure disorders (epilepsy) must continue to take anticonvulsants during pregnancy, because a seizure is more dangerous to the fetus than these medications. A careful appraisal of anticonvulsant drugs prior to attempting conception can significantly reduce the risk of birth defects in these individuals. An obstetrician will put the woman on the lowest possible dose of the safest drug, thus providing maximum safety for both the mother and fetus.

Certain antibiotics, particularly tetracyclines and chloramphenicol, should not be used during pregnancy because of their effects on developing teeth. Others, however—including penicillin, ampicillin, and cephalexin—appear to be safe. The indications for use and stage of pregnancy are important determinants in the use of antibiotics in pregnancy.

Anticancer drugs (for example, fluorouracil) are known to cause a high incidence of malformations in infants. These agents inhibit the growth of tumors by disrupting cell growth and killing actively growing cells. Embryos and fetuses, which have many growing cells, are particularly vulnerable to the toxic effects of these drugs.

Amphetamines may have the potential to cause birth defects. It also appears that babies born to women who have taken sedatives containing barbiturates during pregnancy may experience symptoms of drug withdrawal.

Synthetic hormones, such as estrogens and progestins, may increase the risk of birth defects when taken during the first 3 or 4 months of pregnancy. The low levels in most birth control pills, however, do not appear to pose a threat. Even so, most obstetricians advise their patients to wait up to 3 months after going off birth control pills before attempting a pregnancy just to make sure that hormonal levels have returned to normal. In addition, a period of post-pill menstrual disturbances may prevent accurate estimation of the date of conception in a pregnancy in the first few months after pill discontinuation.

Before she becomes pregnant, a woman with any chronic condition for which she regularly takes drugs should consult her physician. In some cases, a safer form of medication or altered regimen may be recommended.

OVER-THE-COUNTER DRUGS

EVERY DRUG SOLD over the counter is labeled with the following warning from the FDA: "As with any drug, if you are pregnant or nursing a baby, seek the advice of a health professional before using this product." The warning is protective; it does not mean that the given drug has been proved dangerous to pregnant women or to their babies.

Many nonprescription drugs are not considered "medications" by most people, even though they may have the same potential for adverse reactions as a prescription drug. Megadose vitamins and minerals are prime examples. It is known that very large doses of vitamin A can cause birth defects, yet many women persist in taking megadoses of A, even during pregnancy, because they think it will help clear up acne and other skin problems that may occur at this time. Vitamin A is closely related to Accutane, the prescription acne medication that has been closely linked with an increased risk of birth defects.

The bottom line is that no drug can be considered absolutely safe for a pregnant woman. Not only must the specific drug and the stage of pregnancy be taken into account, but also the woman's particular susceptibility, which is determined by such factors as her genetic makeup and her environment (diet, smoking, drinking, and pollution).

In general, drugs should be considered dangerous unless proved otherwise. Researchers cannot trace the exact cause-effect relationship of most drugs to birth defects, nor are they certain what proportion of birth defects are actually caused by these agents. Complicating the investigation is the fact that women often do not realize they are pregnant during the first few weeks after conception, and so they may fail to keep track of the drugs they take at that time. Further, some defects, such as heart and kidney problems or mental retardation, may not become apparent for months or years after the child is born and a woman may not remember what drugs, if any, she took during pregnancy.

Before even trying to become pregnant, it is advisable to stop using all over-the-counter drugs, including medicated creams and sprays, aspirin products, cough mixtures, and cold and allergy drugs.

VACCINES

LIVE-VIRUS VACCINES, such as rubella vaccine, cannot be given to pregnant women. Certain killed-virus vaccinations, however, are safe later in pregnancy. Vaccinations should be considered and discussed before a woman becomes pregnant, so that she can be adequately protected against potentially harmful infectious diseases. If a woman is already pregnant and there is an epidemic of infectious disease against which she is not protected, she should discuss the pros and cons of vaccines with her physician.

STRESS

STRESSFUL EVENTS accumulate in modern life, with subtle and compounded effects. Stress, for example, may be a factor in some of the complications of pregnancy. A woman under prolonged stress might drink more, use drugs, smoke more heavily, or fail to eat properly, all of which could lead to problems during pregnancy.

It is important for a pregnant woman to find methods to reduce tension that are less potentially hazardous than, for example, taking drugs. It may help to write down the causes of stress or to confide in a friend or counselor. Perhaps a course in yoga or an exercise class should be considered. Gentle and rhythmic exercise, such as swimming, cycling, or walking, is often a good way to reduce everyday tension.

Occupational stress includes such factors as excessive noise, heat, or cold; vibrations; eyestrain; heavy lifting; repetitive hand motions; poor seating conditions; constant deadlines; and overtime. Strained relations with employers or co-workers, sexual harrassment, and concerns about safety, salary, and future employment may all contribute to stress overload. If a woman is pregnant or contemplating pregnancy, it is important that she try to correct to reduce such job-related stress.

RADIATION

HIGH LEVELS of ionizing radiation can cause spontaneous abortion and genetic damage in the fetus. Unless it is absolutely necessary, diagnostic X rays should be avoided during pregnancy, especially during the first trimester. Exposure to high doses of radiation during the second and third trimesters, though less likely to cause malformations, may lead to permanent growth retardation. Fortunately, the risk of producing fetal abnormalities is slight when modern diagnostic X-ray procedures are used conservatively during pregnancy.

HEAT

RECENT EVIDENCE shows that an embryo may be endangered when a newly pregnant woman spends time in a hot tub or sauna. Forty-five minutes or more of exposure to temperatures over 102°F in the very early days of pregnancy (21 to 24 days) has been linked to neural tube defects. Additional reports now indicate that exposure to heat later in the first trimester results in reduction of blood flow to the fetus and may cause brain damage. Ordinary bathing does not pose a risk, but saunas and hot tubs should definitely be avoided during pregnancy.

TOXINS IN THE WORKPLACE

CIGARETTES, DRUGS, AND ALCOHOL are the most common and most dangerous toxins for a developing fetus. These reproductive hazards lie within our control, but other potentially destructive elements are more difficult to counteract. From the moment of their conception, young human beings may now be exposed to chemicals unheard of even 20 years ago.

Pollutants are present in air, food, and water, and there is nothing we can do to avoid them. In recent studies, the most commonly used weedkiller in the nation, herbicide 2,4-D, has been linked to cancer. Even organically grown produce may contain traces of insecticides, pesticides, or other chemicals picked up from water and soil that has run off from neighboring land. Although no solid evidence has yet coupled these common environmental pollutants with problems associated with pregnancy and birth, the connection is considered a possible one.

The most concentrated, and therefore potentially the most dangerous, hazards are found in the workplace. It is estimated that in the United States today over 60,000 chemical substances are in common commercial use, with more than 3,000 new chemicals introduced each year. The long-range effects of exposure to most of these substances are unknown.

Humans may absorb toxic substances through the skin, through the digestive system, and through the lungs. The results may be sudden and severe—blistering of the skin or lungs, vomiting, dizziness—or they may take years to develop and manifest themselves. Lung disease, liver disease, and most cancers may take 15 to 40 years to develop.

It is rare that such effects can be traced to one specific toxin. While scientists generally test substances for toxicity 1 at a time in a laboratory, in real life our bodies usually have to deal with several toxins at once. In combination, 2 or more hazards can produce an effect greater than 1 by itself. Asbestos is the classic example. Asbestos workers run a high risk of cancer, but those who also smoke have the highest risk factor of all.

In the past, research on industrial hazards has centered around increased incidence of cancer, but today there is a growing awareness of potential dangers to reproduction. Unfortunately, when reproductive hazards are recognized in the workplace, they are usually defined as a "woman's problem." In some cases, the threat posed by such toxins has been used to discriminate against women. Some companies have taken advantage of the issue of reproductive health to institute "protective" discrimination policies that include demotion, transfer, and exclusion of women of childbearing age from jobs that might compromise their ability to bear children. Faced with job loss or demotion to lower-paying positions, some women have opted to have themselves sterilized. Thus, the rights women have established through civil rights legislation and court actions may be undermined in the name of fetal health or the protection of female reproductive capability.

But, in fact, any job—or any chemical—that threatens a woman's reproductive potential also threatens a man's. When both partners work, they have twice the chance of exposure to occupational hazards. Banning female workers is an inexpensive solution to the problem, but it does nothing to protect the offspring of male workers and their wives. These fetuses are also at risk from mutagenic substances. Making improvements in the workplace wherever women are employed, rather than restricting women from certain jobs, is a partial solution. If the reproductive hazards of the jobs in question were reduced, men would also benefit, although not necessarily to the same extent.

A more satisfactory alternative would be to protect the health and reproductive potential of all employees, although the high cost of cleaning up reproductive hazards is likely to be resisted by many industries.

TOXINS, STRESS, AND THE MALE REPRODUCTIVE SYSTEM

SEPARATE SYSTEMS control sperm production and sex drive in men. The sperm-generating cells that line the testicles are more sensitive and more likely to become damaged; the cells that make testosterone—the male hormone that governs sex drive—can sustain almost any abuse. Therefore, a man may have poor sperm production and still have perfectly normal sex drive.

The most widely publicized risky jobs for men are those involving radiation. Radiation appears to do its worst damage on the sperm-generating cells. Some of these spermatogonia may survive and continue to produce sperm, but the sperm may also suffer from the radiation. Spermatogonia damaged by radiation seem to have some ability to regenerate in time and to begin producing sperm again. However, even if the spermatogonia revive, their DNA code may be altered. Since the other cells of the testicles usually escape damage, the sex drive is unaffected.

The primary effect of many toxins on the male reproductive system is to lower sperm production. Heavy drinking, for example, appears to depress sperm production in several ways. If the liver is damaged by alcohol it cannot get rid of used hormones, which causes small amounts of female hormone to build up, depressing both sperm production and potency. Alcohol also causes an inappropriate release of the hormone prolactin, which has deleterious effects on sperm production and can also cause male breast development.

Other drugs also may affect sperm production. Substances in marijuana, for example, are known to remain for weeks or even months in body tissues, including the testicles. Marijuana also may cause an inappropriate release of prolactin. Antihypertensives, antidepressives, and hallucinatory drugs can disrupt the brain's hormonal signals to the sperm-generating center of the testicles. Narcotics such as morphine and opium derivatives are known to release prolactin.

As sperm cells grow and mature, they become increasingly sensitive to toxic agents from the environment. A man suffering from environmental toxins or stress may continue to produce sperm, but the sperm may be sluggish or deformed. Sometimes only some of the sperm-producing cells are affected while others remain relatively free from toxic damage.

Extreme stress, anxiety, and tension have a deleterious effect on sperm production. Emotional stress alters the functioning of the lower brain (hypothalamus), which in turn affects the output of various hormones. In animal studies, overstressed male rats showed diminished fertility, and young mice crowded in cages showed delayed puberty. Even though these effects are well documented, most researchers believe that only severe and prolonged stress, not the ordinary wear and tear of daily life, affects human fertility.

Heat is thought to interfere with

sperm production, but it is a question of how much and for how long. Tight briefs that hold the testicles close to the body are unlikely to be a cause of a low sperm count, but this may be a problem for truck drivers who sit for long hours in a hot cab. And welders working inside boilers or storage tanks where the surrounding heat is intense often show a severely depressed sperm count, as do men who regularly have a sauna or a long soak in a hot tub. However, most experts in male infertility believe that heat exposure would have to be continuous over a long period of time to affect sperm production in any important way.

So far, little is known about the extent to which environmental hazards affect a man's offspring. New evidence shows that men who work in hazardous jobs may transfer toxins to their pregnant wives, bringing increased risk of spontaneous abortion. In one recent study, wives of employees in the waste-water treatment plant of an oil refinery reported a rate of spontaneous abortion twice as great as they had before their husbands began working at the plant. How this transfer of toxins from male to female takes place is unclear. Toxins may accumulate in semen and be transferred to a pregnant woman during sexual intercourse, or possibly the male partner carries toxins into the home environment on his shoes, clothing, or skin.

Wives of men who work in operating rooms or with vinyl chloride appear to face an increased risk of miscarriage. There is also some evidence that exposure to chemical solvents by either parent can result in brain tumors in the children, even though the parents exhibit no obvious negative effects.

WORKPLACE TOXINS

Ionizing Radiation

Most workers exposed to ionizing radiation wear film badges that are monitored every 3 months to assess the accumulated dose. Any exposed worker planning a pregnancy should request that her badge be read every month. The recommended dose limit for the 9-month period of pregnancy is 1.5 rem (rad); because of protection provided by the abdominal wall this translates to 0.5 rem or less for the fetus. The dose from any diagnostic X rays should be added to the occupational dose to measure the total exposure to radiation.

Men and women who work in nuclear power plants are exposed to significantly higher levels of radioactivity than the general public. The testes of young men are especially vulnerable to radiation, and sperm damage may occur at levels common in nuclear power plants. Dentists, X-ray technicians, and many kinds of scientific and medical research workers are exposed to high-voltage X-ray machines on a daily basis. Hospital personnel are closely monitored for radiation exposure, but dentists and dental technicians in private offices must monitor themselves.

Most people, however, including those who work in a hospital environment, are not exposed to high enough levels of radioactivity to cause problems. In animal studies, colonies of mice have survived for several generations at 2 rem a day with no increase in birth defects.

Nonionizing Radiation

Nonionizing or radio frequency (RF) radiation is a type of radiation that can raise the body temperature, an effect that may prove dangerous for pregnant workers. Teratogenic effects induced by exposure to nonionizing radiation are probably caused by direct heat damage to the embryo. Animal studies show that fetal malformations are related to both the intensity of the heat and the length of exposure. A level that is harmless after 1 hour may cause serious defects after 2 hours. If the temperature is high enough, however, a brief exposure will cause malformations in animals. Significant malformations occurred in rats when body temperature were elevated up to 3°C above their normal body temperature. It is not known, however, whether this can be extrapolated to humans.

Nonionizing radiation is used in many different industries. Commercial radio and television broadcast stations, citizens band and ham radios, radar, high-voltage power lines, medical diathermy equipment, and a variety of industrial and scientific radio frequency and microwave devices now contribute to human exposure to nonionizing radiation. Although the Occupational Safety and Health Administration (OSHA) recommends limits of exposure, this standard is not mandated by law, and many workers are exposed to significantly higher amounts than the OSHA standard.

In high-tech industries, nonionizing radiation is used to etch and clean silicon wafers. Workers may also be exposed to high-intensity radio frequency radiation while operating heat sealers used to manufacture a variety of products, including book covers, checkbook covers, cosmetic accessories, display boxes, gas masks, handbags, luggage, notebooks, toys, travel cases, and water beds.

One recent study shows that many heat sealer operators are exposed to nonionizing radiation levels that exceed the OSHA standard, but exposure levels varied depending upon the type of heat sealer used. Several manufacturers of this equipment have developed shields and automatic feeding devices to diminish the level of exposure.

Exposure to high-intensity radiation also occurs near active television broadcast antennas. Women working in the upper floors of office buildings that are in close proximity to radio and television transmitters may also be at risk, although this has not been proved.

Radio frequency heating is potentially much more dangerous than conventional heating. Conventional heat sources raise the surface temperature of the body, allowing the body's temperature control system to adjust its internal temperature. Radio frequency radiation, however, penetrates much deeper into body tissues, heating internal organs without a corresponding increase in skin temperature.

Therefore, heat receptors in the skin may fail to activate the body's normal cooling mechanism.

Microwave ovens, color television sets, "electronic" garage door openers, and electric toys all operate on nonionizing radiation, but at such low levels that it is highly unlikely that they would emit enough radiation to damage an embryo or fetus. The FDA regulates the levels of nonionizing radiation emitted from these consumer products.

Chemicals

Certain toxic chemicals do their damage to the reproductive system at concentrations disturbingly close to those allowed in the workplace. And in many instances we do not yet have enough information to determine exactly what is a safe level. While it is impossible to list all the chemicals that might present a reproductive hazard, a few of the most common are described below.

Halogenated Hydrocarbons. These are agricultural and industrial chemicals that include PCBs and PBBs (polychlorinated and polybrominated biphenyls) and vinyl chloride. They are toxic to the liver and kidneys and can cause mutations and congenital defects.

In particular, PCBs are associated with liver cancer, reproductive failure, skin eruptions, nausea, dizziness, eye and nasal irritation, and asthmatic bronchitis. They are readily transferred to breast milk, and nursing infants may appear lethargic and lacking in muscle tone.

Officially banned by the Environmental Protection Agency (EPA) in 1979, PCBs had been used as plasticizers, heat exchange fluids, and insulation material in transformers and other electrical devices. Lubricants, pesticides, cutting oils, adhesives, wax extenders, inks, sealants, caulking compounds, and paper coatings also used PCBs. Although banned from the marketplace, regulations do not prohibit the use of existing supplies, and many products containing PCBs continue to be used and sold.

In addition, industrial and electrical plants have discharged PCBs into nearby sewers and streams, thus introducing the contaminant into the wider environment, where it is absorbed into the food chain. Today, diet is the main source of PCB exposure for most people, and the main dietary source of PCBs is fish that have spent all or most of their lives in fresh water. Although the FDA has set the maximum level of PCBs in fish shipped in interstate commerce, it is a measure impossible to gauge without examining each individual fish. Further, fish sold within state borders are not subject to the regulation. The fish to avoid are freshwater fish, such as bass, carp, whitefish, trout, pike, and catfish, and bottom-feeding estuarine fish such as catfish, sole, and flounder. Ocean fish such as cod, red snapper, halibut, and haddock are usually free of PCBs. While high doses of PCBs are hazardous to a nursing infant, there is no proof that trace amounts in breast milk are detrimental.

Vinyl Chloride. This is one of the most widely used chemicals in the United States. Almost 5 million workers are exposed to vinyl chloride gas in factories producing plastic plumbing pipes and conduits and manufacturing such diverse products as flooring, garden hoses, and clothing. Until it was banned, vinyl chloride monomer, or VCM, was used as a propellant for hundreds of household and cosmetic products.

Vapors from vinyl chloride are linked to brain, liver, lung, and lymph node cancers. Vinyl chloride has also been linked to an increased risk of birth defects in infants whose mothers were exposed to the gas. In some studies, chromosomal aberrations were found, but the chemical significance of these studies is unclear. An increased fetal mortality was also noted among the offspring of male vinyl chloride workers.

Arsenic. This deadly poison is known to cause birth defects in laboratory animals. A by-product of the smelting of ores for various metals (copper, lead, zinc, silver), arsenic is also used in the manufacture of pigments and glass, as well as insecticides, fungicides, and herbicides. More and more semiconductor plants use arsenic compounds to make a new kind of microchip.

When exposed to arsenic, among other tested toxins, pregnant women show an increased risk of miscarriage. However, human studies remain inconclusive because those who work with arsenic are usually exposed simultaneously to other potential toxins such as lead and sulfur dioxide.

Carbon Disulfide. This is a colorless, volatile liquid that vaporizes at room temperature. Carbon disulfide is used in the production of viscose rayon and cellophane, and in the manufacture of carbon tetrachloride. The chemical is also used in dry cleaning, oil extraction, fumigating grain, vulcanizing rubber, degreasing, and chemical analysis.

Carbon disulfide is toxic when the vapor is inhaled or when there is repeated skin contact. In women, prolonged exposure is associated with menstrual abnormalities, a higher incidence of spontaneous abortion, and premature birth. The chemical is also toxic to the male reproductive system. However, in terms of regular work exposure of pregnant women, to date there is no convincing evidence that carbon disulfide causes birth defects in a fetus.

Heavy Metals and Solvents

Industries and jobs where organic solvents and heavy metals are used are known to have dangerous reproductive hazards. Heavy metals can damage the reproductive system and cause birth defects. Lead, mercury, and cadmium are the heavy metals most dangerous to pregnant women. Lead has been linked to increased risk of miscarriage, stillbirth, and birth defects. Women whose partners are exposed to lead in their jobs may also experience an increased incidence of these problems. Exposure to mercury increases the risk of spontaneous abortion and of neurological and renal defects in the newborn.

Glues and solvents used in a wide variety of occupations are also significant reproductive hazards. Glycol ethers, for example, commonly used as solvents in high-tech industries, are known to impair sperm development, causing severe birth defects in offspring of laboratory animals exposed even to low doses.

HAZARDOUS WORKPLACES

AMONG THE WORKPLACES where female and male employees are believed to be at risk for reproductive hazards are:

Leatherworking Factories. In one new study, pregnant women employed in the manufacture of leather products had almost 3 times the usual risk of giving birth to stillborn infants. The suspected toxic agents were glues and cements.

Graphic and Plastic Arts Studios. Hazards include exposure to solvents, enamels, paints, solder, cadmium, clays, glazes, welding and firing fumes, glycol esters, and poor ventilation. While none of these elements has been proved conclusively to endanger a pregnancy, artists should exercise caution. Their workplace should be well ventilated; even better, whenever possible, artists should try to work out of doors.

Hospitals, Medical Laboratories, and Other Health Care Facilities. Jobs in medicine may mean contact with radioactive materials, anticancer drugs, or anesthetic gas. Some studies have indicated that exposure to anesthetic gases in the operating room significantly increases the risk of spontaneous abortion among pregnant physicians and nurses. However, infor-mation on the degree and length of exposure is sketchy, and more careful analysis suggests that the increased risk may be due to other variables associated with working in an operating room, such as stress or exposure to waste products. Dentists and dental hygienists face exposure to most of the same toxins plus mercury.

Nuclear Power Plants, Atomic Plants, and Uranium Mines. Workers are at risk from radiation, which some sources have linked to a broad range of genetic and health hazards.

Metallurgy Plants. Workers may be exposed to heavy metals—copper, lead, arsenic, and cadmium. Metal grinders, lead smelter workers, and lead storage battery workers are also at risk.

Radio and Television Manufacturing Plants. Workers are at risk from exposure to lead solder fumes. A 1980 medical study of 35,000 female factory workers in Finland found an unusually high rate of miscarriages among electronic workers in general, and solderers in particular.

Chemical Laboratories. Workers may suffer repeated exposure to solvents and other chemicals.

Plastic Factories. Workers are likely to be exposed to PVC and solvents.

Hairdressing Salons. Various chemicals, hair sprays and dyes, aerosol sprays, cosmetics, and other preparations can all have adverse reproductive effects. Lung disease in the newborn may result from deep inhalation of aerosol sprays and other chemicals.

Offices. The safety of video display terminals (VDTs), widely used in many businesses, has been called into question, but to date they have not been found to pose a danger to the fetus. Several major studies are currently being conducted to determine if there is a connection between the use of this equipment and problems in childbearing. However, VDT operators may experience neck pains or headaches from sitting in a fixed position for prolonged periods. As a precaution, until more information is available, VDT workers can cover their screens with a specially designed shield that cuts glare while it reduces very low frequency radiation.

Confined office spaces and chemicals released from some ventilation systems may constitute a new environmental threat, which has not yet been assessed.

GETTING INFORMATION

UNFORTUNATELY, people often are unaware of the risks that their jobs pose to their reproductive ability or may underrate them. An experienced worker, for example, may ignore hazards that have become familiar. The American College of Obstetricians and Gynecologists suggests that a woman planning a pregnancy keep an hourly diary for several days, noting all the tasks she performs and the materials she handles. She should describe the physical requirements of her job, as well as the chemicals, radiation, or fumes that both she and her husband work with, and pass this information along to her physician. Such a record is often remarkably revealing, both to the woman and to her doctor.

In light of the information, the physician may suggest that one or both partners switch to another job before pregnancy. However, most physicians know little about the specific chemicals used in a specific job. The range of possibilities and unknown factors is too wide. Thus, getting the facts is often the responsibility of the couple themselves.

Every working person should know the occupational risks he or she is facing. OSHA requires manufacturers, importers, and distributors to provide workers with information on hazardous substances and label chemical containers. This applies to substances that contain 0.1 percent or more of carcinogens or 1 percent or more of hazardous substances. These concentration levels have been criticized as arbitrary and some charge they

Table 6.4
ORGANIZATIONS DEVOTED TO WORKER SAFETY

Occupational Health and Safety Administration (OSHA)

U.S. Department of Labor
200 Constitution Avenue NW
Washington, D.C. 20210
(202) 523-8158

OSHA, a government agency, provides free consultation by industrial hygienists to companies.

National Institute for Occupational Safety and Health (NIOSH)

Department of Health and Human Resources
200 Independence Avenue, SW
Room 714-B
Washington, D.C. 20201
(202) 472-7134

This agency of the federal government provides information and makes referrals to proper government agencies for occupational health concerns.

New York Committee for Occupational Safety and Health (NYCOSH)

275 Seventh Avenue
25th Floor
New York, NY 10001
(212) 627-3900

This is the largest branch of COSH, 25 to 30 labor-based groups situated around the country. COSH advises workers about toxic effects and legal rights with respect to workplace chemicals. The groups serve as networking resources, provide information about workplace hazards, lobby for protective standards, and support strict right-to-know legislation. Local units are listed in the telephone white pages or can be contacted through labor unions.

provide inadequate safeguards to workers.

One problem with this federal standard is that employers may not report to their employees all known facts about a given chemical's dangers. Nor does the rule apply to nonmanufacturing personnel in the chemical manufacturing field, such as office workers. In addition, the manufacturers and importers themselves decide which chemicals are considered hazardous.

The difficulty in getting hard data about hazards has prompted some states to institute workers' right-to-know programs. State right-to-know laws are generally more comprehensive than the federal ruling and cover a larger working population. Most states decide which chemicals are included, and many define "hazardous" more broadly than does OSHA. Currently 31 states* and a number of cities and other localities have passed their own right-to-know laws. These laws require manufacturers to inform employers about the risks of their products and for employers to pass this

---

* Alabama, Alaska, Arkansas, California, Connecticut, Delaware, Florida, Georgia, Illinois, Iowa, Louisiana, Maine, Maryland, Massachusetts, Michigan, Minnesota, Montana, New Hampshire, New Jersey, New York, North Carolina, North Dakota, Oregon, Pennsylvania, Rhode Island, Tennessee, Texas, Vermont, Washington, West Virginia, and Wisconsin.

information on to employees—along with training in protective procedures.

Although management is supposed to provide a safe workplace, the real impetus usually comes from the workers and/or their labor unions or other organizations. Employees who suspect that their working environment might be hazardous should learn as much as possible about the chemicals and other substances they work with; they should then talk to their employers or trade unions. They may ask for the hazard to be removed or request better conditions.

The Council on Scientific Affairs (Division of Personal and Public Health Policy, American Medical Association) has issued reports for physicians ("Professional Awareness of Reproductive Hazards to Pregnant Workers") to guide them concerning risk factors associated with the reproductive health of workers. Further assistance and information can also be obtained from the health professionals working within the company, or from National Institute for Occupational Safety and Health (NIOSH) and OSHA consultants in the region.

Several agencies have been established to help workers and industries assess and correct occupational hazards. (See table 6.4.)

KEEPING THINGS IN PERSPECTIVE

IN THIS CHAPTER, we have briefly outlined some of the more common environmental hazards that can affect reproductive health and the developing fetus. In approaching the question of environmental hazards, it is important to maintain some perspective. At times, it may appear that virtually everything is a potential danger to an unborn baby. Of course, this is not the case; some toxins are so minor that they pose virtually no threat, while others are potent substances that invariably cause birth defects. The majority of environmental hazards fall somewhere in between.

In trying to create as safe an environment as possible for a developing fetus, the couple should concentrate on those potent hazards that are readily avoidable: cigarette smoking, alcohol use, illicit drugs, unnecessary medication, ionizing radiation, and certain workplace chemicals or hazards that are known risks. A commonsense approach should prevail, especially when dealing with unproven or relatively benign risks, such as microwave ovens, color televisions, or VDTs. By focusing on what is the most important, couples can go a long way toward ensuring the safety of their unborn babies.

7 The Pregnant Body

Edward Bowe, M.D.

INTRODUCTION

THE PREGNANT BODY undergoes rather amazing changes in order to prepare for the growth, nourishment, and birth of a child. The uterus grows to 18 times its normal weight, blood volume increases, the rib cage widens, and the pelvic bones soften.

These changes, which are primarily controlled by the hormones estrogen, progesterone, and human chorionic gonadotropin (HCG), may be both positive and negative from the mother's point of view, depending on the trimester. Within each trimester (as the three 3-month periods that make up the pregnancy are called), the mother's physical and emotional changes vary predictably. While this pattern is typical of many pregnancies, at the same time every pregnancy is unique. Even for the same woman, 2 pregnancies may be very different.

Women in the first trimester often become preoccupied with the changes in their bodies and the unusual things that seem to be happening day by day. Physical symptoms of fatigue and pregnancy sickness can be disturbing. In addition, almost everyone feels some ambivalence about being pregnant. Even those who have had trouble becoming pregnant experience moods that swing widely between excitement and anxiety. Both prospective parents are likely to be concerned about the financial and psychological responsibilities that parenthood will bring.

In the second trimester, much of this ambivalence disappears, along with most of the unpleasant symptoms of early pregnancy. The pregnancy is now physically obvious to everyone, and the pregnant woman usually receives positive attention from others. Many women are thrilled when they first begin to feel the movements of the fetus.

The third trimester is a time of expectancy and also a time of some physical discomfort as the fetus grows larger. A strong desire to have the pregnancy finished may be countered by anxiety about labor and delivery. Childbirth preparation classes help lessen the anxiety and also give prospective parents an opportunity to share their concerns and their excitement with other couples.

The last few weeks can be difficult; most women stay close to home, depending on friends and family for both physical and emotional support. Those who are alone should make sure that a friend is on call to help with chores and to be available when labor begins.

The following sections attempt to catalog each of the physical and emotional conditions that might occur during pregnancy. However, it is not meant to suggest that all of them will. For example, even the best known and one of the most widespread complaints—pregnancy sickness ("morning sickness")—affects only half of women, and of those, only a minority actually experience vomiting.

Many women, in fact, find that pregnancy has a positive effect on their health and emotional well-being. Oily hair and acne-prone skin may clear up, for instance, and allergic reactions may lessen. In the end, most pregnancies are remembered as a time of both excitement and contentment. In those whose pregnancies are more difficult, remembering that it will soon be over and recognizing that the changes are necessary for the healthy development of the fetus can help sustain the expectant mother through a very important 9 months.

THE DEVELOPING UTERUS

IN ORDER TO PUT into context the changes that occur within the 3 trimesters, it is useful to have an overall picture of the development of the uterus as it gradually changes over the course of pregnancy. The size of the uterus varies from woman to woman, but before pregnancy it is a pear-shaped organ weighing about 2⅓ ounces; it is approximately 3½ inches long by 2¼ inches at its widest point. At term, it has enlarged to about 13¾ inches by 9 inches in diameter; and its weight has increased by over 1,400 percent to 2¼ pounds.

In early pregnancy, the uterus enlarges as the muscle cells expand. Later in pregnancy, growth is due largely to the expansion of the existing muscle fibers. The blood supply to the uterus and to all the pelvic organs increases rapidly during pregnancy; by term, blood flowing to the uterus accounts for about 25 percent of the total body circulation.

By the twelfth week of pregnancy (counting from the last menstrual period), the top of the uterus can be felt just above the pubic bone. By the twentieth week, it has enlarged until it has reached the umbilicus; and by 36 weeks it is just below the lower end of the breast bone.

By the thirty-sixth week of pregnancy, the uterus has reached its highest point. At this point, the baby is probably lying with the head pointing toward the cervix. Soon the head will descend into the pelvis in preparation for birth.

In about half of first pregnancies, this descent, or engaging, of the baby's head occurs at around the thirty-sixth week. In the other half, it usually happens in the next 2 weeks. In second and subsequent pregnancies, however, the head often does not engage until the fortieth week or even until labor begins.

THE FIRST TRIMESTER

Emotional Changes

Even the most eagerly awaited pregnancy is accompanied by some conflicts and worries, and these may be exaggerated by mood swings during the first trimester. Both prospective parents will probably experience emotions ranging from delight to anxiety, perhaps all at the same time. For some, the anticipated pleasures of parenthood seem to pale beside the responsibilities.

Worries and problems thought to be resolved before pregnancy may reappear. Vivid dreams are sometimes reported during pregnancy, an indication that the mind is working out these problems subconsciously.

It helps to keep things in perspective. It is normal to have negative feelings, even resentment, about the pregnancy and impending motherhood, and it is best to acknowledge these feelings as part of the experience. They in no way affect the ability to be a good mother later.

Ambivalence may be heightened by pregnancy sickness and fatigue at the beginning of the pregnancy. But these symptoms are a result of the bodily changes necessary to provide a proper environment in which the fetus can grow and develop. The symptoms are most obvious in the first trimester and many of them will diminish or disappear in a few months.

Hormonal Changes

Body changes and unpleasant physical symptoms are most profound in the first trimester. Fatigue, nausea, vomiting, constipation, sensitive breasts, indigestion, and diminished or absent sex drive are all common complaints. Many women do not want to be physically touched in these early months.

These symptoms coincide with the sudden increase in levels of estrogen and progesterone, hormones normally present in the female body, but produced in increased amounts during pregnancy. A third responsible hormone is HCG, which only appears during pregnancy and is produced by the placenta. The production of HCG skyrockets in the first trimester, but by the beginning of the second trimester the cell layer that manufactures most of the HCG dissolves, and production of the hormone subsides. When HCG wanes, many unpleasant symptoms disappear as well.

These 3 hormones—estrogen, progesterone, and HCG—and their derivatives are thought to be responsible for virtually all the changes in the body during pregnancy, but the exact mechanism by which they work is not fully understood.

Fatigue

Fatigue is the most widely experienced symptom in the first 3 to 4 months of pregnancy. Even those who manage to sleep extra hours may feel uncommonly tired. They should not assume that it will only get worse as the pregnancy continues. Quite the opposite, it generally improves in the second trimester. In the meantime, getting as much extra rest as possible is important. This can be difficult for those who have demanding jobs, but finding ways to take short breaks throughout the day can help. Going to bed earlier and getting more sleep each night is also a good idea.

Pregnancy Sickness

Another common problem of early pregnancy is pregnancy sickness. In about half of all pregnancies, there is some nausea during the first trimester. Of these, about a third also involve episodes of occasional to frequent vomiting. The common term "morning sickness" is a misnomer—symptoms may occur at any time during the day or may last all day long. Pregnancy sickness is not dangerous to the mother of the fetus, but it makes some mothers especially miserable.

Like other changes of pregnancy,

pregnancy sickness is caused by disturbance of the normal working systems of the body, but the exact cause is still unknown. Because a high level of HCG usually coincides with pregnancy sickness, this pregnancy hormone may be the culprit. Possibly other hormones are also involved. Diet may be another important factor, both before and in the early weeks of pregnancy. Some evidence indicates that sickness may be more likely when the diet is high in protein and low in carbohydrates and vitamin B_6. Emotional stress appears to make pregnancy sickness worse.

Symptoms that continue all day long, especially vomiting, should be reported to the doctor. Although there is no real remedy for pregnancy sickness, nor any currently FDA-approved medication available for acute cases of nausea and vomiting during pregnancy, there are several things that will help minimize illness. Diet, mild exercise, and rest are the therapies that are usually recommended.

A well-balanced diet that emphasizes complex carbohydrates, such as whole-wheat bread and pasta, whole-grain cereals, and wheat germ; bananas; spinach and other green leafy vegetables, usually help minimize pregnancy sickness. This may be because these foods are high in vitamin B_6. In severe cases of pregnancy sickness, some physicians may recommend a vitamin B_6 supplement and yeast extract.

Foods rich in fat, such as fried foods and red meat, tend to make nausea worse. Those who cannot tolerate more sensible foods should eat whatever they can tolerate, even if they just nibble, and drink plenty of fluids. Fasting tends to make things worse. When it comes to curbing nausea, it is better to eat than not to eat. (See table 7.1.)

The bending and stretching that are part of normal exercise routines may make pregnancy sickness worse, and these programs may have to be suspended temporarily. However, fresh air and walking at a relaxed pace are good alternatives.

In terms of nutrition, the fetus does not suffer from its mother's pregnancy

---

Table 7.1

TIPS TO EASE PREGNANCY SICKNESS

Symptoms may be mitigated with these practices:

- Eating several small meals throughout the day, rather than 2 or 3 larger ones.

- Trying to keep some carbohydrate in the stomach at all times, especially in the morning. The old line, "Eat a dry saltine cracker while still in the bed in the morning," is still good advice.

- Eating a snack at bedtime to help alleviate morning nausea.

- Eating the large meal—if there is one—in the middle of the day rather than in the evening.

- Drinking plenty of fluids to help neutralize stomach acids and to prevent the dehydration that can come from vomiting. Chewing on small pieces of ice or sucking on hard candy or caramels may be helpful.

sickness, provided that she was well nourished before conception. Mothers will have time to make up for any deficiencies caused by erratic diet after the pregnancy sickness passes and they resume a nutritious eating pattern.

Heartburn

Although heartburn is most likely to occur during the last trimester, it can also appear early in pregnancy. In this case, it may be caused by the action of progesterone on the cardiac (no relation to the heart) sphincter, the muscle surrounding the lower end of the esophagus, the canal that connects the stomach to the mouth. Progesterone causes the cardiac sphincter to relax, allowing stomach acid to be regurgitated into the lower esophagus, where it causes a burning sensation that is felt behind the breastbone.

The same eating patterns that help alleviate pregnancy sickness can also help relieve heartburn. Substituting several small meals for 1 or 2 large ones, and waiting an hour or so after the last meal before going to bed may be helpful. Eating slowly and drinking plenty of fluids may also help. Sleeping propped up with pillows and avoiding bending and stretching whenever possible may prevent stomach acid from regurgitating.

If these suggestions fail, an antacid such as Gelusil may help. Like all medications, however, these should be taken only on the advice of an obstetrician. Baking soda, which is high in sodium and promotes fluid retention, should be avoided.

Cravings

Although they are most common in the first trimester, cravings for certain foods or drinks can occur at any time during pregnancy. They may take the form of a sudden, intense desire for sour or salty foods; at other times, the craving may be for bland foods or sugar. The origin of these cravings is unknown, but they probably have nothing to do with nutritional needs.

Cravings may be connected to hormonal influences on the sense of taste. Eating the food that is craved usually is not harmful, if not carried to extremes and as long as nutritional requirements are met.

A craving for a nonfood substance—a rare occurence—is called pica. If large quantities of these substances are ingested, they can interfere with the normal absorption of vital nutrients from food and can lead to anemia. Consuming large quantities of ice may also interfere with the absorption of iron and other minerals. For these reasons, any desire for nonfood substances should be controlled.

Aversions

Pregnancy can also bring strong aversions to certain foods, drinks, or even odors. The food should simply be avoided or a substitute found. In the early part of pregnancy, there may be a metallic taste in the mouth that affects the taste of food, but this symptom usually disappears later.

Dizziness and Fainting

Changes in blood volume and distribution, as well as the relaxation of blood vessels, can cause momentary dizziness or fainting early in pregnancy, as well as in the second and third trimesters. The sensation of light-headedness is caused by a momentary reduction in the flow of blood to the brain. Instead, the blood collects in the abdominal region or the legs, a phenomenon sometimes known as vascular pooling. A stuffy or smoky atmosphere, sitting or standing still for too long, standing up too quickly, fatigue, or sudden fear or anxiety can all bring on a fainting spell.

Changing positions rapidly after being still for a long time should be avoided. Taking 3 or 4 deep breaths before rising from a bed or chair can help avoid dizziness. Sitting in the fresh air or lying down near an open window will usually counteract feelings of faintness. Fainting spells should always be reported to the obstetrician.

Constipation

Constipation is a common complaint during pregnancy. This is probably caused by the relaxing effect that pregnancy hormones have on the muscles of the intestinal wall, slowing the passage of the stool. As it enlarges, the uterus also exerts pressure on the bowel, which further contributes to constipation.

Other factors, such as low-fiber diet and iron supplements, may also contribute to the problem. Plenty of fluids and high-fiber foods and fruits, such as prunes

and figs that have a natural laxative effect, should help. However, eating large quantities of unprocessed bran should be avoided, as this can interfere with the absorption of minerals from food. Intake should be limited to 1 or 2 teaspoons of bran a day added to soups and cereals.

Laxatives should never be taken without a doctor's supervision. Strong laxatives can cause the uterus to contract and certain laxatives also interfere with the absorption of vitamins.

Breast Changes

During the early part of pregnancy, tender, sensitive breasts are very common. Some women experience tingling or throbbing in the area around the nipple. Breasts become larger and firmer as hormonal activity causes the glandular tissues to enlarge. An increase of 2 cup sizes is common. By the middle months, when breasts have reached near maximum development, this tenderness usually disappears.

The areola around the nipples may become pigmented and brown. Sometimes raised white areas, called Montgomery's glands, appear. These will secrete oil to keep the nipples lubricated and prevent cracking. In blondes, the areola tends to become pinker. Later on, additional brownish spots, called secondary areolas, may appear on the skin surrounding the areola.

To some extent, wearing a well-fitting maternity bra that gives good support can alleviate breast discomfort. Breasts tend to sag during pregnancy because they contain no muscle tissue to support their excess weight. If proper support is provided, breasts are more likely to return to their former shape after pregnancy. A good bra may also help avoid stretch marks.

Prominent nipples are not necessary for successful breastfeeding nor does the size of the breast matter. Even if the nipples are inverted or retracted, shape has nothing to do with efficient function. Retracted nipples tend to protrude more readily after delivery and are drawn out even farther as the baby latches on securely to breastfeed.

Genital Changes

The external genitals (vulva) may darken and also become enlarged under the influence of the same hormone (estrogen) that encourages breast development. Unlike the breasts, however, which return to their original size after pregnancy, the labia majora, or outer lips, usually do not regress completely, and may remain slightly open or apart. The darkening usually disappears after delivery.

Internally, both the cervix and the vagina produce more secretions. The cervix (the neck at the opening of the uterus into the vagina) becomes shorter and more vascular. The vagina becomes more congested as the cells thicken, and it turns bluish in color with more vasuclar activity.

Skin

The hormones active during pregnancy affect each woman's skin differently. If skin tended to be oily before pregnancy, it may exhibit dry patches. If it was dry, oiliness may develop.

Dry, itching skin is common during pregnancy, particularly where the skin stretches tightly across the abdomen. The cause of this dry skin condition is unknown.

Smooth materials and loose-fitting clothes enhance skin comfort. Bath water should be warm, but never hot. (Saunas and hot tubs should be avoided completely, not only for the mother's comfort, but, more important, for the safety of the fetus.) Adding a little milk to the bath water may be soothing; body lotion, moisturizer, or talcum powder may also help.

Vaginal Discharge

Vaginal discharge increases during pregnancy and is usually white and odorless. There may be increased susceptibility to such vaginal infections as monilia (yeast). The risk of monilia infection can be reduced by allowing air to circulate. Wearing loose-fitting clothing and cotton underwear is advisable; stockings or maternity pantyhose with an open gusset are preferable to ordinary pantyhose. Any vaginal discomfort or a discharge that becomes malodorous or yellowish in color should be reported to the physician.

Vaginal Bleeding

During the first 2 months of pregnancy, spotting and staining are common. In some cases spotting may occur throughout the pregnancy without danger. However, such minor spotting must be distinguished from bright red vaginal bleeding, a serious symptom that should be reported immediately to a physician. In the early months bleeding can be a sign of ectopic pregnancy or threatened miscarriage. Later in the pregnancy bleeding may mean that the placenta has begun to separate from the uterus, threatening the life of the fetus. Late bleeding requires immediate hospitalization.

Polyps or cervical erosion may occasionally cause bleeding from the cervix, a condition that may be aggravated by sexual intercourse.

Nosebleeds

Nosebleeds are common during pregnancy because higher blood volume (as a result of hormonal changes) makes it easy to damage small blood vessels (capillaries). A simple sneeze can cause the nose to bleed. Nosebleeds are not a sign of elevated blood pressure. A little lanolin or petroleum jelly inserted into each nostril at night helps to keep nasal passages from drying out during sleep. To minimize the risk of nosebleeds, the nose should always be blown gently. Frequent or heavy nosebleeds should be reported to the doctor.

Dental Problems

For the same reason they are susceptible to nosebleeds, pregnant women are susceptible to bleeding gums and gum infections, and these can lead to serious dental problems. While it is true that the fetus needs large amounts of calcium for proper development, the old wives' tale that a woman loses a tooth for every pregnancy stems not from the fetus draining calcium from the mother's teeth, but from gum ailments.

During pregnancy, gums become softer and more vascular, making them more vulnerable to inflammation and disease. Gums are now especially sensitive to a buildup of plaque on teeth, which results in irritation and perhaps infection.

Before pregnancy, cleaning by a dentist or dental hygienist is advisable to make sure that the teeth and gums are in good condition. During pregnancy a dental checkup is recommended. Thorough, regular brushing and flossing at home will help prevent serious dental problems. Although gums may swell and even bleed, with proper care there is less likelihood that they will become infected and cause more serious problems. After childbirth, when hormonal balance resumes, teeth and gums should be in good condition.

THE SECOND TRIMESTER

As the pregnancy enters the second trimester, the mother usually begins to feel much better. Compared to the first trimester, the second is almost euphoric.

Most women say that these 3 months are the best of pregnancy. Any pregnancy sickness has probably begun to disappear; swelling and tenderness of breasts subside; bowels are functioning better; and the profound fatigue of the first trimester clears up. Moods lift and spirits rise. It is also the time when the uterus has enlarged enough so that the pregnancy is definitely apparent, swelling below the umbilicus. The breasts reach the point of maximum enlargement.

The sudden change is attributed largely to the decline of the hormone HCG. Although estrogen and progesterone will continue to rise, the body seems to adjust to the presence of these hormones in the second trimester.

Skin and hair improve noticeably, most women look especially beautiful in these months, and sexual activity resumes for most couples. Although positive emotional changes and general well-being may enhance a woman's appearance, the well-known "bloom" or "glow" of pregnancy is actually due to hormones.

If a couple has not already done so by now, this is the time to find out about childbirth classes and reserve a place.

Quickening

In a first pregnancy, the baby's first movements can be felt sometime between weeks 18 and 20; in subsequent pregnancies, or if the mother is normally very thin, movement may be noticed as early as week 18. These first, very gentle fluttering movements are known as "quickening."

Stretch Marks

Pregnancy often means the appearance of pink or brownish red streaks on the abdomen, buttocks, thighs, and breasts. These striations are due to the breakdown of elastic fibers in the skin as the progressing pregnancy causes the abdomen, breasts, and other parts of the body to enlarge. They become pigmented because pregnancy brings a general increase in the pituitary hormone that stimulates pigment-containing cells scattered throughout the body. Stretch marks, or *striae gravidarum*, never disappear completely. After delivery, however, they fade and become much less noticeable. During subsequent pregnancies stretch marks usually become pigmented again.

About two-thirds of pregnant women develop stretch marks, and there is no way to prevent them. They can be minimized, however, by keeping the skin supple, practicing good posture, and providing good support for the enlarging abdomen and breasts.

Varicose Veins

Blood vessels throughout the body are much more visible and dilated during pregnancy. Dilation is caused by the expansion of maternal blood volume (there is 30 to 40 percent more blood circulating in the body by the end of the second trimester). Increased progesterone circulating in the blood allows the walls of vessels to stretch, accommodating the extra blood volume.

During pregnancy, the veins in the hands and arms are more visible than usual. Pressure from the enlarging uterus causes veins in the lower part of the body to dilate further. Valves that normally help blood move upward through leg veins weaken, compounding the effect. All these factors contribute to development of varicose veins in the legs, the external genitals, and anus (hemorrhoids). Development of varicose veins is fairly common, particularly in those who have a predilection in their families. (To a great extent varicose veins are hereditary.)

Varicose veins of the legs, although they regress to a great degree, do not go away entirely following childbirth. With every new pregnancy, there is a new increase of blood volume and stretching of the walls of the veins. Varicose veins established in the first pregnancy will appear again during the next.

Standing for long periods and sitting with the legs crossed promote varicose veins in the legs. Sitting up straight, legs uncrossed, and standing straight can help reduce the severity of varicose veins. Wearing well-fitting support stockings or pantyhose will also help keep varicose veins to a minimum.

Varicose veins that do not regress after pregnancy can be treated with injections or surgery, depending on the location and extent of the problem.

Varicose veins that appear around the vulva sometimes cause severe aching and irritation. Lying down will reduce the pressure on the veins and bring some relief. Holding small pieces of ice wrapped in a plastic bag and a clean cloth against the veins might also help temporarily. These veins tend to disappear rapidly after delivery.

Hemorrhoids

Almost every pregnant woman gets hemorrhoids, a form of varicose veins, in the anal area. Hemorrhoids are temporary and usually disappear within 3 to 4 months following childbirth.

Constipation, and consequent straining to defecate, can worsen hemorrhoids and should be avoided as much as possible. If hemorrhoids occur, an ice pack may help reduce swelling. Although it is important to check with the obstetrician before using any medication, topical ointments (such as Preparation H) for relief of swelling or itching are generally considered safe. If the hemorrhoids are painful, or if they protrude or bleed, the obstetrician should be consulted.

Backaches

Although in the second trimester the fetus is still small, pregnancy hormones are beginning to cause the joints to loosen and ligaments to soften. Stooping, wearing high heels, and poor posture can all contribute to strained muscles, particularly in the back. Walking and standing properly can help avoid aches and pains, as can a regular program of exercise. (See chapter 10, The Pregnant Lifestyle.)

Strain on the muscles supporting increased breast weight can cause pain high in the back. Good posture and a good support bra can help in this case. Even more common in pregnancy is low backache. This generally occurs when a woman thrusts her shoulders back in an attempt to compensate for the increased forward weight of the uterus. Regular back and abdominal exercises are important, as well as attention to posture. Firm back support is advised whenever driving or sitting for long periods of time, and a bed board or extrafirm mattress may be recommended when pain is pronounced.

Round Ligament Pains

The round ligaments help to hold the uterus in place. These ligaments stretch out and may occasionally cramp as the uterus enlarges during pregnancy, usually in the second trimester. This uncomfortable situation is very common during pregnancy and no cause for alarm. The spasms are characterized by sharp pains that occur on one side, and occasionally both sides, of the abdomen toward the groin. Effective remedies include massage and heat application. Sometimes a change of position, especially drawing up the knees into a "fetal" posture may be enough to relieve symptoms.

Leg Cramps

Leg cramps, especially at night, are common during pregnancy. If leg cramps occur frequently, a physician may prescribe supplemental calcium. It helps to stretch out the leg and "point" the heel. Standing and putting weight on the leg may also relieve the cramp.

Leg pain may also occur in late pregnancy when the enlarged uterus presses on nerves that extend from the pelvis into the legs. Hugging the knees to the chest may provide a remedy.

Sciatic Pain

The sciatic nerve runs from the buttocks down the back of both legs. In some positions, the fetus can put pressure on the blood vessels, which in turn press on the nerve, causing a sharp, piercing pain across the lower back and down the legs. The application of heat and a change of position, particularly pulling the knees to the chest, may provide temporary relief.

THE THIRD TRIMESTER

THE LAST 3 MONTHS of pregnancy, the third trimester, bring further changes in both physical and emotional status. Facial features seem to change, becoming fuller and less well chiseled. Hair seems coarser and loses much of its gloss. Noticeable changes in skin color and texture occur. Skin temperature is always warm during the third trimester, as the mother's body radiates fetal body heat that passes through the placenta.

There is no mistaking now that the woman is pregnant, and the baby's kicks are visible to the eye. The movements of the fetus are stronger, but less frequent. If the baby were born now, there would be an excellent chance of survival.

By the begining of the third trimester, the top of the uterus, the fundus, has reached a point about halfway between the navel and the breastbone. By the seventh month, the umbilicus is no longer a depression and in the final weeks of pregnancy it may actually protrude.

The position of the uterus and the weight of the baby account for a number of discomforts likely to be encountered in this trimester. Pressure on the bladder results in a more frequent need to urinate; some women may find that pressure on the stomach makes it necessary to eat smaller meals more often.

From about the thirty-fourth week until the baby's head engages (known as "lightening"), the baby will take up a great deal of room, so that a woman's lung capacity may be less than usual. There is upward pressure on the diaphragm, displacing it by as much as 1 inch. Thus, the mother may experience difficulty in breathing. Sitting up straight and sleeping propped up with pillows may provide some relief.

The enlarging uterus may also press on the main vein that returns blood from the lower body to the heart, causing the blood pressure to fall and sometimes resulting in a feeling of faintness or nausea. Because this is particularly common if the mother lies on her back for more than a few minutes, this position should be avoided in the last trimester. If fainting spells or blackouts occur, they should be reported to the obstetrician.

As the end of the third trimester approaches, waiting may become tedious and the baby's energetic kicking may rob the mother of sleep. She may find it difficult to do ordinary tasks, or even to sit still comfortably. Sometime between 36 and 38 weeks the baby's head engages, bringing some relief. After dropping, there is less pressure on the stomach, ribs, and diaphragm, and it becomes much easier to breathe. There is still pressure on the bladder, however, as well as occasional swelling in the ankles.

The final weeks of pregnancy are often filled with fluctuating emotions. On the one hand, a woman may be tired of waiting and may be looking forward to holding her newborn. On the other hand, she may be anxious about the coming labor and delivery or perhaps, if she is still working, wondering if she will be ready for maternity leave. Prenatal depression is common, but generally short-lived. Talking things over with her partner, obstetrician, or childbirth class instructor can help the mother relieve some of her anxiety.

Sexual Activity

Sexual activity usually diminishes in the third trimester. This may be due to further hormonal changes that cause a decline in libido, but there are also many psychological and emotional factors at work at this time. Many fathers-to-be are afraid to have sex with their wives for fear they will disturb the pregnancy. Waxing and waning of sexual activity and desire are also tied to a woman's feelings about how she looks. Late in pregnancy breasts are heavy, the abdomen is burgeoning, skin pigmentation and striae may be apparent. A pregnant woman in the third trimester may fail to see herself as a desirable sexual person, and sex is often the last thing on her mind.

Diminished sex drive may also have something to do with instructions a couple receive from their physician. Some doctors still believe that intercourse in the third trimester is harmful. In high-risk pregnancy, sexual intercourse and orgasm might contribute to premature rupture of membranes and premature labor, and is usually best avoided. For the normal pregnancy, however, sexual intercourse is generally not harmful.

Emotional Impact on the Fetus

Mothers and aunts have been telling women for years that if they are unhappy and anxious during pregnancy their babies will turn out unhappy and anxious, too. There is no evidence that a mother's emotions affect the fetus so directly.

A fetus is probably unable to respond directly to the mother's feelings. If she feels good about her pregnancy, however, and is looking forward to motherhood, her positive mental attitude may ease labor and delivery. And this positive attitude will help during the emotionally critical adjustments necessary when an infant becomes part of the family.

It is true that infants can sense and respond to unexpressed emotions of their parents. Whether they are aware of such emotions while still in the uterus remains a mystery. Those who tend to be excitable and temperamental during pregnancy, for example, will probably exhibit a similar temperament after the baby is born. To pinpoint the moment at which the baby first begins to respond to a mother's personality is impossible.

Skin Pigmentation

In the third trimester skin pigmentation becomes more apparent, but these changes are reversible and usually disappear after the baby is born. The pituitary gland enlarges in pregnancy, and the particular portion of the pituitary that produces a hormone called melanocyte-stimulating hormone increases its activity. Melanocytes are pigment-containing cells throughout the body, concentrated mostly in the midline, but melanocytes are also present in the nipples and areola, areas that begin to darken early in pregnancy.

Some women develop dark patches on their face, called chloasma, or the mask of pregnancy. This condition is especially noticeable in those with dark hair. It, too, fades after delivery.

Other parts of the body are also subject to skin changes. A dark streak called a *linea nigra* may develop from the navel to the pubic bone. Genital skin also becomes darker.

In general, the sun should be avoided as much as possible. A sunscreen on the face and other exposed areas is always advisable. Skin changes are temporary and camouflage is the best remedy. Bleaches or "scrubs" should never be used in an attempt to erase the patches or streaks.

Changes in Hair

Hair is modified skin. Increased hormonal stimulation of hair follicles causes hair to coarsen for some pregnant women. It also causes hair to grow, even in places where it was never noticeable before. Facial hair, for example, may appear during pregnancy, and hair may grow up on the lower part of the abdomen. There is often more hair on the arms and legs. The hormone responsible is probably progesterone, which has the potential to be metabolized by the body and the placenta into the male-type hormone. The subsequent thickening of skin and hair reflects increasing amounts of circulating androgens. Genetic inheritance also will influence hair growth. Mediterranean women, for example, will probably see more dramatic changes in body hair and skin pigmentation. Fair-skinned women will notice less change.

Hair may react quite differently to dyes or permanents during pregnancy, and so it is probably best to avoid both until at least 6 months after delivery.

Hormonal changes continue to affect the mother's hair after the baby is born. A sudden drop in progesterone after childbirth is most likely the reason that many women lose some hair post partum. Good nutrition and gentle brushing helps. Hair will resume its normal thickness within 3 to 4 months following childbirth.

Digestive Problems

During the last trimester, as the growing fetus puts increasingly more pressure against the mother's stomach, indigestion and heartburn may again become a problem. Eating normal-sized meals may become impossible because of the decreased capacity of the stomach. Small meals throughout the day are the best answer. (See also the section on minimizing heartburn.)

Edema (Swelling)

In the final weeks of pregnancy, the weight of the fetus impedes circulation by pressing on the pelvis, and this can cause the ankles to swell. Wherever possible, the mother should try to sit or lie down to relieve pressure on legs and feet. When she sits, she should prop up her feet on a low footstool or box. Those who must stand for long periods should keep moving, which helps calf muscles to pump up blood and fluids into the rest of the body. If they must stand still, they should prop up one foot and then the other on a footstool.

Lying down with the upper body resting on pillows and the feet supported by firm pillows so they are raised just above shoulder level will help drain fluid from the ankles. Most women gain a measure of comfort by lying on one side with one knee bent; a pillow under the abdomen serves to help support the weight of the uterus.

If the hands or face become swollen, it may be a sign of toxemia and should be reported to the doctor immediately.

Tingling Sensations

Numbness and tingling in hands and fingers may be due to pregnancy-related carpal tunnel syndrome, caused when accumulated fluid in the wrist presses on the median nerve in the forearm as it passes through a tunnel formed by the wristbone (carpals) and a ligament just under the skin. It is experienced most often in the morning.

The numbness can sometimes be eased by raising the hands above the head, then flexing and extending the fingers. Swinging arms in a circular motion can also help, or resting the fingertips on the shoulders and rotating elbows backward may also help.

Late in pregnancy, tingling or a feeling of pressure in the vagina may be caused by fetal pressure on vaginal nerves. Although a little uncomfortable, it is usually nothing to worry about.

Fatigue and Sleeplessness

The physical effort of carrying increased weight often brings a return of the fatigue suffered earlier in pregnancy. The problem is often exacerbated by the inability to get a good night's sleep. The frequent need to urinate, leg cramps, and difficulty in finding a comfortable sleeping position all may disrupt sleep. Rest during the day is recommended whenever possible. Lying on the side with 1 pillow under the abdomen and the other between the legs may make sleeping easier. If sleep is elusive, a warm bath or shower and a cup of warm milk before bed are often helpful.

Leakage from Breasts

During the last trimester, as the breasts prepare for milk production, there may be a discharge from the nipples of a clear or milky substance. This is normal. In the last few weeks before delivery, colostrum, the substance that is the forerunner of breast milk, may begin to leak from the nipples. This is normal also and a woman should not squeeze the nipples in an effort to extract the colostrum.

The breasts can be gently washed with soap and water. If heavy leakage is a problem, breast pads, a folded handkerchief, or a soft tissue inside the bra will prevent the colostrum from staining clothes.

SUMMING UP

TO CREATE AN ENVIRONMENT in which the fetus can be nourished and protected while it grows and develops, the pregnant body undergoes a number of changes, which are primarily controlled by hormones, some of which are present only during gestation. The same hormones may also influence or exacerbate emotional changes, which may range from excitement and anticipation to apprehension and ambivalence.

Physical effects can be both positive and negative from the mother's point of view. On the one hand, the face takes on a special glow, skin problems may clear up, and the mother may enjoy the attention her expanding abdomen brings her. The second trimester in particular can be a period of renewed well-being and contentment. On the other hand, early pregnancy may mean fatigue and pregnancy sickness; the final weeks may bring some discomfort, caused by the weight of the pregnancy and a wish for it all to be over. These changes are temporary, however, and are necessary for the healthy development of the fetus.

8 Medical Care During Pregnancy

Laxmi Baxi, M.D.

INTRODUCTION

CONSISTENT PRENATAL CARE is the hallmark of a healthy pregnancy. Prenatal care should begin as soon as a woman discovers she is pregnant. The number of prenatal checkups a pregnant woman has depends largely on her medical history and the recommendation of her physician. In general, "low-risk" pregnant women, that is, women between the ages of 18 and 35 with no known medical problems, will see their obstetricians once a month until week 28 of pregnancy. As they enter the last trimester, they see their doctors every other week until week 36; and, from then on, every week until the baby is delivered. Women with risk factors may have to see their obstetricians as often as every week from the beginning of pregnancy, depending on the severity of their risk. [Note: The progress of pregnancy is usually measured in weeks calculated from the date of the last period. To calculate from the date of conception (if known), subtract 2 weeks.]

The initial prenatal visit that confirms the pregnancy is usually the most thorough examination, and much time is devoted to taking a thorough medical history and discussing the mode of delivery the couple prefer and the physiological changes the mother can expect. Subsequent visits are primarily to make certain that the fetus is growing adequately and that the mother's general health continues to be stable. These prenatal visits usually take only a few minutes. If a woman has anything she wishes to talk over with her doctor, however, she should take the time to do it. Between prenatal visits a woman should make a note of any minor physical ailments or anxieties she may have so that she will remember to discuss them with her obstetrician at the next checkup.

For a list of other conditions that require more immediate attention, see table 8.1.

THE FIRST VISIT

THE FIRST PRENATAL VISIT begins with a thorough medical history, including a record of previous pregnancies and family medical background if this has not been done in the pre-conception checkup. (See chapter 1, Planning Your Pregnancy.) The following tests are carried out to confirm the pregnancy and evaluate the present health of the mother. Remember, although these tests are now routine, a woman has the right to refuse some of them, if she so desires.

Blood Tests. A blood sample is analyzed to identify blood group and to test for venereal disease, anemia, rubella antibody titers, hepatitis screening, and rhesus (Rh) factor. (See chapter 1.)

If the patient is found to be anemic and she is black or of ethnic background considered at high risk (certain Mediterranean, Asian, and Caribbean island countries), the physician will order a hemoglobin electrophoresis test to detect sickle cell or thalassemia, two hereditary blood disorders. Hemoglobin electrophoresis is a process that separates the different types of hemoglobin in the blood so

Table 8.1
WARNING SIGNS DURING PREGNANCY

Most pregnancies proceed normally and uneventfully through the 3 trimesters, but occasionally problems arise unexpectedly.

General Illness

Common illnesses such as cold or the flu are generally harmless during pregnancy unless accompanied by high fever. Proper treatment of illness will prevent the development of more serious complications. Because over-the-counter medications should not be taken without medical advice, a pregnant woman should immediately report the following symptoms to her obstetrician:

- High fever (any fever above 101°F)
- Frequency of and burning on urination (signals urinary infection, which may trigger premature labor)
- Asthmatic attack
- Diarrhea
- Severe cough or severe cold
- Rash
- Joint pains

Threatened Abortion

Vaginal bleeding in early pregnancy is described as a threatened abortion. At times, it may proceed to an inevitable, spontaneous abortion. A pregnant woman should call the doctor immediately if any of the following symptoms occur:

- Severe abdominal pain
- Any bleeding from vagina
- Abdominal cramps
- Severe vomiting
- Dizziness
- Severe, unexplained pain in the shoulder
- Continuous headache or blurred vision and swelling of hands and face (especially in late second and third trimester)
- Irritating vaginal discharge
- Sudden escape of fluid from the vagina
- Marked decrease in urine output

they can be measured. The formulation of hemoglobin is controlled by genes, and prospective parents with genetic tendencies toward certain types of anemia may be tested and counseled about the risks to their offspring. (For more information, see chapter 3, Genetic Considerations.)

PELVIC EXAMINATION

FOR THE INTERNAL PELVIC exam the doctor gently inserts an instrument called a speculum into the vagina to hold it open so that he or she can see the cervix and vaginal wall. He or she will take a cervical swab for a Pap test and to test for infections.

After withdrawing the speculum, the

doctor inserts 2 fingers into the vagina and pushes them up against the cervix. At the same time, he or she presses on the abdomen with the other hand to feel the uterus and the organs around it.

The internal exam will confirm that the woman is pregnant and that the size of the uterus agrees with the estimated due date of the baby. The exam will also detect any structural abnormalities of the pelvis, vagina, and cervix that might affect the pregnancy or labor and delivery. The fetus is well protected, and the examination will not harm the pregnancy. The pelvic exam is usually not repeated until about week 36 of pregnancy, unless the physician suspects the mother has a vaginal infection, possible premature dilation of the cervix, premature onset of labor, or for a cervical examination.

INFECTIONS

THE PHYSICIAN will take cervical swabs for a Pap smear and to test for the presence of infections.

Chlamydia

Chlamydia trachomatis is now the most common sexually transmitted disease in the United States, affecting 1.6 million women annually. It can infect the eye, the urethra, the anus, and the pelvic organs in women. It is thus the cause of many cases of nonspecific urethritis, cervicitis, and other infections. When it infects the pelvic organs it can cause pelvic inflammatory disease (PID), which may lead to infertility. Gonorrhea is often present along with chlamydia. It is estimated that 40 to 70 percent of infants born to women infected with chlamydia may acquire this organism while passing through the birth canal.

In a newborn, chlamydia may cause eye infections; pneumonia; infections of the middle ear, nose, and throat; stomach and intestinal infections; and poor weight gain. Chlamydia eye infections, which usually do not appear until the second or third week of life, respond to treatment with antibiotic ointments over a period of several weeks, and usually heal without scarring or impaired vision. Some physicians also treat these infections with supplemental doses of oral antibiotics.

Chlamydia symptoms, when present, include burning on urination and urinary frequency, pain during intercourse, and—if the disease invades the pelvic cavity—fever and abdominal pain. However, 60 to 80 percent of infected women do not display any symptoms for years. For this reason, screening tests are becoming a standard part of a thorough gynecological examination, particularly an initial prenatal visit. Chlamydia is a fragile organism that was difficult to identify until recently, when a quick, accurate test was developed. A specimen from the urethra or cervix is collected on a swab, and results are available within hours. Although tetracycline is the treatment of choice for chlamydia, it is not safe for pregnant women, who should receive erythromycin instead. A woman's partner must be treated at the same time in order to prevent reinfection.

Gonorrhea

About 98 percent of women with gonorrhea have no noticeable symptoms and, as a result, many cases of gonorrhea in women go untreated. Without treatment, the infection can spread into the Fallopian tubes, ovaries, and abdominal cavity. When a pregnant woman contracts gonorrhea, however, the progress of the disease is temporarily impeded by a thick plug of mucus that blocks the cervix during pregnancy. The gonorrhea organisms remain in the vaginal vault until the time of delivery approaches, and the mucus plug is discharged. Bacteria can then pass freely through the cervix and invade the pelvis. At the same time, the baby is exposed to the disease as it passes through the birth canal during delivery. Since gonorrhea can have serious consequences for both mother and newborn, women should be checked carefully for the disease early in pregnancy.

Some studies have shown that women who contract gonorrhea during pregnancy have a higher incidence of prematurely ruptured membranes and onset of premature labor. Exposure to gonorrhea during delivery may cause severe inflammation and scarring of the newborn's corneas, which, if not treated promptly, may result in permanent blindness. It has become routine procedure in hospitals to apply preventive silver nitrate drops to the eyes of all babies just after birth. Infants born to mothers with gonorrhea are at high risk to contract the infection; in addition to receiving eye drops, these babies require immediate treatment with an injection of penicillin.

Pregnant women should have a gonorrhea culture performed at the first prenatal visit; the culture is often repeated later in pregnancy. Results are usually available within 2 to 5 days. If gonorrhea is present, the treatment of choice is penicillin, which can be safely given to pregnant women. Women allergic to penicillin-type antibiotics or those with a strain of gonorrhea that is resistant to penicillin may be given spectinomycin or ceftriazone, combined with probenecid. Tetracyclines should not be used during pregnancy.

Syphilis

Syphilis *(Treponema pallidum)* is far less common than chlamydia or gonorrhea. It is almost always transmitted through sexual contact, although pregnant women can also transfer the infection to their babies via the placenta.

The incubation period usually lasts 2 to 4 weeks but a woman may have the disease as long as 3 months before the first sign of infection appears: a hard, painless sore or ulcer on the genitals. Occasionally, the red, protruding ulcer, called a chancre, will show up in the rectum or on the tongue, lips, or breast. If the chancre develops out of sight in the vagina or cervix, it may go unnoticed. The lymph nodes near the chancre may also swell, but a correct diagnosis at this early stage can be made only by examining tissue sample from the chancre under a microscope.

Untreated, the chancre usually heals slowly and disappears. Two to 6 weeks later, the secondary stage of the disease usually develops: fever, headache, loss of appetite, fatigue, and aching joints. Lymph nodes throughout the body may become enlarged, and a rash will appear on the trunk, palms, and soles. Grayish-white patches may appear on the inside of the mouth. All of these skin and mucous membrane lesions are highly infectious. These symptoms mean that the organism has now disseminated throughout the body, and diagnosis at this stage can be made by a simple blood test.

If left untreated, the secondary stage of syphilis also disappears within a few weeks, and there may be no further sign of the disease for 10 or even 20 years. Rarely in the United States does syphilis progress to the third stage, but when it does, it is devastating and sometimes fatal.

Effects on Pregnancy. A fetus may be directly infected with syphilis via the placenta, the connecting link between mother and child. If the mother is in the primary or early secondary stages of infection, syphilis may overwhelm and kill the fetus, or the baby may be born with the disease. Symptoms may not appear for several weeks or even months; the usual signs of infection are skin lesions, a runny nose, severe tenderness over the bones, and deafness. Proper antibiotic therapy can cure the disease in an infant

and prevent serious aftereffects.

Several different lab tests can diagnose syphilis. The most frequently used is the Venereal Disease Research Laboratory (VDRL) or the rapid plasma reagin (RPR). These 2 blood tests detect an antibodylike substance in the blood if syphilis is present. One of these screening tests is often performed during early pregnancy. The tests are not always accurate, however. When the VDRL or RPR is positive, a fluorescent treponemal antibody absorption (FTA-ABS) test, a more sensitive blood test, is usually used to confirm the presence of syphilis. If the screening test is negative, it may be repeated in several weeks to be sure an early infection was not missed.

If sores are present, a diagnosis may be made by obtaining a sample from an ulcer and examining it under a microscope against a special dark field. This darkfield examination, available in only a few clinics, may reveal the characteristic corkscrew-shaped organisms of syphilis.

Genital Herpes

There are 2 types of herpes simplex virus. Type 1 causes cold sores and fever blisters, usually in the mouth and around the lips. In women, type 2, or genital herpes, causes sores or blisters on the labia and around the rectum, as well as in the vagina and on the cervix. There is often watery discharge and pain during urination. In the first episode, there may also be low-grade fever, headache, generalized muscle ache, and tender, swollen lymph nodes in the groin. The entire episode lasts about 3 weeks.

Once begun, the disease usually comes and goes in sporadic outbreaks of lesions that may vary from a slight red bump to clusters of blisters. Although there is no drug that cures an infection, acyclovir lotion applied to the blisters helps relieve the pain and may reduce the period during which the virus is contagious.

A woman who contracts herpes for the first time during the early weeks of pregnancy has a greater chance of spontaneous abortion than an unaffected woman. The first infection is usually more virulent than recurrent episodes and is therefore more dangerous to the fetus.

If the herpes is inactive at the time of vaginal delivery, the child will not contract the disease. A child born at the time the mother has an active episode of herpes, however, has a 50 percent chance of contracting the disease as it passes through the birth canal. A child who contracts herpes during delivery has a significant chance of brain damage, blindness, or death. If a pregnant woman knows she has herpes, careful observation, appropriate blood tests, and cesarean delivery may prevent the virus from being passed on to the child.

To avoid unnecessary cesarean delivery, any pregnant woman who has ever had genital herpes should be carefully examined as she approaches term. Her physician should perform a weekly culture during the last period of her pregnancy. If symptoms appear, a cesarean delivery can be performed. Unfortunately, these precautions are not foolproof. The most reliable test for herpes is a culture, a process that usually takes 7 to 10 days to complete. In that time, an inactive herpes lesion may erupt. To avoid such a possibility, some physicians recommend cesarean delivery for any woman who has a history of herpes virus infection. Recent data, however, show that it is *not* necessary to deliver asymptomatic patients by cesarean who had a positive herpes culture from before.

AIDS

THE RAPID SPREAD of autoimmune deficiency syndrome, or AIDS, in certain high-risk groups has led to difficult questions of when to test for the disease. Studies to date have found that about half of the babies born to mothers who carry the AIDS virus either have the disease or evidence that they, too, harbor the virus. The disease is particularly tragic when it occurs in an infant; thus doctors are recommending that women be tested for presence of AIDS antibodies if there is any chance that they may have been exposed to the virus. Women who are at high risk include:

- Intravenous drug users
- Any women whose sexual partner is an intravenous drug user or bisexual

● Prostitutes or women who have had sexual partners with AIDS or whose background may not be known to them

● Women who had blood transfusions before 1985, or before blood was routinely tested for AIDS antibodies

PERIODIC PRENATAL CHECKUPS

EACH PRENATAL CHECKUP that follows the initial visit includes the same routine tests, whether they are carried out in a hospital clinic or doctor's office. (See table 8.2.) At each visit the mother's blood pressure is recorded and her urine tested. These routine tests are performed primarily to avoid problems.

Urinalysis. Routine urinalysis will pick up any traces of glucose, protein, or white blood cells, which might indicate developing gestational diabetes, urinary tract infection, or any tendency to develop pre-

eclampsia. (See chapter 14, Complications in Pregnancy.)

Blood Pressure. During pregnancy some women's blood pressure is always slightly above their normal prepregnant level. Other women may have a temporary rise caused by mild anxiety on the day of the prenatal visit. These fluctuations are usually not reason for concern. An elevated blood pressure may, however, be a sign of impending preeclampsia, and it is to guard against development of this complication that blood pressure is carefully monitored throughout pregnancy.

Although gestational diabetes and preeclampsia usually do not appear until the later months of pregnancy, early testing gives the obstetrician a standard against which to measure subsequent test results.

Weight. The mother's weight is also recorded on each visit. The total weight gain during pregnancy correlates with the size of the fetus. Most physicians like to see a weight gain of between 20 and 25 pounds. Ideally, a woman should gain weight steadily throughout the pregnancy, rather than in spurts: about 1½ to 3 pounds during the first 3 months; 1 pound every 9 days after that. A sudden,

---

Table 8.2
SUBSEQUENT VISITS

The following tests are standard for each prenatal visit:

● Urinalysis

● Weight

● Blood pressure

● Examination for edema

● Examination of the abdomen for size of uterus

● Presentation of baby

● Fetal heart sounds

excessive weight gain without a change in eating habits is another sign of preeclampsia. (For more information, see chapter 9, Nutrition During Pregnancy.)

Edema. Any obvious signs of fluid retention anywhere in the body will also be noted at each visit. Some slight edema is normal during pregnancy, particularly in the third trimester. But excessive fluid retention, along with other important symptoms—rapid weight gain and high blood pressure—suggests preeclampsia.

Fetal Heartbeat. The physician or midwife also listens for the baby's heartbeat. The fetal heartbeat can be heard from about week 24 of pregnancy with a standard stethoscope, as early as week 10 or 12 with an electronic instrument. A healthy heartbeat varies from minute to minute throughout pregnancy and ranges from 120 to 160 beats per minute. There is no truth to the old wives' tale that a fetal heart rate above 140 beats per minute means the fetus is a girl, while one below 140 represents a boy.

Blood Tests. During the course of pregnancy, blood tests are carried out for anemia and for antibody detection if the mother is Rh negative and her partner is Rh positive. At about 16 weeks, blood is usually tested for the alpha fetoprotein level.

Abdominal Examination

At each prenatal visit the obstetrician examines the mother's abdomen to assess the height of the fundus (base) of the uterus and determine the position of the baby. The height of the top of the uterus is recorded.

By week 12 of pregnancy, the top of the uterus can be felt in the abdomen, just above the pubic bone. It enlarges at a regular rate (approximately 3 centimeters each month) until it reaches the umbilicus at about week 20 and is just below the lower end of the breast bone at 38 weeks.

A uterus that is growing faster than normal may indicate the presence of twins or a very large baby, while a uterus smaller than expected according to the date it is measured may indicate problems of fetal growth. During the last 3 or 4 weeks the uterine height may suddenly decrease by a few centimeters when the baby's head drops into the mother's pelvis.

During the abdominal examination the doctor uses first 1 hand, then both, to feel the fetus's position by pressing gently around it. At the same time, the doctor tries to feel the fetus move. The abdominal examination gives the doctor a lot of information about the baby, including size, position, and, from week 38, whether the head is engaged. It also gives an idea as to whether the mother's pelvis will be large enough for a vaginal delivery.

Presentation

Throughout the third trimester, the growth of the baby is very important. Beginning around week 26 the obstetrician will carefully observe the presentation of the baby on each prenatal visit.

Most babies adopt a longitudinal lie, with head or buttocks pointing toward the cervix. About 96 percent of babies adopt a head-down (vertex or cephalic) presentation, which is the easiest and safest way of delivery. The uterus is wide at the top, and so a baby in the cephalic presentation has more room for its legs and buttocks. A baby that is in another presentation may pose a more difficult delivery.

Breech Presentation. At week 32 of pregnancy, about 25 percent of all babies present buttocks first (breech). However, most of these babies turn themselves around naturally by week 38, and only about 3 percent of babies born at term are in breech presentation. Breech presentations are much more common in premature births.

A breech presentation does not necessarily require a cesarean delivery, but vaginal delivery will need experienced medical personnel and careful supervision. If the baby has not turned naturally by week 38, the doctor may try to turn the baby from the outside, a maneuver called external cephalic version. This maneuver must be done by a skilled person because there is the risk that the placenta will separate from the uterine wall. At times, uterine-relaxing agents (such as ritodrine) may be necessary to facilitate this procedure.

If the doctor attempts to turn the baby, the woman will be asked to lie on the examination table with her knees slightly bent and her abdominal muscles relaxed. Medication is sometimes given to relax the muscles in the wall of the uterus. The doctor then uses both hands to exert gentle pressure on the baby's body. If the turning is successful, a normal vaginal delivery can follow. Often, however, the baby will return to the breech position. If the procedure is not successful, it may indicate that the pelvis is small for the size of the baby or that there is a malformation of the uterus.

Transverse Lie. If the baby lies obliquely in the uterus, the part that presents to the cervix is usually the shoulder. This occurs in about 1 in every 500 labors. If this sideways lie persists in labor, a cesarean section is required. (See chapter 15, Labor and Delivery.)

These are the basics of each prenatal visit. Perhaps the most important element is the personal rapport between doctor and mother. The mother will always be asked how she is feeling, and these visits are the time to mention any physical problems. Equally important, they provide an opportunity for the mother to discuss any worries or anxieties she may have about the pregnancy.

ADDITIONAL TESTING POINTS DURING PREGNANCY

As a PREGNANCY develops, additional tests may be performed at certain critical points:

At 16 weeks, an alpha fetoprotein (AFP) test is carried out on a routine blood sample. If indicated, ultrasound scan and amniocentesis may also be performed at 16 weeks.

At 26 weeks (approximately) a glucose challenge test (GCT) routinely is recommended to detect gestational diabetes. If the mother is at high risk for this disease the test may be performed earlier, at 16 weeks. It may also be used at any time during the pregnancy that a urine sample is found to contain sugar.

If the test is abnormal, a more definitive test, the glucose tolerance test (GTT) is performed. This test, which requires eating well for 3 days and then fasting overnight preceding the test, measures the body's response to a large dose of sugar (glucose). Fasting blood and urine samples are taken to establish a baseline; then the woman is asked to drink a concentrated sugar solution. Additional blood and urine samples are then taken at regular intervals over the next 3 to 5 hours, and glucose levels measured. High levels of glucose in urine or blood are associated with diabetes.

At week 32, blood counts may be repeated to make sure that iron intake is sufficient. Also around week 32 a cervical culture may be repeated if the mother has excessive vaginal discharge or a history of premature labor.

Between weeks 30 and 36, the mode of delivery can usually be determined.

Between 36 and 38 weeks, the pelvic examination is repeated to confirm the presentation of the baby, in order to determine if the baby's head has dropped and if the pelvis is adequate.

AN EXPLANATION OF SPECIAL TESTS*

PRENATAL TESTING can detect many, although unfortunately not all or even most, birth defects. In the future, however, surgeons may be able to correct birth defects while the fetus is still developing in the uterus. The most common prenatal tests performed today are ultrasound and amniocentesis. Other new tests, such as chorionic villus biopsy and cordocentesis (see following sections) are even more promising for the future.

Alpha Fetoprotein Testing

Alpha fetoprotein (AFP) is a protein that is produced by the baby's liver and then passed into the mother's blood via the

---

* Some of these tests reveal the baby's sex. Women undergoing these procedures should tell their doctors beforehand if they do not wish to learn the baby's sex in advance. Further, a primary reason for testing is to offer the parents the option of abortion if the results show that the fetus has a serious anomaly. If a couple would not choose to have an abortion no matter what the results, they must consider whether it would be appropriate to have the test.

placenta. When a woman is about 16 weeks pregnant, the AFP level in her blood can be measured by a routine blood sample. A certain level of the protein in the blood is a sign that the fetus is developing normally, but a high or low level suggests a number of possible problems. An abnormally low level of AFP in the mother's blood may indicate Down syndrome. A high level may be a sign of a threatened abortion, or it may indicate that the mother is carrying twins. A very high level of AFP may warn of a gap in the baby's skin that exposes blood vessels (neural-tube defects such as spina bifida, "open spine") or an obstruction in the gastrointestinal tract of the fetus). Detection of open neural tube defects is the primary reason for measuring the AFP level.

Alpha fetoprotein is most accurately measured between weeks 16 and 19 of pregnancy. The accuracy of the test can vary, however, and an abnormal level does not necessarily mean a baby is abnormal. If the level is high, the reading is confirmed by repeating the test. If the second test is also abnormal, the fetus may be examined with an ultrasound scan, which can detect gross abnormalities. If it is low, amniocentesis (which measures the protein level in the amniotic fluid surrounding the baby) is recommended to rule out chromosonal anomalies, such as Down syndrome. Together, these tests can detect about 85 percent of all babies with spina bifida.

X Rays

Although X rays should be avoided whenever possible during pregnancy, they are sometimes necessary to determine if a mother's pelvis is large enough to allow a vaginal birth in case of breech presentation at term.

Ultrasound Scans

An ultrasound scan uses pulsed sound waves that vibrate at high frequencies to obtain a picture of what is happening under water or inside a structure. When directed into the uterus, the sound waves bounce off the baby's bones and other tissues; the echoes are converted into an image, called a sonogram, that builds up on a television monitor.

This simple procedure usually takes only a few minutes. The pregnant woman's abdomen is covered with a thin film of jelly or oil and the radiographer passes a small device, called a transducer, back and forth across the abdomen. An image appears on the screen that, as the fetus moves, can be identified even by the untrained observer.

Ultrasound, which does not involve X rays, is considered a safe procedure. Although some physicians recommend that all pregnant women have an ultrasound scan to detect malformations in the fetus, the incidence of malformations is 1 in 1,000. Although there has been scattered speculation about potential harm to the fetus, this has not been established. Therefore, the American College of Obstetricians and Gynecologists recommends ultrasound to assess the overall condition of the pregnancy only if any of the following risk factors are present:

• If the size of the fetus does not correspond to the stage of the pregnancy (if the uterus is much larger or much smaller for the number of weeks)

• If the woman has not been followed closely through pregnancy

• If a previous child was born with malformations

Ultrasound can:

• Show the position and viability of the fetus

• Reveal any severe abnormalities, such as spina bifida, and malformations of the brain, heart, kidneys, or bowel

• Detect multiple pregnancies

• Monitor fetal growth later in pregnancy to determine if the baby requires early delivery

• Sometimes determine baby's sex if at risk to inherit sex-linked disease

• Assist 2 other prenatal diagnostic tests, amniocentesis and fetoscopy, by showing the position of the fetus.

Amniocentesis

There are 2 major uses of amniocentesis. It may be performed early in pregnancy (16 weeks) to detect some birth defects or later in pregnancy to establish the maturity of the fetus and help in the management of a problem pregnancy.

Amniocentesis is recommended to assess fetal health in the following circumstances:

• When the mother is over age 35

• When alpha fetoprotein levels are abnormal

• When family history reveals risk of certain severe birth defects or metabolic disorders

• When a premature delivery is anticipated

Amniocentesis is most often used to detect Down syndrome when the mother is over age 35, but the test can also detect structural defects such as spina bifida and anencephaly (incomplete development of the brain). More than 100 different biochemical tests also can be carried out on the fluid sample to detect rare inherited metabolic disorders.

Unfortunately, many of the most common birth defects, such as congenital heart disorders, cleft lip and palate, and certain types of mental retardation, cannot be diagnosed by this test. For the average couple without known risk factors, it is unlikely that amniocentesis would detect a serious birth defect. Because there is a risk from the procedure itself, as well as considerable expense ($600 to $900 for the procedure and full evaluation), amniocentesis is reserved for couples known to be at risk for specific genetic disorders.

Amniocentesis may be recommended for a woman in whom a premature delivery is anticipated. The procedure can assess the maturity of the baby's lungs and help determine whether it is mature enough to survive. If the membranes rupture prematurely, amniocentesis also can be used to determine if an infection has reached the amniotic fluid. When a Rh-negative mother is carrying an Rh-positive baby, amniocentesis may be performed at intervals during the last half of pregnancy to determine whether the Rh incompatibility is affecting the baby and whether early delivery is required. The cost of amniocentesis for problem pregnancies is considerably less (between $125 and $200) because extensive laboratory analysis is not required.

The Procedure. Amniocentesis takes only 15 to 20 minutes to perform, but additional time is necessary for preparation and recovery. The procedure involves removing a small amount of the fluid from the amniotic sac surrounding the fetus. Between weeks 14 and 18 of pregnancy the amniotic sac contains about 250 milliliters (ml) of fluid, so that a small amount (20 to 30 ml or 1 to 2 tablespoons) removed is not significant and is quickly replaced.

Amniocentesis is generally a very safe procedure. There is a slight chance of triggering a spontaneous abortion and a slight possibility of introducing an infection or injuring the fetus. Ultrasound is used to monitor continuously throughout the procedure so that the needle can be inserted in a safe location; the fetus usually floats away from the needle tip.

The mother is given a local anesthetic that renders the procedure painless; the physician then inserts a long, thin needle through the abdomen into the amniotic sac and withdraws a small amount of fluid. (See figure 8.1.) After amniocentesis, the fetus is again examined by ultrasound to guarantee that the baby is unaffected.

Amniotic Fluid. The amniotic fluid, contained within the amniotic sac that surrounds the baby from early development, protects the fetus from shocks and allows unhindered growth and free movement, at least in the early months. Amniotic fluid also maintains the fetus at a constant temperature and equalizes the pressure exerted by uterine contractions. It discourages the growth of bacteria and guards against infection. The fetus excretes urine into the fluid and also swallows some of the fluid. The fluid is not static, but flows freely between the mother and the fetus via the placenta.

Amniotic fluid makes an ideal testing medium because it contains fetal cells, as well as protein, fats, enzymes, carbohydrates, hormones, and fetal urine. Cells in the fluid are cultured in a laboratory, and the cells are carefully analyzed to look for the proper number and arrangement of chromosomes. The fluid is also tested for various chemicals. In addition to certain birth defects, the examination of the cells reveals the baby's sex, which is important if there is a family history of sex-linked disorders such as hemophilia or muscular dystrophy.

The disadvantage of amniocentesis is that it cannot be performed until between weeks 14 and 16 of pregnancy, and it usually takes 2 to 4 weeks for the laboratory analysis to be completed.

Fortunately, in over 95 percent of cases the results of such testing show no abnormalities and the parents can proceed with the pregnancy without undue anxiety. Because only a few disorders can be detected, however, a normal amniocentesis does not guarantee a normal child.

Chorionic Villus Sampling

The prime advantage of this relatively new test, chorionic villus sampling (CVS),

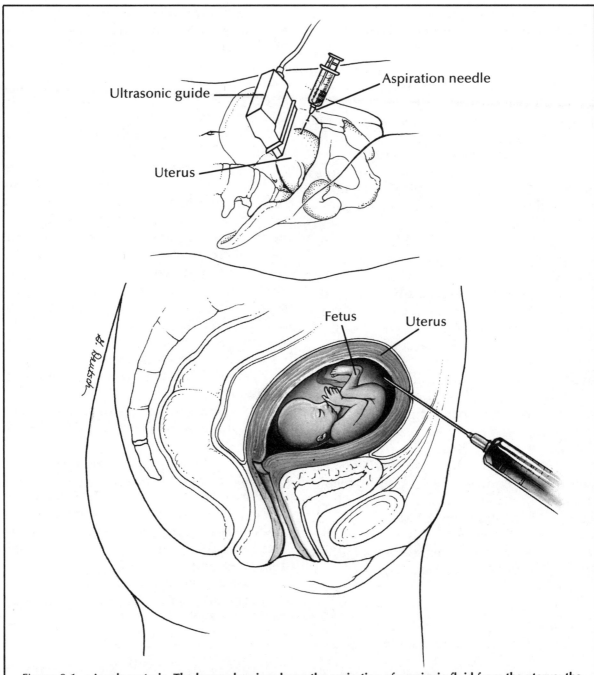

Figure 8.1. **Amniocentesis. The larger drawing shows the aspiration of amnionic fluid from the uterus; the smaller drawing shows the ultrasonic guide that is used to make sure that the fetus is not harmed.**

is its speed. The test (sometimes called chorionic villus biopsy) can detect birth defects between weeks 8 and 12 of pregnancy, much earlier than amniocentesis. Preliminary results, which will reveal the presence of Down syndrome, are available within 48 hours; a more thorough analysis, comparable to that offered by amniocentesis, takes 2 weeks.

Early test results mean that if a woman chooses to have an abortion she can do so in the first trimester. (An abortion after amniocentesis would take place in the second trimester, when there are more potential complications.)

The disadvantage of villus sampling is that it carries a higher risk of miscarriage, between 1 and 2 percent, with some researchers putting it as high as 8 percent. Amniocentesis has a risk of 0.02 to 0.05 percent. However, wide-scale testing has not yet been completed, and physicians have not had as much experience with it as they have with amniocentesis. Another disadvantage is that it is not as comprehensive a test as amniocentesis and must be supplemented by an alpha fetoprotein test. If the protein level is high, amniocentesis may be recommended.

Chorionic villus sampling, which takes about 20 minutes to perform, does not require an abdominal incision. A thin tube (catheter) is introduced into the mother's cervix under ultrasound guidance. The physician then gently aspirates (withdraws) a small sample of the tissue from the finger-shaped protrusions (villi) on the chorionic plate, the tissue that will ultimately become the placenta.

Although the tissue does not actually touch the fetus, it does contain fetal cells. Analyzing the tissue gives the same information as amniocentesis, including the gender of the fetus, and appears to offer the same degree of accuracy.

Only a few hospitals around the nation offer chorionic villus sampling but, depending on the results of long-term studies, within the next several years many more hospitals may offer this test as an alternative to amniocentesis.

Cordocentesis

Cordocentesis, also called percutaneous umbilical cord sampling (PUBS), is a relatively new procedure available only on a limited basis in major medical centers. It has replaced fetoscopy as a testing method. Cordocentesis is used if there is a known risk of a severe genetic blood disorder, such as sickle-cell anemia, thalassemia, or hemophilia, and rapid evaluation of fetal chromosomes is needed.

As with amniocentesis, a woman usually receives a local anesthetic before cordocentesis is carried out. Under ultrasound guidance, the physician inserts a thin needle into the abdomen and withdraws a small sample of blood from the umbilical cord. The blood cells can then be tested for the presence of disorders.

In Utero Surgery

Only rarely can a problem in the fetus be corrected while it is still developing in the womb. Two important operations can be carried out on the fetus: blood transfusions for a severely anemic fetus (as happens when an Rh-positive baby receives Rh antibodies from an Rh-negative mother), and catheterization to help a fetus suffering from a blocked urinary tract.

A blocked urinary tract, discovered by ultrasound scan, is usually a developmental problem. Such blockages cause a buildup of urine in the bladder, which can lead to irreparable kidney damage. Surgery is carried out by threading a fine catheter through the mother's uterus into the bladder of the fetus. The fetal urine can then drain into the amniotic fluid as it should. The catheter remains in place until after the baby is born. After delivery, the tube is removed and the blockage corrected by surgery.

Unfortunately, not every fetus with a blocked urinary tract will benefit from this type of in utero surgery and the major problem is to select those who will. In the future many more life-threatening birth defects may be corrected in utero.

PREPARED CHILDBIRTH CLASSES

PREPARED CHILDBIRTH CLASSES usually begin in the third trimester of pregnancy. Their goal is to familiarize both partners with the sequence of events of normal labor, so they will know what to expect when labor begins. The mother will learn how she can help herself during the various phases and her partner will learn how to help her.

The wide variety of available classes means that a couple needs to take time to explore ahead of time so that they will be able to reserve a place in the class of their choice. Couples should try to make this choice and reserve a place by the end of the first trimester.

A couple should look for a program that offers a balanced approach and discusses many different childbirth options. Some childbirth classes teach a specific point of view, to the exclusion of other options. A good class provides a medical view and considers a woman's emotional needs. It is educational in tone, inviting couples to ask questions and share their feelings and concerns. It should stress that every labor is different and every individual is different.

Although some classes offer different techniques, such as the Bradley method, most classes incorporate various breathing and relaxation techniques into a generalized program based on the Lamaze method. The class should be practical as well as theoretical. The teacher should give basic information about the physiological changes of pregnancy, explain about different modes of delivery, anesthesia, and pain relief, and include open discussions about various childbirth and hospital procedures. Specific medical interventions such as episiotomy and cesarean sections should be described; both partners should know what kind of medical response to expect if complications arise during labor or delivery. Ideally, time should be set aside at the end of the course for instruction on breastfeeding and bottle-feeding.

Regardless of the kind of obstetrical care a couple has chosen, learning more about pregnancy, as well as different ways of coping with labor and birth, is beneficial. Even those who have been through the process before will want to know about any changes in obstetric procedures since their last baby was born. Prepared childbirth classes also give couples the opportunity to meet other prospective parents with whom they can discuss their anxieties, plans, and hopes.

Prepared childbirth classes are based on the principle that education minimizes fear, which normally creates physical tension and thus makes pain worse. This observation was first made in the 1920s by Dr. Grantly Dick-Read, an English physician who developed the earliest theories of natural childbirth. Dr. Dick-Read observed hundreds of women in labor and noted that women who had not acquired a fear of labor did not experience the pain normally associated with childbirth. Frightened women appeared to suffer more.

Dr. Dick-Read believed that fear could be eliminated by simple instruction, but he did not claim that childbirth was pain free or that medication did not have a place in complicated labor. His approach became popular in Britain and the United States, but in the 1950s was gradually superseded by the Lamaze method.

French physician Dr. Fernand Lamaze based his technique on the Pavlovian principle of conditioned response. Lamaze observed that the whole body instinc-

tively tenses during a labor contraction. With training, however, a woman can learn to relax the rest of her body when a contraction occurs. This deliberate relaxing minimizes residual tension throughout the body, making subsequent contractions less painful. The Lamaze method emphasizes the active participation of the mother and her partner in a sequence of trained responses.

More recently the Bradley method, with even more emphasis on the intimate participation of the husband in all phases of the pregnancy and birth, has become popular. Over an extensive 6-month course a pregnant woman and her partner are taught to recognize any sign of tension in her body and how to eliminate it by touch and massage techniques.

Although the emphasis is on being awake and aware during this significant life experience, prepared childbirth is not necessarily "painless" childbirth, nor is a woman expected to go through labor and delivery without medication or medical help. Training techniques rarely abolish pain completely, nor are they equally effective for everyone. The ability to cope with pain varies considerably from person to person, as does the intensity and duration of pain itself.

In most classes, pain relief medications are fully described and are regarded as tools to aid labor. Again, good preparation is knowing what options are available. Most teachers of prepared childbirth classes advise that no matter how much a woman wants to remain in control, she should never be ashamed to ask for or to accept pain relief when she feels the pain is more than she can tolerate. In extreme versions of prepared childbirth classes women are made to feel they have failed if they ask for help. Excessive anxiety and stress during labor and delivery can sometimes be worse than the possible side effects of medication.

Prepared childbirth classes may be offered by a hospital, a community organization, such as the YMCA/YWCA or by individual instructors. The teacher is often an obstetrical nurse, although this is not necessary. She should, however, provide details about her qualifications and experience. If a couple is uncertain about the kind of class they want, they can ask individual instructors to let them observe a class.

Classes are usually limited to 10 couples or fewer. Most 2-hour classes meet once a week for 6 weeks. Sometimes, early classes are offered (in the first trimester) to help couples deal with the physical changes and emotional adjustments of pregnancy.

Every prepared childbirth class should be a shared experience, with everyone having a chance to participate. Ideally, the teacher will guide discussions and offer an all-around, unbiased insight into childbirth and parenthood.

The Labor Companion

A basic tenet of prepared childbirth classes is developing a close working relationship between partners. The childbirth partner fulfills a crucial role, providing companionship, comfort, and support for the mother during labor, and also acting as her advocate before hospital and medical personnel. The exercises learned during class are the tools the partner uses to sustain the mother during labor and delivery.

The labor partner is usually, but not always, the baby's father. If the father will not be the partner, the woman should choose a labor companion early in pregnancy. She may want to ask her mother or sister or a close friend, male or female, to be her companion. Whoever she chooses should attend the childbirth classes with her and be willing to learn the breathing techniques. The labor partner should also be free to be with her on a moment's notice as the time for labor approaches.

Even if a woman does not have a labor partner available, she should consider taking prepared childbirth classes. She will find the information helpful and most instructors will be willing to act as a partner during class. During the birth itself, the obstetrical nurse will generally serve as her coach.

Despite well-made plans, there is always the possibility of unexpected, last-minute circumstances that prevent the labor partner from participating in the birthing experience. Every woman should be prepared for this possibility and feel confident that she will be able to manage with the help of health care professionals attending the birth. (For more information, see chapter 15, Labor and Delivery.)

9 Nutrition During Pregnancy

Mary Ann Jonaitis, R.N., M.Ed.

INTRODUCTION

GOOD MATERNAL NUTRITION helps ensure the best possible physical and mental development of the fetus—and builds up the woman's reserves for labor, delivery, and breastfeeding later on. Doing all the eating for her growing fetus as well as herself, the woman should seek out a variety of foods of high quality, not just quantity. Ideally, the woman's concentration on good eating starts even before her pregnancy.

159

NUTRITION BEFORE CONCEPTION

A WOMAN SHOULD take a careful look at her weight and overall nutrition while she is still only planning to have a baby—at least 2 or 3 months before conception, if at all possible and, ideally, during all of her reproductive years. Nutrition has many effects on health: Indeed, malnourishment is one cause of infertility.

Anyone contemplating pregnancy may want to have her nutritional status evaluated professionally before adjusting it. (If so, she may ask her physician, the local chapter of the American Dietetic Association, or her state or local health department or Cooperative Extension Program for a referral to a maternal nutritionist.) Through analysis of diet records, a maternal nutritionist can calculate the intake of nutrients.

There are 2 main reasons for getting an early start on nutrition for pregnancy: establishing good eating habits and getting close to optimal weight. (See chapter 1, Planning Your Pregnancy.)

Breaking Bad Habits

The earlier a woman attempts to establish good eating habits—and break bad ones—the better chance she has of maintaining high-quality nutrition throughout the pregnancy and beyond it. The good habits should not stop at delivery. For many women, pregnancy is just the start of a healthier lifestyle that they enjoy for the rest of their lives.

The goals of nutrition before, during,

and after pregnancy are familiar from everyday dietary precepts: eating a varied, well-balanced diet that includes a variety of foods from all 4 food groups. Ideally, about 55 percent of calories should come from complex carbohydrates, with emphasis on fresh fruits and vegetables, starches, and whole-grain cereals and breads. About 30 percent should come from fats, mostly polyunsaturated and monounsaturated (vegetable sources), instead of saturated or hardened fats (animal sources, palm and coconut oil). The remaining 15 percent should come from protein, both animal and vegetable.

A person who has already established these sound eating habits will not have much to change. However, while planning her pregnancy, she will also want to start curtailing her intake of alcohol and caffeine, and eliminate tobacco if she smokes. An early start is worth it, because powerful dependencies on these substances can take a long time to break. Also, adverse effects of nicotine on the fetus may linger even up to a year after quitting cigarette smoking.

Achieving Ideal Weight

Before conceiving, strive to get within the normal range of weight for height and bone structure. (See table 9.1.) If you conceive while your weight is within the normal range, you will feel more free to gain the weight needed for pregnancy.

Women who are significantly underweight or overweight at conception face several problems. In either instance, achieving pregnancy may be more difficult, because weight extremes can interfere with ovulation and hormonal balance. A woman who starts pregnancy underweight has a great deal of catching up to do. To nourish the fetus adequately, she may be advised to gain enough to meet her ideal body weight—*plus* the 24 to 28 pounds usually advised for pregnancy. Gaining that much weight over a 9-month period can be daunting, especially for someone with a skewed body image, for instance, someone who sees herself as fat, no matter how thin she is. Stressing that the additional nutrients are needed for baby as well as mother is less threatening than focusing on counting calories. With an early start (before conception), the weight gain becomes more manageable.

An overweight woman who fails to lose much weight before conceiving should still gain weight during pregnancy. But being overweight places her at higher risk of developing high blood pressure and gestational diabetes. Her baby may be born quite large for postconcep-

Table 9.1
STANDARD WEIGHTS FOR HEIGHT AND FRAME

This 1983 Metropolitan Life Insurance table shows desirable weight by height and size of frame, for women 25 to 59 years old, wearing 3 pounds of clothing and shoes with 1-inch heels.

Height	Small Frame	Medium Frame	Large Frame
4'10"	102–111	109–121	118–131
4'11"	103–113	111–123	120–134
5'0"	104–115	113–126	122–137
5'1"	106–118	115–129	125–140
5'2"	108–121	118–132	128–143
5'3"	111–124	121–135	131–147
5'4"	114–127	124–138	134–151
5'5"	117–130	127–141	137–155
5'6"	120–133	130–144	140–159
5'7"	123–136	133–147	143–163
5'8"	126–139	136–150	146–167
5'9"	129–142	139–153	149–170
5'10"	132–145	142–158	152–173
5'11"	135–148	145–159	155–176
6'0"	138–151	148–162	158–179

tual age (macrosomic), complicating the delivery and sometimes necessitating a cesarean section. The outcome may not be as favorable if she limits her weight gain during pregnancy: The fetus may actually be malnourished, although the woman started pregnancy overweight. (See chapter 14, Complications in Pregnancy.)

HOW MUCH TO GAIN

DURING THE PAST 20 YEARS, several careful studies have shown that insufficient weight gain during pregnancy raises the risks of a variety of problems—not just while the fetus is still in the womb, but also during and after birth. Specifically, the baby may be born underweight for postconceptual age (time elapsed since conception). Low birth weight remains the single factor linked most closely to infant death and illness.

Accordingly, the pendulum of opinion has swung from smaller babies of 6 to 7 pounds to babies of 7½ or 8 pounds made possible by greater maternal weight gain (of 24 to 28 pounds) and associated with the most favorable infant outcomes. This recommended gain works out to about 3 to 4 pounds per month—¾ of a pound to 1 pound per week—of pregnancy after the first trimester. However, women should not be alarmed if they do not gain weight precisely at this rate. Remember, these are averages. Instead, weight gain often accelerates as the pregnancy proceeds: During the whole first trimester, many women put on only about 2 or 3 pounds or may even lose weight, and then gain 3 to 5 pounds a month. Rates of gain are also important and episodes of rapid gain or weight loss should be evaluated. (See table 9.2 and figure 9.1.)

Gaining the 24 to 28 pounds corresponds to eating an extra 80,000 calories' worth of food throughout 266 days of pregnancy—or an average of about 300

Table 9.2
NORMAL RANGES OF WEIGHT GAIN

Number of Weeks of Pregnancy	Low Side of Normal Weight Gain	High Side of Normal Weight Gain
12	2	4
16	4	8
20	7	13
24	10	18
28	13	23
30	14	25
32	16	27
34	17	30
36	18	32
37	19	33
38	20	34
39	20.5	35
40	21	more than 35

Figure 9.1. **Normal range of weight gain. (A) Suggested minimum weight gain for underweight women. (B) Gain for women near ideal weight. (C) Gain for overweight women.**

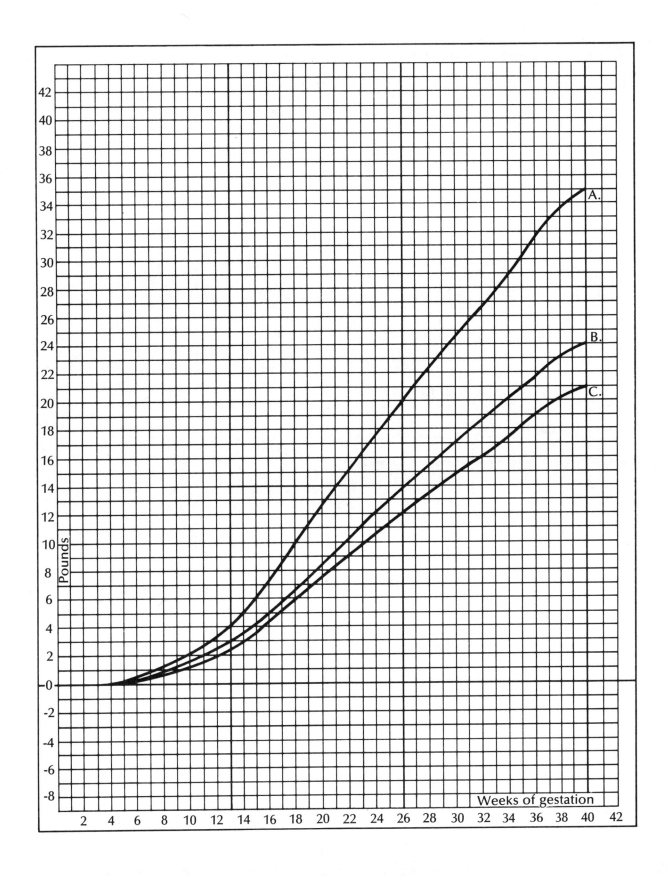

extra calories a day over prepregnancy intake. Like weight gain, calorie intake tends to rise during pregnancy: usually an average of approximately 150 extra calories a day in the first trimester and 350 extra calories a day during the second and third trimesters—or more if the woman is quite active physically. (See table 9.3.)

Fetal and Maternal Needs

It is worthwhile to reflect that the woman's diet is responsible not only for preparing her for childbirth and breastfeeding but also for fueling all the changes that the fetus goes through in the womb—from single cell to fully formed baby. (For more of this concrete evidence of the importance of maternal nutrition, see chapter 12, The Developing Fetus.)

During the second and third trimesters, fetal growth demands more calories, which are provided by an increase in the *quantity* of food consumed. However, there is no reason to alter the *quality* of the food—assuming a balanced diet—as pregnancy progresses through its 3 major stages.

First Trimester. During the first 3 months (or 12 to 13 weeks) of pregnancy, almost all of the fetus's organ systems are formed, but growth to this point has been limited. By week 13, the fetus is only 3 inches long, weighing a mere 1 ounce. The mother may have only gained 2 or 3 pounds (mostly in the third month)—or even less if morning sickness has been a problem.

Second Trimester. In the fourth through sixth months (weeks 14 to 26) of pregnancy, the fetus grows to a height of 14 inches and a weight of 1½ pounds. The woman gains weight at a faster rate— about 3 or 4 pounds per month.

Third Trimester. During the seventh through ninth months (weeks 27 to 38) of pregnancy, the fetus has a 5-fold weight increase, growing to birth weight (about 7½ to 8 pounds, on average)—with an average length of 19 to 20 inches. Weight gain continues at about 3 or 4 pounds per month.

Maternal Stores. Less than half of the weight gained during pregnancy goes directly to the fetus and supporting tissues such as the placenta and amniotic fluid.

Table 9.3
CALORIE INTAKE

**Calorie intake =
acceptable
weight
(pounds)**
$$\begin{cases} \times\, 10 \text{ for light activity} \\ \times\, 15 \text{ for moderate} \\ \qquad \text{activity} \\ \times\, 20 \text{ for heavy activity} \end{cases}$$
$$\begin{cases} -\,0 \text{ (age 25 to 34)} \\ -\,100 \text{ (age 35 to 44)} \end{cases}$$

Then add 300 calories for pregnancy or 500 calories for breastfeeding. For example, a pregnant, moderately active, 37-year-old woman whose acceptable weight is 140 pounds:

[140 pounds × 15 (for moderate activity)] − 100 (for age 35 to 44) + 300 (for pregnancy) = 2,300 calories

Most of the weight is needed for the mother's increased volume of blood and fluid, the enlargement of the uterus and breasts, and fat and protein stores. Most of the maternal fat deposited by the time of delivery is earmarked for energy reserves for breastfeeding. (See table 9.4.)

During pregnancy, the volume of circulating blood rises by about 50 percent, increasing cardiac output (the amount of blood that the heart pumps) and blood flow to the uterus and placenta. Blood volume expands primarily through an increase in plasma, the liquid part of the circulating blood. But there is also a 25 percent rise in the mass of red blood cells, which contain the iron-rich, oxygen-carrying molecule hemoglobin. If a woman does not consume enough extra calories (or nutrients), the volume of the blood does not increase adequately; not

enough blood goes to the placenta, the fetus does not receive adequate nutrition from the mother, and fetal growth is shortchanged.

Overweight Women

Pregnancy is simply no time for weight loss. Even if a woman does not manage to get into her standard weight range before conception, thus starting pregnancy overweight, she should still gain weight during pregnancy. This holds true no matter how obese she is at conception. Any weight reduction regimen she has been following should be cut short as soon as she knows she is pregnant. Fetuses need access to nutrients from fresh food, and no amount of mobilized fat reserves will nourish them adequately. Indeed, burning stored fat can release large amounts of harmful chemicals called ketones. In addition, polychlorinated biphenyls, (PCBs) and other toxic substances may be stored in body fat; breaking down this fat to nourish the fetus increases the risk of exposing the baby to these substances.

A massively overweight woman may, however, be advised to gain weight at a slightly slower rate than the average woman. (Morbidly obese women should seek dietary guidance from a maternal nutritionist.) Figure 9.1 shows a day-by-day suggested weight curve for obese pregnant women, which ends in a 21-pound gain. The reason is that an extremely overweight woman can produce a normal-weight infant by gaining somewhat less than the usually recommended 24 to 28 pounds.

Table 9.4
WHERE THE WEIGHT GOES

Average Weight Gain in Pregnancy (in Pounds)	
The baby	
Fetus	7.5
Placenta	1
Amniotic fluid	2
The mother	
Fat and protein stores	4–6
Increased fluid volume	1–3
Uterus	2.5
Breast enlargement	2
Increased blood volume	4
TOTAL	24 to 28

Underweight Women

If weight falls significantly below the ideal range for height and frame, the mother will have to eat particularly hearty meals, gaining weight at a fast clip throughout pregnancy; otherwise, she runs the risk of producing a baby of low birth weight. An underweight woman should gain up to her ideal weight—plus the usually recommended 24 to 28 pounds. Thus, if she is 10 pounds underweight at conception, she may be advised to gain at least 35 pounds during pregnancy. (See table 9.5.)

Younger Women

An expectant mother who is still young and growing herself needs more calories than an adult woman does. Many adolescents—especially those whose menarche (first menstrual period) occurred only recently—have not yet reached their full growth potential prior to conception. Therefore, it may take a greater weight gain—as much as 35 pounds—for a teenager to produce a baby of normal weight, especially if she is also underweight, than it does for someone in her 20s or 30s. Also, instead of the 4 or 5 daily servings of milk or other dairy products advised for most pregnant women, pregnant teenagers should have 6.

Older Women

There are no nutritional guidelines designed specifically for pregnant women over 35 years old. They should follow the standard nutritional advice, including

Table 9.5
IF YOU NEED TO GAIN MORE WEIGHT

If you continue to have trouble gaining weight after the third month of pregnancy, you may need to try some of the following suggestions:

- Eat 3 small meals with 3 between-meal snacks.
- Use whole milk for drinking and cooking (such as in puddings and cream soups).
- Add margarine, gravy, cheese, or cream sauces to potatoes and vegetables.
- Add nonfat dry milk to soup, gravy, and casseroles.
- Use more margarine, peanut butter, mayonaise, honey, or jam.
- Eat more bread, toast, pancakes, potatoes, tortillas, rice, and noodles.
- Eat more high-calorie nutritious desserts such as puddings, ice cream, malts, fruit sundaes, and yogurt.
- Cut down on coffee, tea, chocolate, and cola beverages.
- If you smoke, make every effort to quit.

gaining 24 to 28 pounds during pregnancy, unless they are underweight or overweight or have any chronic diseases. Individual nutritional counseling is needed for pregnancy complicated by chronic conditions such as high blood pressure, diabetes, and kidney disease, which entail special demands on nutrition.

Multiple Births

Of course, a mother who is carrying 2 or more fetuses will have to eat more than if she were carrying only 1, but precisely how much more has not been established. Various amounts have been proposed for twin pregnancy, including 500 to 600 calories more than usual pregnancy intake, or approximately 300 calories per fetus. Large, rapid gains are not uncommon and should not be viewed as harmful as long as other physical parameters—blood sugar levels, blood pressure, urinalysis, and vision—remain normal. The postpartum weight loss for these women usually occurs at an accelerated rate.

WHAT TO EAT

EVEN MORE IMPORTANT than gaining enough weight is choosing nourishing foods to eat during pregnancy. Like consuming too few calories, inadequate intake of nutrients prevents blood volume from expanding fully during pregnancy. Thus, not enough blood passes to the placenta.

The pregnant woman should try to avoid eating or drinking anything she would not want her fetus exposed to. Almost everything she consumes will cross the placenta and reach the fetus. The exceptions, which are extremely rare, are substances that have a high molecular weight (that is, they are made up of very large molecules) and are not broken down into smaller units that can cross the placenta.

Some drugs can interfere with absorption of certain nutrients, and vice versa. During pregnancy, all medications except those specifically recommended by the mother's doctor should be avoided. (See chapter 6, What Is Safe?)

General Nutrition Pointers

Standard guidelines for healthy eating should be followed throughout pregnancy, favoring fresh fruits and vegetables over processed, whole grains over refined, and baked, poached, or broiled over fried foods.

Pregnant on the Job. Many mothers go out to work throughout their pregnancies, and they may face special challenges when it comes to nutrition. However, with a little extra effort a pregnant working woman can eat well, especially if a refrigerator is available at her job site for storing snacks such as milk, hard-boiled eggs, cheese, and yogurt. Pregnancy is no time for habits such as skipping lunch or dinner in favor of working—or relying on donuts, candies, and other high-calorie, low-nutrient snacks. If the morning race out of the house means not eating breakfast at home, at least bring a peanut butter sandwich—or something else that contains protein, starch, and fat and not much sugar—to eat first thing at work, preventing the late-morning low-energy slump that would occur otherwise. (For more on working during pregnancy, see chapter 10, The Pregnant Lifestyle.)

Read the Fine Print. Many processed foods now carry labels that reveal their contents in detail, and it pays to read these labels carefully. The word "natural," for example, has little meaning, since almost all foods come from natural sources. The question is how much they have been processed and what has been added to them.

It is also a good idea to take into account the various motives of all the sources offering advice to pregnant women: For example, an admonition to drink lots of orange juice during pregnancy loses its authority when one notices that the source is a juice manufacturer. (Juice is preferable to soda, but fresh fruit, such as an orange, is even better. Fruit drinks, on the other hand, are highly processed and loaded with sugar.)

Milk. Each day during pregnancy, the equivalent of 4 or 5 dairy sources should be consumed. Assuming a woman has been eating a well-balanced diet before conception, including 2 glasses of milk a day, she can satisfy 2 of the most important dietary rules of pregnancy—adding 300 calories a day, and drinking at least 4 glasses of milk a day as well as substantially increasing protein intake—simply by adding 2 glasses of whole milk. Each glass of whole milk contains approximately 150 calories. To avoid consuming the entire 300 extra calories in a mere 2 glasses, switch to low-fat or skim milk. Compared with whole milk, skim milk offers a slight addition of calcium—and even more of vitamins A and D—but only about half of the calories, at 80 calories a glass. Milk is also a quality source of protein.

Some people cannot tolerate milk, because they are either partly or completely deficient in lactase, the enzyme needed to break down milk sugar, lactose. However, they may be able to digest other dairy products, such as cheese or yogurt, as well as milk that has been specially treated with lactase. Both the enzyme itself and a variety of lactase-treated milk products are now commercially available.

If a pregnant woman strongly dislikes the taste of milk, she may want to try flavoring it with chocolate. To balance out the extra calories from the chocolate, she should use low-fat or skim milk. Another suggestion may be the addition of skim milk powder to baked goods, pancakes, or casseroles. Calcium supplements should not be automatically used because they do not provide the vitamins A and D or protein found in calcium-rich foods.

Fat. There is a role for fat in the diet: In particular, milk fat may help the pregnant woman absorb vitamin D and calcium. However, the average American diet contains too much fat already—especially the saturated fats found in animal sources, coconut and palm oils, which have been implicated in heart disease. So there is no need to eat extra fat, provided the diet derives about 30 percent of its calories from fats, and the normal dietary fat will assist in absorption of calcium and vitamin D in low-fat and skim milks. The only exception may be the underweight woman who has trouble gaining.

Protein. The growth and development of the fetal tissues and blood demand protein. (See table 9.6 for Recommended Dietary Allowances for protein and other nutrients.) The average meat-eating American obtains more than enough protein. However, strict vegetarians who avoid animal (including dairy) products have to concentrate on eating plenty of protein sources—and on combining them to achieve protein complementarity. For example, they must eat dried beans, peas, or legumes (which contain some essential amino acids) in combination with whole grains, nuts, or seeds (which contain

other essential amino acids) to make sure that they take in all the essential amino acids at the same time. Like all animal food, dairy products are complete protein sources and need not be combined, but are good food choices with which to complement.

Fluids. During pregnancy, at least eight 8-ounce glasses of water or other fluids a day are needed. These fluids should not be supplied in the form of coffee or tea, which are mild diuretics. Instead of replenishing fluids, they get rid of them.

Salt. Like anyone else who is trying to eat well, an expectant mother should avoid processed foods that are laden with salt (sodium) and other added preservatives. However, sodium is now recognized to play a crucial role in the increase of a pregnant woman's blood volume. Therefore, table salt (sodium chloride) may be used, though in moderation, during pregnancy. Iodized salt and sea salt are preferred, because they provide the trace mineral iodine.

No longer is salt restriction recommended in pregnancy. A generation ago, sodium was commonly restricted because of the now-dismissed notion that this practice might prevent the development of high blood pressure and preeclampsia. This condition, whose origin remains obscure, involves high blood pressure, urinary protein loss, visual changes, and swelling between the twentieth week of pregnancy and the end of the first week after delivery. Preeclampsia occurs in about 1 in 20 pregnant women (often those with preexisting high blood pressure or blood vessel disease). If not

---

Table 9.6
RECOMMENDED DIETARY ALLOW-ANCES (RDA) DURING PREGNANCY

Nutrient	RDA Regular (add for pregnancy) = total	
Protein (gm)*	44 (+30)	= 74
Vitamin A (RE)	800 (+200)	= 1000
Vitamin D (mcg)	5 (+5)	= 10
Vitamin E (mg)	8 (+2)	= 10
Ascorbic Acid (mg)	60 (+20)	= 80
Folacin (mcg)	400 (+400)	= 800
Niacin (mg)	13 (+2)	= 15
Riboflavin (mg)	1.2 (+0.3)	= 1.5
Thiamine (mg)	1.0 (+0.4)	= 1.4
Vitamin B_6 (mg)	2.0 (+0.6)	= 2.6
Vitamin B_{12} (mg)	3.0 (+1.0)	= 4.0
Calcium (mg)	800 (+400)	= 1200
Phosphorus (mg)	800 (+400)	= 1200
Iodine (mcg)	150 (+25)	= 175
Iron (mg)	18 (+30–60)	= 48–78
Magnesium (mg)	300 (+150)	= 450
Zinc (mg)	15 (+5)	= 20

From the Food and Nutrition Board, National Academy of Sciences–National Research Council, Washington, D.C., revised 1980.
* Key to abbreviations: gm, gram; RE, retinol equivalents; mcg, microgram; mg, milligram

treated, it can worsen to a condition called eclampsia—manifested by a coma, convulsive seizures, or both.

Vitamins and Minerals

During pregnancy, the demand for specific vitamins and minerals, including folic acid, iron, zinc, and calcium, increases sharply. If not consumed in adequate amounts in the diet, these nutrients may need to be supplemented.

Folic Acid. The need for folic acid, a B vitamin, is twice as high during pregnancy as at other times. Like most vitamins, folic acid is a coenzyme—that is, a substance obtained only through the diet, which enables an enzyme to function. Enzymes that contain folic acid are crucial to growth and development, because they are needed to make nucleic acids—the genetic materials deoxyribonucleic acid (DNA) and ribonucleic acid (RNA)—as well as to metabolize amino acids, the building blocks of proteins. Folic acid deficiency has been implicated in neural tube defects (such as spina bifida).

Many foods that provide iron and protein also help supply folic acid. Green leafy vegetables, broccoli, asparagus, peanuts, mung bean sprouts, and liver are examples of foods that contain folic acid. However, folic acid supplements or a multivitamin containing the folic acid requirement for pregnancy are almost always recommended, even for pregnant women who eat a well-balanced diet that emphasizes these foods.

Other B vitamins include thiamin, niacin, riboflavin, and vitamin B_{12}. They are also needed in higher amounts during pregnancy. However, they are usually provided adequately by a good diet that includes such B vitamin sources as milk, whole-grain bread and cereal, wheat germ, liver, and nuts.

Iron. This mineral is needed for the production of hemoglobin in red blood cells, both in the developing circulatory system of the fetus and in the expanding blood volume of pregnancy. Foods rich in iron include liver, red meat, dried beans, green leafy vegetables, enriched bread and cereals, and dried fruits. Since it is very difficult to get enough iron to meet the increased needs during pregnancy from the diet alone, an iron supplement is usually recommended. However, health care providers may differ in their approach to iron therapy, depending upon serum iron levels.

Zinc. Deficiency of this mineral during pregnancy has been linked to slowed growth of the fetus—and even, tentatively, to some birth defects. Most iron-rich foods also contain zinc, and so emphasizing these foods in the diet tends to make zinc supplementation unnecessary.

Calcium. Pregnant women need extra calcium—for the development of fetal bones and teeth—and they can consume it easily through milk and other dairy products (such as yogurt and cheese).

Other sources include the soft bones of sardines and salmon, and green leafy vegetables. Tofu (bean curd) is another source of calcium, but tofu-based frozen desserts, which contain less than 10 percent tofu, are not.

A few tentative links have been suggested between the lack of certain minerals, including calcium and magnesium, and the development of preeclampsia. However, the cause of preeclampsia has still not been established.

Supplements

Supplements of both folic acid (800 mcg/day) and iron (30 to 60 mg/day of elemental iron, especially for those with iron-deficiency anemia) may be recommended in most pregnancies. To ensure that iron supplements are properly absorbed, they should be taken with citrus juice or another source of vitamin C—never with milk, because the calcium hinders iron absorption.

Calcium and zinc supplements are advised only for those whose diets are low in these minerals. For instance, pregnant vegetarians may benefit from a supplement of 25 mg of zinc per day. And individuals who cannot or will not consume enough dairy products may be given 500 to 1,000 mg of calcium carbonate a day. (See section on Milk, for the importance of choosing alternative calcium sources, before using supplements.) Without calcium supplementation, these women's own calcium stores (in bone) could be threatened during their pregnancy. Some people have theorized that

this may contribute to osteoporosis (porous, brittle bones) later on, but the idea has not been proved. In fact, many experts discount it, noting that pregnancy increases the efficiency of calcium absorption and less is excreted by the kidneys. The increased efficiency of calcium metabolism may actually protect against later osteoporosis, explaining why the disease is more common among women who have never been pregnant.

During pregnancy, the requirements for all other vitamins and minerals increase. (Again, see table 9.6.) However, all of these higher requirements are usually met by eating enough of a well-balanced diet that includes a variety of foods. Taken in the proper amounts, the commercially available prenatal vitamin and mineral supplements probably do no harm. However, it is much better to eat well than to rely too heavily on supplementation.

Megadoses. Although all pregnant women need extra vitamins and minerals, none of them need any "megadoses"—that is, supplementation of vitamins and minerals in amounts vastly exceeding the recommended dietary allowances (RDAs). Megadoses threaten the health of the fetus in several ways.

Excesses of fat-soluble vitamins (vitamins A, D, E, and K) are not easily excreted, and so megadoses of these vitamins are particularly dangerous. For instance, too much vitamin A can cause birth defects, including bone deformities, and excessive amounts of vitamin D can lead to kidney problems.

Nor are megadoses of water-soluble vitamins safe. Excessive amounts of any nutrient can potentially cause the same problems in a fetus as in adults.

Food Groups

Enough weight usually is gained simply by eating to satisfy the appetite, which is heightened during pregnancy. Therefore, most pregnant women need not bother to count calories closely. Instead, they can rely on guidelines like tables 9.7 and 9.8, which suggest numbers of servings per day from the various types of food.

Table 9.7
DAILY FOOD GUIDE FOR PREGNANT WOMEN

Food Group	Need
Dark-green and dark-yellow vegetables	1
Vitamin C fruits and vegetables	2
Other fruits and vegetables	1 (or more)
Breads and cereals	4 (or more)
Milk and milk products	4
Protein foods (animal and vegetable, 2 servings each)	4 (or more)

From "Help Your Baby to a Healthy Start," New York State Health Department, 1984.

Table 9.8
FOOD GROUPS

Food Groups	Number of Servings		
	Pregnant	Pregnant Lacto-ovo Vegetarian	Breastfeeding
Fruits and vegetables			
Vitamin C rich	1	1	1
Dark green	1	1	1
Other	2	3	2
Cereal products (whole-grain or enriched)	4	5	4
Milk and dairy products	4–5	6	5–6
Protein foods			
Animal (poultry, fish, eggs, meat)	2	—	2
Beans, nuts	2	3	2
Fats and oils	2 tbsps	2 tbsps	2 tbsps
Fluids	8 8-oz glasses	8 8-oz glasses	8–10 8-oz glasses

From "Food, Pregnancy, and Health," by the American College of Obstetricians and Gynecologists, Washington, D.C., 1982.

Meal Plans

See tables 9.9, "Sample Menus," and 9.10, "Typical Serving Sizes," for specific suggestions on what to eat. There is no reason to abandon eating any nutritious food that one is accustomed to. For instance, such "ethnic" foods as pasta, kasha, yams, plantains, cassava, corn bread, tortillas, and rice and beans are excellent sources of complex carbohydrates as well as being tasty and nourishing.

Vegetarianism

There are several types of vegetarians. Some will eat fish but no meat. For them, consuming a balanced diet is not a problem. Similarly, lacto-ovo vegetarianism (which includes eggs and milk and other dairy products) in no way precludes a healthy pregnancy, as long as vegetarians make sure they are eating enough protein —which they can get from milk, egg whites, and by matching vegetable protein. This diet, however, may be lacking in iron. Vegans, extreme vegetarians who eliminate not only animal food but also eggs and dairy products including milk, must put out a greater effort to ensure they are receiving enough protein, calcium, calories, and the other essential nutrients. Without supplementation, pregnant vegans are likely to be deficient in a variety of nutrients, including iron, folic acid, zinc, and vitamin B_{12}. Another consideration for a vegan diet during pregnancy is the volume of food that a strict vegetarian must eat to obtain enough calories to promote the fetus's healthy development and to achieve protein complementation.

Eating Problems

Dietary changes can help solve some eating problems encountered commonly during pregnancy. (For more on morning sickness and other pregnancy-related problems, see chapter 7, The Pregnant Body.)

Cravings. Dairy products, fruits, and sweets such as ice cream are the foods for which expectant mothers most often develop sudden urges, or cravings. A strong desire for foods that provide calcium or energy poses no real problem. However, some pregnant women develop a condition called pica: cravings for such non-food items as ice, soil, and cigarette ashes. These women need to be evaluated for iron-deficiency anemia, which might cause—or result from—their unhealthy cravings.

Aversions. Especially at the beginning of pregnancy, nausea and vomiting prompted by certain foods—most often animal products and beverages that contain caffeine or alcohol—may develop. This might be a form of natural protection of the fetus, while its organs are developing, against the threats of toxins from animal fat as well as alcohol and caffeine. There is no choice but to avoid

Table 9.9
SAMPLE MENUS

All 3 sample menus are designed for a woman of 5′4″ who needs 2,300 calories for pregnancy. Adjust for your height and activity level.

FIRST MENU
3 meals and a snack for meat eaters

Breakfast
1 cup whole milk*
½ cup orange juice
½ cup oatmeal
1 slice whole-wheat toast
1 boiled egg
1½ teaspoons butter or margarine

Lunch
1 cup whole milk*
¾ cup fresh strawberries
1 whole-wheat bagel
2 ounces tuna (packed in water)
1½ tablespoons mayonnaise
Lettuce and tomato

Dinner
1 cup whole milk*
1 medium baked potato
1 small whole-wheat dinner roll
1 cup broccoli, steamed
3 ounces broiled chicken
2 teaspoons butter or margarine
1 nectarine

Snack
1 cup low-fat plain yogurt
½ medium cantaloupe
2 graham crackers (2½ inches square)
2 tablespoons peanut butter

* For women whose weight gain is too rapid, skim or low-fat milk may be substituted for whole milk without missing out on any of the important nutrients.

SECOND MENU
3 meals and 3 snacks for meat eaters

Breakfast
½ cup orange juice
1 slice whole-wheat toast
1 boiled egg
1½ teaspoons butter or margarine

Snack
1 cup whole milk*
¾ cup corn flakes

Lunch
1 cup whole milk*
¾ cup fresh strawberries
1 whole-wheat bagel
2 ounces tuna (packed in water)
1½ tablespoons mayonnaise
Lettuce and tomato

Snack
1 slice whole-wheat bread
2 tablespoons peanut butter
1 cup whole milk*

Dinner
seltzer water with lime
½ cup rice
1 small whole-wheat dinner roll
½ cup summer squash, ½ cup carrots
3 ounces broiled flounder
2 teaspoons butter or margarine
1 nectarine

Snack
1 cup low-fat plain yogurt
½ cup fresh blueberries
2 graham crackers (2½ inches square)

these foods—and to concentrate instead on small portions of complex carbohydrates, such as toast, rice or pasta, milk, or broiled fish or chicken.

Morning Sickness. Anyone suffering from morning sickness, which is not uncommon in the first trimester, should try to break the cycle of nausea, eating a few crackers or dry toast when she first wakes up, trying small, frequent snacks in place of large meals or taking small feedings if she wakes up in the middle of the night. If morning sickness drags into the second trimester, it should be evaluated by a physician.

Feeling Full. Especially during the third trimester, the fetus may grow to be quite large, pressing against the woman's stomach and bowels and causing a "full" feeling. If a woman feels full all the time, she can try eating 6 (or even more) small snacks a day, instead of 3 regular meals. She should also avoid drinking fluids and eating food at the same time, as the fluids and food will compete for the limited room. Instead, she can try drinking fluids between the meals or snacks.

Heartburn. As the pregnancy progresses, the fetus may push against the stomach, sometimes causing heartburn— a burning feeling in the chest. Some heartburn may also be related to the hormonal changes of pregnancy. Heartburn is often relieved by eating small, frequent meals—and by relaxing, chewing food

THIRD MENU
For lacto-ovo (milk- and egg-eating) vegetarian

Breakfast
½ cup orange juice
½ cup oatmeal
1 tablespoon blackstrap molasses
1 cup whole milk*

Snack
½ whole-wheat bagel
1 tablespoon peanut butter
½ cup whole milk*

Lunch
2-egg sandwich, 2 slices whole-wheat bread
1 cup vegetable soup with barley
1 medium banana
1 cup whole milk*

Snack
1 ounce peanuts, 1 ounce sunflower seeds
4 ounces seltzer water with 4 ounces apple juice

Dinner
1½ cups lentils over 1 cup brown rice
1 cup Romaine lettuce salad
2 tablespoons oil and vinegar
½ cup broccoli
1 cup low-fat yogurt
8 ounces seltzer water with fresh lime

Snack
1 cup whole milk*
½ cup blueberries

Table 9.10
TYPICAL SERVING SIZES

Food	Amount per serving	Food	Amount per serving
Dark-Green and Dark-Yellow Vegetables		**Breads and Cereals**	
		Bread	1 slice
Broccoli	½ cup	Cooked cereal	½ to ¾ cup
Spinach	½ cup	Pasta	½ to ¾ cup
Greens	½ cup	Rice	½ to ¾ cup
Green salad	1 bowl	Dry cereal	1 ounce
Lettuce	1 wedge	**Milk and Milk Products**	
Carrots	½ cup	Milk	8 ounces (1 cup)
Vitamin C Fruits and Vegetables		Yogurt, plain	1 cup
		Hard cheese	1¼ ounces
Grapefruit	½ medium	Cheese spread	2 ounces
Melon	½ medium	Ice cream	1½ cups
Orange	1	Cottage cheese	2 cups
Tomato juice	¾ cup	**Protein Foods**	
Orange/grapefruit juice	½ cup	Animal	
		Poultry	2 to 3 ounces, cooked
Other Fruits and Vegetables		Fish	2 to 3 ounces, cooked
		Meat, lean	2 to 3 ounces
Banana	1 medium	Eggs	1 to 2
Apple	1 medium	Vegetable	
Grapes	¾ cup	Dry beans and peas	1 to 1½ cups, cooked
Pear	1 medium	Nuts and seeds	½ to ¾ cups
Potato	1 medium	Peanut butter	4 tablespoons
Green peas	½ cup, cooked		

more thoroughly, eating more slowly, and choosing food that is less greasy or spicy. If heartburn persists, a doctor should be consulted rather than taking any antacids, as certain antacids may be harmful to a developing fetus.

Constipation. Sluggish bowels are a common complaint during pregnancy. Constipation can be relieved by drinking more fluids and eating more fiber-containing foods. (Sprinkling wheat germ on cereals or salads is one way to add fiber.) One side effect of iron overdose may be constipation, and so it is possible that excessive iron supplementation may result in constipation in some pregnant women.

Gaining Too Much. Although some expectant mothers have difficulty gaining weight, others may have hearty appetites during pregnancy. They may easily consume 300 extra calories a day—and even more. Excessive weight gain is not as much of a concern as is insufficient gain. However, if a woman who was near her ideal weight at conception gains over, say, 40 pounds during pregnancy, at least some of this weight represents extra fat on both the fetus and herself. This fat can be difficult to take off after childbirth.

It can be harder to control weight gain late in pregnancy, but it is never too late to try to curb excessive gain. One way to curtail extra weight gain, provided it is not excessive water retention, is to switch from whole to low-fat or skim milk. Another is to eat less of other calorie-loaded fats and sugar.

In place of sugary sodas, try seltzer—carbonated water, which by definition contains no calories, sugar, or salt. (In contrast, tonic water contains sugar, and club soda contains salt.) For flavor, add a squeeze of lemon or a dash of fruit juice. Diet sodas should be avoided, because there is concern about the safety of sugar substitutes, including aspartame, for the fetus.

If a woman starts gaining more than 2 pounds a week, she should seek medical attention, to tease out the reasons behind the large weight gain. Especially if multiple births run in the family, she might be evaluated for the possibility that she is carrying more than 1 fetus.

NUTRITION AFTER GIVING BIRTH

Breastfeeding

Breastfeeding demands even more energy than does pregnancy: an average of 800 calories a day, as opposed to 300 calories a day for pregnancy. For the first 3 months after delivery, nursing mothers can use their fat stores to supply about 300 calories a day, but they need to eat an extra 500 calories a day above their prepregnancy diet. Thereafter, they need to eat an extra 800 calories a day above their prepregnancy diet.

Breastfeeding requires even more nutrients than does pregnancy, particularly calcium and protein, but these extra requirements can usually be met by eating a hearty, well-balanced diet consuming plenty of milk and other dairy products.

The outlook changes when a woman becomes pregnant again while still nursing. (Breastfeeding is far from a reliable contraceptive.) If a woman insists on continuing to nurse during her new pregnancy, she must be extremely conscientious about eating enough nourishing food—1,100 extra calories' worth a day—to ensure that the nutrition of the new fetus is not sacrificed. (She should also seek advice from a maternal nutritionist and discuss her decision with her health care provider.)

How to Lose

Pregnancy and childbirth are no exceptions to the advice that weight is best gained and lost gradually. It takes 9 months to gain weight during pregnancy, and it can take almost that long to lose the weight that lingers after childbirth. (About half of the weight gained during pregnancy is lost at delivery.) Postpartum weight loss regimens should not be too drastic, and they should not be started until the baby has been weaned from breastfeeding. (See chapter 17, Getting Back in Shape.)

SUMMING UP

BY THE TIME a woman conceives, she should be as close as possible to the optimal weight for her height and body frame. However, even if she is severely overweight at conception, she should still gain weight during pregnancy: All weight reduction diets are strictly out of the question during pregnancy, because they can seriously harm the fetus.

While pregnant, the woman should eat a varied, nourishing, well-balanced diet (including 4 or 5 glasses of milk a day) and gain at least 24 to 28 pounds. To do so, she will have to consume about 300 extra calories a day—equivalent to 2 glasses of whole milk. Breastfeeding demands eating even more—500 extra calories a day during the first 3 months, and 800 extra calories a day after that. No woman returns to her optimal weight immediately after delivery: The extra pounds that remain should be shed gradually.

10 The Pregnant Lifestyle

Elynne Margulis, M.D.

INTRODUCTION

SOME OF THE QUESTIONS that a woman is sure to ask herself when she first knows that she is pregnant are about the effects of the pregnancy on her lifestyle. How will the pregnancy affect her day-to-day activities at home and at work? Will she be able to continue with her regular workouts and participate in sports as before? What effect will being pregnant have on her relationship with her partner? on her career? How does she feel about the pregnancy now that it is no longer a hope but a reality?

PSYCHOLOGICAL CHANGES

ESPECIALLY during the first trimester, a pregnant woman goes through numerous physiological changes. The hormonal upheaval can cause bouts of depression and euphoria, crying jags, irritability, and mood swings that may startle both the woman and those around her with their strength and volatility. It is normal to be irritable when tired and nauseated and adjusting to the body changes of early pregnancy. It is also completely normal to have negative feelings about the pregnancy. Impatience, apprehension, even resentment of the pregnancy, are to be expected.

By the second trimester, when pregnancy sickness is a thing of the past and a woman is more accustomed to the pregnancy, severe mood swings tend to disappear. During the third trimester, however, many women must deal anew with feelings of anxiety and depression. As the due date approaches, they begin to worry increasingly about how the labor and delivery will go; they may be concerned for their own health, fearful of the pain of childbirth, or concerned about whether or not their baby will be normal. They may wish vehemently that the pregnancy were over—and feel guilty at the thought.

In pregnancy, dreams may be more frequent and vivid than before. Daydreams and fantasies are also more frequent. Some authors have noted a pattern to the dreaming. Early in pregnancy, the dreams often involve water and fish, perhaps reflecting an identification between the woman and the fetus in its liquid environment. Later, dreams are full of anxiety: The baby has been born but has been lost somehow, or the mother has neglected to feed or care for it, for example. Dreaming is one way in which the mind deals with concerns that it does not acknowledge consciously. Concerns about the well-being of the fetus are common in pregnancy; disturbing dreams are entirely normal.

Insomnia is common during the third trimester and may be due to worry, the need to urinate frequently, or difficulty finding a comfortable sleeping position. Fatigue increases the likelihood of irritability and nervousness and can contribute to depression. If a woman is having trouble sleeping at night, she should take every opportunity to lie down and rest during the day.

Remember, psychological changes and bizarre dreams are a normal part of pregnancy and thus only temporary. Mothers concerned about the health of their unborn child can take comfort in the knowledge that, unless there is a specific genetic disease in the family, there is a greater than 97 percent chance of having a perfectly normal baby once the third month of pregnancy is past.

THE FATHER'S FEELINGS

FATHERS , too, experience a number of different feelings during the months of the pregnancy. His worries may be quite different from his partner's. He may be concerned about the cost of raising a child, about his relationship with his partner, about his new role as a father. (See also chapter 11, Role of the Father.)

During the first trimester, in particular, it may be difficult for a man to feel very involved in the pregnancy. His partner may feel nauseated or tired, but there are no visible signs that she is carrying a child. Since she looks the same, some feel that she should also act the same way, continuing to be energetic, finding time to cook and entertain friends, and so on. However, in the second trimester, when the baby has begun to move or the father has heard the heartbeat at a prenatal checkup, he may begin to relate more closely.

Today, men participate in childbirth much more fully than they did only a decade ago. It is not uncommon for a man to attend prenatal checkups, witness the birth, even stay overnight in the hospital with his wife and baby. Some are able to take paternity leave in order to care for the mother and the new baby at home.

Men can prepare themselves by talking with other couples and fathers (both those who were at their babies' births and those who were not); by accompanying their partners to prenatal checkups; by reading some of the literature a woman usually has stacked high next to the bed in preparation for childbirth; and by attending childbirth preparation classes. (See chapter 15, Labor and Delivery.)

Many men fear that they will hurt their partner or the fetus by having sex during pregnancy. This fear is unfounded (see below). Others fear being ineffectual at the delivery or inept with the newborn. There should be no problems so long as the father is prepared for the sight of a delivery. And he should have no more trouble handling the newborn than his partner does—newborns are resilient creatures and cannot be hurt by inexperienced but loving handling.

Going straight back to work after the birth may be a necessity for some fathers. Others may want to take a few days off to care for both mother and baby. Only a handful of companies offer paid paternity leave, but fathers can request a few personal days without pay or take a paid vacation.

SEX DURING PREGNANCY

FOR 1 WOMAN in 4, there is a decrease in sexual interest during the first trimester of pregnancy. This may be the result of nausea, fatigue, breast tenderness, or fear of hurting the fetus.

During the second trimester, interest

in sex usually revives. Breast tenderness, which may have been a turnoff in the early months, usually disappears and is replaced by a pleasantly heightened sensitivity. An increased sense of sexuality and arousal may result from increased blood flow to the pelvic area, including the genitals. However, frequency of orgasm may decline at this time. Difficulty reaching orgasm may be due to the increase in vaginal discharge, which makes the vagina more moist, to a diminished libido on the woman's part, or to difficulty in finding a comfortable position for adequate penetration. Orgasms achieved may be less satisfying to the woman because the blood flow to the pelvic area does not dissipate as it usually does after orgasm.

During the third trimester, sexual frequency may decline again. A woman may feel herself to be unattractive and intercourse may become increasingly awkward as her abdomen becomes larger. Most couples find that positions other than the missionary (man on top) position are more comfortable at this time. A couple can try woman on top, side by side, or rear-entry positions. The on-top position allows better control in the depth of penetration.

With the stress and fatigue of late pregnancy, sex may be the last thing on a woman's mind, but it is as important as ever to find time for intimacy. Sex need not be equated with intercourse: oral sex, massage, and masturbation are ways of lovemaking that many couples turn to if intercourse becomes uncomfortable or if the doctor or midwife advises against it.

A man's sexual interest and pleasure should remain as in prepregnancy days, assuming that he does not find his partner's figure distasteful. While some men see their wives' new body form as voluptuous and sexy, others find the changes upsetting—a once-slim woman now looks distended, with varicose veins and heavy thighs. These men may find it difficult to find their wives attractive and may worry that their feelings will carry over after pregnancy. But because the change is temporary, these feelings pass.

Vaginal secretions, which become more plentiful and thicker, with a heavier scent and taste, may make cunnilungus unpleasant to some men. Some women leak colostrum from the breasts during sex; if this bothers either partner, they can simply refrain from breast play.

Many men are concerned that intercourse may hurt the fetus or their partner. However, it is perfectly safe all through a normal pregnancy. The fetus is protected from possible infection until the rupture of the membranes. Sexual relations cannot hurt it, well cushioned in its amniotic fluid. Orgasm will not cause premature labor in a normal pregnancy.

Sometimes after intercourse light bleeding may be experienced. This is not necessarily cause for alarm as it may be the result of some small injury to the surface of the cervix, which is engorged during the months of pregnancy. Simple avoidance of deep penetration may be the only modification required. However, the woman's doctor or midwife should be contacted to make sure that the bleeding was related to intercourse and not to any problem with the pregnancy.

Abdominal cramps after intercourse are very common. They are usually brief and of no concern. But if they continue to worsen over a period of an hour, a doctor should be consulted. The cramps may indicate that the cervix is dilating in response to prostaglandins contained in the sperm. These hormones can initiate uterine contractions.

The doctor or midwife will usually advise limiting sexual relations if there is unexplained bleeding or a leakage of amniotic fluid. Some may also limit intercourse during the first trimester if the woman has a history of miscarriage. During the last trimester, a couple may be advised to limit sex if multiple fetuses are present or if there is a history of premature labor or signs of threatened premature labor.

TRAVEL

ALTHOUGH TRAVEL IS, for the most part, safe during pregnancy, it may be better to avoid it in the very early and very late months. During the early months, there is the highest risk of miscarriage. Travel in itself will not cause a miscarriage, but it would be unfortunate if this should occur while away from normal medical support, family, and friends. Traveling during the last few months is inadvisable for much the same reason: Should labor occur earlier than the due date, the baby would be delivered with unknown medical personnel in a strange hospital.

When traveling by plane during pregnancy, be sure to sit in the no smoking section. Unpressurized cabins should be avoided—changes in barometric pressure could cause a rupture of the membranes. It is important to drink plenty of fluids, as travel by jet can be dehydrating, and to avoid sitting for long periods of time. Without a doctor's certificate many airlines will not accept a passenger who is more than 32 weeks pregnant.

When traveling by car, it is a good idea to stop at least every 2 hours for a 5 to 10 minute walk or stretch period to promote circulation. Seat belts should always be worn and should be positioned low across the lap, not across the uterus (See figure 10.1.) Many fetal deaths are related to maternal trauma during a car accident in which the mother was not wearing a seat belt.

Figure 10.1. **Proper position for wearing seat belts while pregnant.**

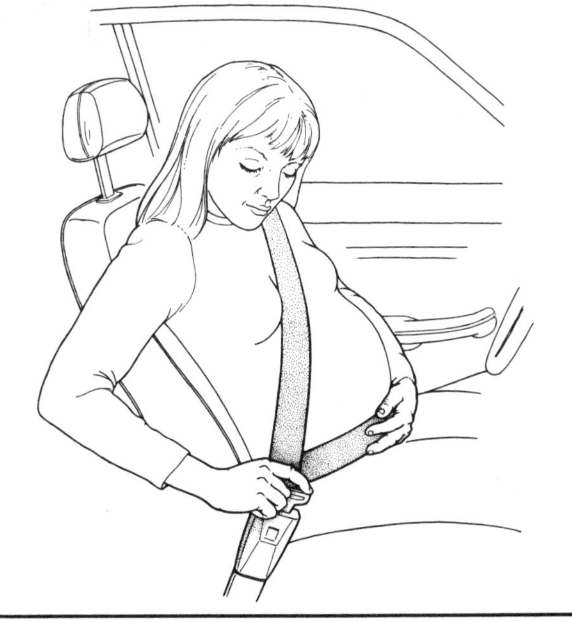

HOUSEHOLD HAZARDS

THERE IS NO RESEARCH on the effect of microwave ovens on a fetus. Microwaves are thought to be safe, but it is advisable to take precautions in any case, making sure that the oven is not "leaking" (meters to check for radiation levels are available), trying not to stand near the oven when it is in operation, and following the manufacturer's instructions carefully.

Women who like to cook should be aware of the danger of toxoplasmosis, a parasitic disease sometimes contracted from raw meat or poultry. Even the handling of raw meat can pose a health threat. Meat should be cooked to at least 140°F and the hands should always be washed after handling raw meat.

Cat feces may also contain toxoplasmosis protozoa and for this reason pregnant women should not clean litter boxes or do gardening in soil frequented by cats. Domestic cats can be tested by a veterinarian to see if they are carrying the disease. A blood test is also available to determine human immunity. An old infection does not pose a threat, but toxoplasmosis contracted during pregnancy does. The symptoms of the disease may be severe—a high fever, rash, and prostration—or much milder, resembling those of infectious mononucleosis. And sometimes they are so mild, an infection may not be suspected. Toxoplasmos early in pregnancy is likely to result in a spontaneous abortion. Infection in the second or third trimester may result in miscarriage, stillbirth, or the birth of a living child infected with the disease.

A number of common household products are best avoided during pregnancy. Strong cleaning products should only be used with adequate ventilation. Aerosols should be replaced with pump sprays. Products whose labels are covered with toxicity warnings—oven cleaners, for example—should not be used. As at any other time, ammonia should not be mixed with chlorine-based products, and gloves should be worn while cleaning.

Insecticides and insect repellants should be avoided. Some have been linked to birth defects.

Paint fumes are basically harmless but may cause nausea; windows should be kept open for ventilation. Paint removers are highly toxic. Ladders should be treated with caution since balance may be unsure during pregnancy and a serious fall could damage the fetus. (See also chapter 6, What Is Safe?)

CLOTHES

IT IS NOW POSSIBLE to find everything from attractive bathing suits and tennis clothes to corporate business suits and evening gowns cut for the pregnant body. Maternity clothes, however, are expensive and some women get by for a long time in their own loose-fitting clothes or their partners' shirts.

When buying maternity clothes, look for comfortable absorbent clothing that will fit both in the fourth and in the ninth month. If the baby is due just as the seasons change, a few more purchases may have to be made toward the end of the pregnancy. Synthetics should be avoided, as pregnancy brings an increase in sweating. Shoes should have low heels. High heels shift the weight of the body forward, accentuating the curve in the lower back and demanding adjustments throughout the body to maintain balance. They are especially problematical in later pregnancy, when the body's center of gravity has itself shifted forward.

Most women continue to wear their regular underwear but for others maternity panties and slips are more comfortable. Wearing regular undergarments may render them useless for postpregnancy wear, since seams and elastic will be stretched. New bras will have to be purchased since breast size increases (usually about 2 cup sizes) during pregnancy. If a woman plans to nurse, it is more economical to buy a nursing bra toward the end of the pregnancy rather than a regular one in a larger size. A padded bra may be more comfortable during the early months, when breasts are tender. Even a woman who does not normally wear a bra should wear one in pregnancy to support her breasts. If colostrum is leaking, special pads can be placed inside the bra. Maternity girdles with good lower back support are available if there are back problems.

Support hose are helpful for aching legs and essential for those with varicose veins. Support hose can be purchased ready-made or can be custom-made according to individual measurements. They can be pulled on before getting out of bed in the morning to help prevent further relaxation of the veins. Since feet tend to swell during the final 2 months, larger size shoes may be needed.

After the birth, most women are anxious to get back into their regular clothes as soon as possible. Usually, the prepregnancy figure has been regained within 2 months, although it sometimes takes up to 6 months.

SKIN, HAIR, AND NAILS

MANY WOMEN look radiant during their pregnancy: Their blemishes clear up and the increased blood volume gives a rosy blush to the cheeks. In others, hormonal changes may cause the skin to become suddenly oily or to develop dry patches.

Oral and topical antiacne preparations containing tetracycline must be avoided during pregnancy as the drug causes discoloration in the child's teeth, both the primary and the permanent ones. Acne medications with steroids such as cortisone can be dangerous with prolonged use.

Some develop what is known as the "mask of pregnancy," or chloasma—brownish patches on the face that are the result of increased activity of the cells that produce the skin pigment melanin. Usually this disappears after pregnancy and, although annoying, is not serious. During the summer, a strong sun block is recommended to prevent the discolorations from darkening. The areola (the area around the nipple) frequently darkens also and many develop a *linea negra*, a dark line from the pubic bone up to the navel. These changes are normal and temporary.

Hair may also change, becoming oilier or drier. The shampooing regimen should change accordingly. Increased perspiration may make the hair limper than usual. A change of hair color should be postponed until after pregnancy. Not only is the safety of hair dyes not established, colors "take" unpredictably during pregnancy.

The nails grow faster than usual during pregnancy. Sometimes, the nails become brittle or develop ridges. Brittleness can be treated with a moisurizing hand cream.

PERSONAL HYGIENE

BATHING AND SHOWERING can continue as usual throughout pregnancy. However, if the waters have broken or there is a leakage of amniotic fluid, a tub bath should be avoided. (If there is a suspicion that the waters have broken, the doctor or midwife should be contacted immediately.)

During pregnancy, douching should be avoided as well. Many commercial douche preparations contain iodine, which is harmful to the fetus. And there is always the possibility that an infection in the vagina could be introduced into the uterus.

EXERCISE

A PREGNANT WOMAN is not fragile. If she is otherwise healthy, exercise will not hurt her, cause a rupture of the membrane, or bring on labor prematurely. Nor will exercise or other strenuous activity hurt the

fetus, which is well protected by the bones of the spine and pelvis, by layers of muscle and tissue, and by the soft cushion of amniotic fluid.

The best time to begin an exercise

program is before becoming pregnant, but it is never too late. A woman does herself a disservice if she allows the fatigue or discomfort of pregnancy to serve as an excuse for not exercising. Those who do not exercise in pregnancy become progressively less fit as time goes on. Exercise in general contributes to a sense of well-being and increases the ability to deal with physical demands of pregnancy and labor. At least some exercise can be incorporated into any schedule or lifestyle. Even if they do not participate in sports or general conditioning exercise, expectant mothers should practice relaxation techniques and incorporate exercises designed expressly for the pregnant body to prevent (or relieve) many of the common discomforts of pregnancy and make labor easier (see section on Exercises for Pregnancy).

General Guidelines

The frequency and intensity of exercise will, of course, depend on medical history and physical condition. A woman should consult her doctor about her exercise program if she has a history of premature labor or suspects premature labor; is carrying multiple fetuses; has heart disease, incompetent cervix, vaginal bleeding, high blood pressure, diabetes, thyroid disease or anemia; or if she is obese.

Sports and Workouts. Anyone who enjoyed jogging or tennis or some other sport before becoming pregnant can continue at much the same activity level through most of her pregnancy. However, exercise in which weight is a factor will take more effort as the pregnancy advances. If a woman listens to her body, she will know whether to continue, cut back, or stop. She should expect a decrease in performance as the pregnancy progresses and she might consider switching to an activity where the effort is less dependent on body weight—swimming, for example.

Exercise should be done in moderation, never to the point of exhaustion. A woman should stop immediately and, if necessary, seek medical attention if she feels pain of any kind, a cramp, contraction, rapid heart rate, palpitations, chest pain, dizziness, bleeding, or nausea. During pregnancy, avoid getting overheated by wearing cool, comfortable clothes, not exercising in the heat of the day, and avoiding completely the use of saunas, steam rooms, and hot tubs. With marked increase in body heat, blood is diverted from the uterus to the skin as the body attempts to cool off.

Dehydration should also be avoided by drinking plenty of liquids—plain water is best—before and after and, if thirsty, during exercise.

Numerous physiological changes occur during pregnancy that may increase vulnerability to exercise injury. For example, as the levels of the hormones estrogen, progesterone, relaxin, and elastin increase, ligaments soften and are more easily stretched, making the joints more susceptible to injury. Bouncing or jerky movements and deep-knee bends, which should be avoided at any time, are especially dangerous now.

After the fourth month, exercise

while flat on the back should be avoided, as it can lower blood pressure and cause fainting. In addition, the pressure of the enlarging uterus can compress major blood vessels, leading to decreased blood flow to the heart and uterus.

Sports that require precise balance and coordination and carry the risk of a hard fall should be avoided, as should those in which becoming overheated is likely. (The list below evaluates a number of sports and fitness regimens in terms of their safety during pregnancy.) Strenuous exercise in the last month appears to increase the risk of low birth weight, still birth, and infant death; exercise should be reduced sharply at that time.

After exercising, a woman should always relax, lying on her left side. In addition to replacing fluid lost in perspiration, she should increase caloric intake to replace calories lost. The appropriate shoes and clothing and a support bra should be worn.

Aerobics. Aerobics may be too strenuous a workout during pregnancy. The pulse should be checked. If the count is 140 beats per minute during class, or if 10 minutes after the workout the pulse has not dropped below 100, the exercise is too vigorous. The jogging and jumping may put extra strain on low back muscles and varicose veins. The extra weight may stress the muscles of the pelvic floor.

Biking. This is a good sport during pregnancy since it does not put weight on the legs and ankles. However, the hard, narrow saddle on most 10-speed bicycles may injure the vulva during sudden stops. Toward the end of pregnancy, when balance is a problem, stationary cycling is an excellent alternative.

Climbing. Abrupt changes to high altitudes should be avoided during pregnancy. The change in a woman's center of gravity in late pregnancy may make her more likely to fall or lose balance.

Contact Sports. All contact sports should be avoided because of the risk of injury from collision.

Cross-Country Skiing. This is basically an aerobic exercise and, as with aerobics, may be too strenuous.

Horseback Riding. An experienced rider can continue to ride, provided she has a healthy pregnancy. Jumping is not recommended. This is not the time to start riding.

Hiking and Walking. This is great exercise but, again, overexertion should be avoided. Day packs should be used rather than the heavier backpacks.

Ice Skating. Experienced skaters may be perfectly comfortable continuing this sport. Most falls on the ice do no harm. The changing center of gravity may make it more difficult to execute the usual turns and moves.

Jogging. Increased circulatory demands may cause dizziness and heat stress and may lower oxygen supply to the fetus. Moderate jogging is appropriate for women who are in good condition, but they should take care that body temperature does not rise more than 2 degrees.

Racket Sports. Tennis and other racket sports are appropriate for pregnant women but excessive exertion raises body temperature and must be avoided.

Scuba Diving. Many obstetricians advise that *all* deep-water diving be avoided during pregnancy. In the first trimester, when nausea and fatigue are problems, diving is inadvisable. Later in pregnancy, the wet suit may be too constricting. In any event, diving depths should be limited to no more than 60 feet and the duration of the dive should be limited to one-half the recommended limits set by the U.S. Navy decompression tables.

Skiing. The body's altered center of gravity during pregnancy can make even a seasoned skier more likely to take a bad fall. Experienced skiers should limit themselves to the easy runs. This is not the time to learn the sport.

Swimming. This is a wonderful form of exercise. Balance is not a problem. All the muscles are exercised without strain and the pregnant woman has the added benefit of feeling light and graceful. Swimmers should not push themselves to do extra laps and should not dive or jump into the water.

Waterskiing. Not recommended. There is the risk of traumatic falls. There is also the possibility that water will rush up the vagina with excessive force during a fall, traumatizing the uterus.

Weight Training. Stronger back and leg muscles are helpful in carrying the extra weight of a pregnancy. Weights should be appropriate to the level of ability.

Exercises for Pregnancy

Exercises for pregnancy generally concentrate on 5 areas:

- *strengthening the abdominal muscles*, to make it easier to support the weight of the fetus, to prepare for labor, and to speed recovery of the figure after delivery
- *strengthening the back muscles*, to help avoid low back pain, which is common in pregnancy when the muscles are strained by the extra weight
- *maintaining good posture*, which also helps prevent and relieve back problems
- *breathing and relaxation techniques*, to keep the muscles well oxygenated, thus increasing the feeling of strength and well-being, and to prepare for labor
- *strengthening the muscles of the pelvic floor* in preparation for labor and to prevent postpartum bowel and bladder problems and uterine prolapse

The pelvic floor muscles, which loop around the urethra, the vagina, and the rectum in a figure-8 shape, are especially important in pregnancy. Strong muscles will support the weight of the uterus and its contents comfortably, will stretch and relax during labor, and will return quickly to good tone after delivery. A good way to locate these muscles is to spread the legs wide apart while urinating, and stop and start the flow of urine several times. Once the muscles have been located, strengthening exercises (sometimes called "Kegels") can be done at any time—while waiting for a bus, sitting at a desk, preparing a meal. The muscles should be contracted hard for about 5 seconds, then gently released. This sequence should be repeated twice. Ideally, the pelvic floor should be exercised at least 20 or 30 times a day. Kegels can be incorporated into other exercise routines, with the pelvic floor being tightened along with the abdominal muscles.

Relaxation techniques include breathing and concentration exercises that help relax body and mind, conserve energy, and increase body awareness. Specific relaxation techniques that are used during labor are taught in most preparation-for-childbirth classes. Some women find yoga instruction beneficial, both during pregnancy and for labor and delivery.

Exercises for pregnancy (illustrated in figures 10.2 to 10.6) can be done at home alone, or in a group with other women. An exercise class has several advantages: a well-designed program, a trained instructor, and companionship. Classes generally meet for an hour, 2 or 3 times a week, in such settings as schools, YMCAs, and church halls. Exercising at home should be limited to a 20- or 30-minute workout daily. Exercises should not be done on a full stomach, and they should not be continued if there is any pain.

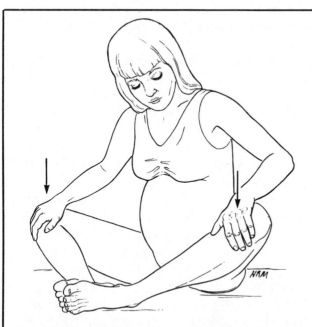

Figure 10.2. **Tailor position and stretches. Sit on the floor, either Indian-style with knees apart and ankles crossed or with the soles of feet together (as illustrated). Back should be straight. Bring soles of feet together, and take a deep cleansing breath. Then inhale and lift knees up; exhale, slowly pressing knees toward the floor. Start with 5 times and work up to 10 or more if comfortable.**

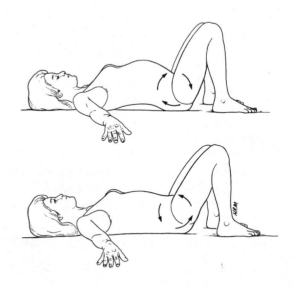

Figure 10.3. **Pelvic tilt. Lie on the floor with knees bent and feet flat on the floor. (The coach can help by sliding a hand under partner's back.) Take a deep breath, then exhale and slowly roll the spine down to the floor, slightly lifting the buttocks. Inhale again, and pressing the buttocks back against the floor, roll the spine gradually back into a normal position. Do this 5 times.**

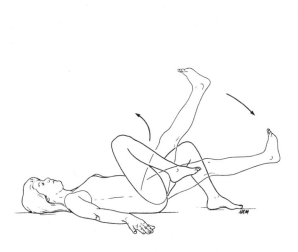

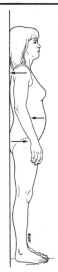

Figure 10.4. **Leg lifts. Lie flat on the floor, and bend 1 leg, keeping the foot flat on the floor. Inhale and slowly lift the straight leg up, with toes pointed forward. Exhale and lower the leg back to the floor, being careful not to arch or twist your back. Try 5 times with each leg and work up to 10.**

Figure 10.5. **Posture check. Stand against a wall with feet flat on floor and heels about 3 to 4 inches from wall. Line up body so that shoulders and buttocks touch wall, with spine as straight as possible. Try to walk in this position, keeping hips and shoulder in line.**

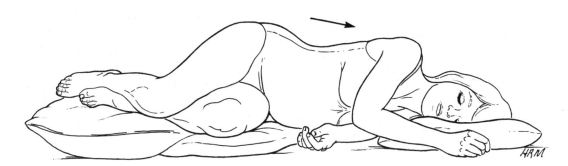

Figure 10.6. **At rest. Toward the end of pregnancy, it often seems there is no comfortable position. When resting, lie on your left side (to ease pressure on the vena cava, the large blood vessel on the right side of the body). Use a pillow or rolled up blanket to raise the legs somewhat higher than the rest of the body. In this position, the blood flows toward the heart and head, thereby helping ease swelling of the legs and ankles.**

WORK

TODAY, pregnancy is no longer considered an illness and the pregnant woman someone who needs to be sheltered from the outside world. She usually continues to work and involve herself in normal activities throughout her pregnancy.

There is no reason that a job should not be continued provided the pregnancy is uncomplicated and the workplace poses no reproductive hazards. A 1977 report from the National Institute for Occupational Safety and Health states: "The normal woman with an uncomplicated pregnancy and a normal fetus in a job that presents no greater potential hazards than those encountered in normal daily life in the community may continue to work without interruption until the onset of labor."

Much depends on the type of job and the environmental hazards of the workplace. Health care workers, for example, should protect themselves against infectious diseases and exposure to X rays, anesthetic gas, and anticancer drugs. Dentists and dental hygienists must guard against exposure to mercury, which may increase the chance of spontaneous abortion and the risk of birth defects. For teachers, the biggest worry is contracting an infectious disease, such as rubella or viral influenza. (See chapter 8, Medical Care During Pregnancy, for further information on workplace materials and their risks to reproduction.)

The American Medical Association (AMA) recommends that women who must stand on their feet for more than 4 hours a day stop working by week 24 of pregnancy. Those who must stand for 30 minutes to 1 hour a day should quit by week 32. The AMA also recommends that women not stay in jobs that require a great deal of lifting, climbing, or excessive bending. It should be understood that these are only recommendations and that individual needs and abilities may

vary. Some women continue working even in very strenuous jobs until near term; others find they must quit early, even though their work does not require excessive physical exertion.

Pregnant women should never deny feelings of fatigue or overwork and should make an effort to rest each day. Even if a nap is impossible, just lying down (on the left side) will help. A pregnant woman who is experiencing stress on the job should talk with her health care team about the particulars of her situation— the time she spends commuting, the number of hours she works, the amount of time spent standing, deadline pressures, smokers in the workplace, noise level in the office, and so on. They can best advise her as to whether or not she should consider quitting, reducing her responsibilities, or asking for a transfer to another department, for example.

Some women work until the onset of labor. Others want some time off before the baby is born, to rest and get the house in order. Some disability plans allow for paid leave to begin 2 to 4 weeks before the due date. (See chapter 2, Choosing Your Health Care Team, for further information.) If a woman wants to remain on the job until the baby is born but would prefer reduced hours, she should talk with her employer to see if this can be arranged. If she needs more time off than the company will pay for, she should consider trying to store up vacation and sick days for use over the maternity leave. (See chapter 2 for discussion of pregnant women's rights at work.)

It is often difficult to predict, before a baby is born, when the mother will want to return to work. She may decide to go back right away (that is, after about 8 weeks) or—particularly if her job is secure and the family's finances permit—she may prefer to wait until the baby is 9 months or even 1 year old.

When deciding whether or when to return to work, a woman should consider whether she wants to breastfeed; whether manual pumping of breast milk during work hours is feasible; whether it would be acceptable to suplement with bottles; how flexible her workday is, or could be; whether it would be possible to work part-time; whether she can find good-quality child care; and whether she feels comfortable in the role of working mother.

Staying at home—maintaining a household and caring for children—is no less strenuous than working in an office. Those who stay home during their pregnancies can usefully follow many of the suggestions outlined for working women. (See table 10.1.) If finances allow, this is a good time to get some extra help with the children, so that the pregnant mother has a chance to rest during the day.

Table 10.1

TIPS FOR WOMEN WHO WORK DURING PREGNANCY

- Wear support hose, especially if you are on your feet a good deal

- Take a rest break before you become fatigued

- Stay out of a smoke-filled work area

- Avoid temperature extremes

- Empty the bladder at least once every 2 hours

- When possible, keep legs elevated

- Take frequent breaks to do stretching exercises

- If possible, lie down during the lunch hour, resting on the left side

- Use a chair with arm rests to ease back strain

- Avoid crossing your legs

- Try to arrange coming in late in the morning if early-morning pregnancy sickness is a problem

- If you work at a VDT, take a break every 30 minutes to avoid excessive back and muscle strain from sitting in one position too long

- Do not try to work until your due date—quit when you find you are getting progressively more tired as the day goes on

11 Role of the Father

Edward Bowe, M.D.

INTRODUCTION

NOT SO LONG AGO, a father was the forgotten man, relegated to the outer circle of the childbirth experience. His presence was unwelcome and unexpected in either the labor or delivery rooms. If he was permitted to observe, he was expected to keep out of the way of the real and important drama enacted between mother and medical staff. Most often, fathers were sent off to their own waiting room where, according to the stereotype of the situation comedy, they chain-smoked, paced up and down, and asked each other foolish questions.

Today, fathers are much more likely to share in the experience of the birth of their children and, in most cases, are fully accepted as an important part of the team. Fathers also accompany their partners to prenatal visits, attend prepared childbirth classes, and come to the hospital with a good working knowledge of the procedures of childbirth. They expect to stay in the labor and delivery rooms and participate fully.

And families have profited by this paternal involvement. Pregnancy and birth bring a couple face to face with the fundamentals of life and death, joy and pain, and the process usually brings a new maturity and depth to each person and to their relationship.

Ambivalence

And yet pregnancy is not without its anxious moments. Couples should not assume that because pregnancy and childbirth are normal events, that it is unnatural to feel anxious about them. In fact, although most couples do look forward to the *concept* of having a new baby, most also have feelings of doubt because more than anything else, pregnancy signifies change. Automatic acceptance of pregnancy is uncommon for either partner, and, for men, acceptance seems to come more gradually than for women.

As they become more closely involved with the pregnancy, both partners may feel apprehensive about the future, fearing change, anxious about the pain of childbirth. It requires a period of adjustment before these concerns can be thought out and integrated comfortably into each partner's life. The changes a woman experiences are heightened by physical changes: Her body shape changes, and the shifting hormonal pattern of early pregnancy creates moods that swing from extreme joy to depression. Because a man does not have to deal with these physical changes, his period of adjustment is usually more submerged and less obvious. Yet the prospect of becoming a father carries new and serious emotional implications. Among them may be concerns about money and sex, and how a baby will alter his relationship with his partner. Not every father can cope with pregnancy. Some may agree that having a baby is a good idea, but they have second thoughts when reality hits.

Many things can bring pressure to bear on a relationship during pregnancy. A newly pregnant woman may feel exhausted and nauseated. At times, she cannot tolerate sexual activity and may resent what she perceives as her partner's lack of sympathy and understanding. The father, trying to adjust to the idea of pregnancy, may feel rejected when she refuses sexual relations. As the pregnancy develops, some men also resent necessary changes in lifestyle: less sex, giving up smoking and drinking, abandoning nightlife, and curtailing other social activities. But these things are preparation for parenthood: It is important to understand that parenthood entails inconvenience along with the pleasure that children bring.

When faced with parenthood many men reexamine their relationship with their own fathers in order to come to terms with their anxieties. This contemplation is helpful, especially if it helps a man more clearly envision what kind of father he would like to be to his children.

Whatever a couple can do now to cement their relationship helps the formation of the expanded family. When both partners can offer support to each other, each can retain emotional strength and stability. Talking to each other, expressing anxieties and fears, as well as hopes and aspirations for the future, helps to create a sense of intimacy and sharing and adds a new dimension to their feelings for each other. Eventually, worries are usually overcome by a new sense of excitement and anticipation as couples look forward to the changes that parenthood will bring.

THE FIRST TRIMESTER

THE FATHER has a vital role to play throughout the course of pregnancy. Men who view themselves as the caretaker of mother and fetus seem to have an easier time making the adjustment. A prospective father who comes to the prenatal clinic or the doctor with his partner is fulfilling this role. On a day-to-day basis, his willingness to help with diet, exercise, and lifestyle changes involves him as an active partner, not merely an interested bystander.

Early Pregnancy Classes

Early pregnancy classes and other parent education programs are a new concept to help couples adjust to physical and emotional changes of pregnancy. These classes are usually offered within the first 3 to 6 months of pregnancy. Unlike prepared childbirth classes, which are offered later in pregnancy, the early pregnancy classes are not about labor and delivery; instead, they are concerned with coping with financial problems, resolving ambivalence, easing anxieties, sustaining marital relationships in the face of dramatic change, and about forming new familial attachments. Discussion is the keynote, although some relaxation exercises are usually recommended. Discussions center on how both partners feel and the physical changes going on in the mother's body. Understanding the physiology of pregnancy gives men a sense of what's happening to their wives.

In a typical class, a leader and a small group of couples meets together for 3 sessions at a hospital, YMCA, or other community center. In a group setting both partners may be more likely to talk about their feelings, and this special interaction among couples is what makes early pregnancy classes so valuable. A man may find talking to another prospective father especially valuable, as it may help him to recognize that he is not alone in his feelings.

Attending Prenatal Checkups

A man can also talk to the obstetrician or midwife supervising his partner's pregnancy, if he accompanies her on prenatal visits. Doctors may not directly ask, "What are your feelings?" but most will ask both partners if they have any questions. This is a cue for fathers and mothers to talk about anything that is worrying them.

A man will also gain an understanding of the physiological process of pregnancy when he attends these prenatal checkups, staying with his partner while she is being examined. When a doctor speaks of vaginal discharge as being normal or of breast tenderness, the father can begin to understand, without feeling rejected, why his partner may not want to make love. The better informed a father is, the better he can cope with some of the changes going on in the marital relationship.

Later on, when the baby's heartbeat is audible through a special amplified stethoscope, the father will be able to share this confirmation that his baby is growing and developing.

THE SECOND TRIMESTER

FOR MOST COUPLES, the second trimester is like a cloud lifting. Both partners have usually grown accustomed to the idea of pregnancy, although the reality may still be a few months away. Sexual relations usually improve. Now partners need to understand that sexual intercourse will not hurt pregnancy. Many couples enjoy a particularly good, intimate relationship at this time.

Attending Childbirth Classes

Late in the second trimester or at the beginning of the third trimester of pregnancy, many couples attend prepared childbirth classes together. (See chapter 8, Medical Care During Pregnancy.) There they learn techniques to cope with each stage of labor and are told what will happen in the delivery room.

Both partners should learn to relax and breathe calmly, because the father's restful attitude will influence the mother. The father should learn to recognize when his partner is completely relaxed and when she is tense so that he can detect any signs of tension during labor and help her to stay calm. Preparing to deal with the delivery together strengthens the bond between parents and helps them to share some of the expectations and responsibilities of pregnancy.

Quickening

Sometime between 16 and 18 weeks after conception, the mother will be able to feel the first fetal movement, an event known as quickening. At first, it will only be a flutter, but as the baby grows stronger, definite movements can be felt. Eventually, distinct kicks will be felt and sometimes can even be seen, as the wall of the mother's abdomen is pushed out.

The mother can help the father share in the excitement of these fetal movements by guiding his hand to the spot where the baby is kicking or pressing.

THE THIRD TRIMESTER

THIS IS THE TIME for making room for the new baby, for buying baby clothes and furniture together. Discussing practical matters and making plans together also help to reinforce the feeling that having a baby is a shared experience. Choosing a name is one good way to occupy the time in the last weeks of pregnancy. Naming him or her also makes the unborn child seem like a very real person. Mother and father begin to imagine a home that includes a new human being for whom they are responsible, who must be outfitted with all the trappings of babyhood, given love and attention and intellectual and psychological stimulation and support.

Relaxing Together

In the final weeks of pregnancy a woman tends to be very uncomfortable. Sexual relationships wane again. Physical relaxation with the help of her partner can ease her discomfort and foster feelings of closeness at the same time.

Massage can be extremely relaxing if done correctly and it is a good way for the father to help ease the discomfort of the last few weeks.

The pregnant woman should lie in a warm room supported by pillows, either on a bed or on a thick towel on the floor, with her partner standing or kneeling beside her. As he massages each area, she should concentrate on relaxing those particular muscles. He should use only enough pressure so it feels comfortable, never irritating or painful. He can use body lotion, body oil, or massage oil to help his hands slide smoothly. These same massage techniques to ease tension spots or relieve pain are also helpful in labor. Massage should not be used over varicose veins, swollen joints, or areas of tender skin.

A man should use sweeping strokes along the length of his partner's back, finishing with firm pressure. He can start by working up her spine and down her arms and hands. Then he should focus on her back, alternating hands or using both hands together.

Spot Massage

The art of spot massage is to move two skin surfaces together, that is, the massaging hand and the receiver's skin, without rubbing or digging. If the base of the woman's spine or the joints in her back between hip bones and spine (sacroiliac joints) are painful, her partner can massage them with his fingertips, the heel of his hand, or a bent index finger. For extra pressure he can press or roll a tennis ball warpped in a sock on the base of the spine.

If an expectant mother suffers edema (fluid retention) in the ankles, she can lie with her feet raised just above shoulder level and supported by a low stool. The upper part of the body should be resting on 2 or more pillows. This position will help to drain the fluid while her partner massages her legs and ankles.

He should place his hands on either side of her feet and slide them along her thigh toward her groin, spreading out his fingers to cover as much of her leg as possible. He should use the weight of his body to make his hands move, without digging his fingers into her flesh.

Couvade (Male Symptoms)

It is common for fathers to become so intimately involved with their partners that they feel some of the physical ramifications of pregnancy themselves. In some cultures a father actually experiences labor pains when a child is born. He may retire to a room or hut to moan for several days, during which time his wife has the baby.

Such sympathy pains are by no means confined to primitive societies. Even in the United States many men suffer from abdominal pains or toothache during a spouse's pregnancy and labor. Some prospective fathers echo the symptoms of their wives throughout pregnancy. A father may gain weight, become easily irritated, take afternoon naps, or suffer backaches.

This phenomenon, known as couvade (from the French word meaning to brood or hatch), may include morning sickness, insomnia, depression, stress, and cravings for a particular food. Men seldom tell anyone about their symptoms, even though these can become very uncomfortable after several months.

Doctors who have observed the phenomenon believe that couvade is a natural way for a father to express a bond of sympathy with the expectant mother, and it is also a way to establish his paternity. So far, no one has discovered any physiological reason for couvade symptoms, nor offered any solutions.

The Father in Labor and Delivery

As the pregnancy approaches its final days, both partners prepare to play their most important and vital roles. Sharing the complete experience of pregnancy and labor and witnessing the birth prepares both partners for sharing all the joys and responsibilities of parenthood. Childbirth is one of the most intense and moving experiences either will ever know, and one that will strengthen the bonds of love between both them and their baby.

Not only can it enhance the relationship between partners when a man sees what it is like to have a baby, but he can be of great help. It may be uncomfortable for the father to watch, but hand-holding and other supportive, loving gestures can seem invaluable to a woman having a baby.

Unless either partner is adamantly opposed, the father should be in the labor room. However, a woman in labor need not accept the presence of anyone she does not want. Some fathers are so uncomfortable seeing their partners in labor that both partners might be better off without the father's presence.

Some women prefer to go through labor without their husbands present. Some do not want their husbands to see them experiencing the pain of labor. Others do not believe that sharing this experience will be beneficial to their relationship. These women may prefer that only the medical staff attend the delivery, or they may choose a mother, sister, or friend to stay with them. A woman who chooses her own mother should be sure it is because she really wants her there, not simply because her mother insists on being there. The important thing is that it is the woman's choice, and she is the one who should be happy with it.

Father as Labor Partner

It is during labor that a man's training in prepared childbirth really pays off. He should be ready to remain calm when his partner is under stress and to offer all the emotional support and encouragement he can.

Because the father knows his partner better than anyone else does, one of his most important roles is to help maintain good communication between her and the medical support people in the labor room. He is the mother's strongest advocate. His role is sometimes that of a go-between; he will be squarely on her side and do everything he can to help her.

The best time for the father to establish himself with the medical staff is when the couple first enters the hospital. His goal is to create friendly, open communication between himself and the staff members who will participate in his partner's labor and delivery. The couple and the hospital staff have the same aim—the safe delivery of a healthy baby.

Labor is hard, exhausting work, and a father may feel his role is a minor one compared with the effort his partner is expending, but there is a great deal he can do to ease her discomfort and help her. He can wipe her forehead, moisten her lips with cool water or ice cubes when her mouth feels dry and parched, and smooth her hair off her face as she rests between contractions. During childbirth preparation courses the partner will be taught how to act as a labor coach.

As labor partner he will follow every contraction with the mother, maintaining eye contact with her during contractions, and helping her change positions. He can watch for tension in her muscles and help her to relax with a gentle massage and encouraging words. If she does not want to be touched, the labor partner will sense that, too. He should not be offended if she complains to him or seems ungrateful. When the contractions are strong, he can remind her that the stronger they are, the sooner the baby will arrive. He can remind her to keep her chin down on her chest as she rises to push with each contraction, and use the right muscles and the right breathing techniques for pushing.

The father's physical support will be essential if his partner wants to adopt a more upright position that will allow gravity to play its maximum part in labor. Partners should practice these holds together beforehand to see which might work best for the mother. For some positions she may need the help of a third person, and so her partner should know when to ask for assistance.

The father can fill an important role for his partner when she is too busy with contractions to notice anything else. If she has complete faith in him as her interpreter and spokesman, she can feel totally free to submerge herself in the process of giving birth.

As labor culminates in birth, the father's time will be divided between encouraging his partner and keeping an eye on the perineum for the first sight of the baby's head. His own enthusiasm at the progress she is making can be a powerful incentive to keep going, even if she has been in labor for a long time. When the baby's head crowns he can help her sit up

to watch the birth by supporting her back and shoulders. If she cannot be propped up, the father may be able to hold a mirror reflecting the perineum so that the mother can see what is happening. After the head has crowned, the father will have to restrain his enthusiasm and help her to do the same so that she can "pant" the head out gently, instead of pushing it forcefully through the vulva. If complications arise during this stage, the father will have to concentrate on talking to the mother about what is happening and why. He must help to keep up her confidence and assure her that she is doing well.

Most women are likely to experience some difficult moments during the course of labor and they may need pain relief. A woman who becomes anxious or alarmed during labor may tense instead of resting as she anticipates the pain of the next contraction. With the support and coaching of her partner, however, nothing should frighten her or cause her to lose confidence. Many women who have had difficult deliveries have nevertheless felt positive about the birth experience because of the supportive role played by their partners. The baby can only benefit from the positive effects of this teamwork between partners during labor.

FATHERS AND BONDING

BONDING FOR BOTH partners often begins before the baby is born. Many women who have sonography, for example, report intense feelings of bonding when they first see their baby appear on the monitor. Fathers who attend the procedure have a similar reaction.

If a mother requires an emergency cesarean delivery, the father can be there to receive the baby while the mother is in the recovery room. In this case fathers have a head start in forming an essential bond.

Bonding between parents and child occurs in many different ways. The key is allowing the father to get to know his baby as soon as possible after the delivery. When fathers are excluded from the mother–baby relationship, the adjustment to a new family relationship is difficult for everyone.

The new father should be allowed to hold and fondle the baby soon after birth and, even while mother and baby are still in the hospital, to participate in the baby's care. Most hospitals permit flexible visiting hours and encourage fathers to handle their babies.

NEW-PARENT LEAVE FOR FATHERS

IN MANY NEW families, the father has a hard time working his way into the intense relationship between mother and baby. This is largely a matter of the quantity of time each parent spends with the infant. Mothers are often on hand around-the-clock, while fathers have only brief periods of time with the baby. This is an unfortunate situation because the father can be a big help during the first weeks of a baby's life, especially if there are already children in the family. Everyone really needs him now, especially because the family's initial adjustment to a new baby is critical.

Unfortunately, anxiety about money and careers may push many new fathers away from their families at this crucial time. Although some corporations (36.8 percent) offer unpaid paternity leave for new fathers, according to one national survey of 420 major companies conducted by Catalyst, a New York-based organization, men rarely take advantage of it. Loss of pay and concern about missing out at work are the given reasons.

New family relationships can be stressful for a man who feels that he, and he alone, should support the family. For some men, it is not enough to be good fathers and good husbands. The outward trappings of success may be important to them. A man may feel bad if his wife has to go back to work. Even when she wants to work, it may be deeply ingrained in a man's psyche that a wife's money should not be used for necessities, only for the "extras." Fortunately, this attitude is changing, thanks to the growing trend for 2-career families as well as the economic realities of meeting the expenses of supporting a family.

In the long run, a man's family needs him for much more than his earning power. The father's active participation in rearing children is gradually becoming more common. If in some way the opportunity is available for a new father to take 1 or 2 weeks off, he should take advantage of it.

WHEN FATHER IS PRIMARY CARETAKER

WHEN BOTH PARENTS work, one partner may take time off to devote to parenting for the first few years of the child's life. The temporary leave-taker has almost always been the mother. The father may actually be in a better position or be more inclined to take time out from his career to care for the child on a day-to-day basis. With growing acceptance of shifts in traditional roles more fathers may choose this option.

A father who stays home with a new baby can expect to encounter the same problems as a mother would—and the same set of emotions. He may feel, "I'm stuck at home with the kids all day, while she's out enjoying her life." This is not a female or male complaint; it is the complaint of a primary caretaker.

WORKING OUT PARENTING ROLES

MARITAL AND FAMILY issues surface as couples try to work out their household arrangements. If both parents work, who stays home when the babysitter is late or when the baby is sick? No matter what kind of child care arrangements the parents can afford, they cannot pay someone to be a psychological parent. Even when both parents work, one or the other usually fills the role of primary caretaker.

Each partner is the other's greatest ally as they embark on this unique adventure. Having children today means understanding the promises of parenthood and being physically and emotionally prepared to cope. The more couples can talk together and work out their anxieties, the easier it will be to create a stable and relaxed environment for their entire family.

12 The Developing Fetus

Jack Maidman, M.D.

INTRODUCTION

FROM THE MOMENT of conception, the fetus develops for about 266 days or 38 weeks. The obvious way to follow fetal development is from the moment that sperm and egg fuse into a single cell. That event almost always coincides with ovulation, which occurs 14 days before the onset of menstruation, and fetal age is dated from the time of conception.

Because the actual moment of conception can only be guessed at, however, doctors date a pregnancy from the beginning of the woman's last menstrual period, although she probably conceived 2 weeks later, depending upon the length of the menstrual cycle. Thus when an obstetrician says the pregnancy is at 20 weeks' gestation, it is 18 weeks' postconception. And when it is said that most babies are delivered at about 40 weeks, the actual

delivery is at 38 weeks. To further complicate dating, this is an "average," not a rule. Some will have perfectly normal pregnancies that deliver 1 or 2 weeks earlier or later.

To follow the progress of fetal development in this chapter, we will begin with the moment of conception and continue to describe the developing fetus according to its actual age within the uterus. (See figure 12.1.) Using that model, pregnancy will be traced for 38 weeks. (If your obstetrician uses the 40-week system, add 2 weeks to each stage.)

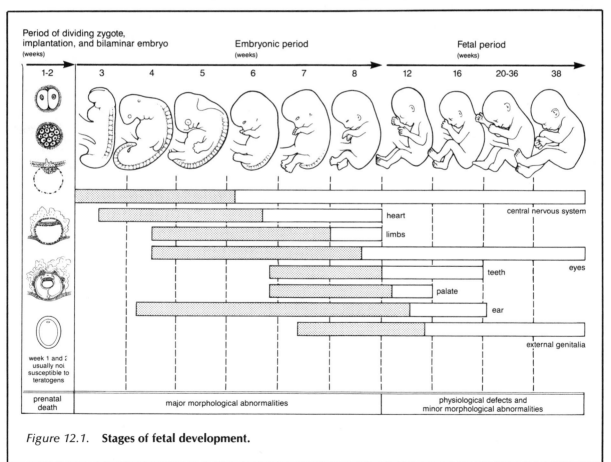

Figure 12.1. **Stages of fetal development.**

THE FETUS IN THE FIRST 12 WEEKS

THE MOST DRAMATIC development occurs in the first 12 weeks of fetal life. For the first few weeks the fertilized egg is known as a blastocyst; from week 4 to week 8 it is called an embryo; and after week 8 it is a fetus.

A fetus develops from a single fused cell, a hybrid formed when egg and sperm join. Immediately following fertilization, this new cell divides within its containing bubble and begins to move down the Fallopian tube toward the uterus. On average, the 2-cell stage is reached within 36 hours of fertilization.

These 2 cells both continue to divide into a mulberrylike cluster of many smaller cells. At about 60 hours, the cell cluster, called a morulla, contains between 12 and 16 cells. The whole cluster is no bigger than the original egg as it reaches the top of the Fallopian tube and enters into the cavity of the uterus.

On entering the uterus, however, the cluster—now called a blastocyst—begins a new phase of development, its physical attachment to the endometrial lining of the uterus.

Implantation

The blastocyst is a tiny hollow sphere of cells bulging at one end. The outer wall of the sphere is called the trophoblast. The inner bulge, the raw material from which the embryo will grow, is the embryoblast.

The blastocyst floats into the cavern of the uterus and catches onto the wall. Sometimes a blastocyst implants in other places—usually with serious consequences. If the cell cluster implants near the bottom of the uterus (the cervix), it can lead to a complication known as *placenta previa*, which causes severe bleeding in the last stages of pregnancy, as well as other complications during delivery.

Other wrongly targeted implantations may lead to dangerous ectopic pregnancies, caused when the blastocyst implants in a variety of inappropriate locations–such as in a Fallopian tube or on the ovary.

Most of the time, however, by about day 5 or 7, the blastocyst buries itself in the plush wall of the uterus, its position marked only by a small clot of blood remaining on the surface. The sphere collapses, and the inner mass of cells takes on a flat, disklike appearance. From this inner disk the foundations of the baby's body will be laid.

The outer layer of cells will become the primitive placenta. The trophoblast is the only tissue, other than malignant tissue, which invades another. At the same time, it is like a tissue graft. Normally tissue grafts from one person to another are rejected, but the trophoblast is not rejected, thanks to changes in the mother's immune system that prevent this from happening.

Week 2

The trophoblast begins to thicken and sends out little finger-shaped projections called villi that poke into the uterine lining, anchoring the blastocyst. At about 2 weeks, these fingers have penetrated maternal blood vessels to such an extent that they can extract blood and nutrients; thus, placental circulation is established. Eventually, this outer cell layer will become a fully functioning placenta and, as the connecting link between embryo and mother, continue to supply blood, nutrients, and oxygen to the developing fetus throughout pregnancy.

When the blastocyst implants, a woman might have slight vaginal spotting as the maternal blood vessels are eroded. This bleeding may be mistaken for signs of a menstrual period, but it is actually one of the earliest signs of pregnancy.

Once the placental circulation becomes established, the unique process of embryonic differentiation begins. The rapidly dividing cells begin selectively to form groups, which eventually become various organs and body systems. By day 9, the inner disk divides into a double-layer plate. The lower layer, the endoderm, will create the inner surface of the body—the digestive tract, the liver, and the lungs. The upper layer, the ectoderm, will give rise to the skin, hair, nails—and then fold inward to make the nervous system.

On the ectoderm side of the embryoblast, a thin-walled amniotic cavity appears. An insignificant little space at this stage, it will later fill with fluid and accommodate the whole baby.

Week 3

By day 15, on the endoderm side, a larger cavity, called the yolk sac, develops. A third cell layer, called the mesoderm, begins to fill in between the 2 original layers and ultimately builds such vital body systems as the muscles and blood. All animals form these 3 layers—ectoderm, endoderm, and mesoderm—as the first step in their development. Each layer, regardless of species, gives rise to the same type of organ. The ectoderm, for example, forms the scales in fish, the feathers of a bird, and the skin in humans.

With differentiation, the disklike cell mass changes from a sheet of undistinguished cells into a distinct head and tail fold. It bends in the middle, losing the flat shape. Two parallel ridges form down the middle of the ectoderm. Between them is a groove or trench, known as the neural groove. This will form the nervous system. The bottom of the groove becomes deeper and wider, while at the top the edges fuse together, so that a tube is formed. This folding in of surface cells (invagination) is the embryologic mechanism for forming hollow tubes. The digestive tract and some of the tubes in the urogenital system will form in the same fashion. In the case of the nervous system, the back of the tube becomes the spinal cord; the front thickens and expands to form the brain. Inadequate fusion of the neural groove at this early stage of development will produce neural tube defects (spina bifida with meningomyelocele).

The essential parts of a human being —the brain and the heart—also start to develop in week 3, and a primitive circulatory system is forming. In the head region a large single tube forms; it will acquire a thick muscular coat and become the heart. Before the complicated 4-chamber human heart is complete, this simple tube will undergo many twists and turns. Nevertheless, even at this rudimentary stage it begins to contract, forcing blood through the primitive embryo and placenta.

By the end of week 3, substantial changes have also occurred in the outer layer of cells. The little pocket of fluid enlarges and now separates the embryo (embryoblast) from its surrounding wall (trophoblast), and a connecting stalk develops between the 2. This body stalk, through which the embryoblast receives nutrients, will later become the umbilical cord. The size of the yolk sac reduces in proportion, as organ development begins in the embryo.

The Embryonic Period

Weeks 4 to 8 of human development are called the embryonic period, dominated by dramatic changes in the nervous system and blood supply. This is a very critical time in the development of the fetus because the basic structure of human life, the nervous system, is being laid down. Other organs are also being formed during this period. It is in these very early days that the embryo is especially vulnerable to environmental damage, such as exposure to drugs or other teratogens that can cause birth defects.

Week 4

From day 20 to 30 the embryo is in the *somite* stage. Early pairs of primitive cells, called somites, align themselves in ladderlike progressions on either side of the neural groove. From these somites will eventually come cartilage, bones, and muscles. The number of somites gives a rough guide to developmental age of the embryo. A 20-day embryo has 1 to 4 somite pairs, a 23-day embryo 10 to 13 pairs, a 24-day embryo 13 to 17 pairs, and a 28-day embryo 26 to 29 pairs. The distribution of somite pairs is the first sign of the two symmetrical halves of the human form. As the embryo enlarges, more somites are added, until eventually there are 44 pairs.

The repetitious pattern of somites down the sides of the embryo suggests an evolutionary link with other vertebrate animals, such as fish, which retain a clearly segmented body. In humans, however, such clear segmentation is seen only in the early weeks of development.

Shortly after the nervous and circulatory systems are laid down, the digestive tract begins to form from the endoderm. A tube develops with another invagination process; the front of the tube pushes forward and will soon break through to form the mouth.

At 4 weeks, the embryo has a head and a tail. The neural groove has fused over completely, and formation of the brain is progressing. In the head, the beginnings of the eye and ear are developing. Thyroid, larynx, and trachea start to develop. The heart, a large bulge on the underside of the embryo, beats rhythmically and can be picked up on ultrasound. Although the rapidly growing embryo is only ¼ inch long, almost all the organs have begun to form.

By the end of week 4, the amniotic

sac expands further and its outer layer merges with the inner layer of the tropho-blast. The body stalk has developed into the umbilical cord, joining the placenta and embryo. Oxygen, carbon dioxide, and nutrients are exchanged through the placenta.

Week 5

In week 5, the lungs are tiny solid organs on either side of the abdominal cavity. The liver and kidneys have begun to form in the middle layer of cells. Of all the or-gans, the kidneys differ in their manner of development. Most organs begin as sim-ple embryonic structures, which become more complex as they develop. The kid-neys, however, seem to develop on the basis of trial and error. A type of kidney similar to that found only in few very primitive fishes and eels develops first. This organ, called pronephros, lasts only a few days, then disappears. Then a sec-ond, more complicated kidney develops, called the mesonephros, or middle kid-ney. This kidney also fails. Finally, a third and even more complex kidney is formed, the metanephros. This structure endures and develops into a mature kidney.

By the end of week 5, the arm and leg buds have begun to form. The arms and hands develop a little ahead of the feet and legs. (See table 12.1.) It was at this stage of development that thalidomide had such devastating consequences. When thalidomide was taken before for-mation of the limb buds began, or after it was completed, no harm was done. If, however, the drug was taken in the sev-eral weeks when the limbs were forming,

Table 12.2
FETAL HAND GROWTH TO 12 WEEKS

- Arms first appear as limb buds late in week 4.

- By week 6, paddles have developed at the end of the arms. Radial ridges and grooves appear in the hands.

- By week 7, the tissue in the radial grooves has broken down and the fingers sepa-rate. The fingertips swell as touch pads develop.

- Fingernails appear during week 10, al-though they will not reach the fingertips until week 32. The thin layer of skin that covers the nails later degenerates, leaving the cuticles.

- By week 12, the hands are fully formed.

development stopped at the limb bud stage, and the infant was born with rudi-mentary arms and legs.

Regional divisions of the brain are recognizable in week 5. The eyes are visi-ble, with a web of skin covering them. Be-hind the eye on either side gill slits develop, embryologic leftovers from an-other species. Parts of these become the facial and neck structures; the remainder regress. Occasionally, remnants are pres-ent at birth. These are benign and can be surgically removed. Depressions for the nostrils are also recognizable. The minute heart begins to push newly formed blood cells around the pea-sized embryo.

At about 4 to 6 weeks, the hormones of the placenta take over from the ovary's corpus luteum.

Week 6

By week 6, the circulatory system becomes established and the heart is beating strongly. The stomach is recognizable. New cells are laid down to form the skeleton and backbone. A little tail is present but does not grow.

The most dramatic changes are seen in the face. The large head, which comprises ⅓ of the embryo's length, seems to bend the embryo over. The embryo begins to take on a much more human appearance. The eyes and nostrils become more distinct. The eyes are at the side of the head, but will gradually move around as the face takes form. The eyes are covered by skin that will form the eyelids, and they will remain closed until week 25 or 26. The inner ear is rapidly growing, but the external ear has not yet formed. The slit beneath the eye will eventually become the ear. The head rests on a large bulge on the undersurface of the embryo, which contains the heart and liver.

By the end of 6 weeks the embryo is about 1 inch long and its main internal organs have finished forming, although they are still in a rudimentary stage. The heart is strongly beating and the circulatory system is well established. The heart parts fuse to form the 4 chambers. A failure of the heart parts to fuse at this time can cause cardiac defects. (See figure 12.2.)

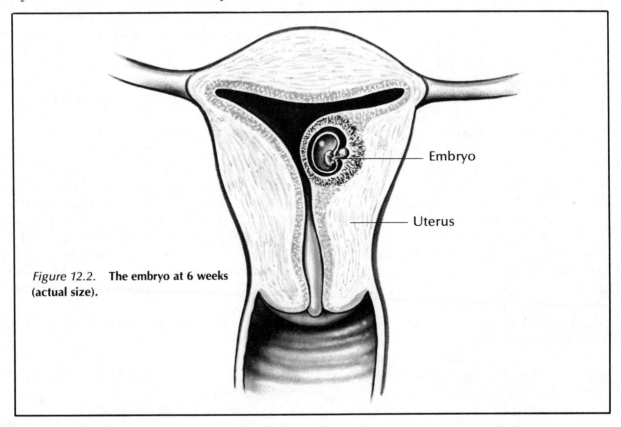

Figure 12.2. **The embryo at 6 weeks (actual size).**

Embryo

Uterus

Week 7

By the end of week 7, the embryo's hands and feet have formed. The beginnings of fingers, toes, and eyelids are evident. The nervous system is forming and muscle fiber begins to develop. Adrenal gland and thyroid cells become more mature. The tail disappears.

Week 8

Centers of bone growth are established and ossification begins. Nose and upper jaw grow rapidly and the 2 sides of the lips and palate fuse. It is at this time that abnormalities of development may lead to such conditions as harelip and cleft palate. After this stage is complete, these defects cannot occur.

THE EMBRYO BECOMES A FETUS

BY THE END of week 8 the embryonic period is complete; the baby now enters the fetal period and is called a fetus, meaning offspring. The fetus is now about 1½ inches long and will grow rapidly until week 20, when the rate of increase in length will begin to slow down. (See box, Measurements of the Fetus.) The head is still large compared with the rest of the body, but the face is more recognizable. The eyes are much larger and have moved to the front of the head. They can easily be seen beneath the skin. The tear ducts have also formed, and the ears, which originated on the neck, continue moving toward the head. Ten tooth buds, which will eventually become "baby" teeth, make their first appearance.

Ankles and wrists are forming, and the fingers and toes can be clearly distinguished, despite still being covered by webbing.

The body first forms a cartilage model of the skeleton. As pregnancy progresses, true calcified bone gradually re-

MEASUREMENTS OF THE FETUS

Ultrasound can be used to monitor fetal growth. (See chapter 8, Medical Care During Pregnancy.) During the first trimester, the length of the fetus from the top of the head to the bottom of the spine will give an estimate of fetal age that is accurate to within 1 to 2 days. From week 12, the spine begins to curve, making it difficult to judge length. The side-to-side diameter of the head is used instead. The expected date of delivery can be predicted within 7 days if the side-to-side diameter is measured before week 24 after conception. After week 24, this measurement also becomes less accurate, but measurements based on the circumference of the baby's head and abdomen, the length of the arms, and possibly specific diameters of the brain can be used.

places the cartilage. This replacement follows a definite pattern and, on X ray, the maturity of a fetus can be gauged by which bones are calcified and which are not.

The muscle structure is developing

beneath the skin, giving the body contours of the fetus a more human form. The potbellied appearance of the 2-month fetus is caused by a relatively large liver, which comprises ¹/₁₀ of its body weight. Some of the neck and trunk muscles begin to contract spontaneously, and the arms and legs move. These movements can be detected by ultrasound, but the mother will not be able to feel them for another few weeks.

THE THIRD MONTH (WEEKS 9—12)

ABOUT THE WEEK 9 the external genitalia begin to appear, although the sex of the fetus cannot be discerned until the fetus is at least 12 weeks old. (See box, Formation of the Sexual Organs.)

At 10 weeks the fetus is about 2¼ inches long and has doubled its length in the previous 3 weeks. The head is more rounded, but still bent forward on the chest. (See figure 12.3.)

The eyelids are properly formed now, and the fetal movements have increased. The fingernails appear, followed by the toenails. The nails develop slowly; they will not reach the fingertips until week 32 and the toetips by week 36. At the time of birth they will project slightly at the tips of the fingers and will have to be trimmed in the first few days of life to keep the baby from scratching itself.

In the third month the larynx, or voice box, begins to form at the upper end of the trachea, or windpipe. The vocal cords—2 delicate bands stretching across the top of the larynx—do not form until much later. Even at birth they are relatively inflexible. The vocal cords are not completely finished until the baby is several months old.

The digestive tract becomes perfected at this early stage, although the fetus will have nothing to digest until it begins to eat after delivery. The liver, in addition to producing digestive juices, also manufactures some red blood corpuscles for the fetus. After birth, the bone marrow will take over this job, but during fetal life the liver is an important manufacturing site.

Cells that produce the insulin hormone also appear in the third month. Insulin controls the metabolism of sugar in the body. When this hormone is lacking, diabetes develops. The fetus of a diabetic mother often has larger and more numerous groups of insulin-producing cells (known as islets of Langerhans), as if to compensate for its mother's lack of hormone. Since insulin acts as a growth hormone in utero, excessive fetal production of it can lead to an oversized baby. Some of these big babies are born with serious problems, and occasionally die shortly before or after birth. Thus, it is important to control a diabetic mother's blood sugar throughout pregnancy to prevent high fetal insulin.

The final kidneys also form and begin to function in the third month, although they will not be fully mature until after delivery. As soon as the fetal kidneys

FORMATION OF THE SEXUAL ORGANS

Every cell in the body has the same 46 chromosomes (44 plus 2 sex chromosomes) that carry the genetic code. Reproductive cells begin to sort themselves out in the early weeks of embryonic life. The female and male gonads (ovaries and testicles) arise from similar tissue—a cluster of reproductive cells that migrates down below the kidneys, together with other support cells.

As the reproductive systems develop, two cords of cells known as the müllerian system move down toward the pelvic floor. In a girl, the lower portions of the cords fuse and hollow out into the vagina and uterus. The upper segments remain separate and later become the Fallopian tubes. A baby girl should be born with an intact vagina, cervix, uterus, Fallopian tubes, and 2 ovaries. The ovaries are equipped with a full complement of ova, more than 400,000.

In a boy, the müllerian cords almost completely disappear under the influence of müllerian-inhibiting factor, which is produced by the testes. Instead, the major ducts of the male gonads are formed from another pair of cords, the mesonephric. The upper portion of the mesonephric cords forms the ejaculatory ducts, and the lower portion becomes the vasa deferentia. In a girl, these cords disintegrate.

For the first 8 weeks it is impossible to distinguish a boy or a girl from the amorphous mass of cells. Then, slowly the external genitals begin to take shape from a small groove near the fetal tail. Under the influence of the hormone dihydrotestosterone, the upper portion of the groove develops into the penis in a boy and becomes the clitoris in a girl.

The testicles of a boy are originally formed just under the kidneys in the abdomen. They usually begin to descend around week 28 of fetal life, and reach the scrotum by week 32. A newborn boy should be born with all his sexual organs in place: penis, testicles, scrotum, accessory glands, and a system of ducts.

Boys born prematurely usually have undescended testicles, as do some boys born at term, but they usually reach the scrotum within 3 months of birth. About 1 of every 200 male babies is born with 1 or both testicles still inside the body proper. At one time physicians advised waiting until puberty to see if the testicles would descend spontaneously. But today if the testicles do not descend naturally the infant is usually given hormones to increase his testosterone level when he is between 6 and 18 months of age. If the testicles do not descend naturally after drug therapy, microsurgery is recommended as early as possible. The younger the boy is when surgery is performed, the more likely his sperm-producing capacity will be intact when he reaches puberty. Two years is considered the optimum age for this type of surgery.

begin to function, the volume of amniotic fluid increases. At term, there is roughly a quart of amniotic fluid. Any excess or deficiency may be caused by an abnormality somewhere in the developing fetus. Too little fluid suggests that the kidneys are absent or that an obstruction exists in the urinary passage. Too much fluid is sometimes traced to a flaw in the swallowing mechanism, caused either by a defect in the brain or an obstruction in the digestive tract.

The Fully Formed Fetus

By 12 weeks after conception, the limbs and internal organs of the fetus are fully formed, although they are not sufficiently developed for it to survive independently. The most sensitive period of the fetus' de-

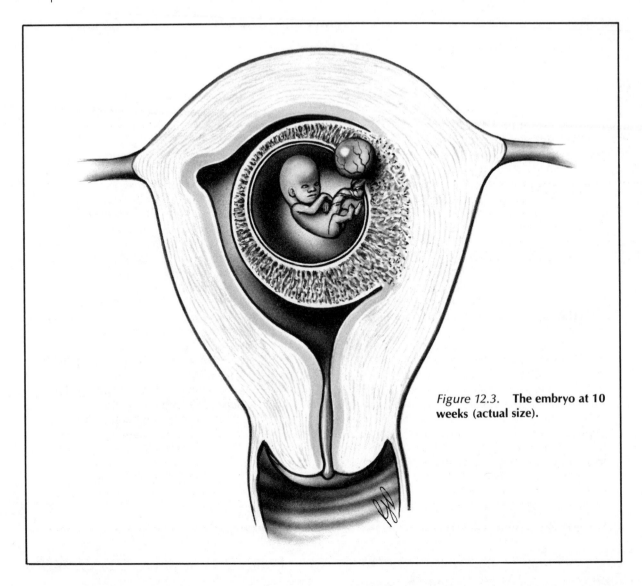

Figure 12.3. **The embryo at 10 weeks (actual size).**

velopment has passed, and risk of gross structural abnormality occurring in the last 6 months is very small. Once organs and limbs have been properly formed, they are no longer subject to teratogenic effects. Should the fetus sustain a heavy bombardment of toxins, however, it is still possible for growth to be inhibited, especially in the brain, which has barely begun to develop.

The fetus is now connected by the umbilical cord to the placenta and comes into contact with the amnion and the uterine wall only by bumping against it. The amniotic sac that surrounds the fetus contains about 12 ounces of fluid and the

3-inch fetus has plenty of room to move about, although the mother cannot feel it move yet. The head of the fetus is now rounded, with the neck and facial features properly formed and the ears in their permanent position on the sides of the head.

The fetus can swallow and move the upper lip, the beginnings of the sucking reflex. Most of the amniotic fluid the fetus swallows is used by the body, but a few drops of sterile urine also are produced; this is removed by regular exchange of the fluid through the placenta and the mother's bloodstream.

The external sex organs are now developed enough for the baby's sex possibly to be determined by ultrasound.

For the next 6 months, the main focus is on the growth of the fetus into a baby capable of surviving outside the protective environment of the uterus. The weight of the fetus will multiply 7 or 8 times in the last 6 months of pregnancy.

The Placenta

The placenta is a complex organ that establishes physiological communication between mother and baby by means of the umbilical cord. The rough, spongy side of the placenta burrows into the lining of the uterus and initiates direct contact with the mother's blood. The fetus is attached to the other, smoother side of the placenta by the umbilical cord, which leads from the placenta to the navel.

The mature placenta is shaped like a flat disk. It weighs a little over 1 pound, is about 8 inches in diameter and 1 inch thick in the center. It usually implants in the upper part of the uterus. Its position is easy to see on an ultrasound scan. If the placenta has implanted too low in the uterus, a cesarean delivery may be required.

What the Placenta Does

The placenta performs 4 crucial tasks:

- It filters oxygen and nourishment from the mother's blood to the baby via the umbilical cord.
- It siphons off carbon dioxide and other waste products from the fetus and carries them back to the maternal blood.
- It blocks the transmission of some infections and drugs, although it cannot screen everything. (The rubella virus, aspirin, alcohol, and many other substances can penetrate the placental barrier. Fortunately, antibodies from the mother's blood can also cross the placenta to provide the baby with immunity from certain illnesses, a protection that persists for a time after birth.)
- It manufactures hormones, chiefly human chorionic gonadotrophin (HCG), progesterone, and estrogen, which help maintain the lining of the uterus and support the growth of the uterus and breasts.

The Umbilical Cord

As 1 side of the placenta develops a maze of blood vessels into the uterus, 3 large blood vessels from the other side grow into the slowly elongating umbilical cord. The placenta is like the root system of a tree and the umbilical cord is the trunk. These three blood vessels—2 arteries and a vein—are surrounded by a gelatinous material called Wharton's jelly.

The arteries carry waste products from the fetus through the umbilical cord and into the placenta; there they are exchanged for oxygen and nutrients from the mother. The vein in the cord then carries these materials back to the fetus. The placenta makes this interchange possible.

Early in pregnancy, the umbilical cord begins to twist spirally and at birth may contain as many as 40 turns. It is also fairly common for the cord to wrap around the fetus. The umbilical cord is about ½ inch thick and often has small bumps, or false knots, along its length. These kinks may be caused by blood vessels or small pockets of Wharton's jelly. True knots occur if the fetus moves through a loop of the cord; as long as the loop is not pulled too tightly, circulation will not be impaired.

At term, the cord is approximately 20 inches long, although its length varies considerably. An excessively long or short cord can lead to problems during labor and may necessitate a cesarean section.

The Circulatory System

The fetus maintains its own circulatory system, separate from the mother. Blood rarely escapes from the fetal circulation; if bleeding occurs at any time during pregnancy it is almost always from the mother.

The work of the fetal respiratory and digestive systems is handled by the placenta. Oxygen and nutrients from the mother's blood diffuse through the placenta, into the umbilical cord, and are absorbed into the fetal circulation. Carbon dioxide and waste products pass back through the umbilical cord to the placenta and are extracted by the mother.

Fetal blood oxygenated in the placenta returns to the fetus via the umbilical cord, where it mixes with some of the deoxygenated blood already in circulation. This oxygen-rich blood is pumped to the head and around the body, losing oxygen as it goes. However, most blood bypasses the lungs. This is because the lungs, which oxygenate blood after birth, do not do so in the fetus. The lungs require only enough blood to enable them to continue growing. The deoxygenated blood returns to the placenta via the heart. The fetal heart functions differently too, since it does not need to pump large quantities of blood to the lungs.

THE FOURTH MONTH (WEEKS 13–16)

THE CHANGES that occur in the remainder of pregnancy are much less dramatic than the early weeks. The basic structure of all the organs is complete, and over the next 6 months they will enlarge and mature.

By now, the risk of miscarriage—

spontaneous abortion—is diminishing. The uterus has now grown to accommodate the pregnancy. If the mother lies on her back and relaxes it is possible for the uterus to be felt as a soft round swelling just rising out of the pelvis.

The amniotic sac holding the baby contains about 100 milliliters of fluid within which the baby has plenty of room to move, although its movements are still not apparent to the mother.

The skin is still thin and red. Later in pregnancy, the skin thickens and loses much of its red color. The skin on the bottom of the feet and on the toes, hands, and fingers begins to develop ridges.

The arms, legs, and head have developed. The body of the fetus looks like a baby except the head is still relatively large in proportion to the rest of the body, and the legs are relatively short. (See figure 12.4.) The head is now quite round and the neck is formed so that the head can move easily on it. The forebrain can be distinguished from the cerebellum and brain stem. The mouth, nose, and eyes are properly developed, as is the outer ear. The sexual organs are essentially formed,

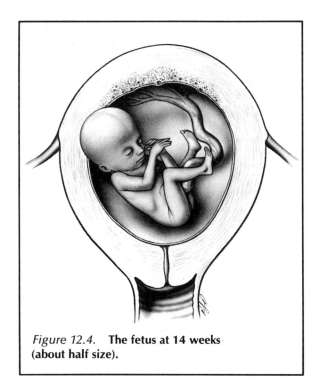

Figure 12.4. **The fetus at 14 weeks (about half size).**

and the fingers and toes are fully separated.

Weighing roughly 6 to 8 ounces at the end of 4 months, and measuring 8 to 10 inches in length, the fetus is still much too small and immature to survive outside the womb.

THE FIFTH MONTH (WEEKS 17—20)

FINE, DOWNY FUZZ called lanugo begins to grow on the eyebrows and upper lip. By week 20 it will cover most of the body. The purpose of lanugo is unknown, but it is later replaced by hair from secondary hair follicles. The soft fuzz is shed before or shortly after birth, disappearing last from the eyelashes, eyebrows, and scalp.

Vernix caseosa, a creamy white substance which acts as a protective covering for the thin fetal skin, has also begun to form—mainly from oil gland secretions in the skin. Vernix caseosa first appears on the back, in the hair, and in joint creases, but will eventually cover the whole body, preventing the skin from becoming waterlogged from the amniotic fluid. Vernix is gradually absorbed by the skin, but some of it is usually still evident at birth.

The fetus is growing rapidly. At the end of week 18, it weighs about 12 ounces and is about 10 inches long.

There is a great deal of fluid around the baby in which it can move and rotate with ease. Some babies are much more vigorous than others; at sometime during the fifth month (usually between weeks 16 and 18), the mother will feel the fetus move for the first time. This is called "quickening." The first felt movement may seem like a flutter, but will continue to gain in strength each day.

The fetus has sleeping and waking cycles. These periods of rest and activity are influenced by sensors in the fetus as well as by the mother's activities. As pregnancy progresses the sleep/wake cycles become more noticeable.

THE SIXTH MONTH (WEEKS 21–24)

GOOD MATERNAL NUTRITION throughout this stage is essential to enhance the development of brain cells. The brain undergoes an important period of growth from the fifth month on. The brain as well as the body of the growing fetus needs the nourishment of a good maternal diet, especially in the last 4 or 5 months of pregnancy. (See figure 12.5, and box, Development of the Senses.)

Eyebrows and eyelashes are evident. The iris, which gives rise to eye color, does not develop pigment until after birth. Consequently, all babies are born with slate-blue eyes.

The ovaries and testes are established, and the tubules of the kidneys branch out. The bronchial tube also continues to branch. At 6 months the fetus is covered with downy lanugo.

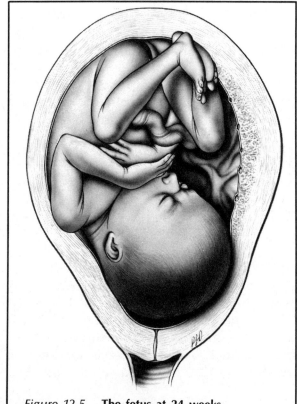

Figure 12.5. **The fetus at 24 weeks (about one-third size).**

DEVELOPMENT OF THE SENSES

The foundation of the fetal nervous system is established in the first few weeks following conception. By 6 weeks, the reflexes are present and electrical brain wave patterns can be recorded. From quite early in life the fetus is responsive to touch, sound, and light. In some limited sense, the baby may be able to learn and remember some sounds that are heard while still in the uterus. That the fetus forms memories and retains some of them seems possible, but is difficult to prove. Research is continuing into the fetus's response to music and memory of it after birth.

The fetus can touch parts of his or her body with the hands and feet and can also be touched all over by the umbilical cord. Experiments have shown that early in pregnancy the fetus tends to move away from things that touch it, but later will move toward them. For example, if the hands touch the mouth, the mouth opens, but the fetus turns its head away. Later, the fetus may turn its head toward the hands, and may even suck a thumb or finger.

As early as week 9, the fetus may turn its head away and frown if its forehead is touched, and will curl up the toes or bend the knees if the soles of the feet are stroked. The whole body becomes sensitive to touch, except the top, back, and sides of the head, which seem to remain relatively insensitive until after birth. This may be a way of protecting the head during birth. Certainly, the changes in heart rate and the increase in movement for a few minutes after amniocentesis suggest that tactile stimuli are sensed in some way by the fetus, although its movement in this situation might be merely a reflex response to a uterine contraction.

The eye muscles are present in early pregnancy, and the fetus moves its eyes while sleeping or changing position. From about week 16, the fetus becomes sensitive to light that penetrates the uterine wall and the amniotic fluid. If a very bright light is shown on the mother's stomach, the fetus may reflexively move away.

The inner ear is totally developed by mid-pregnancy, and the fetus is able to respond to a variety of sounds. In the uterus the fetus is subjected to continuous noise from the mother's intestines and the blood flowing through her blood vessels. External noises, such as loud voices or music, also reach the fetus, who may react to these with movement. The fetus also responds to changes in frequency that are beyond the range of an adult's ear, moving more at the sound of high frequencies and less at low ones.

The fetus is able to swallow amniotic fluid early in pregnancy and is also able to taste. If a sweet substance is injected into the amniotic fluid, the fetus will turn toward it and swallow more.

THE SEVENTH MONTH (WEEKS 25–28)

THE HAIR IS longer, and the eyebrows and eyelashes have grown. The eyes are capable of opening and shutting. The soft fuzzy lanugo has begun to disappear and the skin has started to change from red to a flesh tone because fat is beginning to be deposited under the skin.

The testes in a boy, originally in the abdomen, begin to descend and usually reach the scrotum by week 32.

At 28 weeks, the fetus is about 14 inches long and weighs approximately 2.4 pounds. Further development now is mainly that of greater size. From now until term, the fetus needs only to grow in length, weight, and size.

A fetus born at this stage will be able to cry weakly and breathe with difficulty and has up to a 75 percent chance of survival in intensive care in a special neonatal unit. Chances of survival depend on condition at birth and maturity of the lungs. Many premature babies born at this time will grow up normally. If they are very premature, however, they may require intensive medical care and may, because of their immaturity, suffer from a variety of serious disorders, ranging from intestinal problems to brain hemorrhages and cerebral palsy.

THE EIGHTH MONTH (WEEKS 29–32)

AT 30 WEEKS, the fetus is approximately 16 inches long and weighs about 3½ pounds. A baby born at this time has a good chance of surviving, provided the infant receives special care in a premature baby unit. The lungs are still immature, as are the other vital organs, and the skull is delicate and can be injured during labor. The head is now in better proportion to the body. More fat has been laid down under the skin, but the fetus still looks rather thin. The placenta weighs about 1 pound and there are about 3 pints of amniotic fluid.

The fetal heart can be heard well through a stethoscope, though it sounds rather muffled. The rate varies between 120 and 160 beats per minute, which is about double the mother's pulse rate. Occasionally, a soft blowing sound (funic souffle) can be heard if a fetal stethoscope is placed right over the umbilical cord.

By now the baby is probably lying with the head down toward the mother's pelvis. Although there is less room in which to move about, the fetus still moves vigorously.

THE NINTH MONTH (WEEKS 33–36)

AT THE END of 34 weeks the baby is about 17 to 18 inches long and weighs approximately 5½ pounds. The kidneys are fully mature and lungs almost so. Babies born now have at least a 95 percent chance of survival.

The head and body are in the same proportion as they will be at birth, and the baby has lost most of the wrinkled appearance because of the additional subcutaneous fat that has been laid down. The nails on the hands have reached the fingertips, although those on the feet have not yet reached the ends of the toes. The fetus now fills the uterus and cannot move around freely.

In most cases, the baby is in a head-down, or cephalic, presentation, ready for birth. There is very little room for the baby to move, and the mother may feel very uncomfortable. When the baby's head moves down into the pelvis and becomes "engaged," usually around week 34 to 36, the mother usually feels more comfortable because there is less pressure on the lungs and stomach.

THE LAST 2 WEEKS

AT 38 WEEKS the baby's skin is pink and the body is round and plump. (See figure 12.6.) Most of the down fuzz has disappeared, and scalp hair is usually about 1 to 1½ inches long, although some babies are completely bald at birth. The body is still covered with vernix, except for the mouth and eyes. The vernix is thickest in the creases of the body.

The whole intestine contains meconium, a greenish-black residue that will be passed soon after delivery. In most cases, the testicles of a male baby have descended into the scrotum by term.

The baby's fingernails have grown beyond the ends of the fingers and the toenails have reached the ends of the toes. The eye whites are fairly white, but the iris is still slate blue. The permanent eye color will appear within a few days or weeks after birth.

At term, the baby will probably weigh approximately 7½ pounds. There is a wide variation in the birth weights of normal, healthy babies, but it is unusual for a baby to weigh more than 10 pounds.

Because of the variations in the length of normal pregnancies, there is lit-

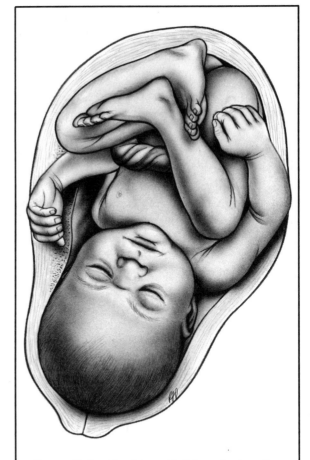

Figure 12.6. **The fetus at full term (reduced).**

tle cause for concern when labor begins 3 weeks before or less than 2 weeks after the estimated due date. Concern begins at 1½ to 2 weeks past the expected date.

Few babies arrive on the day they are expected; in fact, only 1 baby in 20 arrives precisely on the day due. This is hardly surprising since menstrual cycles vary in length and conception may also take place at different times. Even for a woman with a "standard" 28-day cycle (on which estimated delivery date tables are based), the time of ovulation is known only approximately and a precise delivery date cannot be calculated. If a woman has an irregular or prolonged cycle, calculations based on the date of her last menstrual period are sure to be inaccurate.

In addition to the uncertainty of the date of ovulation, it is unlikely that all fetuses mature in precisely the same length of time. The exact cause of the onset of labor at term is unknown, but size of the baby and its maturity may have an effect on how long the pregnancy lasts. For example, a woman carrying twins will very often go into early labor because the combined weight of the babies triggers her body into starting labor.

THE POSTMATURE BABY

PREGNANCIES that last too long can pose problems. The placenta has a limited lifespan. Usually, it grows actively for about 30 weeks, after which it begins to show microscopic signs of degeneration. If labor starts too long after the due date, the placenta may no longer be able to sustain the baby properly. There is a risk of the baby being damaged or dying due to deprivation of oxygen and nutrients before the onset of labor, although fortunately this rarely happens. And if the birth is much overdue, labor may be more difficult because of the baby's increased size.

A baby who is overdue will be monitored carefully. If the mother is well, and monitoring shows that the baby is healthy, too, pregnancy can be allowed to continue until labor begins spontaneously. However, if medical signs indicate, labor can be induced or the baby can be delivered by cesarean section. Induction in the hospital may be initiated by oxytocin—a hormone that causes uterine contractions—in a controlled infusion or by amniotomy, artificial rupture of the membranes.

A baby who is postmature at birth can be readily identified because he or she will have lost fat from all over the body, particularly around the abdomen. As a result, the skin will be wrinkled and may have begun to peel. There will also be little vernix on the body, and the fingernails may be long.

13 The High-Risk Pregnancy

Harold E. Fox, M.D., and Laxmi V. Baxi, M.D.

INTRODUCTION

THE GREAT MAJORITY of pregnancies proceed smoothly through the many changes in a woman's body—and the thousands of coordinated steps involved in developing a new life. When complications do occur, it may be without warning, making regular prenatal care the best insurance that a problem will be detected early and treated successfully. However, health professionals are increasingly able to predict in advance which women are more likely to develop specific complications. By monitoring or reviewing thousands of pregnancies, they have learned that some women, statistically, have a greater chance to develop complications or to deliver a child with specific medical problems. These pregnancies are often labeled "high-risk," with the telltale parts of the health history called "risk factors."

When a pregnancy is labeled high-risk, it does not mean trouble is inevitable. Most women will have no problems in pregnancy and will deliver a healthy, full-term infant. The high-risk label simply means that special care may be necessary to maximize the likelihood of a healthy outcome for mother and baby.

223

Table 13.1
PRENATAL VISIT CHECKLIST

Information provided at initial prenatal visits—or, ideally, during a pre-conception consultation—alerts obstetricians to about half of all pregnancies that might later develop complications. Be prepared to provide answers to the following questions. If the information is not requested, it should be volunteered.

Reproductive and Gynecologic History

- What is the date your last menstrual period started?

- If a home pregnancy test was taken, on what date was it positive?

- What is the usual number of days in your menstrual cycle (counting from day 1 of the menstrual period until day 1 of the next, is it usually 28, 30, 32, irregular, etc.)?

- Have you had any surgery on your reproductive organs?

- Were you exposed to DES in utero?

- If you have had other pregnancies, what was the outcome of each (including tubal pregnancies, therapeutic abortions, miscarriages, and stillbirths)?

- Did you have any complications during pregnancy? at delivery?

- Did you require any special tests, restrictions on activity, or hospitalizations?

- What are the birthdates and birth weights of previous children?

- Did you have any difficulties with delivery?

- Were any born prematurely?

- If you had a cesarean delivery, what was the reason and what type of incision was used on the uterus?

- If known, what is your blood type and that of the baby's father?

- If you are Rh negative, were you given rhesus gamma globulin after every previous pregnancy and abortion?

- Have any previous children had birth defects or required care in the neonatal intensive care unit?

- Has any close relative (mother, sister, aunt) had several miscarriages or stillbirths?

- Does anyone, on either side of the family, have a birth defect or other medical problem that might be inherited?

- Have you had carrier testing for genetic disorders more frequent in your ethnic group (such as Tay-Sachs screening for persons of Eastern European Jewish descent, thalassemia for persons of Mediterranean ancestry, and sickle cell disease for blacks)? (See chapter 3, Genetic Considerations, for more information.)

Infections

- Have you had any sexually transmitted infections, such as gonorrhea, syphilis, genital herpes, chlamydia, or nonspecific urethritis?

- Have you had rubella or been vaccinated against it?

- Are you concerned that you may have been infected with the AIDS virus?

- Are you exposed to infections—such as hepatitis or cytomegalovirus—on the job (health professional, teacher of young children, etc.)?

- Do you have a cat or eat raw meats? (If so, a toxoplasmosis test should be done.)

Medical Care

- Have you had any nongynecologic surgery?

- Do you have any chronic medical conditions, even those not currently being treated? (Some medical conditions, such as asthma, heart disease, diabetes, high blood pressure, lupus, sickle cell anemia, thyroid problems, and epilepsy, require special care during pregnancy.)

- Can you provide the names, addresses, and phone numbers of all health professionals who may have answers or more complete details in any areas of concern? For ongoing medical conditions, copies of medical records may be useful.

Conception

- Was the conception difficult?

- Were any infertility treatments involved, such as medications (Clomid, Pergonal, etc.), artificial insemination, or in vitro fertilization?

- If artificial insemination by donor was involved, was the semen fresh or frozen?

- Was a sperm bank involved?

- What screening tests (for infection, Rh factor, AIDS, and possible genetic disorders) were performed on the donor?

Contraception

- Was the conception planned?

- Were any birth control methods in use at conception (spermicides, IUD, birth control pills)?

Medications

- What medications, prescription and over-the-counter, do you take regularly? occasionally?

- What vitamins or other food supplements do you use? What are the dosages of each?

Lifestyle

- How frequently, if at all, do you use alcohol, tobacco, or drugs not already mentioned under "medications"?

- What is your work environment (hours, materials used, amount of stress) like?

- Does the mother have any unusual eating habits? Any concerns about safe exposures during pregnancy?

This Pregnancy

- Have you had any spotting or bleeding?

- Severe headaches?

- Nausea and vomiting serious enough to interfere with getting enough liquids?

- Chills or fever over 100°F?

- Cramping or abdominal pain?

Risk factors are not all equal. Some are more serious than others, and some risks can be virtually eliminated by proper care. If a health professional designates a pregnancy as high-risk, a thorough explanation of the physician's concerns for mother and baby should be sought, as well as what can be done during pregnancy to reduce the risk.

With many conditions, a woman's knowledge about her own body and understanding of the risk factors play an important part in prenatal care, helping her recognize changes that could be warning signs of problems as pregnancy progresses. In high-risk pregnancy, the prenatal care schedule will usually involve more frequent obstetrical appointments and, in many cases, more testing and specialty consultation than in low-risk pregnancies. For these reasons a high-risk pregnancy can be fairly demanding of the mother-to-be, her partner, and family, making flexibility, support, and good communication with the physician and other health care providers essential.

Patients can be actively involved in assessing risk status. General health as well as reproductive history should be discussed during a prepregnancy or early pregnancy examination. Someone who has had 1 or more pregnancies resulting in stillbirth or who has close female relatives with a history of multiple losses should share this information with her doctor. Previous gynecologic surgery, unusual problems in previous pregnancies, and pregnancies resulting in children with birth defects should also be discussed with the health professional planning prenatal care for the current pregnancy. (See table 13.1.)

Anyone identified as high-risk is not a candidate for delivery at home or in a childbirth center. Although delivery may be by a midwife, prenatal care should be provided in conjunction with a physician and delivery should be in a fully staffed hospital where a physician backup is immediately available. Responsible health professionals will not accept a high-risk woman for delivery outside a hospital.

Although most obstetricians in general practice care for high-risk patients, a woman may choose to see or may be referred to a maternal–fetal specialist experienced in high-risk births for prenatal care and delivery. These specialists are often affiliated with a university medical center or other tertiary care facility.

CAUSES OF HIGH-RISK PREGNANCY

Timing of Pregnancy

Advanced Maternal Age—35 Years and Over. From a purely physical point of view, the ideal time for a woman to become pregnant is when she is 22 years old —after her body is fully mature and before she is subject to the diseases that can come with aging. Obviously, emotional and social circumstances may be much more important considerations in deciding when to start a family. Many women wait until they are well into their 20s or 30s before they have their first baby, often not completing their families until they are in their late 30s or 40s. Between 1980 and 1984, the number of first births to women 35 and over almost doubled.

Most pregnancies after age 35 will proceed uneventfully and result in the birth of a healthy baby. However, the older mother may have to take extra steps to ensure her health and that of her baby.

First, pregnancy becomes more difficult to achieve as time passes. While it takes a 25-year-old woman an average of 2 months to conceive, it takes about twice as long for the average 35-year-old.

Another consequence of maternal aging is the increased risk of genetic defects, particularly chromosomal abnormalities. The risk of having a child with Down syndrome, the most common chromosomal defect, increases from about 1 in every 2,000 births for 20-year-olds to about 1 in 350 babies for 35-year-olds. The presence of a chromosomal defect can be detected prenatally through amniocentesis, which is performed at about 16 weeks of pregnancy, or chorionic villus sampling, an earlier test that is available in some locations. (See chapter 3, Genetic Considerations.)

As women enter their 30s and 40s, they are more likely to have chronic medical conditions that place their pregnancies at increased risk for complications. Hypertension, diabetes, and autoimmune diseases are more common in older women. They are also more likely to be carrying twins or triplets.

Teenage Pregnancy. Women are able to conceive before their bodies are fully ready for pregnancy. Females in the United States, for example, tend to reach menarche (the time of first menstrual flow) between the ages of 11 and 14. For this reason, pregnancies in teenagers are often high-risk for medical, nutritional, or social reasons.

The medical risks are particularly great under age 16. Although life-threatening complications are still rare, anyone who is 16 or younger has more than a 50 percent greater chance of dying during pregnancy and delivery than does a 20-year-old. Women between the ages of 16 and 19 have a 30 percent greater risk of dying. Increased mortality at the younger ages cannot be attributed to any one cause, although the increased occurrence of hypertension in pregnancy in this age group is thought to be partly responsible.

Another serious consequence of pregnancy in very young mothers is stunted growth. In girls, bone growth usually peaks right before menstruation begins and then decreases over the next few years as estrogen levels gradually rise during adolescence. Pregnancy raises the estrogen level and may halt a young teen's bone growth prematurely, leaving her with smaller stature. Anyone who gets pregnant before her own bone growth is complete also may have a pelvis too small to safely allow passage of the baby's head through the birth canal (cephalopelvic disproportion), increasing the chance she will require a cesarean delivery.

Young women often have problems meeting the nutritional requirements of pregnancy. Inadequate, nutritionally deficient diets are common among teenagers, and young women's own rapid growth and development during adolescence places extra demands on their nutritional reserves. Low prepregnancy weight, poor weight gain during pregnancy, and inadequate nutrition contribute to the increased risk of several pregnancy complications in teens, including low birthweight, toxemia, premature labor, and premature separation of the placenta. Diets poor in iron, coupled with heavy menstrual blood loss in young women, make them particularly prone to developing anemia. Iron and vitamin supplements and nutritional counseling are usually necessary to add sufficient calories and nutrients to a pregnant teenager's diet.

Pregnancies Too Close Together. Conception within 3 months of delivery puts the new pregnancy in a high-risk category, because the mother's body has not yet recovered from the physical strains of the first pregnancy. Though conception in the first 3 postpartum months is rare (especially if the new baby is exclusively breastfed), it does happen. Most of these pregnancies result in healthy, normal babies with few ill effects on the mother's health, provided she takes steps to compensate for the extra strain.

If a woman conceives soon after her last delivery, early prenatal care is extremely important. Pregnancy takes a toll on nutritional reserves, and some women find it difficult to put on enough weight and to maintain the protein and iron reserves needed to ensure a healthy second pregnancy. Weaning the older baby, if the mother is still nursing, is often recommended in order to direct all available nutritional reserves to the growing fetus. Rest, exercise, and eliminating other risk factors, such as smoking and drinking, are also important.

Risk Factors Affecting the Current Pregnancy

Contraception in Use at Time of Conception. Nearly 50 percent of pregnancies today are unplanned, many of them the result of failed contraception. Not realizing they have conceived, many women continue to use contraception throughout the early weeks of gestation, inadvertently placing the embryo in an environment that could be harmful. In recent years, there have been suggestions of an increased incidence of birth defects in infants who were exposed to vaginal spermicides early in pregnancy, causing widespread alarm among the estimated 3.4 million users of this birth control method. These fears about spermicide use appear unfounded. A major study conducted at The Columbia Presbyterian Medical Center and involving 13,000 women showed no association with birth defects. Reanalysis of early data questions the true significance of the link found in the initial research. For these reasons, most physicians still consider spermicides a safe method of birth control and do not consider an exposed fetus at any special risk.

The possible adverse effects of using oral contraceptives during early pregnancy have also been the source of much concern. The chance of becoming pregnant while on the pill is very small, increasing slightly with each day a pill is missed. Those who are taking oral contraceptives, but who wish to stop in order to become pregnant, ideally should wait 3 months or 2 normal menstrual cycles before attempting to conceive. This gives the pregnancy-simulating effects of the birth control pill a chance to resolve and lets the body reestablish its natural cycling pattern (which is important for dating the pregnancy).

When a woman becomes pregnant while taking the pill, and therefore continues taking birth control pills during early pregnancy, she may experience nausea and vomiting more severe than that normally associated with morning sickness. Occasionally, jaundice occurs.

Several studies have suggested that oral contraceptives taken early in pregnancy may increase the chance of birth defects. However, no firm evidence has been found for an association and, if there is a risk, it is generally considered miniscule. If the pill is continued into the second month of pregnancy, the risk of genital malformations in female fetuses may be slightly increased. Again, the hazard is so small that it does not significantly alter the likelihood of having a normal outcome in individual pregnancies. Most obstetricians find that even if birth control pills are taken inadvertently early in pregnancy, the infant will be normal.

If conception occurs while an intrauterine device (IUD) is in place, there is a greatly increased risk of spontaneous abortion, infection, and prematurity if the IUD remains in place for the duration of pregnancy. The chance of a normal outcome is greatly improved if the device is in its normal position and can be removed easily as soon as pregnancy is confirmed. If the IUD is inside the uterus or in an awkward position, the decision may be made to leave it in place to minimize the risk of miscarriage. If the pregnancy is continued with the IUD in place, any signs of early pregnancy complication, such as bleeding, cramps, or fever, should be reported to the physician immediately.

Multiple Births. Although the human uterus is not designed to accommodate more than 1 fetus, the presence of twins or triplets is not rare. A multiple pregnancy is always special, drastically changing planning for infant care, enhancing the routine discomforts of pregnancy and increasing the chance of certain complications.

As soon as multiple pregnancy is suspected, an ultrasound examination is likely to be recommended. A sonogram may be suggested if there is an increased risk of a multiple pregnancy. Risk is higher with age and in those who have had many children, who are themselves a twin or who have twins in the immediate family, and who have conceived while taking fertility drugs to stimulate ovulation. Elevated levels of pregnancy-related substances in the blood (particularly human chorionic gonadotropin and alpha fetoprotein) and rapid increases in weight or size of the uterus are signs of possible twins.

Prematurity is the major cause of problems in twins; about half of multiple pregnancies end in preterm delivery. Anyone carrying twins should be instructed in how to detect the subtle signs of early labor. When contractions are detected promptly and the mother treated with rest and, perhaps, medication, contractions can often be delayed to give the babies valuable extra time in the womb.

Twins are likely to be born too small as well as too soon. About half of twins born weigh less than 5½ pounds. To avoid this, the mother must eat more and choose foods carefully in order to maximize fetal growth and to avoid deficiencies of iron and folic acid. If the twins are in the same amniotic sac and share the same placenta, there is occasionally a serious discrepancy in their growth, with 1 twin receiving most of the blood and nutrients. After birth, the smaller twin may develop the complications common to premature infants. The very large twin is at risk for different heart and circulation problems. Both are likely to require treatment in the neonatal intensive care unit.

Other, more frequent complications of multiple pregnancy are premature rupture of the membranes, excess amniotic fluid, toxemia, and gestational diabetes. Decreased activity and sometimes bed rest are recommended as measures that can lessen the increased risk of toxemia and prematurity.

Complications during delivery are also more common and include excessive bleeding following delivery and abnormal presentation of the second twin. In twin pregnancies, both fetuses present head down about half the time and can be delivered vaginally. However, if either twin is not head down, cesarean delivery is sometimes necessary. In certain situations, after the first twin is delivered vaginally it is still necessary to perform a C-section to deliver the second twin safely. In some hospitals multiple births are routinely scheduled to take place in the cesarean delivery room, with an anesthesiologist available, even if vaginal birth is to be attempted. As an added precaution, the mother's blood is often typed and cross-matched since excess blood loss is more common and a transfusion may be necessary.

Maternal–Fetal Blood Group Incompatibility. In most cases, differences between a baby's blood type and that of the mother do not cause any problems during pregnancy. Occasionally, however, a blood factor inherited from the father makes the baby's blood different from the mother's in a way that can be harmful.

The most common serious blood group incompatibility involves the Rhesus (Rh) factor. Most people—85 percent of whites and 95 percent of blacks—are Rh positive because they have a protein called the Rh factor on the surface of their red blood cells. The remainder lack the Rh factor, making them Rh negative. Rh factor status has no effect on a person's own health but can cause serious fetal health problems if a mother is Rh negative and the baby is Rh positive. (For more information, see chapter 14, Complications in Pregnancy.)

Other red blood cell factors, among

the nearly 400 known, can induce maternal antibodies capable of crossing the placenta and destroying fetal red blood cells. Fetal hemolytic disease occasionally occurs when the mother with O type blood has a fetus with A or B type blood. ABO incompatibility is not life threatening, but jaundice is likely after birth and phototherapy or exchange transfusions may be needed. Occasionally, women have antibodies to rare blood factors encountered as the result of blood transfusion before pregnancy (blood is matched for major blood groups only). In the unusual case of the fetus inheriting the same rare blood factor from the father, incompatibility and fetal hemolytic disease can result in the first pregnancy. The most common incompatibility of this type is seen in women with antibodies to a group of red blood cell proteins known as the Kell system. Routine blood tests at the first prenatal visit will reveal whether anti-Kell antibodies or antibodies to any other rare blood group are present. If so, the baby's father will be tested to help the physician anticipate whether hemolytic disease is likely.

Past Reproductive and Gynecological History

DES Daughters. Between 1946 and 1971, as many as 2 to 3 million pregnant women in this country were given diethylstilbestrol (DES), a synthetic estrogen thought to prevent miscarriage and other complications of pregnancy. When the children of these women reached puberty, it became apparent that DES exposure in utero was associated with the development of an unusual type of cancer of the vagina and cervix and structural abnormalities of the reproductive tract in daughters, as well as urinary and reproductive tract defects in sons. Both men and women should inform their physician of exposure to DES, and daughters should have a thorough pelvic exam including a Pap smear (and colposcopic examination, if indicated) at least once a year to check for cancerous changes.

DES daughters are also at risk for complications in pregnancy, primarily because 20 to 60 percent of the women have structural abnormalities of the vagina, cervix, and uterus. Many DES daughters have a small or unusually shaped uterus, making placenta previa and cervical incompetence more frequent. These changes make it more difficult to carry a baby to term, accounting for much of the increased miscarriage and preterm delivery in their pregnancies. For reasons that are not well understood, DES daughters also are more likely to have trouble conceiving.

In order to identify those who may be at risk for complications during pregnancy, some doctors routinely examine the upper reproductive tract of all DES daughters by hysterosalpingography, a technique that involves X-ray imaging of the uterus and Fallopian tubes. Others feel the expense of the procedure and risks of radiation exposure are unjustified, since even if structural abnormalities are identified, they cannot be corrected. Hysterosalpinography is not needed to detect abnormalities of the lower uterus and cervix. If lower reproductive tract abnormalities are found, weekly or biweekly pelvic examinations are done throughout pregnancy so that appropriate therapy can be instituted should premature labor appear imminent. Stitching the cervix closed (cerclage) may be done if it is judged incapable of remaining secure (known as incompetent cervix) before premature labor begins. Evidence from preliminary studies indicates that it may be beneficial to use cerclage as a preventive measure during pregnancy in DES-exposed women, rather than waiting until adverse cervical changes occur. If the mother does go into labor prematurely, medication and bed rest may help delay delivery.

Preterm Labor. A previous premature delivery means a 25 to 50 percent chance of subsequent deliveries being early. Prenatal care will be designed to reduce the risk of preterm labor and to detect premature contractions early so that they can be stopped. Frequent appointments will be scheduled during midgestation, when the mother is most at risk for premature labor.

Those at special risk for preterm labor will be encouraged to practice health habits that promote fetal growth. Proper nutrition will be stressed, as well as avoidance of tobacco, alcohol, and unnecessary medication. Depending on the timing and cause of the last preterm labor, modifications may be made in exercise programs or work schedule. In some cases, bed rest is indicated.

Learning to recognize the signs of impending labor is important; the obstetrician should be contacted immediately if they occur. The signs include 1 or more of the following: a dull ache in the lower back or pelvic area, leaking (or a gush) of amniotic fluid, and contractions that occur at regular intervals increasing in intensity and frequency. (See chapter 15, Labor and Delivery, for additional information.)

Even for those who have never delivered prematurely, certain risk factors may increase the likelihood of preterm labor. These include exposure to DES before birth, previous surgery on the reproductive organs (including D&C and cone biopsy), chronic infections, and repeated kidney or urinary tract infections. Risk is also elevated if the mother is underweight, is under 18 years old, cares for 2 or more preschool children, is a single parent, or is under particular physical or emotional stress. Premature labor can sometimes be triggered by infection, and so prompt recognition and treatment of infections, including those of the urinary tract, should be emphasized.

Medical Conditions

Serious medical conditions such as heart disease, diabetes, hypertension, neurological problems, immune system disorders, and infectious diseases increase the risk for a variety of problems during pregnancy. The hormonal and other changes in body chemistry that occur during pregnancy may exacerbate maternal disease and the disease itself may affect the course of pregnancy and its outcome.

If possible, those with chronic health conditions should consult a knowledgeable obstetrician—one experienced in high-risk pregnancies—before becoming pregnant. Care prior to conception and during pregnancy may be coordinated by an obstetrician and a physician who knows the mother's medical history well. Often a doctor experienced in high-risk pregnancy, with special training in protecting the health of the mother and the developing fetus during complicated pregnancies, will be suggested. Nationwide, there are about 450 physicians who have obtained a subspecialty certification in this area, called maternal–fetal medicine.

Women who rely on medication to control a chronic condition should discuss their medical history and use of medication with a qualified physician who is aware of the pregnancy or plans to conceive. It is *not* safe to stop taking medication without medical advice. Letting a chronic condition worsen through lack of medication is often more risky to the pregnancy than is continued use of the medication.

Chronic Hypertension. Uncontrolled hypertension (high blood pressure) can be lethal during pregnancy, which is why every pregnant woman's blood pressure should be checked regularly throughout the 9 months. Those with chronic hypertension need to be particularly conscientious about having blood pressure checked throughout pregnancy and ideally should have baseline prepregnancy levels established for comparison before conception. Kidney function tests are sometimes done throughout gestation to ascertain whether maternal kidney function is deteriorating.

Consistently high blood pressure can reduce the amount of blood flow to the placenta, limiting the supply of oxygen and nutrients reaching the fetus. Fetal death or intrauterine growth retardation are the most serious consequences. To confirm that fetal growth is proceeding normally, a sonogram is usually done before 24 weeks and again at about 34 weeks. If growth is severely compromised, the fetus may be delivered prematurely and cared for in a neonatal intensive care unit. If growth is normal and pregnancy proceeds without any additional problems, a normal vaginal delivery can be expected.

Blood pressure tends to drop during the first half of pregnancy. Mild hypertension that has been successfully controlled with diet and exercise before pregnancy can probably be sustained without antihypertensive medications. Even mothers who have been on medication for years do surprisingly well. During pregnancy, physicians will select antihypertensive medications that do not interfere with blood flow to the uterus. Because it causes a reduction in blood volume, diuretic therapy is not usually started or continued during pregnancy.

Taking a 2-hour rest each day while reclining on the left side can increase blood flow to the kidney and placenta by 15 to 20 percent. Circulation to the fetus can also be improved by refraining from smoking and getting plenty of rest.

When hypertension occurs for the first time after 20 weeks of pregnancy, it is labeled gestational hypertension. (See chapter 14, Complications in Pregnancy.) Pressure usually returns to normal after the pregnancy—but gestational hypertension can indicate a predisposition to develop hypertension later in life.

Seizure Disorders. Recurrent seizures affect at least 1 percent of those of childbearing age but can be well controlled with medication. The effect of pregnancy on the frequency of epileptic seizures has been argued for many years and even today remains largely unresolved. Studies show that the frequency of seizures remains unchanged in about half of pregnant women with convulsive disorders; another 45 percent have more seizures than usual during pregnancy; and the remaining small minority of patients experience fewer seizures during pregnancy. An initial episode of epilepsy during pregnancy is rare.

Because epileptics vary a great deal in their response to pregnancy, a full evaluation by a neurologist should be done before conception to arrange for treatment supervision throughout pregnancy. Those taking medication to control their seizures should be especially careful to discuss childbearing plans with their physician, because some of the most effective anticonvulsants have been shown to have adverse effects on the fetus and the continuation of pregnancy. For instance, use of very high doses of phenytoin (Dilantin) throughout pregnancy is sometimes associated with a characteristic group of birth defects, including malformations of the face and skull, heart defects, and subtle developmental problems in infancy and childhood. Fetal exposure to valproic acid, another drug commonly used to treat epilepsy, has also been associated with malformations and delayed development.

It may be advisable to substitute another medication for phenytoin or other potentially harmful drugs before attempting to conceive. If a patient has been free of seizures for several years, her physician may recommend a trial without medication before conception. If seizures do not occur, she can continue drug-free throughout pregnancy. When the choice is made to continue medication, blood samples are taken on a regular basis to make sure drug levels are high enough to maintain control over seizures, since severe and uncontrolled seizures are even more dangerous to mother and baby than drugs. For the same reason, medication should not be discontinued without medical advice.

Antiepileptic medication can precipitate folic acid deficiency in women, which may lead to anemia. For this reason, prenatal supplementation with folic acid and iron may be advised. Phenobarbital has been associated with excessive newborn bleeding as a result of a deficiency in vitamin K-dependent clotting factors. If phenobarbital is taken throughout pregnancy, vitamin K may be administered at the onset of labor. Vitamin K will also be given to the baby immediately following delivery, and tests for platelet counts and clotting factor will be performed within 24 hours.

Asthma. Asthma is the most common chronic respiratory disorder in women of childbearing age. The disease is characterized by recurrent bouts of wheezing, coughing, and difficulty in breathing. Attacks are often precipitated by viral infections, emotional distress, exercise, and contact with substances that cause allergic reaction. Although it is usually difficult to anticipate how an individual's asthmatic symptoms will respond during pregnancy, severity of symptoms before pregnancy is often a fairly good predictor. In general, mild symptoms before pregnancy have a tendency to remain fairly stable, while severe asthma will often worsen. If asthma worsened during a previous pregnancy, symptoms tend to be even more severe during subsequent pregnancies.

During pregnancy, medications must be selected carefully out of concern for the fetus. This is especially true during the first trimester, when the fetus is particularly vulnerable to damage. In some cases, the need for medication can be eliminated or minimized if extra care is taken to protect against substances that provoke symptoms. Asthma medication should not be reduced without consulting a physician, however, since an asthma attack itself can cut off oxygen to the fetus. The respiratory burden of pregnancy is greatly increased by bronchial asthma and even mild attacks can be debilitating enough to require medication at some point.

Mild or infrequent attacks may be controlled with an inhalant such as isoproterenol or an oral bronchodilator, such as theophylline. Corticosteroids may be given for severe asthma and for cases that do not respond to bronchodilators. If they are required, the dose is tapered to the minimum needed to control symptoms and the patient is carefully monitored for changes in blood sugar, sodium retention, and blood pressure.

Unless a cesarean delivery is necessary for obstetrical reasons, vaginal delivery is preferred for most women with asthma, as local anesthetics are preferred over general anesthesia.

Systemic Lupus Erythematosus. Systemic Lupus Erythematosus, commonly called SLE or lupus, is a chronic disorder of the immune system that affects about 1 in 500 women of childbearing age. Sometimes, initial symptoms develop during pregnancy. Painful and inflamed joints, weakness, lack of energy, and increased susceptibility to infection are the most common symptoms. Occasionally a butterfly-shaped rash across the nose and cheeks and skin blotches elsewhere on the body are present. The symptoms are so nonspecific that lupus may go undiagnosed for quite some time. Because symptoms vary from patient to patient, accurate diagnosis involves a series of blood and urine tests that may take several weeks to evaluate.

Sometimes lupus is diagnosed during pregnancy. The disease can cause a false-positive reading on the routine test for syphilis given at the first prenatal visit. Rising blood pressure and toxemia before the third trimester of pregnancy may also signal the physician to look for lupus.

There is no consensus as to whether pregnancy adversely affects the course of lupus. Even in the same women, each pregnancy may have its own unique complications and impact on the disease. In general, women without kidney involvement can expect to have relatively uncomplicated pregnancies, while those with renal disease are at slightly increased risk for flare-ups and worsening of kidney function.

Frequent blood tests and kidney and

liver function measurements will be done to detect changes in the activity of the disease during pregnancy and during the period shortly after birth. If steroids or immunosuppressants were taken before conception, they are usually continued throughout pregnancy. The physician may advise a shift to steroid treatment, and away from aspirinlike drugs and other immunosuppressives. In many cases, drug dosage is increased during labor and for several weeks afterward in order to minimize the anticipated worsening of symptoms during this period. Professionals and partners attending the labor and delivery should be aware that lupus can bring on fatigue quickly.

Lupus increases the odds of miscarriage, whether or not it is in remission. Prematurity is also increased, but this risk is minimized when lupus is well controlled during the pregnancy. Although it is still rare, infants born to mothers with lupus have an increased chance of being born with a heart abnormality, congenital complete heart block. This defect is a disturbance of nerve transmission to the heart muscle, causing children to have a slow pulse and a characteristic heart rhythm. Many children with heart block have no symptoms—others become dizzy or faint during exercise or, in the most serious cases, require a pacemaker.

Occasionally a baby whose mother has lupus is born with symptoms of lupus, or transient neonatal lupus. A rash may be present at birth or develop shortly thereafter, and blood tests will indicate the presence of unusual antibodies similar to those seen in the mother. The antibodies are thought to be maternal in origin and typically disappear within a few weeks of birth. The skin rash is usually gone by 6 months.

For the mother with lupus, the decision to breastfeed will depend on energy level and type of medications required. A schedule of breastfeeding for part of the day only, timing feedings to minimize the amount of medication passed to the baby, may be helpful. Those who require immunosuppressants are usually advised to avoid breastfeeding.

Thrombocytopenia. Like lupus, thrombocytopenia is an autoimmune disorder, but it is much more rare. In this condition, which may be a result of lupus, there is a decrease in the number of platelets, special blood cells that are part of the body's blood clotting mechanism. Thrombocytopenia may also result from certain drugs, viral infections, and AIDS, or it may develop as a complication of severe preeclampsia. (See chapter 14, Complications in Pregnancy.) Most cases of thrombocytopenia, however, are of unknown origin and hence are called idiopathic thrombocytopenic purpura (ITP).

Thrombocytopenia can be detected by a blood test, but it is not commonly screened for in pregnancy. Because it affects clotting, there is a significant risk of excess bleeding during childbirth. It can be treated with steroidal drugs and, if the platelet count is high enough at the time of delivery, a vaginal birth is possible. Otherwise, a cesarean section is usually advised. Because thrombocytopenia is an autoimmune disorder, antibodies are formed that can cross the placenta and affect the fetus, causing, in extreme cases, intrauterine hemorrhage.

Diabetes. Before the widespread use of insulin to control blood sugar levels, preexisting diabetes was a dangerous condition for a pregnant woman and the developing fetus. With increased understanding of the importance of tight blood sugar control during pregnancy, and refinement of means to maintain control, the hazards of diabetes for mother and baby have been greatly reduced. Today 1 of every 200 women who become pregnant has diabetes, usually of the insulin-dependent type. Another 4 percent will develop diabetes sometime during pregnancy. (See chapter 14, Complications in Pregnancy.) With careful management, most have an excellent chance of having a healthy baby.

Careful carbohydrate control is the key to improved outcome in diabetic pregnancies. To minimize the risk of miscarriage and birth defects (particularly neural tube defects), good control should be established for the early weeks of pregnancy—in fact, prior to conception. A study recently reported to the American Diabetes Association showed that the rate of pregnancy complications or birth defects was only 2.1 percent in mothers who were in good control before conception. Those who attained control within 21 days of pregnancy had a rate of 4.9 percent, and those who gained control after that time or not at all had a 9 percent chance of having complications or a child with birth defects.

Maintaining tight control during pregnancy is not easy, even for those who understand diabetes well and are adept at adjusting their diet, exercise, and insulin. Hormone fluctuations, nausea and vomiting, and exertion during labor can all affect blood sugar at a time when it should be kept more constant than ever. Careful studies have found that strict control of blood glucose levels to between 70 and 140 mg/dl, with a mean of 80 to 87 mg/dl throughout pregnancy, greatly reduces the risk to both mother and baby. Pregnancies in which glucose levels stayed above 200 have the highest risk.

A glycosolated hemoglobin test, which measures the amount of glucose attached to protein molecules in red blood cells, is a good indicator of the last 2 months' blood sugar control and is often suggested as part of a pre-conception workup. Before pregnancy is attempted, the obstetrician will also check for signs of any diabetic complications, such as kidney problems, retinal damage, high blood pressure, and cardiovascular disease. Diabetic women normally have no more difficulty in becoming pregnant than nondiabetic women.

In selecting an obstetrician, diabetics should look for a physician experienced in the care of diabetic pregnancies and able and willing to work with the patient's regular doctor throughout pregnancy. Hospital choice is also important. Although good blood sugar control minimizes these risks, babies born to diabetics are often large and prone to fetal distress late in pregnancy, as well as respiratory distress and low blood sugar after delivery. Cesarean delivery and newborn care in the neonatal intensive care unit are frequently necessary. A neonatologist or pediatrician who specializes in high-risk pregnancy should be available to examine the baby soon after birth.

After pregnancy is diagnosed, frequent self-testing of blood sugar—usually

6 or 7 times a day—becomes essential, and urine should be tested once a day for ketone bodies. Newer, more sophisticated methods of insulin delivery and monitoring may be recommended during pregnancy. These include a portable pump that delivers a continuous flow of insulin and a glucose meter that gives a numerical readout of the glucose level in a drop of blood. In addition to home monitoring, regular appointments with the obstetrician—weekly or every other week throughout the entire pregnancy—are advisable.

During the course of pregnancy, insulin requirements will change. For those who have been successfully maintained on oral diabetic agents prior to pregnancy, insulin injections are usually recommended. In the early stages of pregnancy, insulin dosage may have to be reduced because the rapidly growing fetus is removing glucose from the mother's blood at a very great rate. As pregnancy progresses, the amount of insulin required by the mother rises. Repeat ultrasound scans are often used to assess the growth of the baby and to check for malformations, and an AFP test for neural tube defects is often done in the first trimester. (See chapter 8, Medical Care During Pregnancy.)

Diabetics have a slightly increased incidence of skin, vaginal, and urinary tract infections, especially during pregnancy. Many physicians do monthly urine cultures during the last trimester to check for a silent infection that could flare up and cause difficulties. With care these infections should not represent a major problem, but they should be treated promptly; left uncontrolled, they can lead to increased insulin requirements. Preeclampsia and excessive accumulation of amniotic fluid around the fetus (polyhydramnios) are 2 other complications of pregnancy seen more frequently in diabetics.

Near-term fetal death can occur in diabetic pregnancies, and doctors may recommend delivering the baby as soon as it is mature enough to leave the supportive environment of the womb. Today, most diabetic pregnancies can be carried to a point where the risk of prematurity is small and the outcome of pregnancy is successful, but to do so requires careful monitoring by both the mother and physician. Toward the end of pregnancy the mother may be asked to keep a careful record of fetal movement and to tell the doctor immediately if movement decreases. During this period, fetal heart rate monitoring is often done weekly or more often in order to make sure the baby is getting enough oxygen. In week 36 or 37, the amniotic fluid may be tested to determine whether the fetal lungs are fully developed. Depending on blood sugar control and the maturity of the fetal lungs, it may be advisable to deliver the baby early, either by inducing labor or by cesarean section.

Once the baby is born, it may require care in a special neonatal unit. These babies often experience a drop in blood sugar soon after birth, but good glucose control during pregnancy will reduce the chance of this complication. If the blood sugar does drop, the baby will be given early supplements of sugar either intravenously or by mouth. Once the baby's blood sugar has stabilized, if no other problems develop, chances are good that the baby can be returned to a regular nursery and the mother.

Soon after delivery, the mother's insulin requirement will drop considerably, frequently within a few hours after the birth. Breastfeeding also tends to decrease insulin requirements, and so those wishing to nurse would be prepared to make minor adjustments in their insulin dosage when they get home. Because breastfeeding also can cause rapid falls in blood sugar, it may be helpful to have a glass of milk, or perhaps a little tea with honey, before nursing the baby, in order to maintain blood sugar.

Multiple Sclerosis. Multiple sclerosis (MS) destroys myelin, an insulating material that covers nerve fibers throughout the central nervous system and is necessary for the normal transmission of electrical impulses. Symptoms of the disease vary considerably from one individual to another, depending on which areas of the brain and spinal cord are damaged by the inflammation and scarring that follows myelin destruction.

Pregnancy does not have any predictable effect on the course of MS, and medical professionals differ in their advice to women with the disease. Recent studies indicate that there may be a remission in symptoms during pregnancy, leading to the impression that symptoms worsen following delivery. Multiple sclerosis does not appear to affect the health of the baby, although the course of pregnancy can be complicated if a severe attack involving the urinary tract develops. In gen-

eral, women with MS who are otherwise in good health can expect to have healthy, full-term babies with no damage to their own health.

Heart Disease. The heart must work harder during pregnancy, beating more rapidly and pumping at least 30 percent more blood than usual. Labor is a strenuous cardiac workout and good circulation is crucial throughout pregnancy to ensure that an adequate supply of oxygen and nutrients reach the developing fetus. In about 1 in 100 pregnancies the mother has a preexisting heart condition—often resulting from rheumatic fever or a congenital heart malformation. It is crucial that the obstetrician be informed of any preexisting heart problems. Unless heart damage is severe, quality care usually leads to a healthy outcome for mother and baby. However, even those who feel well and are usually able to tolerate exertion may need additional monitoring and restrictions of activity during pregnancy. The likelihood of favorable outcome for the mother and baby in pregnancies complicated by heart disease is primarily affected by the extent of disease and the likelihood of other complications that could further compromise the heart's function. Women who have heart disease amenable to surgical correction who want to get pregnant should plan to have the operation before attempting to conceive.

The treatment of heart disease in pregnancy varies, depending on the type and severity of disease. Evaluation by a cardiologist before pregnancy and several times during pregnancy is often recommended. Prenatal care will be aimed at avoiding any complications that increase the heart's work load. It is especially important to avoid excessive weight gain, minimize salt intake (to avoid fluid retention), and get adequate iron from food and supplements (to avoid anemia). Plenty of rest, along with avoidance of all unnecessary exertion, is important even among those who have not had to limit their activity level before pregnancy. The support and cooperation of family members and employers is especially important in order to minimize physical and emotional stress.

Antibiotics may be prescribed as a preventive measure at several points during pregnancy—if dental work is needed, during labor and delivery, or at the first sign of infection. Contact with people with respiratory infections should be avoided and even a mild cold should be reported to the physician immediately. Some doctors also recommend immunization against pneumonia and influenza.

In spite of the physical effort required in labor and delivery, vaginal delivery is safer and less likely to be complicated than cesarean section. If labor is prolonged, continuous epidural anesthesia and other analgesics are often used to relieve pain, and forceps may be used to assist delivery during the bearing-down stage. Proper positioning and use of oxygen can also ease the heart's workload during labor. Postpartum hemorrhage, infection, and thromboembolism occur much more frequently in women with heart disease, even when there has been no indication of heart failure during pregnancy, labor, or delivery. Therefore, the mother will be advised to remain in the hospital for close monitoring after delivery.

In general, heart disease in pregnancy poses a greater risk to the mother than to the fetus. Important exceptions are types of heart disease that interfere with the transport of oxygen to the fetus —which can slow the baby's growth and, in severe cases, can lead to miscarriage and premature delivery—and those that must be treated with beta-blocking drugs that cross the placenta. Digitalis (and its derivatives) and quinidine do not appear to affect pregnancy; however, if a woman is taking quinidine, she is usually advised not to breastfeed.

Sexually Transmitted Diseases

Screening for common sexually transmitted diseases, such as syphilis, gonorrhea, and chlamydia, is part of comprehensive prenatal care. Some viral infections cannot be eliminated from the body, and their presence requires special attention during future pregnancies. (See also chapters 5 and 8.)

Herpes Simplex Virus. Genital herpes, which is caused by the herpes simplex type II virus, is on the increase in this country among adults of all social and economic classes. Spread by any form of sexual contact, the virus does not disappear when the symptoms go away. Instead, it travels along the nerves into the nerve centers at the base of the spinal cord, where it remains inactive or latent until reactivated. Upon reactivation the virus travels back down the nerves, causing new sores in the same area involved in the initial attack. The causes of reactivation are not well understood, but attacks are most frequent in people with chronic illnesses or under a great deal of emotional or physical stress.

Pregnancy is thought to be a precipitating factor for recurrence of active infection, and pregnant women with herpes should be alert for signs of active infection. The herpes virus does not appear to travel across the placenta to reach the embryo or fetus and is not a known cause of malformations. However, it can be the cause of severe disease in the newborn if the virus is transmitted to the fetus immediately prior to or during delivery. Herpes infection in the newborn period can lead to blindness, neurological problems, mental retardation, and even death. Neonatal herpes is very difficult to treat successfully and for this reason, most efforts are directed toward preventing fetal contact with the virus during delivery. Cesarean section is usually recommended if there is a danger of passing the infection to the baby.

Babies of mothers known or suspected of having herpes are usually separated from other infants in the newborn nursery while tests for herpes are done. In order to ensure that herpes does not develop, these babies may be kept under close observation for several weeks. A new mother with herpes should be especially careful to avoid passing the virus to the baby after birth by avoiding contact between her sores, her hands, and the baby. Good hygiene is particularly important if the mother is going to breastfeed the baby.

Human Immunodeficiency Virus. The virus that causes acquired immune deficiency syndrome (AIDS) can cross the placenta and infect the developing fetus. Prenatal exposure to the virus—now known as human immunodeficiency virus or HIV—may cause a characteristic group of malformations and leads to the breakdown and failure of the immune system seen in adults with the disease. Although many of the infections these children get can be treated, the virus itself cannot be eliminated from the body. Most children who acquire AIDS prenatally die within the first few years. Many children born of infected mothers appear normal, but studies have found that 25 to 60 percent of the children have the virus.

Because many people infected with HIV have not developed AIDS, it is possible for a woman who feels perfectly well to pass the virus to her fetus. Women who are concerned that they may have been infected with the AIDS virus can receive counseling and testing for viral antibodies. Women at special risk for infections include those who:

● have used intravenous (IV) drugs for nonmedical reasons

● are or have been sexual partners of IV drug users, bisexual men, men with hemophilia, or men who show any evidence of HIV infection

● have any symptoms of HIV infection, such as chronically swollen lymph glands, weight loss, and frequent infections

● have been rejected as a blood donor because of a positive HIV antibody screening test

● have engaged in prostitution

• received a blood transfusion during the years 1977–1985, before it was possible to screen blood for the virus

The AIDS virus will not be passed to the baby in all pregnancies, but there is currently no way to prevent it or to determine its passage during pregnancy. Because the body's immune system defenses are somewhat diminished in all pregnancies, physicians have been concerned that HIV-infected women will become seriously ill during pregnancy, but studies so far have not indicated that this occurs.

Hepatitis B Virus.   Hepatitis B virus can be transmitted from the mother to her fetus, usually during delivery or after birth. The virus does not appear to travel across the placenta to infect the fetus; however, infants may pick up the virus through breastfeeding. Some infected infants do not show evidence of disease, while others develop rapidly progressing liver disease that can result in death. Still others become chronic carriers of the virus, which puts them at risk for transmitting the virus to others. Chronic hepatitis B virus carriers are also more likely to develop liver cancer later in life.

This form of hepatitis is transmitted most often through contaminated blood and blood products, and in saliva, semen, and vaginal secretions. Some physicians routinely screen all pregnant women for hepatitis B. Others reserve the test for those who are more likely to have been exposed to the virus, including health care workers, IV drug users, and their sexual partners. If a pregnant woman is found to harbor the virus, infection in the newborn usually can be prevented by immunizing the infant with a very effective vaccine against hepatitis B virus soon after birth. Those who may be exposed to the virus in their work or homes should discuss immunization against hepatitis B with their physicians regardless of their plans for pregnancy.

SUMMING UP

IN EARLIER YEARS, women in many of the situations described in this chapter often would have been told not ever to get pregnant. With increasing knowledge and the availability of special care, women must seldom be given such heartbreaking advice. Now the outcome of high-risk pregnancies is most often a happy one.

Women with any chronic medical condition or lingering doubt about their ability to carry a child safely may benefit from consultation with a specialist in high-risk pregnancy. It will help them to make a decision about pregnancy that is based on full information about their risks and options and—if pregnancy is undertaken—will guide them in preparing appropriately for the pregnancy and in obtaining proper medical care to protect the pregnancy and their own health.

14 Complications in Pregnancy

Laxmi V. Baxi, M.D., and Harold E. Fox, M.D.

INTRODUCTION

ALTHOUGH MOST PREGNANCIES proceed smoothly and without incident, complications sometimes occur. Complications may arise spontaneously in an otherwise healthy woman with no apparent risk factors, or they may be the result of known risks such as age, inadequate nutrition, smoking, or a family history of disease. (For information on known risks in pregnancy, see chapter 13, The High-Risk Pregnancy.) With consistent prenatal care throughout pregnancy, most complications are caught early, appropriate treatment is started immediately, and in many cases the pregnancy proceeds normally. Some situations, however, require emergency delivery of the baby, either vaginally or by cesarean section. Described below are some of the more common complications of pregnancy.

SPONTANEOUS ABORTION

PHYSICIANS GENERALLY define abortion as the loss of a pregnancy before week 20 of gestation, but definitions vary. Delivery between weeks 20 and 38 is known as premature birth. (Spontaneous abortion is often called miscarriage to distinguish it from induced abortion, which may be done to safeguard the health of the mother, or for nonmedical reasons at any time up to week 24 of gestation.)

It is estimated that 20 percent of all pregnancies end in early miscarriage, most often between weeks 6 and 10, and many of these go completely unnoticed. Recent studies suggest that the figure may actually be as high as 30 to 50 percent.

Slight bleeding or spotting of dark blood may signal an impending miscarriage. Some miscarriages are completely painless, and so any vaginal bleeding during pregnancy, even if there is no pain, may be a warning. Other signs are cramps, severe abdominal pain, and dizziness.

Bed rest is the most common treatment for an impending spontaneous abortion, although physical stress is not believed to play a major role in this complication. With rest, the cramping and bleeding may stop and the pregnancy proceed normally to term.

A threatened abortion, however, may advance to become an inevitable abortion. This means that a miscarriage cannot be prevented. Bleeding becomes heavy, painful contractions cause the cervix to dilate, the membrane ruptures, and the fetus, amniotic sac, and placenta are expelled. If all the so-called products of conception are expelled, the abortion is termed complete. Pain then ceases, bleeding subsides, and the uterus contracts firmly. If any tissue remains in the uterus, the abortion is incomplete. To prevent the possibility of serious infection and continued bleeding, a dilation and curettage (D&C) may be done to remove all remnants of tissue from the uterus.

A missed abortion is one in which the fetus dies in the uterus but is not expelled. Signs of a missed abortion are lack of menstrual periods combined with the cessation of the signs of pregnancy. The death of the fetus will be confirmed by ultrasound. If a missed abortion occurs early in the pregnancy, a D&C will usually be performed to evacuate the uterus. Later, it may be necessary to induce labor. It is estimated that a missed abortion occurs once in every 100 pregnancies.

Among the causes of miscarriage are fetal abnormality, a hormone imbalance in the mother, structural defects of the uterus, infection, and abnormalities of the immune system. A fall seldom results in miscarriage, as the fetus is well protected by the bones of the spine and pelvis, layers of muscle and tissue, and the cushioning amniotic fluid. In the great majority of cases, the fetus is found to be abnormal. Genetic defects, drug and alcohol use, and exposure to environmental toxins—heavy metals, chemicals, and radioactivity, for example—are associated with an increased risk of miscarriage. In its way, the high incidence of abnormalities in miscarried fetuses provides some reassurance that a pregnancy reaching the sixth month will most likely result in a healthy child.

If the mother has rhesus negative (Rh−) blood, she should be given an injection of rhesus gammaglobulin (RhoGAM) within 72 hours of spontaneous or induced abortion. Generally, a genetic evaluation of the parents is recommended only if the mother has had repeated spontaneous abortions (3 or more), or if she or her partner has a family history of birth defects.

A miscarriage is not automatically a sign of inability to carry a pregnancy to term. In most cases a subsequent pregnancy is perfectly normal. Several consecutive miscarriages (habitual abortion), however, may be due to hormonal imbalance or some other treatable condition. Tests should be done to try to determine the cause.

Intercourse can be resumed within 2 to 4 weeks after a miscarriage, or when the cervix has closed. There is no rule about the best time to try to conceive again. Physically, the body usually is prepared for another pregnancy after 1 or 2 normal menstrual periods have passed. Emotionally, however, many couples have to wait much longer. Miscarriage at any stage of pregnancy can be a devastating experience. Feelings of grief may be complicated by guilt, leading to tension between the partners. They may feel that they did something wrong (had sex too often, exercised too hard, were careless in some way), but such factors rarely cause a miscarriage. The aftereffects of a miscarriage are long lasting and there is often renewed grief at the time when the baby would have been born. It is important that a couple allow themselves adequate time to recover before trying to conceive again.

ECTOPIC PREGNANCY

AN ECTOPIC (TUBAL) pregnancy is one in which the fertilized ovum does not complete its descent to the uterus but implants instead in 1 of the Fallopian tubes; occasionally it may start to grow in the mother's abdominal cavity, on the ovary, or in the horn of the uterus. (See figure 14.1.) Ectopic pregnancies are dangerous:

They always result in the loss of the fetus and, if undiagnosed and untreated, pose a threat to the mother's life.

An ectopic pregnancy can happen to any woman at any age, but the risk is greater among women who have a history of pelvic inflammatory disease, endometriosis, pelvic surgery or appendicitis, have used IUDs for contraception, or have had a previous ectopic pregnancy. Strictures inside the Fallopian tubes are the contributing cause.

The major concern is that the tube (or ovary) will rupture before the condition is diagnosed. Early warning signs—cramps and spotting beginning around the eighth to tenth week, often before the pregnancy has been confirmed—are easily overlooked. The next warning sign is more bleeding and severe pain in the lower abdomen, often on 1 side. These symptoms may be confused with those of a spontaneous abortion, or with appendicitis or pelvic inflammatory disease. A blood test for human chorionic gonadotrophin (HCG), ultrasound examinations, and a pelvic examination may confirm the diagnosis. Ultrasonogram and laparoscopy may be helpful in locating the gestation.

Once ectopic pregnancy is confirmed, surgical treatment must be undertaken right away. Delay may result in rupture, followed by severe hemorrhage, which may prove fatal. Early intervention will save the life of the mother and may also preserve the integrity of the reproductive organs. If there has been no rupture, it may be possible to preserve the tube. Often, however, the whole Fallopian tube, occasionally with the adjacent ovary, may have to be removed. Nonsurgical treatment of ectopic pregnancy is currently being studied. In cases where hormonal levels in the blood show that resorption of the conceptus has taken place, surgery to remove it may not be necessary.

Many women who have had an ec-

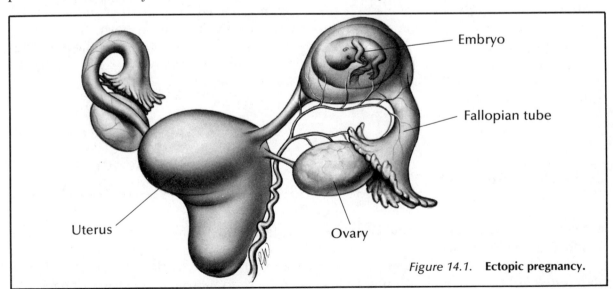

Uterus

Ovary

Embryo

Fallopian tube

Figure 14.1. **Ectopic pregnancy.**

topic pregnancy can conceive and carry successfully. A woman who has had a previous ectopic pregnancy should seek medical care early in any subsequent pregnancy so that the doctor can determine the location of the fetus.

CERVICAL INCOMPETENCE

IN SOME WOMEN, an abnormality of the cervix prevents it from performing its function during pregnancy of keeping the fetus securely inside the womb. This condition, known as incompetent cervix, can be caused by previous trauma to the cervix, but may also be due to a malformation. The incidence of malformation is higher in DES daughters. (See chapter 13, The High-Risk Pregnancy.) Trauma may be due to a tear in the cervix during a previous delivery (either because the delivery was difficult or where delivery was normal but onset of labor was very rapid and forceful), a forced dilation of the cervix during an abortion procedure, or a cone biopsy.

Cervical incompetence may be known ahead of time or may be diagnosed during the pregnancy. Sometimes, dilation of the cervix may be detected during pregnancy. Or the woman may have a rapid premature delivery. In other cases, there may be no signs until the woman experiences a painless, bloodless premature delivery in the second or early third trimester.

Without treatment, it is generally not possible for a woman with cervical incompetence to carry the pregnancy to term. Sometimes, bed rest is prescribed successfully. Another method, which has gained popularity because it allows the woman to continue more of her normal activities, is surgical closing of the cervix. This procedure, known as cerclage, is generally performed after week 12, when the incidence of spontaneous abortion drops. Since the procedure requires general anesthesia, it is safer for the fetus at this time. Cerclage is not recommended in the third trimester. If the incompetency becomes apparent late in pregnancy, bed rest is usually prescribed.

The suture will be removed at about 37 or 38 weeks' gestation, when the baby is viable, or immediately at the onset of labor. The condition is chronic and it may be necessary to repeat the cerclage with each successive pregnancy.

GESTATIONAL DIABETES

GESTATIONAL DIABETES is a condition that develops only during pregnancy; it disappears after the baby is born. However, women who have gestational diabetes have an increased risk of developing diabetes at some later date. Overall, about 2 to 5 percent of pregnant women develop gestational diabetes, which occurs as a result of changes in glucose metabolism, due in turn to the action of various hormones, mainly human placental lactogen (HPL).

Gestational diabetes usually does not appear until late in the second or early in the third trimester of pregnancy. (See chapter 13.) Nevertheless, the complications of gestational diabetes are similar to, but perhaps not as profound as, those of preexisting diabetes: abnormally large babies (macrosomia), preeclampsia, complications during delivery, and greater risk of prematurity. The goal of treatment is the same for both conditions: to reduce the risks of macrosomia and preeclampsia and to sustain the pregnancy as close as possible to term. As with other pregnancies where complications are a factor, the obstetrician must balance the risk of continuing the pregnancy against the risk of delivering a baby whose lungs may be immature. With proper medical management, the pregnancy can be successfully carried to term.

It was traditionally believed that a woman's risk of gestational diabetes increases if she has a family history of diabetes; if a previous baby weighed more than 9 pounds at birth; if she previously gave birth to a stillborn baby or one with a congenital abnormality; if she has high blood pressure, is obese, or is over 35; or if she has traces of sugar in her urine at any time during the pregnancy. While these factors may increase the risk, it is now known that any woman may develop gestational diabetes; hence, all pregnant women should be screened for it.

Initially, gestational diabetes may be treated by changes in diet and increased exercise. Complex carbohydrates, fiber, and perhaps extra protein, are added to the diet; simple carbohydrates are eliminated or minimized. If the disease does not come under control with these measures, insulin injections will be required. Insulin is administered at the outset to women with high blood sugars.

Women who develop gestational diabetes require more frequent prenatal checkups and extra care at delivery, although not as frequent as for those with preexisting diabetes. Frequent self-testing of blood sugar—several times a day—may be necessary. In addition, the urine may be tested regularly for ketone bodies.

When the mother is diagnosed early and receives good medical care, there is only a nominal increase in complications during delivery, and nearly 98 percent of the babies are healthy.

GESTATIONAL HYPERTENSION

LIKE DIABETES, hypertension, or high blood pressure, can be a preexisting condition or can develop during pregnancy.

Normally, blood pressure drops 5 or 10 points, usually during the second trimester. Hypertension that develops after 20 weeks of pregnancy is known as gestational hypertension. The cause is unknown, but it is more likely to happen in first pregnancies in women over 35, in those who are poorly nourished, and in those who have had many children. The presence of diabetes or renal disease also increases risk.

If the hypertension is mild, medication probably will be avoided. A minimal reduction in sodium (salt) in the diet may control it. If it is more severe, carefully chosen drugs may be used. Diuretics will generally be avoided.

Most gestational hypertension disappears after delivery, although it may indicate that the woman is at risk of developing high blood pressure later on, in the absence of pregnancy.

RHESUS INCOMPATIBILITY

THE RHESUS (Rh) factor is a protein substance found on the surface of red blood cells, named for a similar substance found in the red blood cells of rhesus monkeys. Most people are Rh-positive (Rh+), meaning that their red blood cells carry the rhesus factor. About 15 percent of the population, however, does not have it and is said to be Rh-negative (Rh−). Rh− blood is relatively rare among blacks and Asians.

Problems can arise when an Rh− woman becomes pregnant by an Rh+ man. If the man has both Rh+ and Rh− genes, there is a 50 percent chance that the fetus will be Rh− and that no problems of incompatibility will arise, and a 50 percent chance that it will be Rh+. If the man has only Rh+ genes, the fetus will be Rh+ also.

In a first pregnancy, where an Rh− mother is carrying an Rh+ fetus, there will be no incompatibility problems unless she has already been sensitized to the Rh factor by an earlier transfusion of Rh+ blood. (Sensitization means that antibodies to the Rh factor have formed, as explained below.) During that first pregnancy, however, some of the fetus's red blood cells will seep into the mother's circulation, and at delivery, with the separation of the placenta from the uterus, there will be considerable transfer of blood from fetus to mother. Her immune system will read the unfamiliar protein on the blood cells as "foreign" and start to produce antibodies against it.

Once the antibodies are established in the bloodstream, they are ready to attack any future pregnancy that is Rh+; with subsequent pregnancies the level of antibodies rises, increasing the danger to the fetus. Even so, the chance that an Rh− mother will have an affected child is only about 1 in 20, and then only in a third or later pregnancy.

An affected child will be born severely anemic, since the fetal red blood cells have been destroyed in utero by the maternal antibodies. Sometimes the child will be stillborn or will die soon after birth. Those who do survive may be mentally retarded and have hearing loss.

With the modern techniques available in hospitals equipped to care for difficult pregnancies, it is possible to prevent this damage to the fetus. If blood tests show a high level of maternal antibodies to the Rh factor, the health of the fetus will be assessed by amniocentesis. A high level of bilirubin in the amniotic fluid indicates that many of the fetus's red blood cells have been destroyed and the fetus is in danger of dying in utero. Intrauterine exchange blood transfusions will then be given every 10 days to 2 weeks until about 32 to 34 weeks of the pregnancy, at which time the baby will be delivered by induced labor or cesarean section. This may be done using a new technique (available primarily at major medical centers) called percutaneous umbilical blood sampling (PUBS) or cordocentesis. (See chapter 8, Medical Care During Pregnancy.) An exchange blood transfusion may be done immediately after birth.

When the potential incompatibility problem is discovered before maternal sensitization to the Rh factor—which today is usually the case—the problem can be circumvented. Within 72 hours of the delivery of a child, an injection of rhesus gamma globulin (RhoGAM) will be given. The drug destroys the fetal red cells in the mother's circulation and thus the antibodies that would affect subsequent pregnancies are not produced. Rh− women should have an injection of Rhogam after every pregnancy, whether it goes to term or ends in a miscarriage or abortion. They should also receive rhesus gamma globulin at about week 28 of pregnancy to prevent occasional cases of sensitization in the third trimester. Thanks to this drug therapy, problems with rhesus incompatibility are now quite rare.

PHLEBITIS

PHLEBITIS IS A general term meaning inflammation of a vein. This inflammation is often accompanied by a clot (thrombus) that forms in the vein, preventing blood from flowing freely, a condition known as thrombophlebitis. Superficial thrombophlebitis is painful but not life threatening, unlike the deep thrombophlebitis that involves an interior vein and may be fatal if a clot breaks away and travels to the lung, resulting in a pulmonary embolism.

Superficial thrombophlebitis in the legs is relatively common in pregnancy. As the enlarging uterus puts pressure on the blood vessels that drain blood from the legs, return blood flow is inhibited, the veins become inflamed, and clots may develop. The leg (usually only 1 is involved) will be heavy, swollen, and painful; the pain will be eased when the leg is elevated, greater when it is lowered. A red streak may mark the inflamed vein.

If bed rest is required during pregnancy there is an increased risk for thrombophlebitis. The risk is also higher if the mother is carrying twins (because of the size of the uterus), has varicose veins, or has a clotting disorder.

The best prevention is exercise, which promotes good circulation in the legs. If a clot does develop, the leg should be elevated and warm compresses applied to reduce the swelling. An anticlotting medication such as heparin may be necessary (in deep-vein thrombosis) to prevent the clot from becoming larger.

PREECLAMPSIA AND ECLAMPSIA

Preeclampsia

The cause of preeclampsia—also called toxemia of pregnancy—is not known. It occurs only in pregnancy, specifically after week 20. It is more likely to occur in first pregnancies or where there is a history of high blood pressure or vascular disease. Age (under 20 or over 40 years), the presence of diabetes or kidney disease, a family history of high blood pressure, and a mother or sister who had preeclampsia are also risk factors. Fortunately, a woman who develops it once is unlikely to develop it again in a subsequent pregnancy. A well-balanced diet and good prenatal care provide some insurance against preeclampsia, but it occurs nevertheless in about 5 percent of all pregnancies.

The classic symptoms of preeclampsia are high blood pressure, swelling of the face and hands, and protein in the urine. In severe cases, there is significant reduction in urine output. These symptoms may develop over the course of a few days or may appear suddenly in a 24-hour period. They may appear together, or separately, and in any order. Rarely, vomiting, pain in the upper abdomen, and blurred vision accompany the other symptoms. A physician should be consulted immediately if any of these symptoms occur.

Each prenatal visit includes procedures to screen for preeclampsia: blood pressure check, urinalysis (to test for protein), weight (to detect hidden fluid accumulation), and physical exam to detect swelling or fluid accumulation. If undetected and untreated, preeclampsia can develop into eclampsia, a dangerous condition that puts both mother and baby at risk. Early treatment usually forestalls this serious development.

If the condition is relatively mild, bed rest at home is usually recommended. Lying in bed, on the left side, helps to increase blood flow through the kidneys, increases urination, and so relieves fluid retention. In more severe cases, hospitalization will be needed. If the condition is serious and develops near the time of delivery, intravenous medication will be given to lower the blood pressure and prompt delivery will be considered.

A major complication of preeclampsia is abruptio placentae, or placental separation (see below). Therefore the baby will usually be delivered as soon as possible after the mother's condition has been stabilized. If vaginal delivery seems possible, labor will be induced; if not, a cesarean section is done.

Eclampsia

If preeclampsia progresses without treatment, eclampsia may develop, although sometimes this serious condition arises rapidly and without warning. Blood pressure soars and there may be convulsions. Coma, severe headache, confusion, and visual disturbances may precede or follow other signs. Eclampsia is life threatening and immediate treatment is required to save both mother and child. As in severe preeclampsia, medication is given to lower the blood pressure and prevent (or treat) convulsions. Delivery will often be accomplished as soon as possible.

Preeclampsia progresses to eclampsia in 1 case in 200, but this rarely happens with good prenatal care.

BLEEDING IN THE THIRD TRIMESTER

Abruptio Placentae

Abruptio placentae, or placental separation, is the partial or complete separation of the placenta from the wall of the uterus. The severity of the condition depends on how much of the placenta has torn away: The separation may be very small or may involve the whole placenta. Blood may escape from the cervix and become apparent as vaginal bleeding (external hemorrhage), or it may remain hidden in the uterine cavity (concealed hemorrhage); sometimes there is a mixture of both types. Bleeding may be slight, with little or no pain, or there may be abdominal discomfort and considerable bleeding. If hemorrhage is severe, the blood may collect in the uterine cavity, causing it to become markedly turgid and tender and possibly causing the woman to go into shock.

The cause of abruptio placentae is unknown, but in about 25 percent of cases the mother also has preeclampsia, hypertension, anemia, or, rarely, impaired kidney function. Occasionally it follows severe trauma, such as an automobile accident. It appears that smoking may predispose a woman to abruptio.

Any bleeding or abdominal pain during the third trimester of pregnancy is potentially serious and hospitalization is always necessary, if only to discover the cause. If the bleeding from the placental separation is slight, bed rest may be all that is required. Provided the fetal heart tones are normal, the mother may be allowed to return home. If the bleeding is severe, speedy delivery is in the best interest of both mother and child. If the cervix is "ripe," labor will be induced; otherwise, a cesarean section will be done.

Placenta Previa

Placenta previa means that the placenta is attached unusually low in the uterus and covers the cervical os (the opening from the uterus to the vagina) partially or completely. Placenta previa occurs in about 1 in 250 pregnancies, usually in a first pregnancy or where there is an abnormality of the uterus that prevents normal implantation of the placenta.

The primary symptom of placenta previa is painless vaginal bleeding during the last 12 weeks of pregnancy. Usually slight "warning" losses of blood occur, but sometimes the bleeding is severe from the beginning.

When symptoms develop, the mother will be admitted to the hospital and the exact site of the placenta located by ultrasound scan. She is likely to be kept in the hospital because bleeding with this condition can be serious, threatening the lives of both mother and child.

If delay poses no risk, the pregnancy will be allowed to continue as close as possible to term. When the placenta completely covers the os, the only safe way to deliver the baby is by cesarean section.

PRETERM LABOR

IN ABOUT 5 percent of all pregnancies, labor begins before—sometimes well before—the due date. The outcome for the baby depends on birth weight and state of development, and on the care given after birth. At a tertiary-care center, babies born at 25 weeks' gestation, weighing slightly under 2 pounds, have a 20 to 50 percent chance of survival, with excellent neonatal care. At a birth weight of 3 pounds, almost all survive. Every ounce in weight and day in time make a difference—so, when labor begins prematurely, treatment is directed at stopping it and prolonging the pregnancy as long as possible to give the baby the best possible chance.

A history of preterm delivery poses the highest risk for preterm labor. Inadequate nutrition and prenatal care, multiple fetuses, maternal age (under 15 or over 40 years), or exposure to DES in utero all increase risk. Specific causes include preeclampsia, thyroid disease, diabetes, and placental abnormalities. Recent evidence suggests that cervical or vaginal infection is an important contributory factor for premature labor. Incompetent cervix seems to be yet another factor responsible for this problem.

Only very rarely does preterm labor begin after a fright or sudden emotional upset. Even when it does, it is difficult to know whether the event was the real cause or only a coincidence. In half the cases of preterm labor, the cause is completely unknown.

The principal sign of premature labor

is the onset of contractions. It is normal for the uterus to contract occasionally during pregnancy, but these contractions, known as Braxton-Hicks contractions, normally last for only 20 to 30 seconds and stop spontaneously after 1 or 2 hours (or sooner with a change in position or mild exercise, such as walking). True contractions last 40 seconds or more and gradually occur at shorter and shorter intervals. Five or more contractions in 1 hour is a sign of labor, preterm or otherwise.

Other signs that indicate preterm labor include low, dull backache and pelvic pressure, a leakage of amniotic fluid, and vaginal bleeding or spotting. Spotting may indicate that the mucus plug sealing the neck of the uterus has dislodged. Amniotic fluid leaking from the vagina indicates rupture of the amniotic and chorionic sac (the membranes). Labor usually follows rupture of the membranes within 24 hours. If it does not, and the fetus is near term, labor will usually be induced, because of the risk of infection and complications of fluid loss. If the membranes rupture before 35 weeks, an attempt to delay labor may be made, to allow the fetus to mature further. The mother is kept in bed and followed carefully. If infection is obvious, antibiotics will be given and the mother may be delivered promptly.

If indications of preterm labor appear, the obstetrician should be called immediately and preparations made to go to the hospital. If the labor is very premature, the doctor may arrange an admission at a hospital with neonatal intensive care facilities. While she is in the hospital for observation, the uterine contractions will be monitored and her cervix will be checked for the degree of dilation.

If the cervix is only minimally dilated, if the membranes are intact, and if there is no bleeding or other complication, bed rest alone may succeed in stopping the labor. The mother may also be given medications to delay the labor, as well as drugs (glucocorticoids) to speed up maturation of the baby's lungs (breathing difficulties due to immature lungs are the most common problem for premature babies). The baby's chances of survival increase dramatically if labor can be delayed to 30 weeks or more.

If dilation and effacement (thinning out) of the cervix has begun, labor cannot usually be stopped. The goal then is a gentle, nontraumatic birth. A cesarean section may be considered, in the presence of abnormal presentation (for example, breech or transverse lie), to minimize the risk of injury to the baby. If the delivery is vaginal, every effort may be made to keep the membranes intact for as long as possible, to cushion the baby. The mother may have to have an episiotomy and a forceps delivery to reduce pressure on the baby's skull, which is more fragile than that of a full-term baby. During labor and delivery, the baby's heart rate will be monitored continuously by an electronic monitor. Usually, a neonatal specialist will be present at the birth to give the baby immediate attention and to arrange any further treatment that may be necessary.

15 Labor and Delivery

Richard U. Levine, M.D.

INTRODUCTION

OVER THE LAST few decades, there has been a quiet revolution in our approaches to labor and delivery. Natural childbirth, fathers and other family members in the delivery room, and other practices that are so commonplace today were unheard of just 25 or 30 years ago. There are still a few physicians who may grumble at the new practices, but most doctors today welcome the increased parental involvement in the birth of their baby—certainly one of life's most memorable moments.

There has also been an explosion in technology surrounding childbirth and labor. Today, most major medical centers boast neonatal intensive care units that routinely save babies who were previously doomed. Many serious problems can now be diagnosed and corrected before birth. Fetal monitors, ultrasound, and other high-tech apparatus are now standard equipment.

These parallel developments of new technologies and greater parental in-

volvement in the birth process have not been without problems, many of which still defy solution. New parents may complain that the obstetrician has become overly preoccupied with gadgets and technology at the expense of an open doctor–patient relationship. These issues are beyond the scope of this book, but are worth mentioning since they do have an important bearing on the entire birth experience.

It should be stressed that the vast majority of childbirths are without serious complications. And when problems arise, most can be readily resolved. Still, it is important to know signs of possible trouble and what action to take. This chapter describes modern approaches to childbirth as well as the stages of labor and delivery, possible complications, and special considerations. The emphasis is on the normal course of events; more detailed discussions of complications can be found in chapters 13, 14, and 16.

APPROACHES TO CHILDBIRTH

PREPARATION is probably the most important aspect of modern childbirth, with education being the focal point for both *mother and father*. Couples who are prepared for childbirth are more likely to find it a rewarding and happy experience. Knowledge is the best defense against both fear and pain. A woman who goes

into labor knowing what to expect is more relaxed, and that relaxation helps to ease her tensed, pained muscles. A calm, knowledgeable couple will be able to respond better to the instructions of a doctor, nurse, or midwife, and will be more in control of the birth process.

Today, most hospitals with active obstetrics units offer childbirth preparation classes, and prospective parents should strongly consider enrolling in such a course. A thorough class will include instructions in breathing and relaxation techniques, muscle-strengthening exercises for childbirth, and thorough, practical information about labor and delivery. Both mother and father (or an alternative partner if the father is not available) should be involved. If the hospital does not offer these classes, a couple can ask their doctor to recommend one or inquire at the local Family Services office.

Breathing Techniques

Many of today's childbirth preparation classes incorporate the specific techniques of the Lamaze method—named for the pioneer in so-called natural childbirth. The Lamaze method encourages both parents to take an active role in the birth. The coach (usually the prospective father, but a friend or relative can fill this role, too) attends classes with the prospective mother and along with her learns various breathing techniques that are to be used in synchronization with the uterine contractions. The purpose of the breathing techniques is twofold. (See table 15.1.) First, they are designed to keep the oxygen supply flowing both to the baby and to the contracting uterine muscles, thus helping to ease discomfort. Second, they give the woman something to concentrate on other than any pain caused by the contractions.

In addition to concentrating on her breathing techniques, the woman is also encouraged to use a focal point—that is,

---

Table 15.1
BREATHING TECHNIQUES FOR LABOR AND DELIVERY

The type of breathing is dictated by the stage of the contraction and also the stage of labor. Specific techniques are:

- *Deep, cleansing breathing.* This is a long exaggerated breath taken at the beginning and the end of each contraction.

- *Slow chest breathing.* These are breaths taken about 8 times per minute, and are used during the early, milder contractions.

- *More rapid chest breathing.* The technique is the same as for slow chest breathing, but the rate is doubled to 16 breaths per minute. It is used as the contractions increase in frequency and forcefulness.

- *Shallow chest breathing.* This is a light panting, done at the rate of 60 breaths per minute, and is used at the peaks of the more intense contractions.

- *Variation or combinations of techniques.* During active labor, when the most painful contractions come very quickly, the more complicated breathing techniques are employed. Shallow chest breathing is slower at the beginning and end of each contraction and sped up at the peak. Varying rhythmic patterns, for example, inhale/exhale, inhale/exhale, inhale/exhale, inhale/blow, are used for the most difficult contractions.

---

to concentrate on some object in the room, or something she has brought with her for that purpose, while she is doing her breathing during a contraction. This is to help her concentrate and also to give her brain a strong stimulus aside from any pain her body is experiencing. As her contractions become more intense, the woman correspondingly employs a more difficult breathing method.

The coach can help her by calling out encouragement, instructing her on which breathing technique to use, or even breathing along with her. Between contractions, the coach can massage her back, give her ice chips to suck on, and help her relax any tense muscles.

Relaxation Techniques

The relaxation techniques taught in most childbirth classes consist mostly of the woman learning to relax a muscle in response to the coach's touch. The couple practice relaxation responses together in class and at home. The woman lies in a comfortable position on the floor with her knees bent and her feet flat on the floor. (This position helps keep the back straight and free from strain.) To begin, the coach might instruct her to tense her arm. He will then ask her to relax it at his touch or signal. This is practiced over and over again for all parts of the body. Later, when the woman is in labor, her partner can recognize the signs of tension and help her relax by using their prearranged signals. This can give the laboring woman some measure of relief.

Alternatively, some childbirth classes teach a type of self-hypnosis in which the woman learns a special kind of concentration that helps block out pain but does not interfere with her ability to respond to her partner's or physician's instructions. Many people mistakenly equate hypnosis with sleep; in reality, hypnosis is the opposite of sleep in that the person's full attention is concentrated on a specific object or sensation.

Exercise Techniques

Exercise is another important aspect of childbirth preparation. The object is to strengthen the muscles that are most stressed during labor and delivery. In childbirth classes, exercises to strengthen the back, abdomen, and pelvis are taught. Before attempting any exercises the pregnant woman should check first with her physician. She should also know to stop immediately if an exercise is giving her any pain. A deep cleansing breath, in through the mouth and out through the nose, should be taken before each new exercise. (For more information, see chapter 10, The Pregnant Lifestyle.)

SIGNS OF IMPENDING LABOR

DURING THE LAST few weeks of pregnancy, most women feel unwieldy, uncomfortable, and anxious to be done with it. Very few babies arrive exactly on their due date, but there are signs that pregnancy is entering its final stages.

Engagement

One of the first occurs when the baby engages or "falls." This is a sign that the fetus is beginning to settle into the birth canal. Suddenly, the woman feels she can again breathe, as the baby moves lower and eases pressure on the lungs.

Burst of Energy

Many women experience a burst of energy at about this time, and an old wives' tale says that an urge to wax the kitchen floor, clean out the closets, or undertake some other project that was unthinkable just the week before is a sure sign of impending labor.

Dull Ache

Some women experience a dull ache, either in the lower back or in the pelvic area, where it may resemble menstrual cramps.

Show

During most of the pregnancy the cervix is elongated; it is firm and plugged with mucus and has only a very small opening in the center. However, late in pregnancy the cervix starts to soften and efface (shorten and thin out). When labor is beginning, or soon to begin, some women notice a slightly blood-tinged mucous discharge. This is the so-called show or bloody show, and it indicates that the mucus plug is breaking down and being expelled.

Rupture of the Membranes

While not common to all pregnancies, another possible sign of the imminence of labor is the rupture of the amniotic sac that contains the amniotic fluid, also known as the "breaking of the bag of waters." When her "water breaks," a woman will experience anything from a slight trickle to a gush of fluid. This is the amniotic fluid, which is both colorless and odorless. Labor should start within the next 12 or so hours after the membranes have ruptured. The time should be noted and the doctor notified as soon as this occurs. Because the amniotic fluid protects the fetus, the longer it takes to get to labor and delivery, the greater the risk of infection. Some doctors prefer to admit their patients to the hospital once the amniotic sac is broken, or even with the first sign of leakage.

Contractions

Uterine contractions are a dependable sign of labor, but they can also be misleading. Mild, irregular contractions called Braxton-Hicks contractions often occur throughout pregnancy and can increase in intensity and frequency in the third trimester. These contractions can be easily confused with the real contractions of labor. The differences are that Braxton-Hicks contractions will subside, especially when the woman relaxes or drinks a glass of warm milk. They are usually not painful and tend to go away after 1 or 2 hours.

True labor contractions may appear

to originate in the lower back, with the sensation working its way around to the front. They will become increasingly regular and intense. (See table 15.2 for a comparison of true and false contractions.)

Table 15.2

CONTRACTIONS OF TRUE LABOR	CONTRACTIONS OF FALSE LABOR
• Occur at regular intervals	• Occur at irregular intervals
• Intervals gradually shorten	• Intervals remain long
• Intensity gradually increases	• Intensity remains same
• Discomfort in back and abdomen	• Discomfort chiefly in lower abdomen
• Cervix dilates	• Cervix does not dilate
• Contractions are not stopped by sedation	• Usually relieved by sedation

---

WHEN LABOR BEGINS

LABOR is a distinctly individual experience, varying from woman to woman and from pregnancy to pregnancy. Many women are surprised to find that their second experience with childbirth can be different than the first, and both births can differ greatly from another woman's experience.

Many factors can contribute to a woman's response to labor and delivery, including overall health, her feelings about the birth, how problem-free or difficult the pregnancy was, the position and size of the baby at the time of the labor, and other unpredictable circumstances. First deliveries tend to take longer than subsequent ones, but this does not always follow—some women who have a short first labor may have a longer second one, especially if the baby is larger or in a different position from the first. In any event, the couple's physician should be notified when labor begins and the couple should make final preparations to go to the hospital or birthing center.

Going to the Hospital

Most hospitals have preadmissions for obstetrical patients so that much of the necessary paperwork can be done beforehand and the woman in labor will not be delayed in the waiting room. If the birth is going to take place in a birthing center, the center should be called beforehand so arrangements can be made.

When the woman arrives at the hospital, she is admitted into a labor room and is seen by a nurse, who will first take a history. The nurse will ask about the pregnancy itself, whether there have been previous pregnancies and their outcome, the date of the last menstrual period, the due date given by the obstetrician, whether there have been any special problems, any special plans for the delivery, specific questions about any previous medical illnesses or surgery, any allergies, when the last meal was eaten and what it consisted of. The nurse will also want to know what signs of labor brought the woman to the hospital. Blood pressure, pulse, respiration, and temperature will be measured and recorded. Then the physical examination will be done by either a staff physician, the woman's own physician, a resident (if it is a teaching hospital), or in some places a nurse or nurse-midwife.

The Physical Examination

The examining person will listen to the chest and heart and then examine the abdomen by doing what are called Leopold's maneuvers. The doctor or nurse will examine the abdomen in 4 specific places, feeling for the baby's head, buttocks, and sides, to determine the size, approximate weight, and position. A pelvic examination will be done to confirm that true labor has in fact begun and to see how dilated and effaced the cervix is. A set of numbers will be recorded: Dilation is expressed in centimeters from 1 to 10, with 10 being the widest; effacement is expressed as a percentage, with 100 percent being fully thinned or effaced; and the station, or position of the baby's head in the pelvis, is expressed in numbers ranging from -4 (the head is still high in the pelvis) to 0 station (engagement) to $+4$ (the head has descended).

The pelvic examination may be done 1 of several ways. Very often, a speculum is inserted gently into the vagina to examine it and the cervix. The cervix could be cultured for bacteria at this point or this could have been done during a recent obstetrical visit. A digital exam is done to see where the baby's presenting part is, how dilated and effaced the cervix is, and to make sure there are no abnormalities in the cervix or vagina. The doctor will also check for ruptured membranes. If the membranes have not ruptured, the physician will usually wait until the active phase of labor to rupture them manually.

An IV solution may be started at this time. The purpose is to prevent dehydration during labor and also to provide ready access for drugs used during delivery or for blood in case of emergency. It does restrict freedom of movement, however. If a woman is still in early labor and wants to be free to walk around, she might ask that the IV be postponed until later.

In the past, women were routinely given an enema to prevent inadvertant expulsion of stool while pushing during labor. Also, the perineal area was shaved (prepped) or clipped. Most doctors now consider both these practices unnecessary.

Fetal Monitoring

If everything seems fine and the woman feels up to it, she can be up and about during labor, and fetal monitoring can be done intermittently. Most external monitoring is done by ultrasound, which picks up the fetal heartbeat and also records contractions on a paper printout. The machines usually have wide belts that go around the abdomen. If there are any signs of potential problems, or if the mother is 2 weeks past her due date, internal fetal monitoring may be indicated. A catheter is threaded through the vagina and a small electrode is placed on the baby's scalp. (See figure 15.1.) This gives more accurate readings on both the fetal heart rate and the maternal contractions than an external monitor.

Most doctors feel that the advantages of fetal monitoring far outweigh the disadvantages. In about 40 percent of cases of fetal distress or death, there are no warning signs that would indicate the need for careful observation. In many of these cases, fetal monitoring can pick up distress while it is still early enough to save the baby or prevent disability. Internal monitoring in high-risk pregnancies has proved to be warranted and the risks are very minimal. Routine external monitoring carries no risk but does restrict movement and some feel that it is not

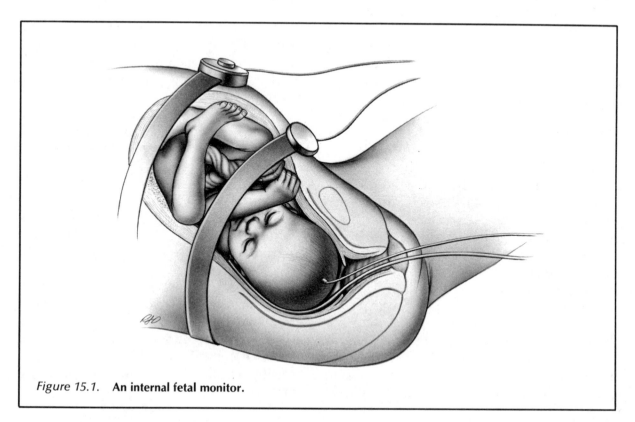

Figure 15.1. **An internal fetal monitor.**

necessary in low-risk pregnancies. If a woman is strongly opposed to monitoring, she should discuss her feelings with her doctor ahead of time.

Another test sometimes used to check fetal well-being during labor is called the fetal scalp sample. A cone-shaped tube is placed inside the cervix so the examining physician can see the baby's scalp. Then, a tiny nick is made with a microscalpel and a capillary tube is used to take a fetal blood sample for testing. This will tell if there is adequate oxygen circulating in the baby's blood and indicate other possible signs of fetal distress.

STAGES OF LABOR

ALTHOUGH labor varies widely from woman to woman, it generally has 3 distinct stages: The first stage starts with the onset of contractions and ends with the full dilation (widening) of the cervix. The second stage, sometimes called the stage of expulsion, starts when the cervix is fully effaced and dilated (to about 10 centimeters, or about 4 inches) and the woman feels the urge to push and ends with the delivery of the baby. The third stage of labor starts after the delivery of the baby and ends with the delivery of the placenta, or "afterbirth" as it has been commonly called.

The First Stage

The first stage of labor is the longest, starting with the onset of contractions and ending when the cervix is fully dilated. (See figure 15.2.) It averages 13 hours for a woman having her first baby, 8 hours for subsequent deliveries. This stage can be broken down into 3 phases. In the early phase, also called the latent or prodromal phase, the first contractions

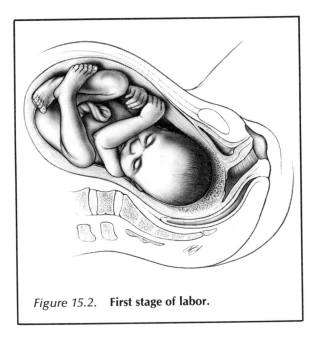

Figure 15.2. **First stage of labor.**

begin. The contractions are usually mild and brief, perhaps lasting only for 10 to 20 seconds and occurring approximately every 20 to 30 minutes. They might even stop for a while and then start again. However, real labor is progressive. The contractions will return and they will start to come more regularly, closer together, and with increasing intensity.

As the labor progresses, the contractions become rhythmic and defined. They are stronger, last longer (perhaps 30 to 60 seconds), and occur more frequently, about every 5 to 15 minutes. At this point in the labor, the cervix is effacing and shortening, and the force of the contractions make it open or dilate. The cervix must eventually open wide enough to allow the baby's head (and the rest of his or her body) to pass through it.

At the end of the latent phase, the effacement has been completed and the cervix is dilated approximately 3 to 4 centimeters. By this time the woman should be on her way to the hospital or birthing center. Typically, new mothers recall feeling very elated, with perhaps an overlay of normal anxieties about the impending birth. The active phase is next, marked by contractions lasting about 60 seconds, coming every 3 to 5 minutes. The peak of each contraction, that is, the point of maximum intensity, is now longer. The cervix is dilated beyond 3 or 4 centimeters, usually in the range of 5 to 7 centimeters.

Transition is the final phase of the first stage of labor. It can be both the shortest and the most intense phase. During this time the cervix completes its dilation to its widest, 10 centimeters. The contractions are very intense, lasting 60 to 90 seconds, every 1 to 3 minutes.

The Second Stage and Normal Birth

After the intensity of the transition phase, the second stage of labor can offer some relief. The cervix is effaced and dilated to its full 10 centimeters—the painful stretching is completed. (See figure 15.3.) Now the pressure of the baby's head on the pelvis creates the urge to push or bear down with each contraction. In fact, these voluntary pushing efforts, combined with the normal expulsive forces of the contractions, help the baby through the pelvis to be born.

Effective pushing is taught in childbirth classes, and using these techniques, the mother can help hasten the baby's delivery. Good preparation, along with attentive coaching and encouragement, can make the second stage go faster. The woman needs to *work* during this stage and not to get discouraged. A deep breath before each contraction helps provide the energy needed for the physical exertion of pushing. If she is not too tired from a prolonged first stage, the second stage of labor can be a time of mounting excite-

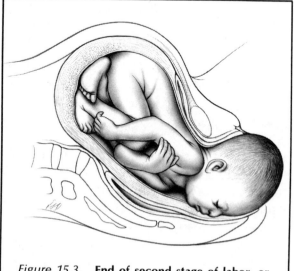

Figure 15.3. **End of second stage of labor, or beginning of delivery.**

ment and anticipation as each push brings the mother closer to the baby's birth. A more difficult second stage can lead to frustration after hours of pushing without delivery.

One factor over which there is no control is the position of the baby at the time of the birth. If the baby's head is well flexed and turned away from the front of the mother's body (in the anterior position) so as to fit into the pelvis and exert even pressure on the cervix, the delivery will be easier. If the baby enters in the posterior position, with the back of the head pointing toward the mother's back and the head pressing into her lower back, the urge to push will not be as great and the second stage could be prolonged.

Another factor is the size of the child in relation to the mother—a big baby can take longer than a small one. A first child also tends to take longer to be born than subsequent children. After the second or third hour of pushing, the doctor will decide whether alternative measures should be considered to help the delivery along.

As the second stage progresses, the perineum (the area between the vagina and the rectum) will begin to bulge. This means a small portion of the top of the baby's head can be seen during a contraction. When the full diameter of the head becomes visible during and after a contraction, the baby's head is "crowning" and the delivery is not far off. The woman is moved from the labor room to the delivery room at this point, unless she is in a special birthing room, where she will remain until after the baby is born. She may be asked not to push if she is being moved; light panting can help her resist the urge to push until she is instructed to do so.

Episiotomy

At this point (especially if it is the mother's first delivery) the doctor may perform an episiotomy, an incision in the bottom of the vagina when the baby is crowning to aid the delivery and to prevent tearing caused by the excessive stretching of the perineum. After a local anesthetic is administered in the woman's perineum, the incision will then be made in 1 of 2 ways. (See figure 15.4.) A midline or median epi-

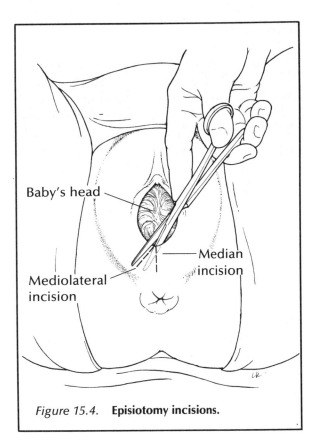

Figure 15.4. **Episiotomy incisions.**

siotomy is a straight cut from the middle of the bottom of the vagina toward the rectum. The mediolateral episiotomy, a diagonal incision, constitutes a very small proportion of all episiotomies done today because it is more difficult to repair, more prone to complications, and also more uncomfortable. The mediolateral episiotomy prevents splitting to the rectum and is indicated when the physician needs extra room, such as in a breech delivery or the delivery of a very large baby. Both procedures must be carefully inspected and sutured after the delivery of the placenta.

The Birth

The baby's head emerges slowly, usually face down. After the whole head is out, it turns spontaneously to the side in what is called external rotation so the baby's shoulders can follow 1 at a time in a sideways position. When the head is delivered, the physician will make a quick check to be sure the umbilical cord is not wrapped around the child's neck and perhaps to clean out the nose and mouth with a suction bulb.

After the shoulders are out the mother will feel a sensation of relief. The body is then quickly and easily delivered along with the remaining amniotic fluid. The baby can be immediately placed on the mother's abdomen, as some mothers and doctors prefer, for immediate warmth and contact. The baby may take a first breath and cry or it may need to be stimulated by gentle back rubbing. (Con-

trary to popular belief, the newborn is not held by the heels and slapped on the back.) Sometimes additional suctioning of the nose and mouth is required to enable the baby to breathe freely.

The umbilical cord connecting the baby to the placenta can be clamped and cut as soon as the delivery is complete or several minutes later, depending on the doctor's preference. The baby's eyes are then treated with either silver nitrate or erythromycin ointment to prevent possible gonorrheal infection in accordance with most state health laws. The baby may also be given a shot of vitamin K, which aids in blood clotting. The baby will be footprinted and 2 hospital identification bands will be attached, 1 to the wrist, 1 to the ankle, and an identical band will be attached to the mother's wrist. After the baby's general condition is checked, he or she can be given directly to the mother. If the room is very cool, the baby might, for its own welfare, be put into a warmer and dried before being given to the mother.

The Third Stage

The third stage of labor begins after the delivery of the baby and ends with the delivery of the placenta, the organ that for 9 months has brought fluids, oxygen, and nourishment to the fetus. Contractions to deliver the placenta should come within a few minutes after the delivery of the baby. If the placenta is not expelled naturally after 30 minutes, the physician may want to remove it by hand, a procedure that may require some anesthesia.

After the delivery, the uterus can bleed quite heavily from where the placenta had been attached. The woman may be given an injection of pitocin, a synthetic hormone that causes the uterus to contract and helps control the bleeding. Breastfeeding also helps stem bleeding by stimulating the secretion of oxytocin, a hormone that causes the uterus to contract as well as promotes the flow of milk.

Analgesics and Anesthetics

The question of the use of painkillers during labor and delivery is a subject of continuing controversy. Proponents of completely "natural childbirth" scorn the use of analgesics or anesthetics on the grounds that these drugs blunt the experience for the mother, and, more important, can depress the baby's respiration and heart rate. In general, the less painkillers given to the mother during labor and delivery, the better it is for the baby. But there are exceptions, and taking a dogmatic stance can result in needless suffering for the mother.

Analgesics relieve pain by depressing the nervous system and raising the pain threshold. Demerol is the most commonly used analgesic during childbirth; it relaxes the mother and eases pain, which can help her rest between contractions. The medication can be administered either through an intravenous drip or by intramuscular injection. Demerol is also a narcotic—it can cause feelings of relax-

ation and sleepiness, or feelings of nausea and a drug "high." Any adverse reactions can be controlled by administering the drug in small doses.

Demerol's effectiveness depends on timing: given too early it can slow and prolong labor; given too close to the birth it can depress the infant's heart and breathing. All analgesics circulate throughout the entire body and cross the placenta. In small doses, they should cause few or no ill effects in the baby. In the case of narcotics that have caused the baby to be lethargic and unable to breathe well, there is a narcotic antagonist called Narcan (nalaxone) that, when given to the newborn, quickly reverses the effects of the drug.

The use of local anesthesia means that a numbing medication, such as Novocaine or Lidocaine, is injected into the perineal tissues. This numbs the immediate area and is usually used before the episiotomy.

A pudendal block is administered with a longer needle in through the vaginal wall to get the medication through to the pudendal nerve, where it courses through the pelvis on its way to the perineal skin, thereby covering a wider area. The pudendal block numbs the entire area.

Regional anesthesia eliminates pain from the entire lower half of the body. The most widely used form of regional anesthesia is the epidural because it deadens the pain but only partially affects motor function. The woman can feel pressure and, more important, help push. The epidural can also be given continuously. The anesthetic is injected through a small catheter through the vertebrae and into a hollow space in the lower spine. An IV drip usually accompanies an epidural to increase fluid volume and prevent the sudden drop in blood pressure that can accompany administration of the anesthesia.

AFTER THE BIRTH

The Apgar Score

The Apgar score, named for the late Dr. Virginia Apgar of the Columbia-Presbyterian Medical Center, is a uniform system for rating the well-being of a baby at birth. The Apgar score is taken at 1 minute and again at 5 minutes after birth. The baby's heart rate, respiration, muscle tone, reflexes, and color are all checked and rated on a scale of 0 to 2. These numbers are then added up to give the total Apgar score, the best score possible being a 10 (2 points in each of the 5 categories). A newborn given a 1-minute Apgar score from 7 to 10 is in excellent condition, from 5 to 7 means the newborn is mildly depressed, a lower score indicates severe depression and the need for resuscitation. The 5-minute test is a better indicator of a serious problem. A low score on the 1-minute test will often improve on the 5-minute test, indicating that the problem was only transient, such as an obstructed airway that was subsequently cleared by medical personnel. (See table 15.3.)

Table 15.3
THE APGAR SCORE

Criteria	Score 0	Score 1	Score 2
Color	Blue, pale	Body pink, extremities blue	All pink
Heart rate	Absent	Less than 100	More than 100
Respiration	Absent	Irregular, slow	Good, crying
Reflex response to nose catheter	None	Grimace	Sneeze, cough
Muscle tone	Limp	Some flexion of extremities	Active

BONDING

BONDING is the important process of forming the deep attachment between the newborn baby and the parents. During the first hour after birth the baby is responsive and aware. In fact, the newborn instinctively turns toward the mother's voice, as if recognizing the sound from inside the uterus. Newborn infants have also been known to recognize their father's voice because they were exposed to it frequently late in the pregnancy (the fetus can hear outside sounds in the later stages of pregnancy). The baby can also distinguish forms at a distance of about 1 foot and so can make eye contact with both the parents. Both parents should hold, caress, and talk soothingly to the infant as soon as possible after birth. Half an hour in the recovery room with the infant is invaluable in establishing the feelings of closeness as a new family and helps pave the way for the responsibility and caring parents exhibit for their children. Fathers who have been involved in the birth and bonded with their baby do not seem to experience the same sort of alienation as "waiting room fathers." Studies have found they also tend to spend more time with the baby later on.

After the parents have had time with their newborn in the recovery room, the baby will be taken to the nursery where it can be watched carefully for any symptoms of trouble and the mother will go to her room for much-needed sleep. She should not attempt to get up the first time unattended because she could become weak and dizzy from the strain, lack of food, and loss of blood. Most hospital stays after a healthy, normal birth are about 2 or 3 days. This allows some time for the uterus to contract and the bleeding (lochia) to lessen.

The nurses will provide the new mother with sanitary pads and instructions on bathing. They will also check the bleeding, examine the skin around any episiotomy stitches for infection or inflammation, take vital signs, and make sure there is normal urinary output. If needed, sitz baths, hemorrhoid preparations, pain medications, and nipple cream will be provided. She may experience afterpains, or slightly painful contractions of the uterus, especially if she is nursing the baby because of the increased oxytocin.

Many hospitals now offer "rooming in," which allows for the baby to stay in the room with the mother at all times. Some also have facilities for the father. In general, visitors, except for the father, are discouraged. Birthing centers usually do not have overnight facilities; the parents take the newborn home with them shortly after the birth.

COMPLICATIONS OF LABOR

As STRESSED earlier, most labors and delivery proceed smoothly without complications. There are, however, a number of warning signs that all pregnant women should be aware of. The more common are discussed below. (For more detailed descriptions, see chapter 14, Complications in Pregnancy.)

Meconium

Sometimes near the end of pregnancy or during labor, the amniotic fluid, which is normally colorless, may appear greenish-brown. This indicates the presence of meconium, which is actually a fetal bowel movement in the uterus. It is a sign of possible fetal distress, and an indication to call the doctor as soon as possible.

Abnormal Presentation

An *abnormal presentation* is one in which the baby is not in a vertical position with the head pointing down into the pelvis so that the upper body emerges first. (See figure 15.5.) Some 3 to 4 percent of all births in the United States are breech pre-

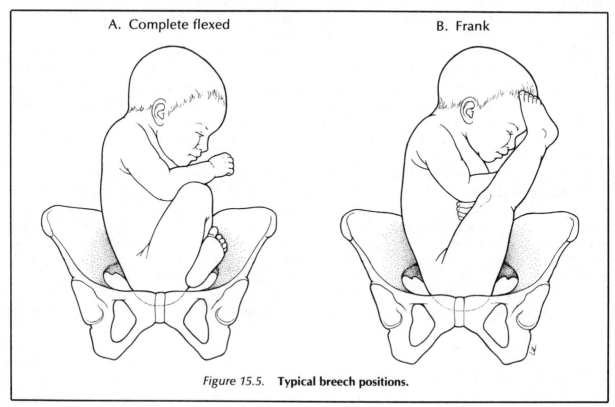

A. Complete flexed

B. Frank

Figure 15.5. **Typical breech positions.**

sentations: The baby is in a vertical position but the legs or buttocks are the presenting parts; that is, the legs or buttocks will present first and the head last. The breech presentation can be detected when the doctor palpates the abdomen, during a vaginal exam, or through ultrasonography. In some hospitals, it is felt that all breech deliveries should undergo cesarean section because when the baby's legs or buttocks are delivered first, the physician cannot know whether the mother's pelvis will be able to accommodate the bulkiest part of the baby's body. However, many physicians have had experience with the safe vaginal delivery of breeches. Important factors to consider are the size of the baby's head, whether the feet or the buttocks are coming first, and if the mother is experiencing effective labor. Breech births do carry a higher risk for injury.

One in 400 of all term babies in the United States are in a transverse or oblique lie. This means the baby is lying perpendicular to the mother, across the abdomen, or that neither the head nor the legs or buttocks have entered the pelvic canal. If labor does not push the baby into a vertical position, a cesarean section delivery must be performed.

Abnormal Bleeding

Typically, the mucus show will be tinged with blood, but any heavy bleeding that is more than a menstruallike flow is a warning sign to seek immediate medical attention. If the bleeding is accompanied by pain, it could indicate the premature separation of the placenta from the uterus (placental abruption). If a portion of the placenta is detached, labor may begin.

If the placenta is completely torn away from the uterine wall, the fetus will be cut off from its essential supply of oxygen and nutrients. This is a life-threatening condition for both the mother and the baby. Fortunately, in most cases, the amount of separation is minimal and the labor can continue normally. If the bleeding is not painful it could be caused by placenta previa, which means the placenta is implanted low inside the uterus and is either partially or completely covering the cervical opening. A cesarean section is required for a safe delivery if the cervix is completely covered. An examination by the physician can tell whether the problem is a low-lying placenta instead of a placenta previa. A low-lying placenta does not necessarily indicate a cesarean. (See chapter 14.)

Premature Rupture of the Membranes

As noted earlier, this can be a sign of imminent labor, and most women will go into labor within 24 hours. If after that time labor has not begun, it can pose a problem for the safety of the fetus, which is no longer in the protection of the amniotic fluid.

A woman should notify her doctor as soon as she notices the leak or gush of fluid, if possible describing the volume and color of the liquid. The fluid should be clear or slightly blood tinged, perhaps with white flecks of vernix (the slippery substance coating the fetus as it floats in the amniotic fluid). A yellow, yellow-brown, or green-brown color indicates meconium and possible fetal distress.

Treatment depends on the woman's particular situation, the number of babies she has had, how close to term the pregnancy is, and the status of the cervix. Some physicians will observe the patient and allow her to go into labor spontaneously; some will set a limit on the duration of time before they will induce labor to avoid the possibility of infection. If there are signs of infection, labor may be induced earlier, or a cesarean section may be performed.

Premature Labor

The onset of labor before week 37 of pregnancy is considered premature, and, depending upon the circumstances, attempts may be made to stop it. In general, premature labor associated with bleeding or rupture of the membranes may be impossible to stop. Otherwise, about half of the premature labor without bleeding or membrane rupture can be stopped by bed rest alone. When necessary, magnesium sulfate or a drug called ritodrine is given. (See chapter 14 for a more complete discussion.)

Indications for Cesarean Section

A cesarean section is the surgical delivery of a baby through an incision in the abdominal and uterine walls. Although emergency cesarean sections are performed with the patient under general anesthesia, today planned C-sections can be done with regional anesthesia and the mother awake for the baby's birth. Fathers also can be in the delivery room during a cesarean delivery, although the field of surgery usually will be shielded from his view.

Abnormal presentations, fetal distress, placenta previa, toxemia, or any medical complication that requires immediate delivery may indicate the need for a cesarean section. Sometimes a previous C-section, even with a transverse incision, becomes the reason for subsequent C-section deliveries, although many doctors will consider a trial of labor to determine whether the mother can undergo a vaginal delivery. (For more information, see chapter 16, Once a Cesarean. . . .)

Inducing Labor

A physician might decide to induce labor for a number of reasons: to reduce the risk of infection after the premature rupture of the placental membranes, to deliver the baby who is more than 2 weeks overdue when the placenta can no longer provide adequate oxygen and nutrition, or to reduce the stress of pregnancy on maternal conditions such as diabetes, hypertension, or toxemia.

Labor is usually induced by giving pitocin, a synthetic form of oxytocin, the hormone that stimulates uterine contractions during labor. Pitocin is given as an intravenous drip in which the rate of flow is very carefully monitored so that the patient receives the minimal amount required to produce effective contractions. The contractions are monitored both clinically and often with electronic monitoring devices that measure their strength and duration as well as the fetal heart rate. The contractions should be strong enough to produce a change but not so long and frequent as to compromise the baby's blood supply.

Augmenting Labor

Pitocin is not only used for induction of labor but also for mothers experiencing dysfunctional labors in which the contractions are not effective or have not established a regular, normal pattern. If the doctor perceives that the baby is not in jeopardy but the labor is simply not progressing, he or she might then decide to augment or help the labor along by administering pitocin by intravenous drip.

Stillbirth

In rare instances, an examination by the doctor will fail to detect a fetal heartbeat and further testing may confirm that the baby has died before birth. In such instances, the labor may be induced and the stillborn baby delivered and examined to determine the cause of death. One of the most common causes for a stillbirth occurs when the umbilical cord becomes knotted or wrapped around the baby's neck. Other causes include gestational diabetes, extreme prematurity or low birth weight, injury to the central nervous system, or placental abruption. (See chapters 14 and 16.)

OTHER SPECIAL CONSIDERATIONS

Forceps

Forceps, stainless steel instruments similar to a pair of large, connected spoons, are not used as much today as in the past. In a forceps-aided delivery, the physician fits the rounded parts of the instrument over the sides of the baby's head and helps guide the baby through the birth canal. Although forceps are associated with a increased risk of birth injury, in skilled hands they can be safely used when the baby's head is low enough during the second stage of labor and the mother is having difficulty pushing the baby through to be delivered on her own.

In most cases where the mother has been having a prolonged and difficult second stage of labor, the judicious use of forceps would be preferable to an emergency cesarean section provided the doctor has had experience in their use and the baby's head is in the right position for a safe vaginal delivery. Other indications for forceps delivery include maternal conditions such as eclampsia, severe toxemia, heart disease, separation of the placenta, infection, shock, bleeding, or other medical situations in which it would be dangerous or too difficult to push.

Forceps deliveries are classified according to where the baby's head is in relation to the perineum or bottom of the mother's vagina: A low forceps means that the instrument is applied once the baby's head is sitting on the mother's perineum. In a midforceps delivery, which is far less common, the head is engaged but not down on the perineum. When the baby is in this position in the midportion of the pelvis, the forceps are used to help pull and guide the baby's head through the birth canal and sometimes to rotate the head into the proper position for delivery. Some obstetricians feel confident about performing safe midforceps when indicated, while others are in favor of performing a cesarean at this point. The physician's particular skill would affect his or her decision. A forceps delivery requires anesthesia and the performance of an episiotomy.

Vacuum Extraction

Some doctors prefer vacuum extraction to forceps when there is a difficulty getting the baby through the birth canal. A small suction cup is placed on the baby's scalp, a vacuum is created, and the doctor is able to draw the baby. This avoids pressure on the sides of the head as with forceps.

Multiple Births

Approximately 1 in every 90 pregnancies is a multiple gestation, mostly twins. Twins are most common among older women, families that have a history of twins, and among women who take fertility drugs.

Most multiple births today are detected before labor and delivery, thanks to the development of ultrasound tests. Still, about 20 percent do go undetected until birth. The delivery of twins depends on the gestational age, the size, the respective positions of the babies, and the obstetrician's experience. Some physicians feel that, if the twins are not too large and everything else is fine, they can be delivered vaginally. Other physicians feel that twins and other multiple births should be delivered by cesarean section. (See chapter 13, The High-Risk Pregnancy.)

ALTERNATIVE CENTERS

Labor Room versus Birthing Room

Many hospitals now offer birthing rooms for the woman with a healthy, uncomplicated pregnancy as a more natural alternative to the usual labor and delivery rooms. Generally, a woman would remain in a labor room until she is almost ready to deliver, at which point she would be transferred to a delivery room.

The delivery room is very much like a regular operating room, with an anesthesia machine, oxygen tanks, and large overhead lights, and it can be a bit intimidating for anyone who has never seen one. One advantage of the delivery room is that anesthesia is readily available. Also, in some situations, such as delivering a large baby or where a forceps delivery becomes necessary, the obstetrician might find it easier to be in a delivery room with the woman on a standard delivery table with her feet resting in stirrups, giving him ample room to work and to help the birth go safely.

The husband is allowed to remain with his wife and to continue coaching her throughout the birth in the delivery room, unless the doctor asks him to leave during an emergency situation such as an emergency cesarean section delivery. In the case of an emergency or complication with the birth, it is an advantage to be in the delivery room where the doctor can get to work quickly without the mother having to be moved.

A birthing room is an acceptable alternative for the couple who have been adequately prepared and do not fall into a high-risk group. A birthing room can be considered if the pregnancy and labor are relatively problem free and if the woman intends to proceed with little or no anesthesia. Also, the birthing room should have ready access to a regular labor room or operating room if an emergency arises. Some birthing centers are free standing

and transporting the mother and baby to a hospital, even one that is nearby, can result in the loss of precious time.

Birthing room facilities differ from hospital to hospital, and so it would be advantageous for the expectant couple to visit the facilities in advance. If regular tours are not available for prospective parents, the couple's doctor can arrange for a visit to the hospital before the birth. Birthing rooms tend to be homier and less clinical in appearance, with labor and delivery taking place in the same bed. Some even permit siblings or other family members to attend the birth.

Special birthing beds (or even birthing chairs) allow for comfort and a variety of positions for the birth. The birth may go faster if the woman is in sitting up or semireclining position with her back supported by the bed rather than lying completely prone, although this is also possible. The end of the birthing bed can drop away for the delivery.

At-Home Deliveries

Most deliveries take place in hospitals or special birthing centers, but in recent years, there has been a trend to return to home deliveries, often with a nurse-midwife in attendance. Even under the best of circumstances, most obstetricians discourage home deliveries. Unforeseen emergencies can arise, with tragic results. The risk of infection is greater in a home delivery where sterile conditions are difficult to control. If a couple are absolutely determined to have their baby at home, it is vital that the mother have adequate prenatal care throughout pregnancy, and that a qualified health professional be in attendance. Plans also should be made for speedy transfer of the mother and baby to a hospital should something go wrong. (See chapter 2, Choosing Your Health Care Team.)

SUMMING UP

THE BIRTH OF A child is a momentous event, and one that should be pleasurable for all involved. Knowing what to expect and advance preparation through childbirth classes and self-education can remove the fear and mystique from childbirth. Most of the time, there are no complications, but when something does go wrong, knowing the warning signs and the appropriate actions can ease the trauma and even avert a tragedy.

16 Once a Cesarean . . .

Mortimer G. Rosen, M.D.

INTRODUCTION

OVER THE PAST 20 years, the cesarean birthrate in the United States has quadrupled to above 22 percent and the upward trend continues. In many hospitals 1 in 4 births is a cesarean; in others, the rate nears 1 in 3. In fact, the cesarean section has become the most common surgical procedure performed on women in this country.

There are some good reasons for the high cesarean rate, and some not so good. Advances in medical care and technology have made the procedure safer and easier; hence the clinical decision is more easily made. In the past, the risk of a cesarean often outweighed any potential benefit to the mother or baby. Today, however, electronic fetal monitoring, improved blood transfusions, better anesthetic agents, and greater control of maternal illnesses such as diabetes and high blood pressure have all made maternal death from cesarean delivery a rarity.

Some have suggested that the increased cesarean rate is largely attributable to the defensive medicine practiced by physicians who fear the threat of malpractice suits for a "less than perfect" baby. At a time when medical insurance costs have skyrocketed, obstetrics and gynecology as a specialty has been particularly hard hit. The likelihood of an obstetrician-gynecologist being sued is 2½ times the national average. And most obstetrical malpractice cases are either for failure to recognize fetal distress or failure to perform a cesarean section soon enough.

The long-held tenet "once a cesarean, always a cesarean" has also fed this rapid increase in the number of repeat cesarean births. Nearly 1 in 18 babies is delivered by scheduled repeat cesarean section. It was Dr. Edwin Craigin, a Columbia University obstetrician at the Sloane Hospital for Women, who urged his colleagues in 1916 (when the cesarean rate was less than 1 percent) to limit cesarean delivery for a first baby because "the usual rule is, once a cesarean, always a cesarean." Ironically, his phrase, intended to restrain cesareans, has become a major reason for the rise in the cesarean rate. Now it is time to lay the dictum to rest.

WHY SO MANY CESAREANS ARE PERFORMED

STUDIES INDICATE that cesarean delivery improves the outcome of various complications of pregnancy. For example, women with active herpes infections at the time of delivery have a cesarean in order to prevent vaginal viral infection of the baby.

Obstetricians favor surgical relief for babies too large or too small, or those in an abnormal position. Sometimes the mother's pelvis is simply not large enough for the baby to fit, although this is quite uncommon. Uterine contractions may be too infrequent or too weak, or for other uncertain reasons, progress in labor does not sustain a vaginal delivery. Such problematic labors, called *dystocia*, are responsible for 40 percent of primary cesarean deliveries and they represent the largest contribution to the overall rise in the primary cesarean rate. (Table 16.1 lists indications for a cesarean.)

Repeat Cesarean

A previous cesarean section is the second major reason for the high cesarean delivery rate at the present time. More than 95 percent of women in the United States undergo a repeat cesarean in any subse-

---

Table 16.1
INDICATIONS FOR CESAREAN SECTION

The following conditions are often associated with a cesarean section (few are absolute):

- Fetal distress
- Dystocia (failure of labor to progress)
- Previous C-section delivery with classical (vertical) incision (almost always a cesarean)
- Maternal infection (herpes, if an active lesion is present)
- Unusual presentation (transverse lie, brow presentation)
- Too large a baby (after a trial of labor)
- Placenta previa
- Abruptio placentae

The following conditions usually, but not always, require a cesarean:

- Breech position
- Multiple births
- Prolapse of the umbilical cord

---

quent pregnancy. Based on maternal and neonatal mortality rates, the practice of repeat cesarean remains less a question than patient care patterns suggest.

A cesarean section should never be considered casually, as it involves considerably more risks than a vaginal birth. Among them are problems of anesthesia for mother and fetus, blood loss (twice that during vaginal delivery), prolonged patient recovery time, and greater chance of postoperative infection.

The likelihood of maternal death from a repeat cesarean is 2 to 3 times greater than it is from a vaginal delivery. The outcome for the fetus is excellent in the vaginal birth group and vaginal birth following a primary cesarean should be an option.

Fetal Distress

The diagnosis of fetal distress is another large contributor to the cesarean rate increase. Problems such as a compressed umbilical cord, unusual uterine contractions, a placenta that separates before delivery of the baby, or a slowdown of the fetal heart rate may place the baby at risk and often result in a cesarean.

Suspicion lingers that fetal distress may be diagnosed too hastily because of the inappropriate use of electronic fetal heart rate monitoring during labor. Some believe that too much information may do more harm than good. The heart rate decelerations often respond to oxygen treatment or to changes in the mother's position, thus avoiding a cesaren delivery. Unfortunately, the heart rate does not easily tell us what is happening in the fetal brain.

Breech

Cesareans are often performed for another, more controversial reason—the baby is breech, with its feet or buttocks ready to come out first. This condition may be apparent in advance or it may surprise both doctor and patient alike. Since the head is the largest part of the baby, and the last to come out, any significant delay in its emergence could cause brain damage, or localized nerve trauma or seizures.

When the breech position is discovered, a cesarean delivery is commonly planned. It is possible, however, for breech babies to be delivered vaginally by an experienced obstetrician. In fact, the National Institute of Child Health and Development recommends vaginal delivery of breech babies so long as the mother's pelvis is large enough and the baby is not judged to be of excessive size.

Age Factor

Because some physicians still consider the woman over 35 a high-risk patient, there is a tendency to perform a cesarean more readily on this patient. While she may be more likely to have specific problems such as high blood pressure or diabetes, or to carry a fetus with Down syndrome, the majority of pregnancies in these years are normal.

VAGINAL BIRTH AFTER CESAREAN

ASIDE FROM the risks of a repeat cesarean, vaginal birth after a cesarean section (sometimes known as VBAC) is an acceptable and worthwhile mode of delivery for most women. Very often the situation that prompted the first cesarean birth does not repeat itself. Dystocia, breech baby, fetal distress, multiple birth, and separation of the placenta are all so-called nonrecurring reasons. In general, each pregnancy is a separate entity and should not influence another.

A report by a National Institutes of Health task force encourages physicians not to rule out vaginal delivery under "appropriate circumstances." The circumstances refer to a fully equipped medical setting with open blood bank, full-time operating room, and full-time anesthesiologist in case an emergency cesarean must be performed.

Types of Incision

In most hospitals 1 cesarean delivery automatically means another. This practice began at the turn of the century when physicians feared that labor contractions would cause the uterus to rupture along the scar of the previous cesarean section. The risk of rupture, a separation of the cesarean scar, is quite small. Instead of a classical incision, which involves a vertical incision in the upper part of the uterus, physicians now make a horizontal cut in the lower segment of the uterus. More than 90 percent of cesareans today are performed with the low transverse incision, which is much safer and less likely to rupture in the future.

At times, because of fetal size (very large or very small), fetal position (transverse or breech), or other maternal problems, a low vertical incision is made rather than a low transverse. This is essentially a modified classical and may carry similar risks for the future. (See figure 16.1.) On occasion, the obstetrician finds that the baby cannot fit through the low transverse incision and a second vertical cut, known as an inverted-T incision, must be made.

A trial of labor is not recommended for women who have had either a classical, low vertical, or inverted-T incision during their first cesarean. In these cases labor is more risky because the data to document complications is not available. The type of incision (and subsequent scar)

the woman has on her skin bears no relation to the incision on her uterus. This can only be learned from the patient's records from the first cesarean or by speaking to her physician.

Uterine Rupture

The term "rupture" sounds very serious, but is more like a separation or a hernia in a muscle. Although this is a major medical problem, only on rare occasions does the uterus rupture completely and in such a way as to cause the mother danger. Because most uterine ruptures occur long before labor begins, even a planned re-

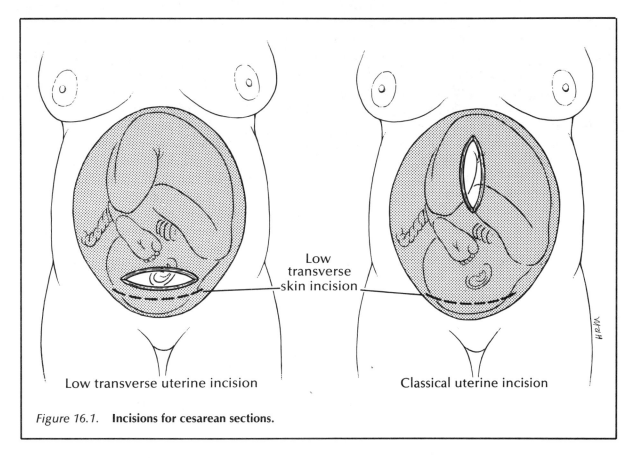

Low transverse skin incision

Low transverse uterine incision

Classical uterine incision

Figure 16.1. **Incisions for cesarean sections.**

peat cesarean will not help to avoid them. Low transverse scar ruptures of varying severity have been reported in 1 to 2 percent of subsequent pregnancies. Over 90 percent of these ruptures are "silent and incomplete" and happen before labor. The mother may experience some bleeding and slight pain. Indeed, should the uterus rupture at the time of labor, the obstetrician generally has time to perform the emergency cesarean.

TRIAL OF LABOR AFTER A CESAREAN

BEFORE 1978, a trial of labor after a cesarean birth was uncommon. A growing number of hospitals, provided they are properly equipped, are allowing a trial of labor, and their success rates are encouraging. Over the past 5 years, between 60 and 80 percent of women who chose a vaginal birth after a previous cesarean had safe, normal deliveries. Although controversy remains as to the prerequisites for a safe trial of labor, there is no doubt that far fewer cesareans will be performed if labor is allowed after a prior cesarean delivery. Slowly, we may come to a stage where the vaginal delivery after cesarean section is the rule rather than the exception.

Allowing a woman a vaginal birth rather than a repeat cesarean eliminates serious problems for the fetus as well, namely those resulting from iatrogenic prematurity. This means that the physician was unable to determine the baby's true due date accurately and has scheduled a repeat cesarean too early. Even with ultrasonography, the doctor may not be able to "date" the baby as well as he or she would like—hence some babies are born prematurely. In fact, iatrogenic prematurity remains a significant cause of admissions to the neonatal intensive care nursery.

Good advice for any woman considering pregnancy would be to keep precise records of her menstrual periods, as this is key to ascertaining the day the baby is due. Should a woman require a cesarean, her obstetrician will aim to deliver the baby as close to full term as possible.

Psychological Rewards

Psychologically, there is a great satisfaction in having attempted a vaginal birth; when a vaginal birth is successful, the entire family enjoys a sense of accomplishment. Cesarean mothers may view their childbirth experience quite negatively. The feelings of disappointment are strongest in women whose cesareans were a surprise. Feelings of anger, failure, guilt, and loss of control may take the place of the happiness the mother should enjoy. Because of the surgery, initial mother–infant contact is often delayed, which may reinforce the mother's sense of inadequacy.

For women planning to have a second child, the thought of a trial of labor and normal delivery can help ease the pain sometimes felt over the first cesarean birth. It is most important for expectant mothers to understand the guidelines and options so that they choose the environment in which they wish to deliver. Some patients are so upset by the first cesarean that they do not want even to anticipate a trial of labor. An anxious patient is urged at least to attend childbirth classes to better understand the cesarean and the alternatives. Most hospitals sponsor predelivery classes for women who have undergone a cesarean.

Hospital Policy

While the mother's choice of delivery has top priority, the hospital's capabilities play a critical role in her decision. A trial of labor is recommended to take place in a hospital where an emergency cesarean can be done within 30 minutes after that decision has been made. The American College of Obstetricians and Gynecologists proposes this guideline for patients who are candidates for vaginal birth after a cesarean.

Many hospitals, particularly smaller centers in rural areas, for instance, are simply not prepared for a trial of labor. They may not have separate labor rooms, nor the nursing and anesthesiology staff needed. Here, the woman really has no choice unless she travels to another city to have her baby.

Any expectant mother can request a tour of the labor and delivery facilities when she is scheduled to deliver and she is advised to learn about the hospital early in her pregnancy. Key questions to ask hospital personnel are:

● Are childbirth classes given at the hospital? Is the father included?

● Do attending physicians deliver vaginally after a previous cesarean?

● What is the attitude of the nursing staff toward vaginal birth after a cesarean?

● Is an anesthesiologist available for labor at all times?

● Is an epidural (regional) anesthesia used for a cesarean birth?

● Is the cesarean birth room available for immediate use at all times?

● Can fathers be present at a cesarean delivery?

● Is breastfeeding immediately after birth encouraged?

● How soon is the baby brought to the mother for feeding after a vaginal birth? after a cesarean section?

If the answers to these questions do not suit her, the expectant mother may decide to seek another hospital or another doctor.

CHOOSING AN OBSTETRICIAN

THE MAJOR ROLE a patient can play in avoiding a second cesarean birth is to ask physicians the right questions before se-lecting an obstetrician. If the cesarean rate the physician quotes seems high, it may be a signal that some cesareans are questionable. It also may indicate that the obstetrician specializes in high-risk mothers, such as diabetics, who often have a high cesarean rate.

Another question to ask is whether the physician requests a second opinion, whenever possible, before performing a cesarean section. This, too, is a recommendation of the American College of Obstetricians and Gynecologists and serves as an important safeguard against unnecessary cesareans. In emergency situations, such as hemorrhage or severe fetal distress, a cesarean must be performed without another doctor's concurrence.

In these discussions, the physician's attitude toward vaginal birth after cesarean should become clear. If he or she does not wholeheartedly favor a trial of labor, another physician may. More and more obstetricians are suggesting a trial of labor for patients who have had a previous cesarean.

Women have changed doctors during their pregnancy, some just weeks before they were due to deliver. If the patient is not happy and feels she must change physicians, she should contact her former obstetrician and request in writing that her records be transferred.

The Supportive Physician

Although there is no reason for her to fear a trial of labor, the woman who had a previous cesarean is undoubtedly apprehensive about her second delivery. In addition to good routine prenatal care, the following reflect a genuinely supportive physician:

- Willingness to answer all questions clearly
- A discussion of drugs and anesthesia
- Referral to childbirth preparation classes, preferably couple-oriented ones
- A full explanation of any tests or diagnostic procedures
- A discussion of breastfeeding and support for the woman's decision, whether it is to breastfeed or bottle-feed
- Strong support for the patient's choice of delivery

Where to Turn for Help

A number of educational organizations and support groups have formed over the past few years in response to the growing cesarean rate. Their goal is to provide moral support for women who have had cesarean births and to help dispel the "once a cesarean . . ." myth.

Through its 42 chapters around the country, the Cesarean Prevention Movement maintains an extensive network. The organization helps women locate physicians in their community who are known to encourage vaginal birth after a cesarean. The International Childbirth Education Association also has information regarding obstetricians and appropriate childbirth classes for women who have had a cesarean. (See table 16.2.)

The Father's Role

Two issues are paramount in the minds of many women facing a repeat cesarean: Will I be awake when my baby is born?

Table 16.2

ORGANIZATIONS PROVIDING INFORMATION ABOUT VAGINAL BIRTH AFTER CESAREANS

Cesarean Prevention Movement
P.O. Box 152
University Station
Syracuse, NY 13210
(315) 424-1942

C/SEC, Inc.
22 Forest Road
Framingham, MA 01701
(617) 877-8266

The International Childbirth Education Association, Inc.
P.O. Box 248
Minneapolis, MN 55420
(612) 854-8660

Will my husband be with me during the delivery? For more and more women, the answers are yes. The preferred form of anesthesia for cesarean delivery today is regional (epidural or spinal), which leaves the woman pain free, but alert to her surroundings and to the events of her childbirth.

While many hospitals have accepted the father's presence during a normal, vaginal birth, some centers may draw the line at his observing a cesarean. Reluctance stems from the potential for increased infection, fathers fainting, and lack of space in crowded operating rooms. Experience in hospitals that do allow the father in the operating room during a cesarean delivery indicates no real problem. On the contrary, his presence and reassurance ease the mother's anxiety and are psychologically and emotionally beneficial.

SUMMING UP

FOR MOTHER AND INFANT, the vaginal birth after a previous cesarean section is the procedure of choice. Many physicians, as well as expectant mothers, are coming to recognize more and more that vaginal delivery is the normal and accepted approach to childbirth, regardless of past experience.

For every cesarean delivery, there are immediate and long-term risks of major surgery. In addition to the initial rewards of a vaginal birth after cesarean, women who do not fear a repeat cesarean may choose to have larger families. Most women who have had a cesarean birth do have a second child, but not a third (unless the second was delivered vaginally).

While exceptions to a vaginal birth after cesarean do exist, the woman is entitled to her choice of childbirth based upon her physician's guidance and the hospital's capabilities. Although pregnancy is a natural process, neither the parents nor the physician can guarantee a perfect outcome. It is most important, however, that a well-informed patient help in good decision making.

17 Getting Back in Shape

Pamela Tropper, M.D.

INTRODUCTION

A NEW MOTHER who has delivered in a hospital will remain there until her condition is stable and her obstetrician is certain that all is going well with her. Before she goes home, her temperature and blood pressure must be normal, and her general health stable. A woman who has delivered a first baby vaginally after an uncomplicated pregnancy will probably be able to leave the hospital by the third or fourth day. If she has had a cesarean, the stay will be longer—5 or 6 days, in most cases. If the baby was delivered at a birthing center, mother and child will leave within 24 hours.

PHYSICAL RECOVERY

A WOMAN'S BODY spent 9 months undergoing changes in preparation for childbirth. The return to the prepregnancy body is much more rapid, with the greatest changes occurring in the first 6 weeks after delivery, the postpartum period or puerperium. In addition, a new mother can expect some relatively minor physical problems following delivery, including aching muscles, edema, hemorrhoids, and constipation.

Postpartum Bleeding and Vaginal Discharge

Postpartum bleeding is normal; it usually lasts 4 or 5 weeks but may continue lightly for up to 8 weeks. This discharge, called lochia, is residual blood coming mainly from the placental site. After the first 4 or 5 days the lochia will change from a bright red to a brownish color, and staining will gradually lessen until it stops completely. Sanitary napkins, rather than tampons, should be used for the bleeding.

If the lochia stops a week or 2 after delivery and then suddenly returns at a heavier rate, it may be a sign that the uterus has relaxed, allowing some of the blood vessels that had closed to reopen. This should be taken as a sign to reduce activity and get more rest. Nursing mothers tend to bleed while their babies are feeding because the same hormone (oxytocin) that lets down milk also causes the uterus to contract.

Most physicians recommend that new mothers continue iron supplements for a while to compensate for the blood loss. Although bleeding is normal, lochia with bad smell or an elevation in temperature may be signs of infection. A new mother who develops a fever should call her doctor or midwife.

After postpartum bleeding stops, there may be a white, sticky vaginal discharge. This is normal. However, if it becomes abundant, green or yellow, or frothy, it is possible that an infection is present. The doctor should be informed about this. Douches should not be used except when recommended by the doctor.

Afterpains

Immediately after delivery, the uterus can be felt as a hard lump midway between the navel and the pubic bone. By the third day it will have begun to descend into the pelvis, and by the fifth day it is about an inch above the pubic bone and can scarcely be felt. Whereas at the time of delivery it weighs about 2 pounds, by the time of the postpartum checkup it will weigh only about 2 ounces. This shrinkage of the uterus occurs in part as a result of contraction of its muscle cells, sometimes felt as cramps or afterpains.

In the first few days after delivery, cramping may be severe and uncomfortable; it is often at its worst when the baby nurses. Most doctors prescribe pain medication, which must be properly selected for nursing mothers. Such severe cramping usually subsides within 2 or 3 days. Cramps tend to be worse with subsequent pregnancies.

Sweating and Hot Flashes

A drop in hormone production following delivery is responsible for hot flashes, which are accompanied by profuse sweating. The sweating helps the body get rid of retained fluid, but it can be inconvenient. In winter, night sweating may lead to chills, and it is advisable for new mothers to keep a fresh nightgown at the bedside.

Fatigue

It takes time for the body to recover from the physical stress of pregnancy, labor, and delivery, and fatigue is one natural response of the postpartum period. When the new demands of around-the-clock childcare are added to the physical stresses of recovery, new mothers are likely to feel exhausted in the first weeks after delivery.

A new mother needs plenty of rest, yet getting enough sleep can be hard during the first weeks of a baby's life. To cope with fatigue, she should try to adjust her waking and sleeping hours to fit the baby's, taking advantage of those daytime moments when the baby is asleep to rest herself. She should try to schedule 2 naps a day for the first 2 weeks and an afternoon nap for at least the next 2. She should also neglect household chores in favor of taking a nap, or reading a book or watching television with her feet up.

It is important for new mothers to have someone at home—their partner or a relative, a friend, or housekeeper—to help with all the other things around the house besides baby care. The situation is eased when the new father can take some time off from work after the baby is born. There is plenty to keep 2 parents busy in the weeks immediately following childbirth.

The Perineum and Episiotomy

The site of an episiotomy or a tear that required suturing will probably feel tender and painful for the first few days. Healing begins immediately, but it takes about a week before the discomfort subsides, and up to 4 weeks before the underlying tissues are strong. Stitches dissolve in place and do not have to be removed.

The process of birth will have caused a great deal of stretching of the vagina and the muscles of the perineum, even if an episiotomy was performed. Much of the pain in the area is due to a reflex tensing of the perineal muscles. An ice pack on the area in the first 24 hours helps decrease swelling. After that, the area should be kept scrupulously clean and pressure on the perineum should be avoided by sitting sideways on a cushion. Inflatable "doughnut" cushions, which can cause the wound site to swell, should be avoided. Any reddening or swelling may be a sign of infection and should be reported to the doctor immediately.

The discomfort of an episiotomy often gets worse before it gets better. As a new mother becomes more active, stands, and moves around more, she will feel the pain more. Warm showers and sitz baths (sitting in a shallow tub of warm water) will stimulate blood flow, help healing, and ease some of the discomfort. A cup of warm water poured over the site while urinating will relieve stinging. Pain medication (acetaminophen) can also help. Tub bathing can resume after 2 weeks.

Constipation

Constipation is a common complaint in the postpartum period. A newly delivered mother may be afraid to push too hard because she is afraid that the episiotomy will hurt or tear. The stitches used to close an episiotomy, however, will not rip. Usually, if she follows a diet that includes plenty of fresh fruit and vegetables, at least 6 to 8 glasses of fluid daily, plus a small amount of bran, constipation will not be a problem. It is also helpful to get out of bed and walk around as soon as possible after delivery. The first bowel movement usually occurs on the third to fifth day after delivery.

Hemorrhoids

Hemorrhoids often become worse after delivery as a result of pressure on the rectum and anus during late pregnancy and childbirth. Cream or suppositories will ease the discomfort. Cotton pads soaked with witch hazel (such as Tucks) are soothing, and are especially soothing if kept refrigerated. Constipation exacerbates the discomfort of hemorrhoids. If the usual dietary remedies do not adequately prevent constipation, a stool softener will help. Lying down relieves pressure on dilated veins and will speed recovery.

Hemorrhoids usually subside in about 1 month, although persistent hemorrhoids sometimes require more radical treatment. Once a woman develops hemorrhoids, however, she will always have a tendency to develop them again during another pregnancy.

Urinary Problems

Increased frequency and urgency are common during the postpartum period, as the body gets rid of retained fluid. Burning during urination at this time usually is not due to an infection but to inflammation of the bladder walls and urethra resulting from pressure put on them during the birth process. These tissues are particularly sensitive to concentrated urine. A woman should drink plenty of water, to dilute her urine until it is almost clear in color. This should quickly relieve the burning sensation.

Because the muscles of the pelvic floor have been stretched by childbirth, many women suffer from the leaking of urine when they exert themselves, or even sneeze suddenly, after the birth. Time usually solves the problem. Kegel exercises also help. (See section on Postpartum Exercises.)

Hair Loss

Hair seems to fall out in clumps with each brush stroke 4 to 6 months after delivery. This is a natural event following childbirth. Normally, hairs grow in different cycles—some are growing while others are resting, preparatory to being shed. In pregnancy, hairs appear to synchronize in the same cycle so that large numbers enter the resting stage together and hair loss becomes noticeable. With time, the cycle readjusts itself and the normal pattern of hair growth and loss resumes.

Recovery after a Cesarean Birth

After a cesarean, most patients feel weak and unwell for a day or 2 after the delivery, and the incision will be sore. In most hospitals, the mother will be fed intravenously for the first 24 to 48 hours; a catheter to drain the bladder may remain in place for the same length of time. The intestines will be sluggish for several days and gas will accumulate, causing considerable discomfort. Passing gas is a sign that the intestines are becoming active again; at that point the IV tube will be disconnected and the diet will be gradually returned to normal.

Today, women who have had cesareans are generally on their feet within 2 days. It may be painful to walk, but this gentle exercise helps to prevent the formation of clots in the legs and is useful in getting the digestive system active again.

The stitches will usually be removed on the fifth day. In the meantime, there is no need to try to keep them dry—a woman can take a shower as soon as she feels steady enough to do so.

Postpartum exercises for the feet and legs can be started right away and gentle exercise for the abdominal muscles after a week. Heavy lifting and strenuous exercise should be avoided for at least 6 weeks. Some doctors advise patients who have had a cesarean not to drive a car for a month.

Menstruation

If a woman does not breastfeed, the menstrual period will usually return within 8 to 12 weeks after delivery. If she does nurse, there is great variation. Most do not menstruate while they are nursing and some do not begin again until 6 or 8 months after the baby is weaned from the breast. However, others begin to menstruate 2 months after the birth, even though they are nursing. Periods may be lighter or heavier than they were before pregnancy and may be irregular for some time.

Sometimes the return to normal hormone production after childbirth is very slow and the uterine lining becomes very thick. When ovulation finally occurs, the sloughing off of this thick lining produces an extremely heavy period. If a heavy flow (requiring the use of 1 pad an hour) continues for longer than 6 or 7 hours—or if it is necessary to change pads every half hour—the doctor should be called.

The Beginning of Lactation

The breasts become full and swollen (engorged) on the third or fourth day after delivery, partly because of the beginning of heavy milk production, partly because the breast tissue itself swells as blood flow to the area increases. Engorgement will continue until the milk begins to flow freely, in another day or 2. Local heat or cold, whichever feels best, will ease the discomfort.

If a woman does not plan to breast-feed, binding the breasts tightly and using ice bags will help relieve the engorgement, which will last for about 3 days before easing off.

Whether she is nursing or not, a woman should wear a bra to support her breasts. They are heavier than usual at this time and tend to pull at their ligaments.

Sore Breasts

Swelling, redness, or a painful lump can mean a plugged milk duct. This may be due to poor letdown of milk, infrequent nursing, or stress and fatigue. Hot compresses, gentle massage of the area, and more frequent nursing usually relieve the discomfort.

If fever and flulike aches accompany the swelling, a breast infection (mastitis) may be present and a doctor should be contacted. More rest also may be needed. Occasionally a breast infection develops into an abcess that must be drained surgically, but early treatment usually prevents this.

POSTPARTUM EXERCISES

THE TIME it takes for a woman to regain her body tone after pregnancy depends on her physical condition before delivery, how much weight she loses during and immediately following the birth, and how much exercise she does after the birth. Regular, nonstrenuous exercise—not dieting—is the best way to get back into shape.

All new mothers should limit their physical activity for about 2 weeks, although some gentle exercises can be started right away. Those who have had cesarean deliveries should limit their physical activity for 4 to 6 weeks.

Early Postpartum Exercises. A new mother can begin these exercises in the earliest days postpartum and continue them after she goes home. A woman who has had abdominal stitches will have to support the scar with her hand before she moves (or coughs, sneezes, or laughs).

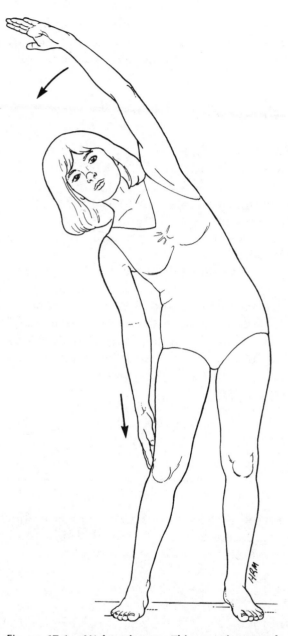

Figure 17.1. **Waist trimmer. This exercise stretches the back and helps firm the waist. Stand straight with feet about 8 to 10 inches apart. Raise 1 arm over head and at same time, stretch opposite arm as far as you can down your leg. Start with 5 on each side and work up to 15 per session.**

Figure 17.2. **Donkey stretch. This exercise firms abdomen and tones upper body. Start by kneeling on floor on hands and knees. Slowly raise 1 arm and swing it under body until you can touch as far as you can on your upper back. Repeat with opposite side. Start with 4 and work up to 10 to 15.**

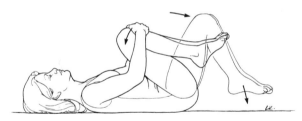

Figure 17.4. **Knee to chest. This exercise helps tighten abdominal muscles. Lie on back with knees bent. Make sure spine is flat against the floor. Slowly lift knees until you can clasp them and pull them to chest. Start with 4 and gradually work up to 10 per session.**

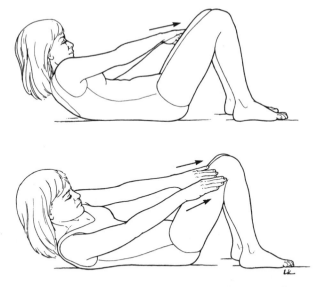

Figure 17.3. **Half sit-ups. This exercise strengthens abdominal muscles and helps tone upper body. Lie on back with feet flat on floor and knees bent. With hands touching, gradually lift shoulders and upper body until you can touch one leg; lie back and repeat on opposite side. Start with 4 and work up to 10 per session.**

Vaginal Tightening Exercise (Kegel).
Start this exercise immediately, while still in the hospital. It can be done lying down, with the knees up, slightly apart, and bent at a right angle. Later, it can be done sitting or standing—in fact, anywhere at any time.

Squeeze the muscles around the urethra and anus as if holding back both urine and a bowel movement. Hold tightly for a few seconds, and relax. Repeat the exercise at least 10 times, 5 times a day.

Progress can be checked while urinat- ing, by stopping and starting the flow several times in midstream. This may be difficult at first, but as muscles regain their strength and elasticity it becomes easier. However, it is important to make sure that the bladder is completely empty before leaving the bathroom; women who have developed a kidney infection should not do this exercise while urinating.

Legs and Feet. Exercising legs and feet will help improve muscle tone and circulation, thus helping prevent leg cramps and varicose veins. Lying flat, press the backs of the knees down on the bed, then relax. Repeat several times. While sitting or lying in bed, flex and stretch the ankles. Point feet upward, and flex and stretch toes. Circle feet outward, then circle inward.

Head Lift for Abdominal Muscles. Lie flat on back on a firm surface and lift head (not shoulders), then relax again gently. Repeat this with a slight twist of the shoulders, lifting head to look to one side and then the other. Do this head lift 10 times per session, three times a day.

Posture. When getting out of bed, stretch the spine. Set shoulders back and down, and balance weight equally on both feet.

Later Postpartum Exercise. After about 2 weeks, most new mothers feel strong enough to move on and do more demanding exercises. Exercise for at least 10 minutes per day, gradually moving on to more strenuous ones as the weeks pass. Figures 17.1 to 17.4 show gentle beginning exercises that most new mothers can do. These beginning exercises are designed to help new mothers get back into shape. Once a woman is feeling back to normal, she can resume active sports or the exercise program she followed before pregnancy. She should remember, however, that it often takes 6 months or longer to completely regain her prepregnancy figure, and even then, hips may be a bit wider than before, and breasts may be either larger or smaller.

NUTRITION

GOOD NUTRITION is vital for new mothers. Women who ate carefully during pregnancy should not have too much weight to lose afterward. Weight loss in delivery and the first 10 days post partum is usually about 15 pounds—the weight of the baby, the placenta, and a considerable amount of fluid. A certain amount of excess fat (about 11 or 12 pounds) remains stored to provide extra calories for making breast milk. This fat will be used up over 3 months or so and the weight should then be back to normal.

New mothers should not go on crash diets. Most want to lose weight at this time, but caring for a new baby puts strenuous demands on the body, even if a mother is not breastfeeding, and stringent dieting can lead to fatigue, poor health, and depression. The goal should be a loss of no more than 1 pound a week.

A woman who is not nursing should resume her normal prepregnancy diet, with an emphasis on complex carbohydrates, fresh fruit, and vegetables, and an adequate amount of protein, and a deemphasis on fats. Iron supplements should be continued because of blood loss in the first few weeks post partum.

Nursing mothers have additional nutritional requirements. Mothers who breastfeed should drink 2 to 3 quarts of fluid daily, 1 quart of which should be milk (whole, low-fat, or skim), and continue on iron and vitamin supplements. Calorie intake is especially important. The body burns nearly 1,000 calories a day to produce milk, and so the mother must eat more than usual.

Most nursing mothers continue the diet they followed during pregnancy but they need even more calories than before

—about 300 to 500 calories a day more than they consumed during pregnancy. The diet should be varied—high in calories and protein. Small, frequent meals will help keep the milk supply constant, but if it drops fluids and calories and rest should be increased.

RESUMING SEXUAL RELATIONS

MANY FACTORS influence the timing and the nature of sexual relationships after childbirth. Most doctors advise couples to wait until after the postpartum checkup before resuming intercourse. The skin edges of the episiotomy will be healed by the fifth or sixth day after delivery, but the underlying tissues do not regain their strength until about the fourth week. Intercourse should not be resumed—nor anything be put in the vagina—until all danger of uterine infection is passed, that is, until the cervix is closed and normal mucus is being secreted. In most women (95 percent) the cervix is back to normal by the end of the fourth week post partum.

After the episiotomy heals, the vagina may become rather tight. An understandable wariness may make a woman tighten it still further. For the first few times after childbirth, intercourse should be very slow and gentle, with patient manipulation to ease vaginal tightness. If pain persists, medical advice should be sought, as this may be a sign of infection or that the episiotmy has not healed properly.

Many new mothers find that they are completely uninterested in sex in the weeks following childbirth. This temporary loss of desire is unrelated to breastfeeding, although it is probably partly hormonal in origin. The body has been overwhelmed by the last months of pregnancy and the stresses of childbirth. Fatigue and tenderness in the perineal area can make sex the last thing a woman wants to think about. In addition, many new demands are placed on new mothers: They are on constant call for the baby, sleep is frequently interrupted, and adjusting to new routines can be exhausting. If a new mother is nursing, intercourse can be uncomfortable as a result of vaginal dryness. This occurs because the ovaries produce little or no estrogen during breastfeeding, and without estrogen the vagina may become abnormally tight and dry. A lubricating jelly may be helpful, but if dryness continues to be a problem, a doctor should be consulted. Within 4 to 6 weeks, however, the body has usually regained its strength, new household routines are established, and sex drive gradually returns to normal.

Resuming sexual relations is a personal matter that depends on both emotional feelings and physical well-being. Sometimes, even after resuming sexual relations, it may take a few weeks before sex is as satisfying as it was before or during pregnancy. Often, however, the intimacy and intensity of the shared birth experience makes a couple all the more loving.

CONTRACEPTION

AT THE POSTPARTUM checkup a couple will have the opportunity to discuss contraception with their physician. If they have sexual relations before then, they should use a condom and contraceptive foam.

Although breastfeeding generally inhibits ovulation, it does not do so invariably and should not be relied on as a method of contraception. Nursing mothers who wish to space their children should also use contraception. A new mother's menstrual cycle may take time to regulate itself and may even be slightly different after childbirth. This makes the rhythm method even more unreliable.

Condoms and Contraceptive Foam. These forms of contraception can be used anytime and are especially recommended for nursing mothers.

Oral Contraceptives. Women who breast-feed should not take oral contraceptives, because the hormones from the pills are excreted in breast milk and the long-term effects are unknown. Those who do *not* breastfeed should avoid the pill immediately following delivery because there is some evidence of increased blood clots during this period. Unless the doctor advises otherwise, the pill can be resumed after the postpartum checkup.

Diaphragm. A diaphragm cannot be fitted immediately after a birth because the muscles of the vagina are slack and the episiotomy swollen and tender. The partner can use a condom until a diaphragm can be fitted, usually about 2 months after delivery. Those who used a diaphragm before pregnancy will have to be refitted, as childbirth may alter the size of the vaginal canal.

POSTPARTUM DEPRESSION

EMOTIONAL CHANGES should be expected in the weeks after childbirth. Approximately 90 percent of all new mothers suffer some degree of postpartum depression, ranging from an emotional anticlimax following the euphoria of birth ("the baby blues") all the way to severe depression.

Typically, a new mother suffering from the baby blues feels that nothing is working out as it should, that she cannot go on trying to cope, that she is exhausted, and that all she wants to do is to sit down and cry. Not uncommonly, she may also feel hostility toward the baby and resentment about her new responsibilities. Guilt may accompany these feelings, intensifying the depression, but they are shared by many women and are normal at this time.

In more severe cases, depression interferes with a woman's ability to meet her responsibilities to herself, her husband, and the baby. Her responsibilities to herself include good hygiene and a proper diet; to her husband, keeping the lines of communication open; and to her child, providing love, food, and shelter. The most extreme form of depression, puerperal psychosis, affects about 1 in 500 and usually requires hospitalization.

The evidence suggests that postpartum depresison—of any degree—is due to hormonal changes following delivery, in combination with fatigue and emotional tension. Estrogen and progesterone levels drop precipitously immediately after the birth and it seems probable that the changed hormonal levels contribute to mood swings. Lack of REM sleep (the stage of sleep at which dreaming occurs), due to broken nights, is also thought to play a part.

Necessary adjustments within the family make for emotional tension. After the baby's birth, the focus of attention shifts from mother to child—just when the woman herself may need attention. Her days are filled with chores, her nights are disrupted by the baby's feedings, and her partner may have ambivalent feelings about fatherhood. Those who have left their jobs feel the lack of a world outside the home. The more severe forms of depression seem to be more likely to occur if there was something abnormal about the pregnancy, or if there has been a prior history of emotional disturbance, an unstable marriage, or a deep anxiety about parenthood.

For most, the feelings of depression are minimal and transitory. The best help for postpartum blues is for a new mother to get plenty of rest, to try not to isolate herself, and to receive the loving support of friends and family. Talking about their feelings is one good way that new mothers can deal with the baby blues. It is also very helpful to get some time for oneself, even if it means hiring someone to watch the baby so that she can take an uninterrupted nap, a long walk, or a relaxing bath without worrying if the baby cries. Women who are breastfeeding should consider having a sitter give the baby an occasional bottle so that they can get out of the house.

Postpartum blues may last from a few days to a few weeks. If the depression does not lift within 6 weeks—at which time the hormonal balance is back to normal—psychotherapy and medication may be recommended to help break the cycle of sleepless nights, anxiety, and irritability. By no means should the depression go on untreated.

POSTPARTUM CHECKUP

THE FIRST POSTPARTUM checkup usually takes place 4 to 6 weeks after delivery although some doctors see their patients as early as 3 weeks and others wait until 8. If a new mother has any problems—chills or fever, increased vaginal bleeding, abdominal pain, bleeding nipples, tenderness or lumps in the breasts, for example —she should call her doctor before the scheduled appointment. Even an apparently minor complication can become serious if 2 or 3 weeks go by.

The postpartum checkup includes:
- blood pressure
- examination of the breasts
- palpation of the abdomen to make sure the uterus is back to its normal size and position and an internal examination to make sure that the vaginal area has healed properly and that the cervix is tightly closed

The uterus, cervix, and vagina will remain slightly larger than they were before pregnancy. Any increased pigmentation of the nipples is probably permanent, as are any stretch marks, which now appear as brownish lines across the thighs and abdomen and will fade further with time.

Medically speaking, the postpartum checkup concludes the pregnancy. The results become part of the woman's medical record and will be an important consideration in her next pregnancy. In some ways the postpartum checkup also represents the end of the period of adjustment to motherhood. The baby is probably settled into a sleeping and waking routine by now and breastfeeding should be well established. However, the woman's body still has physical adjustments to make. It may take 6 months or more before her physical and hormonal balance is completely restored.

GOING BACK TO WORK

PHYSICALLY a new mother can go back to work as soon as she feels well enough, usually in about 3 weeks. The decision about when to return to work, however, is also based on emotional preparedness, financial considerations, and the availability of childcare. Six weeks to 2 months seems a good interval for most mothers, both physically and emotionally. The average leave time is 6 weeks after delivery.

Going back too late can be emotionally wrenching. Many mothers report that the longer they waited to return to work, the harder it became. When a woman returns to work within a month or so after childbirth, she may have some difficulty leaving the baby, but the infant usually makes a fairly smooth transition. When she waits 5 or 6 months, however, the baby will associate its care with her and returning to work may be hard on both mother and infant.

Going back early, on a part-time basis, seems to be the most desirable solution. Those mothers who return to work on part-time schedules begin to balance their work responsibilities and their home life early and can gradually build up to a full-time work schedule, whereas going back full-time after several months at home is jarring. Many new mothers, however, do not have options. While some jobs lend themselves to flexible scheduling, others are more demanding.

Nursing mothers can continue to nurse on a part-time basis, breastfeeding in the morning and evening, and having their babies bottle-fed in between. Or they can express milk during the lunch hour, chill it, and reserve it for the following day. (If refrigerated, breast milk is safe for 48 hours.) The body will usually adapt itself to a part-time nursing schedule. If a nursing mother cuts down too much, however, she may not have adequate milk.

Working mothers, regardless of the type of job they do, should anticipate the rigors of their dual roles. To keep from being overwhelmed by work obligations and childcare responsibilities, they have to take special care to get enough rest, and find some small slivers of time for themselves.

18 Before the Baby Is Born

Fredric M. Bomback, M.D.

INTRODUCTION

DURING THE LATTER PART of pregnancy, many women (and some men) experience an urge to prepare for the baby's arrival that is popularly known as the "nesting instinct." Happily, it tends to inspire parents to do all they can to make life safer and healthier for the baby after birth.

CHOOSING A PEDIATRICIAN

THE MOST SENSIBLE TIME to choose a pediatrician is in advance of delivery. Most parents-to-be schedule a prenatal visit with a pediatrician or several pediatricians late in the last trimester of pregnancy. At this interview, they may decide which pediatrician they wish to select, or if they have made that decision, ask questions about baby care.

The relationship parents develop with their child's pediatrician is often unique. Over the years, through checkups and crises, most get to know the pediatrician better than any other physician. Thus, meeting the pediatrician in advance is important. For mothers, it helps provide a smooth transition from the rapport with her obstetrician, with whom she shared her concerns during pregnancy, to that with the pediatrician who will be a partner in her child's health care. For the father, this is an opportunity to begin to share as an equal partner in parenting.

Prenatal visits are recommended for all parents, but especially for those with high-risk pregnancies, complications, multiple gestation (twins, triplets), and those who have previously experienced miscarriage or stillbirth. Usually there is no charge for this visit, although some pediatricians will send a bill if the parents choose not to use them later on.

The pediatrician views the prenatal visit as an opportunity to establish a relationship with the family, to obtain medical information (such as how the pregnancy has been, the parents' medical histories, and the family history), and to stress the importance of safety issues—in particular, the need for a car seat on the trip home from the hospital.

Parents may wish to discuss preparations for the baby's arrival, issues surrounding the delivery and hospital stay, including childbirth classes, rooming-in, and circumcision. This is a good time to ask questions about the pediatrician's role at and after delivery, office and telephone procedures, and approach to the type of feeding (breast, bottle, or both) that the parents favor. In addition to obtaining specific information, this is a valuable opportunity to gauge the physician's overall attitude and personality so that the parents can decide whether they will feel comfortable with the doctor in the context of their relationship.

In today's mobile society, new mothers and fathers are often unable to turn to their own parents for advice or support, and they often have had little experience with or exposure to children. As a result, pediatricians are often pressed into a role much like that of the old "family doctor." With the increasing awareness among parents of the importance of the child's emotional health, the pediatrician is often turned to for advice in areas that go beyond direct health-care questions.

For this reason, the parents should feel that the pediatrician is responsive to their concerns. No parent should feel ill at ease about asking questions. Nor should parents be made to feel ignorant for their queries. Some pediatricians schedule specific telephone hours each morning, others answer questions throughout the day. Many have the office nurses field some of the questions and direct others to the doctors. But none should object if the parents call at night with a real problem. There is no need for parents to feel guilty or foolish about their anxieties—pediatricians themselves have plenty of anxiety about their own children.

THE PEDIATRICIAN AT THE BIRTH

THE PEDIATRICIAN'S ROLE at the time of the birth depends primarily on the procedure followed by the hospital and the obstetrician. The obstetrician will inform the pediatrician of any condition that may call for his or her attendance at the birth. These may include maternal diseases (such as toxemia) or chronic medical conditions (hypertension, pulmonary disease, or diabetes); fetal prematurity (birth before 37 weeks of gestation), or postmaturity (after 42 weeks); conditions that may require a cesarean section; an abnormal fetal heart rate; meconium-stained amniotic fluid; multiple births; an abnormal pattern or length of labor; or unusual presentation (such as a breech birth).

Virtually all tertiary-care facilities require a pediatrician to be in attendance in the case of a cesarean section. But in a smaller community hospital, pediatricians may not be as readily available, and the obstetrician and anesthesiologist are invariably experienced in newborn resuscitation. The fact that a pediatrician is called in to attend a birth should be no cause for alarm—9 times out of 10, this is nothing more than a precautionary measure.

QUESTIONS THE PEDIATRICIAN MAY ASK

(These may be asked personally or by means of a questionnaire that the parents fill out in the office before the interview.)

- Are there any genetic diseases or birth defects in the parents' families?

- Does either parent have any allergic, metabolic, neurologic, heart, or lung disease?

- Has this been an "easy" pregnancy or have any problems developed?

- Are the parents married? How long have they been married?

- Is this the couple's first pregnancy?

- What have the parents read about baby care?

- Are the parents attending prenatal classes?

- Is the mother planning to breastfeed?

- Who lives in the parents' household?

- Who will help with the housework and siblings when the baby comes home from the hospital?

- Do the parents smoke?

- Have the parents bought a car seat?

- Are there smoke detectors or fire extinguishers in the home?

- What is the educational background of the parents?

- What do the parents do for a living?

- Are both parents planning to return to work after the birth? If so, how soon afterward?

- Have the parents decided about circumcision if the baby is a boy?

- Was this a convenient time for the parents to have a baby?

- How do the parents think having a baby will change their lives?

- Do the parents plan to bring up the baby as they were raised? What do they intend to do differently?

- Any special worries?

THE PRENATAL VISIT WITH THE PEDIATRICIAN

QUESTIONS FOR PARENTS TO ASK

- What are the usual intervals for routine examinations and immunizations?

- What are the pediatrician's office hours? Do the hours accommodate working parents?

- Is the pediatrician willing to attend to a child accompanied by a caretaker other than the parents? If so, is previous authorization required?

- Does the pediatrician have a telephone calling hour? If not, are there particular hours when he or she prefers to be called?

- With which hospital or hospitals is the pediatrician affiliated?

- What are the usual fees?

- Who is on call when the pediatrician is not available?

- If this is a group practice, may the parents choose which physician to see?

- What is the policy concerning insurance?

- Is the pediatrician willing to participate in early discharge (through early examination of the baby and follow-up exams during the first few days)?

- What is the pediatrician's attitude toward breastfeeding?

- What if the mother can't breastfeed?

- Will there be someone to help the mother with breastfeeding in the hospital?

- If the baby is a boy, should he be circumcised?

- Does the pediatrician recommend any parenting classes in the area?

- Does the pediatrician recommend any books for parents to read or have on hand?

- How does the pediatrician assess appropriate weight gain in infants?

- When does the pediatrician start infants on solid foods?

The baby will be examined extensively by the pediatrician within 24 hours of delivery. (The pediatrician may see the baby sooner, but if the birth occurs right after pediatric rounds, the baby will be seen on the next rounds.) But parents can rest assured that the baby will be examined at least twice during the first 24 hours—for such things as a healthy skin color, activity, and crying—by the nursing staff and the obstetrician or midwife. From then on, the pediatrician will examine the baby at least every other day until the time of discharge, assuming the baby is his only patient in the hospital nursery. If he has others there, he will often see each one daily.

If the baby is a boy, a circumcision may be performed in the hospital after he has had some time to recover from the trauma of birth. Before the due date, parents should discuss with the pediatrician whether or not they wish to have a boy circumcised. According to the American Academy of Pediatrics, circumcision is almost never needed for medical reasons—in fact, in the presence of certain conditions it may actually be contraindicated—and, as with any surgery, there are associated risks. If circumcision is performed, it is for religious or social reasons. Circumcisions are usually performed by the obstetrician, but during the prenatal interview the pediatrician should provide parents with enough information to enable them to make a rational decision.

(Note: An expanded discussion of "Before the Baby Is Born" appears in *The Columbia College of Physicians and Surgeons Complete Guide to Early Child Care*.)

Glossary

Abortion The interruption of pregnancy through expulsion of the fetus before it can survive outside the uterus (generally before week 20 of pregnancy). Abortion may be either induced (also called therapeutic) or spontaneous. An inevitable abortion occurs when the fetus dies in utero and miscarriage is unavoidable. In missed abortion, the fetus dies but is not expelled from the uterus. In an incomplete abortion, not all the products of conception are expelled.

Abruptio placentae partial or complete separation of the placenta from the uterine wall.

Abscess a localized buildup of pus due to the breakdown of tissue by bacteria.

Achondroplasia An inherited form of dwarfism characterized by short limbs and average-sized head and body.

Active phase The second phase of the first stage of labor, during which contractions last about 60 seconds and occur every 2 to 5 minutes, dilating the cervix to 10 centimeters.

Adhesion The abnormal union of body surfaces caused by fibrous scars formed when tissues heal.

Adrenal glands Endocrine glands that are situated just above the kidneys and that secrete important hormones. Among the hormones secreted are epinephrine (adrenaline), which affects heart rate and blood circulation and is instrumental in the body's responses to physical stress, and cortisone, a natural anti-inflammatory.

Afterpains Cramps caused by uterine contractions in the first few days after birth, as the uterus returns to its normal size.

Agammaglobulinemia A disease marked by abnormally low levels of antibodies, leading to frequent infections.

Agglutination Clumping together of cells in response to certain antibodies.

AIDS (Acquired Immune Deficiency Syndrome) An incurable disease transmitted sexually and by blood that attacks and weakens the body's immune system, leaving the patient open to "opportunistic" infections and disorders that are normally warded off.

Alpha fetoprotein (AFP) A protein produced by the fetal liver and passed into the mother's blood via the placenta. Higher than normal amounts in the mother's blood indicate the presence of neural tube defects.

Amino acid The nitrogen-containing components of protein used by the body to build muscle and other tissue. Some essential amino acids must be supplied by eating high-protein foods while others are synthesized in the body.

Amniocentesis The extraction of a small amount of amniotic fluid in order to determine genetic and other disorders in the fetus. *See also* amniotic fluid.

Amnion Amniotic sac. The bag of waters in which the fetus and amniotic fluid are contained during pregnancy.

Amniotomy Artificial rupture of the amniotic sac.

Amniotic fluid Water in which the fetus "floats" within the uterus.

Amphetamine A drug that stimulates the central nervous system.

Analgesic Any substance that gives temporary relief from pain.

Androgens Hormones, such as testosterone and androsterone, which are produced mostly in the testes (and also by the adrenal glands) and are responsible for male characteristics. They are also produced normally in small amounts in females.

Anemia A deficiency in the hemoglobin, the number of red blood cells, or in the amount of blood. Anemia is usually a symptom of an underlying disorder.

Anencephaly A congenital defect, fatal before or shortly after birth, in which most of the brain does not develop.

Anesthesia Loss of sensation or feeling. General anesthesia involves the whole body, while local anesthesia involves only a particular area. Regional or epidural anesthesia affects the entire lower half of the body.

Anesthesiology The branch of medical science that deals with the administration of anesthesia.

Anesthetic gas A gas that produces general anesthesia when inhaled.

Antepartum Before labor or childbirth.

Anterior position The head position most babies assume during birth, with the back of the head turned toward the front of the mother's body.

Antibody The components of the immune system that eliminate or counteract foreign substances (antigens) in the body.

Apgar score A uniform system for rating the well-being of a baby at birth. Heart rate, respiration, muscle tone, reflexes, and color are rated on a scale from 0 to 2, and these ratings are totaled to determine the Apgar score.

Areola A round pigmented area around a raised center, such as the nipple of a breast.

Arthritis Inflammation of a joint.

Artificial insemination Depositing semen from the husband or a donor into the cervix via a plastic tube to achieve conception.

Aspartame A sugar substitute marketed under the brand name NutraSweet and used to sweeten many products, including diet soda.

Aspiration The removal of fluid from the body cavities. A suction or siphoning implement is used.

Asthma A reversible disorder of the respiratory system due to bronchial spasm that results in breathing difficulties.

Autistic Withdrawn from reality and absorbed in self-centered mental activity.

Autoimmune disease Any disease in which the body manufactures antibodies against itself. The body regards its own tissue as a foreign body and acts accordingly to eliminate it.

Barbiturate A drug that produces sedation, hypnosis, anesthesia, or sleep.

Basal temperature The body's lowest temperature in the course of a day, which is reached during sleep and measured immediately upon awakening.

Beta thalassemia A recessive blood disorder, the gene for which is carried by 1 in 25 people of Mediterranean (e.g., Italian or Greek) origin. The disease causes severe anemia (see Cooley's anemia), enlargement of the liver and spleen, and frequent infections.

Bilaminar embryo The stage of embryonic development at which the embryoblast consists of a double-layer plate, the endoderm, and ectoderm.

Bilirubin A pigment formed by the destruction of red blood cells.

Birthing room A homelike room in which both labor and delivery take place.

Bladder A sac that contains fluid or gas.

Blastocyst The earliest stage of embryonic development, lasting for the first few weeks after fertilization.

Blood pressure The force exerted by the blood against the arterial walls. A sphygmomanometer measures both the systolic pressure (when the heart is at maximum contraction) and diastolic pressure (when the heart is relaxed between beats).

Blood sugar The glucose that is circulated in the blood. It is the end product of carbohydrate metabolism (although protein and some fat also may be converted to glucose) and is the body's major fuel.

Bloody show Blood-tinged, mucous discharge that is a sign of impending labor.

Bonding The development of attachment between 2 human beings.

Bone marrow The soft substance that fills bone cavities. Red marrow is responsible for red blood cell production. Yellow marrow is marrow that is no longer involved in making blood cells.

Bradley method A method of prepared childbirth pioneered by Robert Bradley, an American obstetrician. The method emphasizes the role of the husband as labor coach and the use of slow, rhythmic breathing and relaxation for pain management.

Brain stem The pons and medulla oblongata, located at the base of the brain and leading into the spinal column.

Braxton-Hicks contractions Mild, irregular uterine contractions lasting 20 to 30 seconds and occurring at any time during later pregnancy. Distinguished from contractions of true labor by their shorter duration and cessation after several hours.

Bronchi The 2 airways or tubes that carry air from the trachea to the lungs.

Bronchitis Inflammation of the bronchi.

Bronchodilator An agent that opens up a bronchus or bronchial tube.

Bronchus Singular of bronchi.

Caffeine A substance that stimulates the central nervous system. It is present in coffee, tea, chocolate, and certain soft drinks.

Calcium An essential mineral. Calcium is the main material in the teeth and bones and vital to proper function of the heart, other muscles, and other body tissues.

Cannula An open-ended metal tube that can be inserted into a cavity to withdraw fluid.

Capacitation The wearing away of the membrane that covers the head of a sperm cell as the cell travels toward an egg.

Capillary Minute thin-walled blood vessel, which in a network facilitates the exchange of substances between the surrounding tissues and the blood.

Carbohydrates Organic compounds of carbon, hydrogen, and oxygen. They include starches, cellulose, and sugars and are divided into 3 groups: monosaccharides (simple sugars), disaccharides (containing 2 different sugars), and polysaccharides (complex sugars).

Carbon disulfide A colorless liquid chemical that exudes toxic vapor.

Carbon monoxide A colorless, odorless poisonous gas formed by the combustion of carbon.

Carcinogen Any agent that is capable of causing cancer.

Cardiac output The amount of blood pumped by the heart.

Cardiovascular Pertaining to the heart and blood vessels.

Carpal tunnel syndrome Pain, tingling, burning, and numbness in the hands caused by compression of the median nerve, which passes between the wristbones from the forearm.

Cartilage The white, elastic tissue located in joints, the nose, and the outer ear.

Catheter A small, flexible tube that can be inserted into the body to withdraw or introduce substances.

Cephalopelvic disproportion A condition in which the mother's pelvis is too small for the fetal head to pass through.

Cerclage Stitching the cervix closed.

Cerebellum The movement-coordinating part of the brain.

Cerebral palsy A defect of movement and coordination caused by brain damage.

Cervical os The opening from the uterus to the vagina.

Cervix The neck, or narrow part of the uterus.

Cesarean section Delivery of a baby through the abdominal wall by means of a surgical procedure.

Childbirth center An out-of-hospital childbirth facility staffed by nurse-midwives.

Chlamydia trachomatis A sexually transmitted disease caused by spherical, nonmotile organisms. Infection may be asymptomatic but may also cause urethritis, cervicitis, and pelvic inflammatory disease.

Chloasma Irregularly shaped brown patches appearing on facial and other skin areas during pregnancy. Sometimes called mask of pregnancy. Also may be caused by birth-control pills.

Chorion The outermost membrane enclosing the fetus, part of which (the chorionic plate) becomes the placenta.

Chorionic villus sampling (CVS) Extraction and examination of a small fragment of the early placenta between weeks 8 and 11 of pregnancy to detect genetic abnormalities in the fetus.

Chromosome Any one of the rod-shaped

bodies in the nucleus of a cell that carry hereditary factors.

Cilia   Hairlike extensions from cell surfaces.

Circumcision   Surgical removal of the foreskin.

Classical incision   A vertical incision made in the upper part of the uterus in cesarean delivery.

Cleft palate   Congenital defect of the mouth in which the palate bones fail to fuse and result in a groove in the roof of the mouth. Harelip is often associated with cleft palate.

Clotting factor   Any of various components in plasma that are involved in the clotting process.

Colon   Large intestine that extends from the small intestine to the rectum. Undigested food that is not absorbed by the body passes from the small intestine into the colon; water is extracted from the waste, which is eventually eliminated from the body in the form of a bowel movement.

Colostrum   A thin, whitish fluid—the forerunner of breast milk—secreted in the last few weeks of pregnancy and the first few days after birth.

Colposcopy   Examination of the cervix and vagina via a magnifying device called a colposcope.

Conception   Impregnation of the ovum by the sperm.

Conceptus   Embryo.

Congenital   Existing at birth or before.

Congenital complete heart block   A birth defect in which nerve transmission to the heart is disturbed, causing a low pulse rate and abnormal heart rhythm.

Constipation   A condition of infrequent and difficult bowel movements.

Contraception   Prevention of conception. Birth control.

Contraction   The rhythmic tightening of the uterine muscle fibers to dilate the cervix gradually during labor.

Convulsion   A violent spasm.

Cooley's anemia   A severe, eventually fatal anemia that results from beta thalassemia.

Cordocentesis (percutaneous umbilical cord sampling)   A method of sampling fetal blood by inserting a needle through the uterine wall and into the umbilical cord. Used to detect genetic blood disorders.

Corpuscle   A small mass of protoplasm. Red corpuscles are called erythrocytes and white corpuscles are called leukocytes.

Corpus luteum   A shell remaining in the ovary after a mature egg has ruptured its follicle. The corpus luteum secretes progesterone, which helps the endometrium prepare to receive a fertilized egg.

Couvade   The custom, in primitive cultures, of a father's undergoing a period of confinement similar to his wife's when she gives birth. May also refer to symptoms a man develops when his partner is pregnant.

Cowper's glands   A pair of small glands in the male reproductive system that are believed to secrete the clear fluid that appears before ejaculation.

Crowning   The appearance of the full diameter of the baby's head in the vaginal opening during the second stage of labor.

Cryobank A facility at which frozen sperm are stored.

Cunnilingus Oral stimulation of the female genitalia.

Cytomegalovirus A disease-causing agent related to the herpes virus that can be passed from mother to child during birth.

Dehydration Inadequate amount of fluid in the body caused by removal of, abnormal loss of, or failure to ingest fluids.

Deoxyribonucleic acid (DNA) The fundamental component of all living matter that controls and transmits the hereditary genetic code.

Depression An organic disease characterized by profound feelings of sadness, discouragement, and worthlessness unexplained by life's events. Depression is often recurring and interrupted by feelings of extreme euphoria, a condition referred to as bipolar depression or manic–depressive state.

Diabetes mellitus A chronic condition characterized by an overabundance of blood sugar due to insufficient insulin production in the pancreas or inability of the body to utilize insulin.

Diaphragm (1) The large muscle between the chest and the abdomen. (2) A dome-shaped rubber cap inserted vaginally to cover the cervix in order to prevent conception.

Diethylstilbestrol (DES) Synthetic estrogen hormone once used to prevent miscarriages. Its use is believed to have resulted in a higher incidence of vaginal and reproductive abnormalities, including difficulty in achieving or maintaining a pregnancy, among daughters born to women who took it. Sons may also suffer reproductive abnormalities.

Differentiation Specialization; acquisition of distinct functions.

Dihydrotestosterone A hormone that causes the development of external genitalia in the fetus.

Dilation Expansion of an organ or passageway (e.g., the cervix). May occur naturally or be artificially induced for diagnostic or therapeutic purposes.

Dilation and Curettage (D&C) Artificial opening of the cervix and removal of the uterine contents with a curved instrument called a curette.

Dilation and Evacuation (D&E) Therapeutic abortion via dilation of the cervix and suction curettage, performed between the weeks 18 and 20 of pregnancy.

Diphtheria An infectious febrile disease marked by the formation of a false membrane in the throat.

Down syndrome (formerly called Down's syndrome) A congenital condition that may include mental retardation and physical malformations caused by abnormal chromosomal distribution. Also called Trisomy 21. Formerly called mongolism.

Dominant inheritance The pattern of single-gene inheritance in which only 1 copy of a particular gene will give rise to the trait encoded by the gene.

Douche A liquid propelled under pressure into the vagina to cleanse or medicate it. Pregnant women should not use douches.

Dystocia Difficult labor.

Eclampsia A sudden convulsive attack

caused by toxemia during pregnancy.

Ectoderm The outer layer of embryoblast cells from which the skin, hair, nails, and nervous system develop.

Ectopic pregnancy Pregnancy in which the fertilized egg begins to develop outside the uterus, usually in the Fallopian tubes.

Edema Swelling of body tissue caused by a buildup of fluid.

Edwards syndrome *See* Trisomy 18.

Effacement Thinning out of the cervix.

Ejaculation Emission of semen from the penis during the male orgasm.

Ejaculatory duct The duct formed at the junction of the vas deferens and the seminal vesicle and leading into the urethra.

Embryoblast The inner cells of the blastocyst, from which the embryo will grow.

Embryo transfer A fertility enhancement method in which the husband's sperm are used to fertilize the egg of a donor via artificial insemination. After conception, the embryo is transferred to the wife's uterus for gestation.

Endocrinology The branch of medical science that deals with disorders of the endocrine glands, which produce hormones that control the digestive and reproductive systems, growth, metabolism, and other processes.

Endoderm The innermost layer of embryoblast cells, which eventually develops into the digestive tract, liver, and lungs.

Endometrial biopsy Removal and examination of a small sample of endometrial tissue for diagnostic purposes.

Endometriosis A gynecological disease in which tissue normally found in the uterus grows in other areas.

Endometritis Inflammation of the uterine lining.

Endometrium The lining of the uterus in which the fertilized ovum is implanted and which is shed during menstruation if conception has not taken place.

Endoscopy Diagnostic procedure using an illuminated optical instrument to examine a body cavity.

Epididymis The duct through which sperm move from the testicle to the vas deferens.

Epidural anesthesia A type of local anesthesia that numbs the nerves that carry pain messages from the lower part of the body to the brain. An anesthetic is injected into the epidural space (the area just outside the membrane that covers the spinal fluid), between 2 vertebrae at the base of the spinal column. May be given in a single injection or administered continuously through a catheter inserted into the epidural region. Also called regional anesthesia.

Epilepsy A disease of the nervous system characterized by convulsive seizures as a result of an imbalance in the electrical activity of the brain.

Episiotomy An incision made in the final stages of childbirth from the vagina downward toward the anus.

Estrogen A primarily female sex hormone produced by the ovary, adrenal gland, and placenta. In women, it controls development of secondary sex characteristics, menstruation, and pregnancy. A small amount of estrogen is produced in the testes of the man, and also in fat tissue.

Euphoria A feeling of well-being.

External cephalic version Turning the fetus so that its head is down by manipulating the outside of the uterus.

External rotation The spontaneous sideways turn of the baby's head when it exits the birth canal.

Fallopian tubes The 2 tubes extending from either side of the uterus through which an egg must pass after release from the ovary. Also called oviducts.

Familial high cholesterol (hypercholesterolemia) Excessive amounts of cholesterol in the blood, due to an inherited metabolic disorder in which the body manufactures too much cholesterol or cannot process it correctly.

Family-centered childbirth An approach to obstetrical care that treats childbirth as a natural process by such means as allowing a partner to participate in labor, relaxing visiting hours for family members, and offering birthing rooms and rooming in.

Fetal alcohol syndrome (FAS) A constellation of mental and physical defects caused by alcohol damage to the fetus.

Fetal hemolytic disease The destruction of fetal red blod cells that may occur when a mother and fetus have incompatible blood cell factors, giving rise to maternal antibodies that can cross the placenta and attack the fetal cells.

Fetal monitor An instrument that measures uterine contractions and fetal heart rate during labor. The monitor may be external, or internal, using an electrode placed on the baby's scalp during a vaginal examination.

Fetoscopy Visual examination of the fetus by means of a slender, periscope-like device that is inserted through the uterine wall. Fetal skin and blood samples can be obtained through fetoscopy, and fetal surgery may be performed.

Fetus An unborn baby after week 8 of pregnancy.

Fiber (1) Body tissue composed mainly of fibrils, tiny threadlike structures. (2) The plant cell components that are indigestible by humans. Dietary fiber. Roughage.

Fibroid A benign tumor of fibromuscular tissue, usually occurring in the uterus.

Fimbria A fringelike structure.

Folic acid A B-complex vitamin, used to promote blood regeneration in cases of folate deficiency. Occurs naturally in liver, kidney, leafy green vegetables, and yeast.

Follicle A small sac or tubular gland.

Follicle-stimulating hormone (FSH) A hormone secreted by the pituitary gland and responsible for maturation of reproductive cells in both sexes.

Forceps Surgical instrument used to grasp or compress tissue. Obstetrical forceps may be used to help guide the baby through the birth canal. In low forceps delivery, the instrument is used once the baby's head is resting on the mother's perineum. In midforceps delivery, the baby's head is higher up in the birth canal.

Forebrain Also called prosencephalon;

the anterior portion of the fetal brain, which develops into the cerebral hemispheres, the thalamus, the olfactory nerve, and other mature brain structures.

Fragile X syndrome An X-linked inherited disorder that, in 80 percent of cases, causes mental retardation.

FTA-ABS (fluorescent treponemal antibody absorption) A highly sensitive blood test used, after a positive VDRL or RPR, to confirm syphilis.

Fundus The portion of a hollow organ farthest from its opening.

Funic souffle A blowing sound, synchronous with the fetal heartbeat, that can be heard through the uterine wall using a stethoscope placed directly over the umbilical cord.

Gamete intrafallopian tube transfer (GIFT) A method of conception that involves removing mature ova from a woman's ovary, combining the ova with sperm, and reintroducing the mixture into the Fallopian tube, where conditions for fertilization are optimal.

Gene A part of the chromosome that determines hereditary characteristics.

Gene mapping Finding the locations of genes on chromosomes.

Gene marker A piece of genetic material that is usually inherited along with a particular gene.

Genetic counseling A medical specialty that combines analysis of family medical history with certain laboratory tests to help couples concerned about the risk of inherited disorders to plan their families.

Genitals, genitalia Reproductive organs.

Gestation Pregnancy.

Gestational diabetes Diabetes mellitus appearing during pregnancy, usually later pregnancy, precipitated by hormonal changes of pregnancy.

Gestational hypertension High blood pressure occurring for the first time after 20 weeks of pregnancy.

Glans The head of the penis.

Glucose (dextrose or blood sugar) The most common monosaccharide (simple sugar) and the main source of energy for humans. It is stored as glycogen in the liver and can be quickly converted back to glucose.

Glucose challenge test (GCT) Screening test for gestational diabetes characterized by an oral dose of 50 grams glucose, and testing blood sugar levels.

Glucose tolerance test (GTT) A test of the body's ability to utilize carbohydrates. It involves ingesting a large amount of sugar in a fasting state, then taking blood and urine samples every half hour to determine glucose levels. Abnormal levels may indicate diabetes or hypoglycemia.

Glycol ether Alcohol compounds commonly used as solvents in high-tech industries.

Glycosolated hemoglobin test A blood test that measures the amount of glucose attached to protein molecules in red blood cells. The test indicates how well a diabetic's blood sugar has been controlled over the preceding 2 months.

Gonad Primary sex gland. Ovary in the female; testis in the man.

Gonorrhea A common venereal disease caused by the gonococcus bacterium and characterized by inflammation of the urethra, difficulty in urination (in males), and cervicitis (in females).

Graafian follicles. Tiny vesicles in the ovaries that contain ova before release (ovulation).

Gynecology The branch of medical science that deals with the normal functioning and diseases of women's reproductive organs.

Hallucinogen Agent capable of producing hallucinations. Psychedelic drug.

Halogenated hydrocarbons Toxic chemicals used in agriculture and industry.

Harelip Congenital defect of the lip due to a failure of bones to unite and thereby causing a split from the margin of the lip to the nostril.

Heart The muscular organ that pumps blood through the body. It is situated between the 2 lungs and behind the sternum.

Heartburn Burning sensations in the upper abdomen or behind the sternum. Usually caused by regurgitation of gastric juices into the esophagus.

Hemoglobin The red pigment contained in red blood cells and combining the iron-containing heme with the protein-containing globin. Hemoglobin is responsible for transporting oxygen to body tissue and removing carbon dioxide from body tissue.

Hemoglobin electrophoresis A process that separates the different types of hemoglobin in the blood by means of a device that moves substances through an electric field.

Hemophilia An inherited blood disorder in which the blood is unable to clot, causing severe bleeding from even minor wounds. The disease only affects males but is passed on by female carriers.

Hemorrhage Abnormal bleeding due to rupture of a blood vessel.

Hemorrhoids Varicose veins in and around the rectal opening. Hemorrhoid symptoms include pain, bleeding, and itching.

Hepatitis B Inflammation of the liver due to infection with the hepatitis B virus, which is transmitted through blood and blood products, saliva, semen, and vaginal secretions.

Hernia The abnormal protrusion of part or all of an organ through surrounding tissues.

Herpes simplex Recurring infection caused by herpes virus. Type 1 involves blisterlike sores usually around the mouth and referred to as "cold sores" or "fever blisters." Type 2 usually affects the mucous membranes of the genitalia and can be spread by sexual contact. In unusual circumstances, either type can cause damage to other parts of the body, such as the eyes or brain. Also, the distinctions between type 1 and type 2 herpes are not as clear as once thought; either virus can cause genital or oral sores.

HMO (Health Maintenance Organization) A medical insurance plan that provides all services, including hospitalization, for a single monthly or yearly fee.

Hormone Secretion from an endocrine gland transported by the bloodstream to various organs in order to regulate vital functions and processes.

Human chorionic gonadotrophin (HCG) A hormone secreted by the placental tissue after implantation in the uterine wall. It is the substance sought in pregnancy tests. Its function is to signal the brain and pituitary to continue production of luteinizing hormone to keep the endometrium intact.

Human placental lactogen (HPL) A peptide produced by the placenta that is important in metabolism and fat breakdown.

Huntington disease A dominant inherited neurological disorder that becomes apparent in adulthood. Characterized by spasmodic involuntary movement and progressive mental impairment.

Hyperactivity Term used to refer to a childhood syndrome of excessive, uncontrollable movement and inappropriate behavior.

Hypercholesterolemia High blood cholesterol.

Hypertension High blood pressure. A condition in which the arterioles constrict and cause the heart to pump harder in order to distribute the blood to the body, thus elevating the blood pressure.

Hypospadias A congenital malformation of the urethra.

Hypothalamus The part of the brain just above the pituitary gland. It has a part in controlling basic functions such as appetite, procreation, sleep, and body temperature and may be affected by the emotions.

Hysterosalpingogram X ray of the uterus and Fallopian tubes after radiopaque dye is injected into the uterus through the vagina and cervix.

Hysteroscopy Visual examination of the inside of the uterus via an endoscope inserted through the vagina and cervix.

Iatrogenic Caused as an unintended side effect of a physician's prescribed treatment.

Iatrogenic prematurity Premature scheduled delivery, usually by cesarean, of an infant whose gestational age has been determined inaccurately.

Immunization The procedure by which specific antibodies are induced in the body tissue.

Immunosuppressants Agents that suppress immunologic response.

Implantation The attachment of the fertilized egg to the uterine wall, which occurs about 1 to 9 days after fertilization.

Incompetent cervix Inability of the cervix to remain securely closed, a condition that may induce premature labor. May be caused by trauma to the cervix or by a malformation.

Infertility Inability to reproduce. A couple is considered infertile if they have been unable to achieve pregnancy after 2 years.

Inflammation The reaction of tissue to injury, infection, or irritation. Affected area may become painful, swollen, red, and hot.

Insomnia Inability to sleep. Can be chronic or occasional.

Instillation abortion Therapeutic abortion between weeks 16 and 24 of pregnancy, induced by injection of saline, prostaglandin, or urea into the amniotic sac.

Insulin The hormone produced and secreted by the beta cells of the pancreas gland. Insulin is needed for proper metabolism, particularly of carbohydrates, and the uptake of sugar (glucose) by certain body tissues.

Invagination Folding together 2 sides of the same object to form a sheath.

Inverted-T incision A vertical incision made above a low transverse incision that is not large enough for the baby to pass through in a cesarean delivery.

In vitro fertilization (IVF) A method of conception that involves harvesting mature ova from a woman, combining them with sperm, and implanting any eggs that are thereby fertilized in the uterus. This technique is mainly reserved for women with damaged Fallopian tubes.

IPA (Individual Practice Association) A type of HMO in which private physicians bill the prepaid plan for services to its members.

Iris The round, colored portion of the eye that surrounds the pupil.

Iron The essential mineral micronutrient of hemoglobin.

Islets of Langerhans The group of cells (alpha and beta) in the pancreas that secrete endocrine hormones.

IUD (intrauterine contraceptive device) Device made of inert plastic, silkworm gut, or plastic with copper, which is inserted by a physician into the uterus to prevent pregnancy.

IV A catheter or needle inserted into a vein through which fluids, medications, and nutrients can enter the bloodstream.

Jaundice Yellow discoloration of the skin and eyes caused by excessive amounts of bile pigments in the bloodstream.

Karyotype A picture of an individual's chromosomes usually produced from a micrograph of a cell nucleus and arranged with chromosome pairs together, from largest to smallest.

Kegel exercises Pelvic floor exercises to strengthen the muscles.

Kell system A group of red blood cell proteins that, if present in fetal red blood cells, may give rise to maternal antibodies that could cause incompatibility problems in later pregnancies.

Ketones Harmful, highly acidic chemicals that can be released when the body burns fat.

Klinefelter syndrome Chromosomal abnormality in which an individual has 2 X and 1 Y sex chromosomes. As a result, the individual appears to be male but has oversized breasts and underdeveloped testes, and is sterile.

Labia Liplike organs. Labia majora: 2 folds of skin and fatty tissue that encircle the vulva. Labia minora: The smaller folds inside the labia majora that protect the clitoris.

Labor (parturition) The rhythmic muscle contraction in the uterus in the process of childbirth.

Lactase The enzyme that splits lactose, the sugar in milk, into 2 other sugars.

Lactation Production and secretion of milk by the breasts.

Lactose A sugar contained in milk.

Lamaze method A method of prepared childbirth pioneered by a French obstetrician, Dr. Fernand Lamaze. The technique emphasizes the use of complicated exercises and breathing patterns designed to help a woman, with the assistance of a labor coach, pass through each stage of labor.

Laminaria japonicum Water-absorbing dried seaweed inserted into the cervix to achieve dilation for induced abortion.

Lanugo Fine, soft hair that covers the fetal body.

Laparoscopy Visual examination of the abdominal organs via a telescopic instrument inserted through a small incision.

Larynx Voicebox. A cartilaginous structure containing the apparatuses of voice production: the vocal cords and the muscles and ligaments that move the cords.

Latent phase The first phase of the first stage of labor, marked by regular, moderately strong uterine contractions, occurring every 5 to 15 minutes and lasting 30 to 60 seconds. This phase usually effects effacement and dilates the cervix 1 to 4 centimeters.

Laxative Any agent that encourages bowel activity by loosening the contents.

Lay midwife A midwife with no formal training in nursing or obstetrics who has, traditionally, assisted in childbirth in areas where medical care is not available.

Leboyer delivery A natural childbirth technique that emphasizes a calm, quiet delivery room atmosphere and avoidance of procedures such as suctioning the infant. The method, pioneered by French physician Frederick Leboyer, is aimed at reducing the pain of birth for the infant.

Leopold's maneuvers Examination of a pregnant woman's abdomen to determine the baby's presentation, position, and descent.

Libido Term used by Freud for the desire for sensual satisfaction. Commonly used to mean sexual desire.

Ligaments The tough, fibrous tissue that connects bones.

Linea nigra A dark streak running from the navel to the pubic bone. Many women develop linea nigra during pregnancy.

Liver The largest internal organ in the body. Among its many functions are secreting bile and digestive enzymes, neutralizing poisons, synthesizing proteins, and producing several blood components.

Lochia Vaginal discharge of blood, mucus, and tissue after childbirth.

Low transverse incision A horizontal incision in the lower part of the uterus in cesarean delivery.

Low vertical incision A vertical incision in the lower part of the uterus in cesarean delivery.

Luteal phase (progesterone phase) The phase in the menstrual cycle dominated by the luteinizing hormone and the hormone progesterone.

Luteinizing hormone (LH) A female sex hormone, secreted by the pituitary, that stimulates ovulation.

Macrosomic Having an abnormally large body.

Magnesium An essential mineral, deficiency of which has been tentatively linked to preeclampsia.

Marfan syndrome An inherited disorder marked by abnormally long bones as well as eye and circulatory disorders.

Mastitis Infection of the breast.

Masturbation Manipulation of the genitals for the purpose of deriving sexual pleasure.

Meconium The greenish-brown residue that fills the fetal intestine and is passed soon after birth.

Megadoses Supplementation of vitamins and minerals in amounts that vastly exceed the recommended daily allowances.

Meiosis The special process of cell division undergone by sperm and ova to reduce their number of chromosomes from 46 to 23.

Melanocyte A pigment-producing cell in the skin.

Melanocyte-stimulating hormone A peptide hormone, secreted by the pituitary, that causes darkening of the skin.

Menarche The onset of the first menstrual period.

Meningomyelocele Protrusion of part of the spinal cord through a defect in the spinal column.

Menopause The period of time in which ovulation and menstruation decreases and finally stops. The change of life after which a woman is no longer able to reproduce.

Menstrual extraction A type of suction abortion performed with a very narrow cannula, between 1 and 4 weeks after conception.

Menstruation The discharge of blood and tissue from the uterus every 28 days and lasting 4 or 5 days.

Mesoderm The middle layer of embryoblast cells from which such body systems as the muscles and blood develop.

Mesonephric cords Embryonic ducts that drain the mesonephric tubules. In males, they become the ejaculatory ducts and vas deferens; in females, they become vestigial.

Mesonephros A kidney that appears and functions briefly during embryonic development. It is eventually replaced by the metanephros, which develops into a mature kidney.

Metabolism The combination of chemical and physical changes in the body essential for maintaining life processes. Basal metabolism is the minimum energy required to sustain life while resting.

Metanephros The first permanent kidney in the developing embryo, preceded by 2 less complex organs.

Microsurgery Surgery performed on extremely small areas viewed through a surgical microscope.

Miniabortion Menstrual extraction.

Miscarriage Spontaneous abortion, usually before week 20 of pregnancy.

Mittelschmerz Pain at the time of ovulation.

Moniliasis Yeast infection that is usually caused by *Candida albicans* and affecting the mucous membranes such as the lining of the vagina, mouth, and gastrointestinal tract.

Mononucleosis, infectious A communicable disease in which the number of monocytes in the bloodstream increases. Symptoms include fever, swollen lymph nodes, and general malaise.

Montgomery's glands Small, rounded, oil-secreting skin glands on the areola of the breast.

Morning sickness Previous term for pregnancy sickness. Characterized by nausea and vomiting; usually worst in first trimester and multiple births.

Morula The cluster of cells resulting from the early cell divisions of the fertilized ovum. About 60 hours after conception, the cluster contains 12 to 16 cells.

Mucus The viscid secretion of mucous glands that moistens body linings.

Müllerian cords Two embryonic tubes extending along the mesonephros that, in females, develop into the vagina, uterus, and Fallopian tubes. In males, they disappear almost completely.

Müllerian-inhibiting factor A substance released by the embryonic testicles, causing the disappearance of the müllerian cords.

Multifactorial inheritance An imprecise pattern of genetic inheritance in which messages from several genes, as well as environmental influences, interact to produce certain conditions such as cleft palate and neural tube defects.

Multiple sclerosis (MS) A degenerative disease affecting the central nervous system and brain, characterized by increasing disability.

Muscular dystrophy A disease appearing in childhood and characterized by wasting of the muscles.

Mutagens Agents that can cause changes in the DNA of egg or sperm cells.

Mutation A change in the character of a gene.

Mycoplasma A type of bacterium found in the genital tract and anal passage of humans.

Neonatal Pertaining to the newborn (up to 1 month old).

Neonatologist A physician who specializes in treatment of premature babies or infants up to 1 month old.

Nervous system The network of nerve fibers and cell bodies through which motor and sensory impulses are carried. The central nervous system consists of the brain, spinal cord, and optic nerve. The autonomic nervous system innervates internal organs and glands. The peripheral nervous system comprises most nerve fibers and cell bodies outside the central nervous system.

Neural groove The trench that forms down the middle of the ectoderm as the embryo differentiates. The groove eventually becomes the central nervous system.

Neural tube defects Birth defects caused by faulty formation of the spinal column during gestation.

Neurofibromatosis A dominant inherited disorder marked by the development of multiple benign tumors beneath the skin.

Niacin A B-complex vitamin.

Nicotine A poisonous substance derived from tobacco and responsible for most of the physiologic effects of smoking.

Nurse-midwife A registered nurse who has specialized training in childbirth and is certified by the American College of Nurse-Midwives.

Obstetrics The branch of medical science dealing with pregnancy, childbirth, and perinatal care.

Orchitis Inflammation of the testicles.

Orgasm Sexual climax.

Ossification The process of becoming

bone or the change of cartilage to bone.

Osteoporosis A condition in which bones become porous resulting in increased fragility. Associated with the aging process.

Ovulation The release of the ovum from the ovarian follicle, occurring 14 days before menstruation.

Ovum The egg cell. The female sex cell, which, when fertilized by the male sperm, grows into a fetus. The egg contains 23 chromosomes that pair off with 23 chromosomes in the sperm to make a complete set of 46 needed to start a new life.

Oxytocin A pituitary hormone that is secreted during childbirth for the stimulation of uterine contractions and milk secretion. A synthetic form of oxytocin is administered sometimes to induce or hasten labor.

Papanicolaou smear (Pap test) The microscopic examination of cells shed from body surfaces; used routinely to screen for cancer of the cervix or uterus.

Patau syndrome *See* Trisomy 13.

PCBs (polychlorinated biphenyls) A class of halogenated hydrocarbons, toxic chemicals used in agriculture and industry. The chief source of human exposure to PCBs is fish from contaminated water.

Pediatrics The branch of medical science dealing with children and the diseases affecting them.

Pedigree A family tree used in genetic counseling containing medical information about prospective parents' blood relatives.

Pelvic inflammatory disease (PID) Infection of 1 or more of the internal female sex organs often caused by gonorrhea or chlamydia, untreated cervicitis, or an intrauterine contraceptive device (IUD). May affect the uterus, Fallopian tubes, ovaries, or the lining of the abdominal cavity and is a frequent cause of infertility.

Pelvic floor muscles A group of muscles surrounding the urethra, vagina, and rectum.

Penis The external male sex organ through which urine is passed and semen is ejaculated.

Percutaneous umbilical cord sampling (PUB) *See* Cordocentesis.

Perineum The area between the anus and the genitals.

PGP (prepaid group practice) A type of HMO in which the physicians who treat members are paid a salary by the HMO and act as its employees.

pH The degree of acidity or alkalinity of a solution.

Phlebitis Inflammation of a vein.

Physician extender Health professional such as a nurse-midwife or nurse practitioner who sometimes handles routine medical care.

Physiology The study of cells, tissues, and organs, their functions and activities.

Pica The craving or consumption of unusual substances that ordinarily are not food, such as dirt, chalk, or paint chips.

Pitocin A synthetic oxytocin that causes uterine contractions.

Pituitary gland The pea-sized gland located at the base of the brain. It is controlled by the hypothalamus and, in turn, controls the hormone production in many other endocrine glands.

Placenta The structure developed on the uterine wall about the third month of pregnancy. Through the placenta, the fetus receives nourishment and oxygen and eliminates waste products. It is expelled from the mother after childbirth. The afterbirth.

Placenta previa Implantation of the placenta in the lower segment of the uterus, extending over the opening of the cervix.

Plaque Patch or film of organic substance on tissues such as teeth or in arteries.

Polar body Duplicate egg cell containing 23 chromosomes, formed through the process of meiosis.

Polydactyly The presence of extra fingers or toes.

Polyhydramnios An excess of amniotic fluid.

Polyp A nodular tumor, usually benign, that grows on a mucous membrane.

Posterior position A head position assumed by some babies during birth, with the baby's face turned toward the front of the mother's body.

Postpartum After childbirth.

PPO (preferred provider organization) A group of physicians who, under contract with an employer or insurance company, provide medical services at reduced cost.

Preeclampsia A toxic condition of pregnancy characterized by high blood pressure, edema, and protein in the urine.

Premature labor Onset of labor between weeks 20 and 38 of gestation.

Prenatal diagnosis Identifying genetic disorders or chromosomal abnormalities in a fetus through amniocentesis or chorionic villus sampling.

Prepared childbirth Any of the various prenatal education programs designed to teach expectant parents about the physiological changes of pregnancy, the stages of normal labor, and pain management during birth.

Presentation The part of the fetal body that is the first to emerge from the birth canal. In a breech presentation, the buttocks emerge first. In a cephalic presentation, the head emerges first.

Prodromal labor The earliest phase of the first stage of labor, in which contractions are mild and brief and occur approximately 20 to 30 minutes apart.

Progesterone The female sex hormone that causes the thickening of the uterine lining and other body changes before conception.

Progestin A substance that produces the same biological changes as progesterone.

Prolapse Downward displacement of an organ from its usual position.

Pronephros A rudimentary, primitive kidney that appears briefly during embryonic development.

Prostaglandins A group of hormonelike substances, secreted by a wide range of body tissues, that perform varying functions in the body. They are instrumental in stimulating uterine contractins during labor and birth and are also important in muscle function.

Prostate gland The gland located at the base of the bladder in males.

Protein Complex nitrogen compound made up of amino acids. Most of the tissues of the body, especially the muscles, are composed primarily of protein.

Protozoa One-celled organisms, the smallest type of animal life. Amoebae and paramecia are protozoa. Some protozoa can cause disease.

Pudendal block A type of local anesthesia administered via a needle inserted in the vaginal wall to numb the entire pelvic area.

Puerperal psychosis Extreme postpartum depression requiring hospitalization.

Puerperium The first 6 weeks following childbirth.

Quickening The stage of pregnancy in which the first fetal movements are felt by the mother, usually around week 18 of pregnancy.

Radioactive Emitting rays or subatomic particles with the release of large amounts of energy.

Recessive inheritance The inheritance pattern of genes expressed, or evident, only when a child inherits a copy of the gene from both parents. Examples of recessive disorders are Tay-Sachs disease and sickle cell anemia.

Retina The layered lining of the eye that contains light-sensitive receptors (the rods and cones) and conveys images to the brain.

Rheumatic fever A disease that can occur in children recovering from streptococcal infection. Causes fever, arthritis, and heart inflammation, which can permanently damage the heart valves.

Rh factor A group of antigens in the blood. Some people lack the Rh factor and are therefore designated as Rh negative. Complications can occur if an Rh-negative mother conceives and has an Rh-positive baby.

RhoGAM Rhesus gamma globulin. A drug that destroys Rh-incompatible red blood cells in the mother's circulation, thus preventing development of antibodies that could cause problems in further pregnancies.

Riboflavin Vitamin B_2.

Ribonucleic acid (RNA) A molecule found in all cells that, along with deoxyribonucleic acid (DNA), encodes genetic information.

Rooming-in The practice of keeping a newborn in the mother's hospital room around the clock.

RPR (rapid plasma reagin) A group of blood tests for syphilis.

Rubella German measles. An infectious disease that can cause birth defects in children whose mothers are infected during pregnancy.

Rupture A tear or bursting of a part.

Sacroiliac The joints connecting the base of the spine to the upper part of the hip bone.

Sciatic nerve The largest nerve in the body. It branches out from the base of the spinal cord (where it is attached) to form the motor and sensory nerves of the legs and feet.

Scrotum The pouch that holds the testicles in the male.

Seizure A convulsion.

Semen The thick, whitish secretion produced by the male testes and sex glands and containing the male reproductive cells, the sperm.

Seminiferous tubules Structures within the testicles in which sperm are generated.

Sensitization The process of developing an immune or antibody response to a particular substance.

Sickle cell anemia A hereditary type of anemia caused by malformed (crescent-shaped) red blood cells.

Silver nitrate An antiseptic compound used to prevent gonorrheal eye infections in newborns.

Single-gene inheritance The inheritance pattern of traits encoded by a single gene. May be either dominant or recessive.

Small intestine The portion of the digestive tract extending from the stomach to the large intestine.

Somite A paired embryonic cell alongside the neural groove. The number of somite pairs increases as the embryo develops.

Sonogram A picture of internal structures, such as the fetus within the uterus, produced through ultrasound.

Speculum An instrument used to dilate a body passage in order to examine the interior, such as the examination of the vagina and cervix during a pelvic examination.

Spermatid An immature sperm cell with 22 single-strand chromosomes and one sex chromosome that is produced by the division, then subdivision, of a spermatocyte.

Spermatocyte A cell produced by a sperm-generating cell. Each spermatocyte, through the process of meiosis, gives rise to 4 immature sperm cells.

Spermatogonia Primitive cells that line the testicles and, by division, generate sperm.

Sphincter A ring of muscle that encircles and controls the opening of an orifice.

Spina bifida A congenital defect in which some of the vertebrae fail to close and therefore expose the contents of the spinal canal.

Spotting Loss of small amounts of blood from the vagina.

Station A number that describes the progress of the baby's head in its descent through the pelvis during labor. Station ranges from −4 to +4, where −4 indicates that descent has not begun and +4 indicates that the descent has been completed.

Stein-Leventhal syndrome (polycystic ovary syndrome) A condition characterized by enlarged ovaries, hirsuitism, obesity, and menstrual irregularities.

Steroids (corticosteroids, cortisone) Natural hormones or synthetic drugs that have many different effects. Some steroids are anti-inflammatory and are used to treat arthritis, asthma, and a number of other disorders.

Stethoscope An instrument that amplifies bodily sounds.

Stillbirth Birth of a dead fetus after 20 weeks of pregnancy.

Striae gravidarum Stretch marks, or brownish-red streaks caused by the breakdown of elastic fibers in the skin in areas such as the abdomen, which enlarge during pregnancy.

Suction abortion Dilation of the cervix and evacuation of the uterine contents by means of an electric suction pump. The technique is used in first trimester therapeutic abortion.

Sudden infant death syndrome (SIDS) Crib death. Sudden and inexplicable death of an apparently healthy infant.

Suppository Medicated substance in solid form for insertion into a body opening, usually the vagina or rectum, and which melts inside the body to release the medication.

Surrogate parenting A fertility enhancement method in which a couple makes a contract with a woman who agrees to become pregnant via artificial insemination with the husband's sperm, carry the pregnancy to term, and give the infant to the couple for legal adoption.

Syphilis A sexually transmitted disease caused by the organism *Treponema pallidum*. The disease progresses in 3 stages, terminating in central nervous system and cardiovascular damage.

Systemic lupus erythematosus (SLE) An inflammatory autoimmune disease that causes deterioration of the body's connective tissues.

Tay-Sachs disease A congenital disease affecting the fat metabolism and the brain and characterized by progressive weakness, disability, and blindness, and finally death.

Teratogens Agents that can damage a developing fetus.

Testicles, testes The pair of primary male sex glands enclosed in the scrotum. They produce the male sex hormone testosterone and the spermatozoa.

Testosterone The male sex hormone that induces the secondary sex characteristics.

Thalassemia An inherited disorder of hemoglobin metabolism. Several types exist, ranging in severity from barely detectable blood cell abnormalities to fatal anemia.

Thalassemia trait (thalassemia minor) A single copy of an abnormal gene that, when inherited with another such gene, causes the blood disorder thalassemia. Individuals with thalassemia trait do not have the disease but can, if they have children with another trait carrier, pass the disease to their offspring.

Thalidomide A drug that, when taken early in pregnancy, may cause birth defects, particularly curtailed development of the arms and legs.

THC (9-tetrahydrocannabinol) The active ingredient in marijuana.

Thecal cells The external estrogen- and androgen-secreting cells of a mature ovarian follicle.

Thermogram A picture showing areas of elevated temperature in the body or in an organ.

Thiamine Vitamin B_1, one of the B-complex vitamins.

Threatened abortion Cramping and vaginal bleeding that may precede spontaneous abortion.

Thromboembolism Blockage of a blood vessel by a blood clot dislodged from a vein.

Thrombophlebitis Inflammation of a vein accompanied by formation of a blood clot.

Thrombus Clot.

Thyroid gland The ductless gland located in the neck. The secretions of the thyroid gland control the rate of metabolism, among other functions.

Titers The amount of a substance needed to produce a reaction with a given amount of another substance.

Toxemia (blood poisoning) A condition in which poisonous compounds (toxins) are present in the bloodstream. Toxemia of pregnancy is another term for eclampsia or preeclampsia.

Toxin A poisonous substance produced by bacteria that may have serious effects in humans. Examples include toxic shock syndrome and botulism.

Toxoplasmosis A disease transmitted from animals (especially cats) to humans by parasite-infected feces or by eating undercooked meat containing the parasite. Infection during pregnancy can cause birth defects or fetal death.

Trachea The windpipe. The tube that extends from the larnyx to the bronchi.

Transducer A device that converts energy from one form to another.

Transient neonatal SLE A condition that occasionally affects infants of mothers with systemic lupus erythematosus, characterized by a skin rash and the presence of unusual antibodies in the blood.

Transition The final phase of the first stage of labor, during which the cervix reaches its full dilation of 10 centimeters. contractions last 60 to 90 seconds and occur every 1 to 3 minutes.

Trichomoniasis Inflammation, usually of the vagina but also may affect the urethra; caused by a protozoan (single-celled) parasite.

Trimester One of the 3 three-month periods into which pregnancy is divided.

Triple X syndrome A chromosomal disorder in which females have 3 X chromosomes instead of 2.

Trisomy 13 (Patau syndrome) A congenital condition caused by an extra thirteenth chromosome, which gives rise to severe abnormalities in the brain, ears, eyes, and hands, and internal organs. Usually fatal in the first month of life.

Trisomy 18 (Edwards syndrome) A congenital abnormality caused by an extra eighteenth chromosome, which gives rise to mental retardation and heart defects, and is usually fatal in early infancy.

Trisomy 21 *See* Down syndrome.

Trophoblast The outer wall of the blastocyst.

Tubal pregnancy Ectopic pregnancy in the Fallopian tube.

Tuberculosis (TB) An infectious disease affecting the lungs most often but also other parts of the body. It is caused by the tubercle bacillus and symptoms include cough, chest pains, fatigue, sweating, and weight loss.

Tubule A small tube.

Turner syndrome A chromosomal disorder in which a female has 1 X chromosome instead of 2, causing short stature and underdevelopment of the ovaries.

Ultrasound Sound waves of very high frequency used for diagnostic purposes. The echoes of the ultrasound are registered with devices that construct pictures showing internal organs. When directed into the uterus, the sound waves bounce off the baby's bones and other tissues.

Umbilical cord The tube that connects the fetus to the placenta and through which the fetus is nourished and wastes are disposed.

Umbilicus The navel. The round scar in the middle of the abdomen left by the cutting of the umbilical cord after birth.

Urethra The tube through which urine passes from the bladder to the outside. In the female, it is about 1½ inches long; in the male, it is 8 to 9 inches long.

Urinalysis Examination and analysis of the urine for diagnostic purposes.

Urogenital system All the reproductive organs and organs involved in the production and passage of urine.

Urology A surgical subspecialty dealing with disorders of the urinary tract and the male genitourinary system.

Uterus The hollow, pear-shaped muscular organ where the fertilized ovum develops during pregnancy. It normally weighs about 2 ounces but enlarges to about 30 ounces during pregnancy.

Vacuum curettage A type of suction abortion in which the cervix is dilated and uterine contents extracted by means of an electric suction pump.

Vagina The muscular canal lined with mucous membrane that extends from the vulva to the uterus. Sometimes referred to as the birth canal.

Varicocele Varicose or swollen veins in the spermatic cord.

Varicose veins Abnormally swollen, dilated veins in which the valves are weakened and therefore allow the backflow of blood. Areas most commonly affected are the lower legs and the rectum.

Vascular Pertaining to, or supplied with, vessels, usually blood vessels.

Vas deferens The duct through which sperm move from the testicles to the urethra.

Vasectomy A method of sterilization of the male. The passageway of the vas deferens is cut off so that the spermatozoa cannot enter the semen.

VDRL (Venereal Disease Research Laboratory) A blood test for detecting an antibodylike substance that indicates infection with syphilis.

Venereal diseases Diseases transmitted through sexual contact.

Vernix caseosa A fatty, white substance secreted by oil glands in the skin of the fetus.

Vinyl chloride One of the toxic halogenated hydrocarbons widely used in industry, particularly as a gas.

Vitamin K A fat-soluble vitamin essential for the formation of prothrombin, a substance necessary for the clotting of blood.

Vocal cords Two ligaments in the larynx, vibrations of which produce the sounds of the human voice.

Vulva The external genitalia of the female including the clitoris and vaginal lips.

Wharton's jelly The mucoid connective tissue surrounding the blood vessels in the umbilical cord.

Whooping cough An infectious disease of children characterized by spasmodic coughing. Pertussis.

X-linked inheritance The pattern of inheritance of traits encoded by genes on the X chromosome, which is the female sex chromosome. X-linked defects do not usually affect the women who carry them, but when they are passed from mother to son, they become apparent. Examples include hemophilia and color blindness.

XYY syndrome A chromosomal disorder in which males have 2 Y chromosomes instead of 1.

Yolk sac The inner cavity of the embryoblast, which develops about the fifteenth day of conception.

Yeast A term used to describe the single-celled fungi such as *Candida albicans*, which commonly cause inflammation of the mucous membranes.

Zinc A mineral essential to good nutrition and usually found in iron-rich foods such as red meat and leafy green vegetables. Zinc deficiency during pregnancy has been linked to slow fetal growth.

Zona pellucid The tough inner membrane of the ovum, which must be pierced by a sperm cell for fertilization to take place.

Zygote The fertilized egg before division.

Index